Running qmail

Richard Blum

A Division of Macmillan USA
201 West 103rd St., Indianapolis, Indiana, 46290 USA

Running qmail

Copyright © 2000 by Sams Publishing

International Standard Book Number: 0-672-31945-4

Library of Congress Catalog Card Number: 00-101803

Printed in the United States of America

First Printing: August 2000

03 02 01 00   4 3 2 1

Trademarks

Warning and Disclaimer

ASSOCIATE PUBLISHER
Michael Stephens

ACQUISITIONS EDITOR
Neil Rowe

DEVELOPMENT EDITOR
Tony Amico

MANAGING EDITOR
Matt Purcell

PROJECT EDITOR
Christina Smith

COPY EDITOR
Gene Redding

INDEXER
Heather McNeill

PROOFREADER
Tony Reitz

TECHNICAL EDITOR
Russell Sutherland

TEAM COORDINATOR
Pamalee Nelson

MEDIA DEVELOPER
Dan Scherf

INTERIOR DESIGNER
Anne Jones

COVER DESIGNER
Aren Howell

ILLUSTRATORS
Steve Adams
Tammy Ludwig

Overview

Contents

PART II   Installing and Configuring qmail

6   Installing qmail   137

7   Changing qmail Operational Parameters   161

8   Using qmail   187

About the Author

Rich Blum has worked for the past 11 years as a network and systems administrator for the U.S. Department of Defense at the Defense Finance and Accounting Service. There he has used UNIX operating systems as an FTP server, TFTP server, email server, mail list server, and network monitoring device in a large networking environment. Rich currently serves on the board of directors for Traders Point Christian Schools and is active on the computer support team at the school, supporting a Microsoft Windows NT network in the classrooms and computer lab of a small K–8 school. Rich has a bachelor of science degree in Electrical Engineering, and a master of science degree in Management, specializing in Management Information Systems, both from Purdue University. When Rich is not being a computer nerd, he is either playing electric bass for the church worship band or spending time with his wife Barbara and two daughters Katie Jane and Jessica.

Dedication

This book is dedicated to my wife, Barbara. Thanks. "That if you confess with your mouth 'Jesus is Lord,' and believe in your heart that God raised him from the dead, you will be saved." Romans 10:9 (NIV)

Acknowledgments

First, all glory, honor, and praise go to God, who through His Son all things are possible, and who gave us the gift of eternal life.

I would like to thank all of the great people at Macmillan for their help, guidance, and professionalism. Thanks to Neil Rowe, the acquisitions editor, for offering me the opportunity to write this book. Also, thanks to Gene Redding, the copy editor, for correcting my poor grammar. The technical editor of this book, Russell Sutherland, an avid qmail administrator, did an excellent job of pointing out my technical goofs and setting me straight when necessary. Of course, any remaining goofs in the text are solely my responsibility. Many thanks to the interior design group at Macmillan for turning my scribbles into great looking pictures. And an extra thanks goes to Tony Amico, the development editor. Thanks again for your support and mentoring for this project.

Finally, I would like to thank my family. My parents, Mike and Joyce Blum, for their dedication and support, and my wife Barbara and daughters Katie Jane and Jessica for their love, faith, and understanding, especially while I was writing this book.

Tell Us What You Think!

As the reader of this book, *you* are our most important critic and commentator. We value your opinion and want to know what we're doing right, what we could do better, what areas you'd like to see us publish in, and any other words of wisdom you're willing to pass our way.

As an Associate Publisher for Sams Publishing, I welcome your comments. You can fax, email, or write me directly to let me know what you did or didn't like about this book—as well as what we can do to make our books stronger.

Please note that I cannot help you with technical problems related to the topic of this book, and that due to the high volume of mail I receive, I might not be able to reply to every message.

When you write, please be sure to include this book's title and author as well as your name and phone or fax number. I will carefully review your comments and share them with the author and editors who worked on the book.

Fax: 317-581-4770

Email: opsys_sams@macmillanusa.com

Mail: Michael Stephens
            Associate Publisher
            Sams Publishing
            201 West 103rd Street
            Indianapolis, IN 46290 USA

Email Services

IN THIS CHAPTER

The use of email has grown significantly over the past few years. What once was considered a luxury item now is almost a necessity, especially in the corporate environment. When personal email use in the home became popular, an entire new industry of Internet service providers (ISPs) was created to provide email services to home Internet users.

As email use grew, so did email systems. What was once a simple mainframe application suddenly became a monster application that required dedicated hardware and high-speed Internet connectivity. Often large corporations purchased expensive email software packages to support the email environment within the corporation. Besides complicated server software, many email packages require complicated client software so that users can access their mail on servers located on the corporate network.

The increasing demand and complexity of email systems brought about advancements in email protocols. The Simple Mail Transfer Protocol (SMTP) was designed to transfer messages between remote computers efficiently. The Post Office Protocol (POP) and Interactive Mail Access Protocol (IMAP) were designed to allow users who were located remotely from their mail hosts to access messages in their mailboxes.

This chapter describes the history of email services and functions, outlining the functional requirements that have grown as email matured. Also, this chapter describes the many protocols and software packages used to implement email on the Internet.

Early Mainframe Email Systems

Email systems didn't start out so complicated. The large mainframe environment initiated requirements for messaging systems. Email started out as a convenience for mainframe users to contact other users using a simple messaging system.

Mainframe Messages

Figure 1.1 shows an example of the simplest form of message communication. Two mainframe users, each on a different terminal connected to a common mainframe, want to share information between them. The simple solution was to create a system that could send text messages directly to the terminal of the other user, sort of like a primitive chat session.

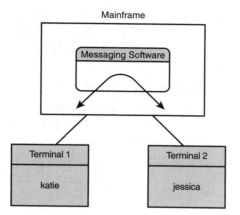

FIGURE 1.1

A mainframe messaging system.

The downside to this system was that it required both users to be logged into the mainframe at the same time. As mainframe messaging systems became more popular, users wanted to be able to send messages to other users who weren't logged into the mainframe. A system of storing messages for individual users was created. Figure 1.2 shows a message storage system.

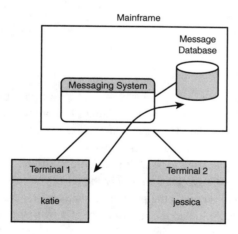

FIGURE 1.2

A mainframe message storage system.

The main advantage of the message storage system was that messages could be sent to users who were not logged into the mainframe. Of course this made the mail software more complicated, because it needed to devise a system of storing and recovering messages on the system.

One disadvantage to those systems was that they transferred only text messages. There were no systems capable of transferring binary data such as executable programs from one user to another.

Multiple-Mainframe Email Systems

As mainframes matured, so did their communications systems. Before long it was possible to transfer data between mainframes using complicated proprietary protocols. Figure 1.3 shows a diagram for a sample mainframe communications system.

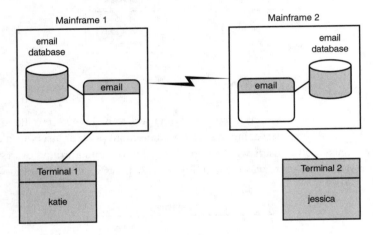

FIGURE 1.3

A multiple-mainframe messaging system.

One thing that became a necessity in the multiple-mainframe environment was a standard naming convention for users. As mainframes were added to the communications system, each computer required a unique name to be identified. If user katie wanted to send a message to the user jessica on the same mainframe, the messaging software only needed to find jessica's mailbox on the system and place the message there. With multiple mainframes connected, the messaging software was required to know not only the userid, but also on which mainframe the userid was located. There was also the possibility that several remote mainframes could contain the same userid. This initiated the requirement of a two-part email address. Both the userid and mainframe names were required for the messaging system to be able to successfully deliver the message to the right user on the right mainframe.

UNIX Email Systems

As UNIX machines became more popular in replacing mainframes, UNIX email systems became more popular. UNIX changed the way email software was approached. One of the main goals of UNIX was to modularize software. Instead of having one gigantic program that handled all the required pieces of a function, smaller programs were created, each program handling a smaller piece of the total functionality of the system. This philosophy was used for email systems. Figure 1.4 shows how email software was modularized in the UNIX environment.

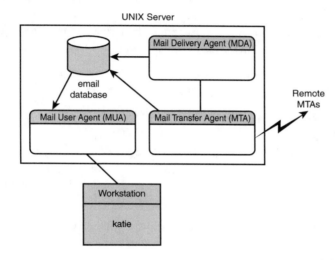

FIGURE 1.4

UNIX modular email environment.

The main portion of the email functionality was located in the Mail Delivery Agent (MDA) software. It was the MDA's responsibility to deliver a message to a user on the local UNIX machine. If a message was intended for a user on a remote system, the MDA passed off the message to a Mail Transfer Agent (MTA) program. The MTA's responsibility was to determine how to connect to the remote host and transfer the message to a user on the remote host. Some programs combined the functionality of two agents into one program. Often the MDA and MTA were treated as a single module—messages for local users are passed to the MDA section of the program, and messages for remote users are passed to the MTA section.

Another piece of the UNIX email puzzle is the Mail User Agent (MUA). The MUA software is responsible for allowing users to read their mail messages. With the increase in the number of networks, MUAs were modified to allow remote network clients to read their mailbox messages. With the availability of high-powered network clients, many MUA programs have incorporated fancy graphical front-end designs to help the client read and organize mail messages.

The following sections describe the different email agents that were implemented in UNIX systems in more detail.

UNIX Mail Transfer Agent Programs

The Mail Transfer Agent software is responsible for transferring both incoming and outgoing mail messages. For each outgoing mail message, the MTA determines the destination of the recipient addresses. If the destination host is the local machine, all the MTA must do is pass off the message to the local MDA for delivery. However, if the destination host is a remote mail server, the MTA must establish a communication method to transfer the message to the remote host. For incoming messages, the MTA must be able to accept connection requests from remote mail servers and receive messages for local users.

The UNIX environment has many different types of MTA programs. The following sections describe some of the more popular MTA programs in use today.

The Sendmail Program

The sendmail MTA program is one of the most popular UNIX MTA programs available. Eric Allman wrote the original sendmail program. The Sendmail Consortium (`http://www.sendmail.org`) currently maintains the source code for it. Allman has moved on to Sendmail, Inc., which provides commercial versions of the sendmail program and provides support to the Sendmail Consortium.

The sendmail program has gained popularity mainly from its extreme versatility. Many of the standard features of sendmail have become synonymous with email systems—virtual domains, message forwarding, userid aliases, mail lists, and masquerading.

Sendmail can be used for many different types of email configurations—large corporate Internet email servers, small corporate servers that dial into ISPs, and even standalone workstations that forward mail through a mail hub. Simply changing a few lines in sendmail's configuration file can change its characteristics and behavior.

Besides being able to change its server characteristics, sendmail also has the capability to parse and handle mail messages according to predefined rule sets. The mail administrator often wants to filter messages according to particular mail requirements. To do this, all that is needed are new rules added to the sendmail configuration file.

Unfortunately, with versatility comes complexity. The sendmail program's large configuration file often becomes overwhelming for beginning mail administrators to handle. Many books have been written to assist the mail administrator in determining the proper configuration file settings for a particular email server application.

The qmail Program

The focus of this book is the *qmail* program. qmail is another MTA program intended for UNIX environments. qmail was written and is maintained by Dan Bernstein (`http://www.qmail.org`) and is a complete replacement for the sendmail program.

The main difference between qmail and sendmail is qmail's modularity. Just as the UNIX system divided email functionality between modules, qmail extends that practice to the MTA program. qmail uses several different programs to implement the MTA functionality. This allows each modular program to be smaller and quicker than one large monolithic program.

Another feature that goes with modularity is security. Each module is independent of the others. qmail requires several different userids to be added to the mail server, and each module runs under a different userid. If an intruder compromises one module, it most likely will not affect the other modules. qmail's security is often touted as its best feature.

Still another feature of qmail is its reliability. As each message enters the qmail system, it is placed in a mail queue. qmail uses a system of mail subdirectories and message states to ensure that each message stored in the message queue is not lost. As an added feature, qmail also can use a specialized user mailbox system that makes it less likely that a user message will be corrupted or lost in the message mailbox.

qmail is simple. Instead of one large configuration file, qmail uses a series of files, each file containing information for one module of the system. As you will see in later chapters, adding elements to the configuration files changes the program's behavior.

The Smail Program

The smail program is another popular MTA program available for the UNIX platform. It is maintained by the GNU Project (http://www.gnu.org). The GNU Project is a major software contributor to the Linux and FreeBSD environments and will be discussed in more detail in Chapter 3, "Server Requirements for qmail."

The smail program uses many of the same features as the sendmail program. Its claim to fame is that it is much easier to configure than sendmail. A standard smail configuration file requires fewer than 20 lines of configuration code, which is much less than sendmail requires.

One of the nice features of smail is its capability to forward mail messages without using mail queues. The sendmail and qmail programs place all messages in a queue file to queue them for delivery. For low-volume mail servers, queuing becomes an unnecessary delay. The smail program attempts to deliver the message immediately, without placing them in a mail queue. While this works great for low-volume mail servers, unfortunately this method can get bogged down on high-volume mail servers. To compensate, the smail program is also configurable to use mail queues to handle larger volumes of mail.

The Exim Program

The University of Cambridge (http://www.exim.org) maintains the exim program. Exim has recently gained popularity because it is easily configured to restrict hackers and spammers. *Hackers* are people who attempt to break into sites using well-known security holes in software. *Spammers* are people who send out mass quantities of (usually) unwanted email, mostly for advertisement purposes.

The exim program contains several configuration files that can contain addresses of known hackers and spammers to restrict any messages from those sites to the mail server. After a hacker or spammer has been identified, his address can be added to the configuration files to prevent any more messages from that address from being received.

UNIX Mail User Agent Programs

The UNIX email model used a local mailbox for each user to hold messages for that user. Programs became available that could interface with the mailbox format. Those programs were called Mail User Agents (MUAs).

The MUAs did not receive messages from remote computers; they only displayed messages that were already placed in the user's mailbox. Throughout the years, many different MUAs have been available for the UNIX platform. The following sections describe some of the more popular MUA programs available in UNIX.

The Mail Program

The simplest MUA program is the mail program. The mail program allows users to access their mailboxes to read stored messages and allows them to send messages to other mail users—on both the local mail system and remote mail servers. Listing 1.1 shows a sample mail session. The text in bold represents text entered by the mailbox user.

LISTING 1.1   Sample Mail Program Session

```
1  $ mail
2  Mail version 8.1 6/6/93.  Type ? for help.
3  "/var/mail/rich": 4 messages 4 new
4  >N  1 barbara@shadrach.isp   Thu Feb 10 18:47 12/417 "This is the first tes"
5   N  2 katie@shadrach.isp1.   Thu Feb 10 18:57 12/415 "Second test message"
6   N  3 jessica@shadrach.isp   Thu Feb 10 19:23 12/413 "Third test message"
7   N  4 mike@shadrach.ispnet   Thu Feb 10 19:42 12/423 "Fourth and final test"
8  & 1
9  Message 1:
10 From barbara@shadrach.isp1.net Thu Feb 10 18:47:05 2000
11 Date: 10 Feb 2000 23:47:05 -0000
12 From: barbara@shadrach.isp1.net
13 To: rich@shadrach.isp1.net
14 Subject: This is the first test message
15
16 Hi, This is a test message
```

```
17
18 & d
19 Message 2:
20 From katie@shadrach.isp1.net Thu Feb 10 18:57:32 2000
21 Date: 10 Feb 2000 23:57:32 -0000
22 From: katie@shadrach.isp1.net
23 To: rich@shadrach.isp1.net
24 Subject: Second test message
25
26 Hi, this is the second test message
27
28 & q
29 Saved 3 messages in mbox
30 $
```

Line 1 shows the mail program being executed with no command-line options. By default this allows the user to check the messages in his mailbox. Lines 2 through 7 show the standard greeting for the mail program. A summary of all of the messages in the user's mailbox is displayed. The location of the user's mailbox depends on the particular flavor of UNIX the mail server is using. On FreeBSD servers, the default mailbox directory location is /var/mail, and on Linux it is located at /var/spool/mail.

Each user has a separate file that contains all of his messages. The filename is usually the system username of the user, and it is located in the system mailbox directory. Thus, all messages for userid rich are stored in the file /var/mail/rich on a FreeBSD system. As new messages are received for the user, they are appended to the end of the file.

In the mail program listing, lines 4 through 7 show how information for each message is displayed on a single line. This information includes the message number, the sender of the message, the date of the message, and the Subject: header of the message. Line 8 shows the interactive command-line prompt generated by the mail program. The user must enter a command. By typing a message number, the user can display the text of that message, as shown in lines 9 through 17. Line 18 shows the user command to delete a message. By entering the d command, the user deletes the current message number from the mailbox, and the next message (if any) is displayed. At the end of the mail session the user can use the q command to exit the mail program. Any undeleted messages are moved from the user's mailbox to a special file in the user's home directory. Messages in this file can be retrieved later by using the -f option on the mail program command line.

The Pine Program

As advancements were made to the UNIX environment, MUA programs became fancier. One of the first attempts at graphics on UNIX systems was the ncurses graphics library. Using ncurses, a program could manipulate the location of a cursor on the terminal screen and place characters almost anywhere on the terminal.

One email MUA program that takes advantage of the ncurses library is the pine program. When pine is started it paints a user-friendly menu on the user's terminal screen, as shown in Figure 1.5.

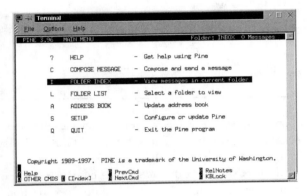

FIGURE 1.5
The pine program main menu screen.

The pine program assigns any messages in the user's mailbox to a special folder labeled INBOX. All new messages appear in INBOX. The user has the capability to create separate folders to hold mail that has already been read, thus making message storage and retrieval easier. As seen in Figure 1.5, pine also includes an address book feature, allowing the user to save important email addresses in a single location.

X Window MUA Programs

Almost all UNIX systems support the graphical X Window environment. Both FreeBSD and Linux use the Xfree86 software to run X Window programs on either the system console or a remote X terminal on the network. There are many email MUA programs that use the X Window system to display message information. The kmail MUA program can be used to read and send messages from an X Window system using the KDE desktop manager. Figure 1.6 shows a sample kmail session screen.

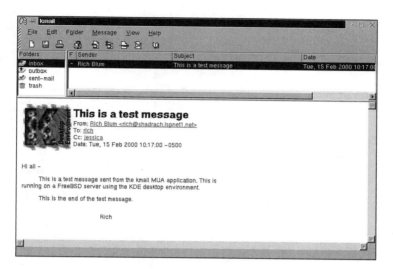

FIGURE 1.6
The kmail MUA program main screen.

LAN-Based Email Systems

In the late 1980s, the computer world was again dramatically changed with the invention of the personal computer. PCs started popping up in corporations, replacing the dumb terminals that were used to communicate with mainframes and minicomputers.

Many organizations used some type of LAN-based network server that allowed network workstations to share disk space on the network fileserver. This created a new type of email server that used the shared network disk space.

Modern email packages such as Microsoft Exchange, Novell GroupWise, and IBM Lotus Notes use programs that access a common disk area containing user mailboxes. The mailboxes are often contained within a single database. To access the database, the MUA programs running on the workstations must be able to read and parse the mailbox database. This method almost always uses a proprietary protocol to access the mailboxes in the database.

The MTA programs often become quite complicated in this environment. Since the email systems use special databases, the method of sending messages to remote systems depends on what the remote system is. If the remote system is the same type as the sending system, then the same proprietary protocol can be used to transfer the message. If the remote system is different, then the MTA must be able to convert the message to a standard format and use a standard email protocol (discussed below) to send the message. Figure 1.7 shows an example of a proprietary email system on an office network.

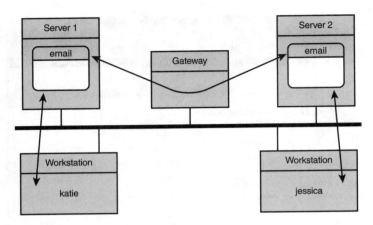

FIGURE 1.7
A LAN-based proprietary email system.

With LAN-based email systems, dedicated workstations are often required to route messages between destinations. This increases the chance of failure, since there is additional hardware and software in addition to the email server involved in the email transfer.

Another possible problem with proprietary email systems is the mail database. All messages are stored in one database, and the database size increases in proportion to the number of messages saved on the system. It is not uncommon to see databases over 1GB in size for a small organization. In this situation, the database can become corrupt, and a database recovery routine must be run. If the routine is unsuccessful, all messages in the database are lost. UNIX-based systems keep individual mailboxes for each user. If one mailbox becomes corrupt, only one user loses his messages, and the rest of the users are unaffected. As stated earlier, qmail even takes this one step further by having the capability to create user mailbox directories, with each message being a separate file in the directory. Thus, one bad message will not corrupt the entire mailbox.

Proprietary LAN-based email systems are very popular. Also, they tend to be very expensive. As the mail administrator, you should weigh all the pros and cons of purchasing a proprietary email system. Often the same functionality can be obtained using a UNIX system such as Linux of FreeBSD with open source programs.

Email Protocols

Using open source email packages means that you must also use open source protocols to communicate messages between packages. There have been many protocols developed to allow messages to be transferred between mail servers and to allow network clients to read their messages from the mail server. This section describes the protocols that are detailed in this book.

Mail Transfer Agent Protocols

MTA programs must be able to transfer messages to users on remote mail servers. To do this, one MTA package must be able to communicate with another MTA package to move not only the mail message, but also the necessary identification information needed for the mail message to be identified by the remote user. MTA programs use the protocols in the next few sections to transfer messages and information between remote hosts.

SMTP

The Simple Mail Transfer Protocol (SMTP) was developed as the primary method to transfer messages across the Internet between MTA servers. Any host connected to the Internet could use the SMTP protocol to send a mail message to any other host.

The SMTP protocol uses simple commands to establish a connection and to transfer information and data between hosts (thus the word *Simple* in the title). Commands consist of a single word with additional information following the command, such as this SMTP command:

```
MAIL FROM: <rich@shacrach.ispnet1.net>
```

This identifies to the remote mail server from whom the message originated. Each command line is transmitted across the Internet in plain ASCII text. After each command, the remote host must send a reply code to the originating host to indicate if the command was successful. Figure 1.8 demonstrates a sample SMTP connection between two hosts.

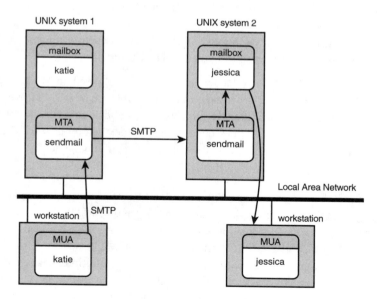

FIGURE 1.8

Sample SMTP connection between two hosts.

No login is required on the remote host, because no functions are performed on the host. It is the responsibility of the remote host to interpret the received message and to decide if to forward it to the appropriate local mailbox. The full SMTP protocol is described in Chapter 5, "SMTP and qmail."

To identify remote hosts, the SMTP protocol uses the domain name system (DNS). DNS is a distributed database on the Internet that allows hosts to be uniquely identified by a name as well as an IP address. Each area within the Internet has a DNS server that is responsible for maintaining the DNS database for that area or zone. Any Internet hosts within that zone that use a registered DNS name have an entry in the database on the DNS server. The entry maps the host's IP address to its official DNS name. Chapter 4, "DNS and qmail," describes how DNS works and how DNS servers are implemented for zones.

ESMTP

As SMTP became more popular, some shortcomings were identified in the original protocol. Rather than create a new protocol, developers decided to extend the basic SMTP commands with new commands. The new protocol was named the Extended Simple Mail Transfer Protocol (ESMTP). The new functionality of ESMTP has proved for the past several years to be more robust and more than capable of supporting the mail transfer environment between MTA hosts.

One important function that ESMTP implemented is the capability for MTA hosts to reverse the SMTP connection. The SMTP protocol was designed to allow only one-way communication between MTAs. One MTA would connect to a remote MTA, transfer any queued mail messages, and then disconnect. If the remote MTA had any queued messages for the originating MTA, it could not transfer them during the SMTP session.

To solve this problem, ESMTP created a new command that allowed an MTA to request a reverse connection. This informed the remote MTA to establish a new SMTP connection to the originating MTA and transfer any queued messages. By establishing a new connection, the remote MTA had a better chance of connecting to the real destination instead of a potential fake. The ESMTP commands are also discussed in more detail in Chapter 5.

QMTP

In addition to qmail, Dan Bernstein created a new mail transfer protocol to replace SMTP. Bernstein recognized that one of the downfalls of SMTP and ESMTP was that each message was transferred individually, thus creating a slow delivery system. To compensate for this problem, he wrote the Quick Mail Transfer Protocol (QMTP). QMTP uses a modified system of sending messages to a mail host that allows the client to send multiple messages before the remote host has to acknowledge receipt of the messages. To use QMTP, both the originating and remote MTAs must be using qmail. Again, this protocol is discussed in more detail in Chapter 5.

Mail User Agent Protocols

The purpose of the MUA protocols is to allow users to read messages from their mailboxes. On a single-user UNIX system this is usually not a problem—the user is logged in to the system from the console. However, in a multiuser environment, there will be multiple users that need to access their mailboxes to read their messages. This would be practically impossible to do from a single console screen.

To accommodate this scenario, protocols have been developed to allow remote network users to log in and read messages in their mailboxes on the network mail server. Each user can connect to his mailbox on the mail server through an MUA program that resides on his workstation. The MUA program uses special protocols to connect to the mail server and manipulate messages in the mailbox. The following sections describe the two most popular MUA protocols in use.

The Post Office Protocol

The simplest MUA protocol is the Post Office Protocol (POP). The current version of POP is version 3, thus the term POP3. MUA programs on the workstation use the POP3 protocol to access and read messages in the user's mailbox. Figure 1.9 shows an example of a workstation using the POP3 protocol to read mail messages.

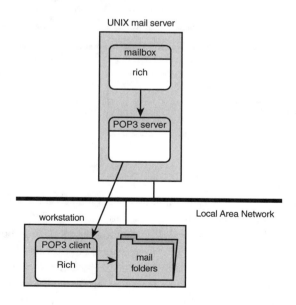

FIGURE 1.9

A sample POP3 connection.

When the POP3 protocol is used, messages for the user are read from the user's mailbox and stored on the local workstation. Usually, the workstation MUA program will delete messages from the server mailbox as they are read, thus freeing up space on the mail server.

The Interactive Mail Access Protocol

Another MUA protocol that is commonly used is the Interactive Mail Access Protocol (IMAP). IMAP is currently at version 4, revision 1, thus the term IMAP4rev1 is often used. MUA programs on workstations can use the IMAP program to manipulate mail messages in folders that reside on the mail server. Figure 1.10 shows an example of a workstation using the IMAP protocol.

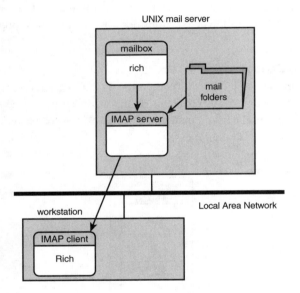

FIGURE 1.10

A sample IMAP connection.

In an IMAP connection, all of the user's mail messages reside on the mail server. Messages are downloaded only to be displayed on the workstation screen. This protocol is useful if the user must access his mailbox from several different computers. Using the POP3 protocol, each time the user accesses his mailbox, the current messages are downloaded to the workstation used for access. This could easily distribute messages between several different computers. IMAP prevents this situation by keeping all messages on the mail server, no matter which workstation is used to display them. While this is more convenient for the user, it makes the job of the mail administrator much more difficult. In this scenario, disk space on the mail server can quickly fill up with undeleted messages and must be watched carefully.

Summary

This chapter discusses the history and functionality of email systems. Email systems started out as nothing more that simple messaging systems that allowed users of a mainframe to exchange quick messages between terminals. As mainframes matured, the email systems allowed increased functionality. Email allowed users to send messages to other mainframe users who weren't logged into the system, storing the messages in an area where the user could retrieve the message when he logged in.

As mainframe networks became mature and allowed inter-mainframe communication, email systems allowed users to send mail messages to users on remote mainframes. The UNIX operating system changed the way email systems operated. Instead of one large email program, the email software was divided into smaller pieces—each piece performing an individual function of the email process. Mail Transfer Agents (MTAs) were used to deliver mail messages to users, both locally and remotely. To deliver messages to remote users, one MTA was required to communicate with another MTA.

Often this communication took place across a network, such as the Internet. To accomplish this communication, protocols were developed that allowed MTAs to successfully pass messages and message information between them. The Simple Mail Transfer Protocol (SMTP) became the most popular of the MTA protocols due to its versatility and simplicity.

The other piece of software used in the UNIX environment was the Mail User Agent (MUA) program. MUAs were used to allow users to read messages from their mailboxes. With the advent of network connected workstations came the necessity for MUA programs that ran on remote clients. These programs needed protocols that allowed them to read user mailboxes on the remote mail server. The Post Office Protocol (POP3) and Interactive Mail Access Protocol (IMAP) were two protocols that allowed remote MUA programs to access messages on the mail server.

qmail Services

IN THIS CHAPTER

One of the more popular email packages available for UNIX systems is the qmail package. qmail was developed by Dan Bernstein to provide Mail Transfer Agent (MTA) functionality for standard UNIX servers. The qmail software is capable of turning a Linux or FreeBSD system into a fully functional email server. The Internet home page for qmail is located at `http://www.qmail.org`.

It is the responsibility of the MTA package to manage messages that come into or leave the mail server. qmail accomplishes this by using several different modular programs and creating a complex system of mail queue directories and message states. Each program processes the message through the various message states until the message is delivered to its final destination. If at any time the mail server crashes during a message transfer, qmail can determine what state the message was last successfully placed in and attempt to continue the message processing.

This chapter details the features and components that make up the qmail software package. qmail was designed to be a complete UNIX MTA mail system, and there are many pieces that must interact for qmail to successfully transfer and deliver mail messages.

The Role of qmail in the UNIX Mail Server

The qmail software package is just one piece of the larger mail server picture. Much like the three blind men trying to describe an elephant, often it is best to take a couple of steps back to view the entire system before looking at the individual pieces.

Figure 2.1 shows a block diagram of how qmail interacts with other system software on the UNIX mail system.

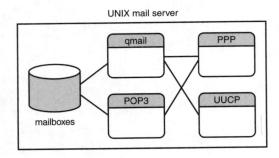

FIGURE 2.1

Block diagram of qmail on a UNIX system.

As shown in Figure 2.1, there are several pieces of software that must be present for qmail to operate on the server. The UNIX server must provide a method to communicate with the remote mail hosts. This communication is most often done using the TCP/IP protocol, across either a local area network (LAN) connection or a dial-up modem connection using the Point-to-Point Protocol (PPP).

Also, there must be a method for users to read messages stored in their mailboxes. The two most common methods for remote users to retrieve their mail messages are the Post Office Protocol (POP3) and the Interactive Mail Access Protocol (IMAP). The following sections describe the pieces that interact to complete a mail server.

The PPP Software

The cheapest method of host communication used today is a dial-up modem. Most home users use dial-up modems to communicate with the remote mail server. Many small businesses also use dial-up modems to communicate efficiently with remote ISPs. The most efficient method of dial-up communication using a modem is to establish a TCP/IP connection with the remote ISP mail host. The PPP protocol is used to transfer TCP/IP packets from the client computer to the ISP host computer. Once the PPP session is established, TCP/IP packets can be transferred between the hosts just as if they were both connected with a LAN (only much slower). Chapters 18, "Configuring a PPP Server," and 19, "Supporting Dial-In Clients," describe the PPP dial-in process in great detail to enable the qmail administrator to configure the mail server to support remote users.

qmail uses the Simple Mail Transfer Protocol (SMTP) to transfer mail messages across the PPP connection to the remote mail host. SMTP uses the TCP/IP connection established with the PPP connection to transfer mail messages to the mail server. Chapter 5, "SMTP and qmail," describes the SMTP protocol in more detail.

The UUCP Software

Besides PPP, the older UNIX-to-UNIX copy protocol (UUCP) can be used to establish a communications link with a remote ISP computer. As shown in Figure 2.1, either method can be used to establish communication with a remote mail server. Often offices that do not wish to have IP connectivity to the Internet for security reasons choose to transfer mail using the UUCP protocol.

Configuring the mail server to support UUCP connectivity to remote hosts is not a difficult task. Chapter 11, "Using qmail as an ISP Mail Server," describes the steps necessary to create a mail server for UUCP clients.

The MUA Server Software

Besides network communications software, MUA server software is also required to allow remote clients to retrieve their mail messages from qmail mailboxes. Most customers require user-friendly GUI application programs to assist them in connecting to the ISP and downloading new mail messages.

The POP3 and IMAP protocols allow remote users to read messages stored in their mailboxes on the mail server and forward new messages to remote Internet users via the mail server. There are several different UNIX implementations of POP3 and IMAP.

One common MUA server program used with qmail is the `qmail-pop3d` program. This allows remote clients to retrieve messages using the POP3 protocol using popular client software packages such as Microsoft Outlook or Netscape Messenger.

Other MUA server software packages include the popular `pop3d` and `imapd` programs from the University of Washington. These programs can support several different types of authentication methods. Chapter 17, "Installing and Configuring POP3 and IMAP Servers," details the use of POP3 and IMAP servers on the mail server.

The qmail Block Diagram

The qmail system itself consists of several executable programs, configuration files, and UNIX environment variables, all interacting with each other to provide mail service. Figure 2.2 shows a block diagram of the qmail pieces.

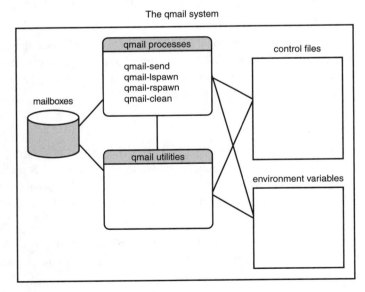

FIGURE 2.2

qmail function processes.

Each piece of the qmail puzzle provides a different function for the whole process. The following sections describe the different pieces of the qmail block diagram.

As shown in Figure 2.3, there are nine core programs used in qmail. The following sections describe the functionality of each of the core programs.

qmail-smtpd

The `qmail-smtpd` program is responsible for receiving mail messages from remote hosts and passing them to the `qmail-queue` program for processing. The `qmail-smtpd` program receives the messages using the SMTP protocol and thus must be prepared to receive messages at any time from the network. However, it does not run as a continual background process. It uses a network helper program to monitor IP connection attempts. The inetd program is a common UNIX program used by both Linux and FreeBSD to monitor IP connections. When an SMTP connection attempt is detected, inetd automatically starts the `qmail-smtpd` program and passes control of the IP connection to it. Also used is the `tcpserver` program developed by Dan Bernstein.

Once the `qmail-smtpd` program establishes an SMTP connection with the remote mail server, the remote mail server can send messages to the qmail mail server.

> **NOTE**
>
> Chapter 5 describes the details of how qmail connects with remote mail servers and transfers mail messages using the SMTP protocol.

To test the `qmail-smtpd` program, you can manually Telnet to the SMTP port (TCP port 25) on the local mail server. Once the connection is established, you can manually enter SMTP commands to communicate with the SMTP server, as shown in Chapter 5. Listing 2.2 shows a sample SMTP session with a qmail mail server using the `qmail-smtpd` program to receive messages.

LISTING 2.2 A Sample `qmail-smtpd` SMTP Session

```
1  $ telnet localhost 25
2  Trying 127.0.0.1...
3  Connected to localhost.isptest.net.
4  Escape character is '^]'.
5  220 shadrach.isptest.net ESMTP
6  HELO meshach.isptest.net
7  250 shadrach.isptest.net
8  MAIL FROM: <barbara@meshach.isptest.net>
9  250 ok
10 RCPT TO: <rich@shadrach.isptest.net>
```

Listing 2.2   Continued

```
11 250 ok
12 DATA
13 354 go ahead
14 From: barbara@meshach.isptest.net
15 To: rich@shadrach.isptest.net
16 Date: January 31, 2000 19:30:00
17 Subject: Let's get together for a meeting
18
19 Hi Rich,
20
21     Let's see if we can coordinate a meeting sometime this week.
22
23 Barbara
24 .
25 250 ok 949355489 qp 1534
26 QUIT
27 221 shadrach.isptest.net
28 Connection closed by foreign host.
29 you have mail
30 $
```

Line 1 shows an attempt to establish an SMTP connection with the local mail server as a test. Line 5 shows the standard SMTP greeting that is sent by the qmail-smtpd program when it takes control of the IP connection. Lines 6 through 27 demonstrate a standard SMTP session to send a message to a user on a remote mail server. In line 26 the SMTP session is terminated by the client, and in line 27 the qmail-smtpd program sends a closing banner and terminates the SMTP session. As can be seen in line 29, the mail message has been properly passed off to the mail queue and picked up by the appropriate local mail handler to deliver it to the intended local user.

qmail-inject

The qmail-inject program is used to accept a locally generated mail message and pass it off to the qmail-queue program. Often messages are passed to qmail-inject from Mail User Agents (MUAs) on the UNIX system, such as mail, pine, and elm.

Before passing the incoming mail message to the qmail-queue program, qmail-inject scans the message to ensure that it has appropriate RFC822 headers. RFC822 describes a standard message header format that provides information regarding the sender, recipients, date, subject, and other technical details of the message.

> **NOTE**
>
> The complete RFC822 message header format is described in detail in Chapter 5.

`qmail-inject` checks the sender address fields to ensure that any addresses listed are in the proper RFC822 format. Table 2.2 shows a list of RFC822 sender header fields.

TABLE 2.2   RFC822 Sender Header Fields

Field	Description
From:	The author of the message
Sender:	The sender of the message if different from the author
Reply-To:	The address to reply to if different from the author
Return-Path:	The route used to send a message back to the author
Return-Recipient-To:	The address to send the reply to besides the original author of the message
Errors-To:	The address to reply to if errors occur in processing the message
Resent-From:	The address of an author who was used to relay the message
Resent-Sender:	The address of a server that was used to relay the message
Resent-Reply-To:	The address to reply to the server that relayed the original message

If no RFC822 sender header fields are detected, `qmail-inject` inserts a From: field in the message header with the name of the UNIX user that invoked the `qmail-inject` process.

Besides sender addresses, `qmail-inject` also checks recipient addresses to ensure proper formatting. Table 2.3 shows the possible RFC822 recipient header fields.

TABLE 2.3   RFC822 Recipient Header Fields

Field	Description
To:	The main recipient of the message
Cc:	Any additional recipients included
Bcc:	Any recipients that do not wish to be identified in the message

TABLE 2.3 RFC822 Recipient Header Fields

Field	Description
Apparently-To:	The message recipient, as determined by the email package
Resent-To:	The main recipient of a message that has been relayed
Resent-Cc:	Any additional recipients of a message that has been relayed
Resent-Bcc:	Any recipients that do not want to be identified in a message that has been relayed

If no To: or Cc: fields are detected, `qmail-inject` adds a Cc: header field formatted as

`Cc: recipient list not shown: ;`

If any Bcc: fields are detected, they are deleted from the message in accordance with RFC822 rules.

The last two RFC822 header fields that `qmail-inject` also scans for are the Date: and Message ID: fields. If no Date: field exists in the message, `qmail-inject` adds a Date: header field with the current date and time using GMT. Every RFC822-compliant email message must have a Message ID: field uniquely identifying the message. If no Message ID: field exists, `qmail-inject` adds one.

qmail-send

Once a message has been successfully placed in the mail queue, the `qmail-send` program is used to process it. `qmail-send` checks the status of each message in the mail queue. Messages that have failed on a previous mail attempt are identified, and it is determined if they are in a temporary or permanent delivery failure status. Messages in a temporary delivery failure status are tried again. Messages in a permanent delivery failure status are passed to `qmail-clean` for deletion. Messages that have not been sent are forwarded for sending.

`qmail-send` uses the `qmail-lspawn` and `qmail-rspawn` programs. Any messages with a recipient address determined to be local to the mail server are passed to `qmail-lspawn`. Any messages with a recipient address determined to be on a remote mail server are passed to `qmail-rspawn`. Once the message is passed to either of those two programs, `qmail-send`'s job is done.

The `qmail-send` program is run as a background process on the mail server. When `qmail-send` starts, it reads the qmail control and configuration files. To determine if qmail is running on your mail server, you can use the UNIX `ps` command. Listing 2.3 shows the output from a `ps` command.

LISTING 2.3   Displaying the qmail Processes

```
1 $ ps ax | grep qmail
2    232 con- I+   0:00.34 qmail-send
3    236 con- I+   0:00.07 splogger qmail
4    237 con- I+   0:00.05 qmail-lspawn |preline -f /usr/libexec/mail.local -r
5    238 con- I+   0:00.02 qmail-rspawn
6    239 con- I+   0:00.04 qmail-clean
7 $
```

Line 1 shows the command used to display the qmail processes currently running on the mail server. Lines 2 through 6 show the qmail processes running on the mail server. Line 2 is the qmail-send program running as a background process. Standard UNIX signals can be sent to the running qmail-send process to control its behavior. To have the qmail-send process attempt to deliver all messages in the mail queue immediately, the root user can send a SIGALRM signal to the process as follows:

```
kill -ALRM pid
```

pid is the UNIX process ID (PID) of the running qmail-send program. The PID of the program can be determined from the ps command. In the ax command-line options, the PID is the first parameter listed. As shown in Figure 2.2, the PID of the qmail-send program in this example is 232. To stop the qmail program on the mail server, the root user can send qmail-send a SIGTERM signal as follows:

```
kill -TERM pid
```

When the qmail-send program is stopped, it terminates all qmail processes running in background.

qmail-clean

The qmail-clean program is used to remove unsent messages from the mail queue that appear to have failed. qmail uses a multi-state system of identifying messages in the mail queue. Each message traverses several states while it is being processed. If at any time the mail server crashes, the qmail-send program can detect the last successful state of the message and continue processing the message. If qmail-send is unable to process the message due to either server errors or the message being undeliverable, the qmail-clean program is called to remove the message from the mail queue.

Like the qmail-send program, qmail-clean runs continually as a background process.

qmail-rspawn

The qmail-rspawn program is called by the qmail-send program when a message is determined to be for a user on a remote mail server. qmail-rspawn attempts to schedule the message for delivery by the qmail-remote program, then asynchronously invokes qmail-remote. One job of qmail-rspawn is to determine the destination mail server for each of the recipients of the message. qmail-remote is called once for each remote destination host.

Again, like qmail-send, qmail-rspawn runs continually as a background process.

qmail-remote

The job of the qmail-remote program is to deliver mail messages to remote users via the SMTP protocol. Messages are passed to qmail-remote via the qmail-rspawn program described in the previous section. qmail-remote can connect to only one remote host each time it is invoked. However, it can deliver the mail message to multiple recipients on the same remote host at one time. It is the responsibility of qmail-rspawn to call qmail-remote multiple times, depending on the destination mail servers.

During processing, qmail-remote scans the body of the mail message to determine if it is in the proper SMTP format. A single period (.) at the beginning of any line is changed to two periods (..) per normal SMTP conventions. Also, all lines in an SMTP message must terminate with an SMTP-style newline (CR and LF). Any UNIX-style newlines (LF) are prepended with CR to conform to the SMTP format. Listing 2.4 shows an example of manually invoking qmail-remote to send a message saved in a text file (named text) to a user on a remote mail server.

LISTING 2.4   Manually Invoking qmail-remote

```
1  $ cat mailtest | /var/qmail/bin/qmail-remote 192.168.1.1 rich rich
2  rK192.168.1.1 accepted message.
3  Remote host said: 250 ok 949512859 qp 28548
4  $ mail
5  Mail version 8.1 6/6/93.  Type ? for help.
6  "/var/mail/rich": 1 message 1 new
7  >N  1 rich@shadrach.ispnet.net  Wed Feb  2 19:34   17/535
➥    "This is a test message"
8  &1
9  Message 1:
10 From rich Wed Feb  2 12:34:19 2000
11 From: <rich@shadrach.ispnet.net>
12 To: <rich@shadrach.ispnet.net>
13 Subject: This is a test message
14
15 Hi Rich -
16
17     This is a test message from shadrach using the qmail-remote mail
```

```
18 system. I hope that this test works.
19
20 This is the end of the qmail-remote test.
21
22 &
```

Line 1 shows an example of using the `qmail-remote` command manually. The message file is piped to the `qmail-remote` program, using the UNIX pipe command (|). The first parameter for `qmail-remote` is the destination address, the second parameter is the sending username, and the third parameter is the recipient username(s). `qmail-remote` responds with a result code. Table 2.4 shows the possible `qmail-remote` result codes.

TABLE 2.4   `qmail-remote` Result Codes

Response Code	Description
r	Recipient accepted the message for delivery.
h	The recipient reported a permanent rejection of the message.
s	The recipient reported a temporary rejection of the message.
K	The host accepted the message for delivery.
Z	The host reported a temporary failure to deliver the message.
D	The host reported a permanent failure to deliver the message.

One lowercase and one uppercase character are used to define the mail transaction. The uppercase character defines the action taken by the remote host, and the lowercase character defines the action taken for the particular recipient. In the case of multiple recipients, the recipient result code will print in the same order as the recipient listing on the command line. After the result code, a text message appears to further describe the result. As shown in Listing 2.4, line 2, the host accepted the test message for delivery, and the message was delivered to the recipient's mailbox.

qmail-lspawn

The `qmail-lspawn` program is similar to the `qmail-rspawn` program in that it is called by `qmail-send`. `qmail-lspawn` is responsible for scheduling mail delivery when a message is determined to be for a user on the local mail server.

qmail-local

The `qmail-local` program is used to deliver messages to the local mail server. If `qmail-local` detects this address as a *Delivered-To:* header field, it bounces the message. This is used to detect mail message loops often caused by improper forwarding commands.

qmail-queue

The `qmail-queue` program handles messages from the `qmail-inject` and `qmail-smtpd` programs and moves them to a mail queue for delivery. While `qmail-queue` processes the message it scans the sender and recipient addresses. The mail message is passed to the `qmail-queue` program on descriptor 0, while the sender and recipient information is passed on descriptor 1. `qmail-queue` expects the sender and recipient information to be presented in a particular format:

- The sender address is preceded by an `F` character and terminated by a `NULL` character.
- Each recipient address is preceded by a `T` character and terminated by a `NULL` character.
- The end of the recipient list is indicated by an extra `NULL` character.

Per RFC822 rules, the `qmail-queue` program always adds the appropriate *Received:* header line to the mail message header.

Inside the qmail Message Queue

The qmail program uses a unique method of queuing received messages for delivery. Unlike other mail programs that create a single mail directory to handle messages, qmail uses a system of message queue directories to indicate the current state of the message during the queuing and delivery processes.

One feature of qmail is an advanced capability to recover messages after mail server crashes. By determining the current state of the message, qmail can restart processing the message and attempt delivery.

The following sections describe the qmail mail queue structure and the message states that each message must traverse to get through the queuing and delivery processes.

qmail Message Queue Structure

By default the qmail mail queue is located in the `/var/qmail/queue` directory. From this directory, subdirectories are created to hold files that contain different pieces of the message. Each subdirectory is used for a different part of the mail queue process. Each message is saved as a separate file, using the inode number as the filename. Each piece of the same message will have the same filename within the separate subdirectories. Table 2.5 shows the subdirectories that are used in the qmail mail queue.

TABLE 2.5   qmail Mail Queue Subdirectories

Directory	Description
bounce	Contains messages that have had permanent delivery failures.
info	Contains the sender address of the message.
intd	Contains the message header as reconstructed by `qmail-queue`.
local	Contains the message recipient address(es) for the local mail server.
lock	Contains files used to indicate when the messages are available for reading by `qmail-send`.
mess	Contains the mail message to deliver.
pid	Initial holding area for new messages placed in the qmail mail queue.
remote	Contains the message recipient address(es) for remote mail servers.
todo	Contains the complete message header, including sender and recipient addresses.

As a new message is placed in the mail queue, it is assigned a unique filename based on its inode number and placed in the `pid` subdirectory. As the message travels through the various qmail message states, parts are copied to files containing the appropriate information in the appropriate subdirectory. Each file that pertains to a message uses the same unique filename (the inode number of the original file). Thus, a message can have several files in the queue that relate to it.

Each message part represents a different message state that the message is undergoing within the queuing and delivery processes. The next section describes the states that a message traverses.

qmail Message States

After the `qmail-queue` program receives the mail message, the message is placed in the `pid` subdirectory. The `qmail-queue` program processes the message through multiple states to parse information necessary to forward the message to the appropriate destination(s). Each message state extracts or creates information from the message header. As the message passes from state to state, files are created in the appropriate subdirectories, shown in the previous section. If at any time the mail server crashes, `qmail-queue` can determine the last state that a message was in and continue processing the message. This is an extremely good feature of the qmail program—system crash tolerance.

The following sections describe the various message states that the mail message traverses before it is delivered to the final destination.

Message state 1—Message Insertion

The first step in processing the mail message is to store the initial message in the mail queue. When `qmail-smtpd` or `qmail-inject` receives a message, the message is passed to the `qmail-queue` program. `qmail-queue` temporarily stores the message in the `pid` subdirectory as a unique filename in that directory.

After the message has been successfully saved as a file, `qmail-queue` determines the inode number assigned to that file. Each file on a UNIX system is assigned a unique inode number that identifies the file on the file system. To display the inode numbers of files, you can use the `-i` option of the `ls` command. By using the inode number of the original file, qmail ensures that no two messages will have the same filename.

The inode number is used to create a new file in the `mess` subdirectory with the inode number of the temporary file created in the `pid` subdirectory as the filename. At this point the message has completed message state 1 and is ready for message state 2.

Message State 2—Message Storage

In message state 2, the message is copied from the temporary file in the `pid` subdirectory to the file created in the `mess` subdirectory. Each message that is stored in the queue is stored as a separate file in the `mess` subdirectory.

If there is a system crash at any time, `qmail-queue` can tell if any messages are stored waiting to be processed by checking the `mess` subdirectory. Any messages that were passed off to the mail queue from either local or remote users will be in the `mess` subdirectory.

At this point `qmail-queue` creates a file in the `intd` subdirectory with the same filename as the `mess` subdirectory filename. The message is now in message state 3.

Message State 3—Message Header Extraction

In message state 3, the message in the `mess` subdirectory file is scanned and the header information is copied to the file created in the `intd` subdirectory. The header information that is required for `qmail-queue` is the recipient address(es) and the sender address. `qmail-queue` requires this information so that it knows how to pass the message onto `qmail-send`, and where to send a message if the original message bounces.

When the header information is copied to the file in the `intd` directory, the message has completed message state 3 and is passed to message state 4.

Message State 4—Message Queuing and Preprocessing

In message state 4, the message is queued for processing by `qmail-send`. This is accomplished by linking the file created in the `intd` subdirectory to a file of the same name in the `todo` subdirectory. As the two files are linked, an inherent requirement is placed on the qmail mail queue that the `todo` and `intd` subdirectories must be on the same file system. If files are on two different file systems, they cannot be linked by qmail.

After the file is successfully linked to a new file in the `todo` subdirectory, `qmail-queue` has completed its job. The message is queued and ready to be preprocessed by `qmail-send`. At this point, the message is still in message state 4.

The `qmail-send` program scans the `todo` subdirectory waiting for new files to appear (remember, `qmail-send` continually runs as a background process). When a new file appears, that indicates that a message is queued for delivery. `qmail-send` first checks the `info`, `local`, and `remote` subdirectories to determine if any files exist with the same filename as the message file. If any exist, they are deleted.

After scanning the `info`, `local`, and `remote` subdirectories, `qmail-send` reads the `todo` file and creates a file in the `info` directory that contains the header information regarding the sender of the message. After creating the `info` file, `qmail-send` determines the recipients and creates a new file in the `local` and `remote` subdirectories, according to the recipients listed on the message.

All local addresses in the message header are included in the file in the `local` subdirectory. Any remote recipient addresses in the message header are included in the file in the `remote` subdirectory. If no recipients are present for either local or remote delivery, the corresponding file is not created. Once the `info`, `local`, and `remote` files are created, the message has completed message state 4 and is ready for message delivery in message state 5.

Message State 5—Message Delivery

In message state 5, the `qmail-send` program processes the files in the `local` and `remote` subdirectories. Each file in the `local` and `remote` subdirectories contains addresses of recipients that must receive the message. `qmail-send` reads each recipient address and attempts to deliver the message body in the `mess` subdirectory to the recipient. `qmail-send` marks each recipient in the file as being either DONE or NOT DONE, depending on the status of the delivery attempt.

Recipients marked as DONE have successfully received the message and do not need further processing. When all the recipients in the file are marked as DONE, the file is deleted from the subdirectory. If `qmail-send` attempts to deliver a message to a recipient and receives a temporary delivery failure, it marks the recipient as NOT DONE so that it can be processed again. If the delivery attempt receives a permanent delivery failure, `qmail-send` marks the recipient as DONE and appends a note to a file in the `bounce` subdirectory. If no file exists in the `bounce` subdirectory for this message, a new file is created.

Messages in the `bounce` subdirectory are treated as new messages. The information in the `bounce` file and the `mess` file is combined to create a new message that is re-inserted into the `qmail-queue` process and sent to the original message sender. Once the new message is created, the file in the `bounce` subdirectory is deleted.

Once all of the recipients are completed and the `local` and `remote` files are deleted, the message is complete. If a `bounce` message exists, it is processed and deleted as previously described. Next, the file in the `info` subdirectory is deleted, temporarily placing the message back in message state 2. Finally, the file in the `mess` subdirectory is deleted, returning the message to message state 1 and completing the message process. At this point, the message no longer is in the mail queue, and qmail considers the message delivery complete.

Message Clean-Up

Due to server or qmail process crashes, it is possible that a mail message may get stuck in an intermediate process. Under normal operating conditions this is not a problem. Both `qmail-queue` and `qmail-send` operate on any files that appear in the appropriate message states, no matter when they were placed there.

If for some unexplained reason a message is stuck for more than 36 hours, qmail assumes that a catastrophic error has occurred and attempts to delete the message. First, if the file in `intd` exists, it is deleted. Next, the file in the `mess` subdirectory is deleted. Also, if any files remain in the `pid` subdirectory for more than 36 hours without being processed, they are deleted.

qmail and Sendmail

The granddaddy of all UNIX email systems is the Sendmail program. Its use has been so widespread that most UNIX implementations install it as default. The qmail system was designed to be a complete replacement for the Sendmail system, and qmail can replace all functions and features of Sendmail on a UNIX system. Some of the compatible Sendmail features that qmail supports are

- The use of `.forward` files in the user `$HOME` directories.
- The use of a system `/etc/aliases` table.
- The use of a system `/var/spool/mail` or `/var/mail` mail queue.
- Support of virtual domains and receiving mail for multiple hosts.
- Support of mail relaying (and even more importantly, mail relay blocking).
- Support for all standard UNIX Mail User Agents (MUAs).

By supporting all of the features of Sendmail, qmail makes it easy for a mail administrator to completely replace an existing Sendmail system with a qmail installation. Chapter 14, "Migrating from Sendmail to qmail," describes the process of converting an existing Sendmail server to a qmail server.

Summary

The qmail program can be used as a complete UNIX MTA mail system. It has features that make it an attractive email alternative for mail administrators. qmail's strengths are in higher security, higher reliability, and higher performance than other MTA packages.

A qmail system is comprised of several different pieces, including software to support PPP, POP3, and IMAP functionality on the mail server. The qmail software itself is comprised of several different parts. The qmail package contains several programs that run in background mode to monitor mail queues looking for new messages to send. Also, there are several utility programs that are used by qmail to process messages and retrieve statistics.

The qmail control files and UNIX environment variables are used to configure the qmail system. qmail divides the MTA processes into several separate programs, each with individual responsibilities in the mail-delivery process. The `qmail-smtpd` program is responsible for accepting SMTP connections from remote mail servers and accepting message deliveries for local users. The `qmail-inject` program allows local users to send messages through the qmail system. The `qmail-queue` program is used to process the messages as they enter the qmail mail queue system.

qmail uses a unique method of storing messages in the mail queue. The mail queue is divided into several different directories, each directory holding information for a different message state. The `qmail-send` program processes the messages in the mail queue waiting to be delivered. The `qmail-lspawn` and `qmail-local` programs are used to deliver messages to users on the local mail server. The `qmail-rspawn` and `qmail-remote` programs are used to deliver messages to users on remote mail servers.

The qmail package can be used as a replacement to the standard UNIX Sendmail mail program. It implements the entire standard Sendmail features on a UNIX mail server.

2

QMAIL SERVICES

Server Requirements for qmail

IN THIS CHAPTER

Before you can get your feet wet with qmail, you must have a server available for it to run on. The qmail software package was written specifically for the UNIX platform. There are several features of the UNIX operating system that qmail needs to operate properly. This prevents qmail from running on a standard Microsoft Windows workstation (even Windows 2000).

Often, mail administrators for small organizations are not familiar with the operating system that is used for the mail server. This chapter presents a brief description of the UNIX operating system that qmail requires. It also describes two popular free UNIX implementations, FreeBSD and Linux. If you are new to the UNIX world and have not yet chosen an operating system on which to run qmail, you may want to read this chapter before deciding.

> **NOTE**
>
> The qmail package is an extremely robust software package that can run under any UNIX operating system. I stress that the operating system used must be an implementation of UNIX. There are several features of the qmail system that are not present on other operating systems (such as using inode numbers as filenames). Also, while this chapter discusses only two different UNIX implementations, there are plenty more to choose from.

The UNIX Operating System

The core of the UNIX operating system is the *kernel*. The kernel must control the hardware and software on the system, allocating hardware when necessary and executing software when required. The kernel is primarily responsible for system memory management, software program management, hardware management, and file system management. The following sections describe these functions in more detail.

Memory Management

One of the primary functions of the operating system kernel is memory management. Not only does the kernel manage the physical memory available on the system, it also can create and manage *virtual memory*, memory that does not actually exist.

It does this by using space on the hard disk (called the *swap space*) and swapping memory locations back and forth from there to the actual physical memory. This allows the system to think there is more memory available than what physically exists. The memory locations are grouped into blocks called *pages*. Each page of memory will be located either in the physical memory or the swap space. The kernel must maintain a table of the memory pages that indicates where pages are.

The kernel will automatically copy memory pages that have not been accessed for a period of time to the swap space area on the hard disk. When a program wants to access a memory page that has been "swapped out," the kernel must swap out a different memory page and swap in the required page from the swap space.

To use virtual memory, you must create swap space on the hard disk. This is often done during system installation. The `fdisk` command is used to partition the installed hard drive on the system. The format of the `fdisk` command is

```
fdisk [option] [device]
```

where *device* is the hard disk device that is being partitioned. UNIX systems use different naming standards for hard disk devices. Table 3.1 shows the Linux hard disk naming standard.

TABLE 3.1 Linux Hard Disk Devices

Device	Description
/dev/hd[a-h]	IDE disk drives
/dev/sd[a-p]	SCSI disk drives
/dev/ed[a-d]	ESDI disk drives
/dev/xd[ab]	XT disk drives

The first available drive of a particular type is labeled as drive a, the second one drive b, and so on. Within a particular drive, partitions are numbered starting at partition 1. Listing 3.1 shows a sample partition from a Linux system.

LISTING 3.1 A Sample `fdisk` Partition Listing

```
1  [root@shadrach root]# /sbin/fdisk /dev/sda
2
3  Command (m for help): p
4
5  Disk /dev/sda: 64 heads, 32 sectors, 521 cylinders
6  Units = cylinders of 2048 * 512 bytes
7
8     Device Boot    Start     End    Blocks   Id  System
9  /dev/sda1             1     460    471024   83  Linux native
10 /dev/sda2           461     521     62464    5  Extended
11 /dev/sda5           461     521     62448   82  Linux swap
12
13 Command (m for help): q
14 [root@shadrach root]#
```

Line 1 shows the `fdisk` command being run on the first SCSI disk on the Linux system—
`/dev/sda`. `fdisk` allows the system administrator to manipulate the partition table on the disk
drive. Line 3 shows the command used to print the current partition table. Lines 5–11 show the
information from the disk partition table. Line 11 shows the partition that is available on the
hard drive for the Linux swap area.

After a swap area has been created on a hard drive, the kernel must know that it is available
and activate it. The Swapon program is used to activate memory page swapping. The `swapon`
command sets up the virtual memory information in the kernel. This information is lost when
the server is rebooted, which means that the `swapon` command must be executed at every boot
time. Most UNIX distributions allow for the `swapon` command to be run from a startup script
when the system boots.

On Linux systems the current status of the virtual memory can be determined by viewing the
special `/proc/meminfo` file. Listing 3.2 shows a sample `/proc/meminfo` entry.

LISTING 3.2   A Sample `/proc/meminfo` File

```
 1  [root@shadrach /proc]# cat meminfo
 2          total:    used:     free:  shared: buffers:  cached:
 3  Mem:  31535104 29708288  1826816 31817728  3051520 15773696
 4  Swap: 63942656  2838528 61104128
 5  MemTotal:     30796 kB
 6  MemFree:       1784 kB
 7  MemShared:    31072 kB
 8  Buffers:       2980 kB
 9  Cached:       15404 kB
10  SwapTotal:    62444 kB
11  SwapFree:     59672 kB
12  [root@shadrach /proc]#
```

Line 1 shows the Linux command used to view the `/proc/meminfo` file. Lines 2–11 show the
output from the `meminfo` file. Line 3 shows that this Linux server has 32MB of physical memory. It also shows that about 18MB is not currently being used. Line 4 shows that there is about
64MB of swap space memory available on this system. This corresponds with line 11 in
Listing 3.1, which showed a 64MB swap space partition on the `/dev/sda` hard drive.

By default, each process running on the UNIX system has its own private memory area. One
process cannot access memory being used by another process. No process can access memory
used by the kernel processes. To facilitate data sharing, shared memory segments can be created. Multiple processes can read and write to a common shared memory area. The kernel must
maintain and administer the shared memory areas. The `ipcs` command can be used to view the
current shared memory segments on the system. Listing 3.3 shows the output from a sample
`ipcs` command.

LISTING 3.3   A Sample `ipcs` Command Output

```
1  [root@shadrach /proc]# ipcs -m
2
3  ------ Shared Memory Segments --------
4  key            shmid    owner      perms     bytes       nattch     status
5  0x00000000 0            rich       600       52228       6          dest
6  0x395ec51c 1            oracle     640       5787648     6
7
8  [root@shadrach /proc]#
```

Line 1 shows the `ipcs` command using the `-m` option to display just the shared memory segments. Lines 3–6 show the output from this command. Each shared memory segment has an owner that created the segment. Each segment also has a standard UNIX permissions setting that sets the availability of the segment to other users. The `key` value allows other users to gain access to the shared memory segment.

Process Management

The UNIX operating system handles programs as processes. The kernel controls how processes are managed in the system. The kernel creates the first process, called the *init* process, to start all other processes on the system. When the kernel starts, the init process is loaded into virtual memory. As each process is started, it is given an area in virtual memory to store data and code that will be executed by the system.

Some UNIX implementations contain a table of terminal processes to start automatically on bootup. On Linux systems, when the init process starts it reads the file `/etc/inittabs` to determine what terminal processes it must start. FreeBSD systems use the `/etc/ttys` table.

The UNIX operating system has an init system that uses run levels. A *run level* can be used to direct the init process to run only certain types of processes. There are five init run levels in the Linux operating system.

At run level 1, only the basic system processes are started, along with one console terminal process. This is called *single user mode*. Single user mode is most often used for file system maintenance.

The standard init run level is 3. At this level most application software, such as network support software, is started. Another popular run level in UNIX is 5. This is where the X Window software is started. Notice how the UNIX system can control the overall system functionality by controlling the init run level. By changing the run level from 3 to 5, the system can change from a console-based system to an advanced, graphical X Window system.

3

SERVER
REQUIREMENTS
FOR QMAIL

To view the currently active process on the UNIX system, you can use the ps command. The format of the ps command is

```
ps [options]
```

where options is a list of options that can modify the output of the ps command. Table 3.2 shows the options that are available.

TABLE 3.2   ps Command Options

Option	Description
l	Use the long format to display.
u	Use the user format (shows username and start time).
j	Use the job format (shows process gid and sid).
s	Use the signal format.
v	Use the vm format.
m	Display memory information.
f	Use the "forest" format (displays processes as a tree).
a	Show processes of other users.
x	Show processes without displaying controlling terminal.
S	Show child CPU and time and page faults.
c	Command name for task_struct.
e	Show environment after command line and a +.
w	Use the wide output format.
h	Do not display the header.
r	Show running processes only.
n	Show numeric output for USER and WCHAN.
txx	Show the processes that are controlled by terminal ttyxx.
O	Order the process listing using sort keys k1, k2, and so on.
pids	Show only the specified PIDs.

There are options that are available to modify the ps command output. A sample output is shown in Listing 3.4.

LISTING 3.4   A Sample ps Command Output from a FreeBSD Server

```
$ ps ax
  PID  TT  STAT      TIME COMMAND
    0  ??  DLs    0:08.27  (swapper)
    1  ??  Is     0:02.95  /sbin/init --
```

```
    2  ??  DL     0:14.57  (pagedaemon)
    3  ??  DL     0:00.00  (vmdaemon)
    4  ??  DL   224:58.77  (syncer)
   34  ??  Is     0:00.00  adjkerntz -i
  135  ??  Is     1:04.04  syslogd
  144  ??  Is     0:00.00  /usr/sbin/portmap
  157  ??  I      0:00.00  nfsiod -n 4
  158  ??  I      0:00.00  nfsiod -n 4
  159  ??  I      0:00.00  nfsiod -n 4
  160  ??  I      0:00.00  nfsiod -n 4
  184  ??  Is     0:02.47  inetd -wW
  187  ??  Is     1:28.67  cron
  220  ??  Is     3:39.71  moused -p /dev/cuaa0 -t microsoft
 3382  ??  I      0:06.98  supervise qmail-smtpd
20150  ??  I      0:00.25  /usr/local/bin/tcpserver -v -p -x /etc/tcp.smtp.cdb -
63574  ??  Ss     0:00.10  telnetd
 1933  p0- S      5:14.58  /usr/local/bin/svscan
 1934  p0- I      0:06.28  supervise qmail-send
 1935  p0- I      0:06.95  supervise log
 1937  p0- I      0:06.21  supervise log
 1938  p0- I      0:06.12  qmail-send
 1939  p0- I      0:00.97  /usr/local/bin/multilog t /var/log/qmail
 1940  p0- I      0:00.32  /usr/local/bin/multilog t /var/log/qmail/smtpd
 1941  p0- I      0:00.80  qmail-lspawn |dot-forward .forward\n|preline -f /usr/
 1942  p0- I      0:00.02  qmail-rspawn
 1943  p0- I      0:00.66  qmail-clean
63575  p0  Ss     0:00.12  -sh (sh)
63579  p0  R+     0:00.00  ps -ax
52538  v0  Is+    0:00.03  /usr/libexec/getty Pc ttyv0
 5205  v1  Is+    0:00.03  /usr/libexec/getty Pc ttyv1
  270  v2  Is+    0:00.03  /usr/libexec/getty Pc ttyv2
  271  v3  Is+    0:00.03  /usr/libexec/getty Pc ttyv3
  272  v4  Is+    0:00.03  /usr/libexec/getty Pc ttyv4
  273  v5  Is+    0:00.04  /usr/libexec/getty Pc ttyv5
  274  v6  Is+    0:00.03  /usr/libexec/getty Pc ttyv6
  275  v7  Is+    0:00.03  /usr/libexec/getty Pc ttyv7
$
```

The first line shows the ps command as entered on the command line. Both the a and x options are used for the output to display all processes running on the system. The first column in the output shows the process ID (or PID). Line 4 shows the init process started by the kernel. The init process is assigned PID 1. All processes that start after the init process are assigned PIDs in numerical order. No two processes can have the same PID.

The third column shows the current status of the process. Table 3.3 lists the possible process status codes.

TABLE 3.3   Process Status Codes

Code	Description
A	The process has asked for random page replacement.
D	Uninterruptible sleep.
E	The process is trying to exit.
I	The process is idle.
L	The process has pages locked into memory.
N	A low priority task.
R	A runnable process.
S	The process has asked for a page replacement.
s	The process is a session leader.
T	The process is traced or stopped.
Z	A defunct (zombie) process.
W	The process has no resident pages.
<	A high-priority process.

The process name is shown in the last column. Processes that are in parentheses () have been swapped out of memory to the disk swap space because of inactivity. You can see that some of the processes have been swapped out, but most of the running processes have not.

Device Driver Management

Still another responsibility for the kernel is hardware management. Any device that the UNIX system must communicate with needs driver code inserted within the kernel code. The driver code allows the kernel to pass data back and forth to the device. There are two methods used for inserting device driver code in the UNIX kernel.

Previously, the only way to insert device driver code was to recompile the kernel. Each time a new device was added to the system, the kernel code needed to be recompiled. This process became more inefficient as UNIX kernels supported more hardware, and so a method was developed to insert driver code into the running kernel. The concept of kernel modules was developed to allow driver code to be inserted into a running kernel and removed from the kernel when the device was finished being used.

Hardware devices are identified on the UNIX server as special device files. There are three different classifications of device files:

- Character
- Block
- Network

Character files are for devices that can handle data only one character at a time. Most types of modems are created as character files. Block files are for devices that can handle data in large blocks, such as disk drives. Network file types are for devices that use packets to send and receive data. This includes network cards and the special loopback device that allows the UNIX system to communicate with itself using common network programming protocols.

Device files are created in the file system as nodes. Each node has a unique number pair that identifies it to the UNIX kernel. The number pair includes major and minor device numbers. Similar devices are grouped into the same major device number. The minor device number is used to identify the device within the major device number. Listing 3.5 shows an example of device files on a Linux server.

LISTING 3.5   A Sample Device Listing from a Linux Server

```
1  [rich@shadrach /dev]$ ls -al sda* ttyS*
2  brw-rw----  1 root    disk    8,   0 May  5  1998 sda
3  brw-rw----  1 root    disk    8,   1 May  5  1998 sda1
4  brw-rw----  1 root    disk    8,  10 May  5  1998 sda10
5  brw-rw----  1 root    disk    8,  11 May  5  1998 sda11
6  brw-rw----  1 root    disk    8,  12 May  5  1998 sda12
7  brw-rw----  1 root    disk    8,  13 May  5  1998 sda13
8  brw-rw----  1 root    disk    8,  14 May  5  1998 sda14
9  brw-rw----  1 root    disk    8,  15 May  5  1998 sda15
10 brw-rw----  1 root    disk    8,   2 May  5  1998 sda2
11 brw-rw----  1 root    disk    8,   3 May  5  1998 sda3
12 brw-rw----  1 root    disk    8,   4 May  5  1998 sda4
13 brw-rw----  1 root    disk    8,   5 May  5  1998 sda5
14 brw-rw----  1 root    disk    8,   6 May  5  1998 sda6
15 brw-rw----  1 root    disk    8,   7 May  5  1998 sda7
16 brw-rw----  1 root    disk    8,   8 May  5  1998 sda8
17 brw-rw----  1 root    disk    8,   9 May  5  1998 sda9
18 crw-------  1 root    tty     4,  64 Nov 29 16:09 ttyS0
19 crw-------  1 root    tty     4,  65 May  5  1998 ttyS1
20 crw-------  1 root    tty     4,  66 May  5  1998 ttyS2
21 crw-------  1 root    tty     4,  67 May  5  1998 ttyS3
22 [rich@shadrach /dev]$
```

Lines 1 shows the `ls` command being used to display all of the entries for the `sda` and `ttyS` devices. An `sda` device is the first SCSI hard drive, and a `ttyS` device is the standard IBM PC

COM ports. Lines 2–17 show all of the `sda` devices that were created on the sample Linux system. Not all are actually used, but they are created in case the administrator needs them. Lines 18–21 show all of the `ttyS` devices created.

The fifth column is the major device node number. Notice that all of the `sda` devices use the same major device node (8), and all of the `ttyS` devices use 4. The sixth column is the minor device node number. Each device within a major number has its own unique minor device node number.

The first column indicates the permissions for the device file. The first character of the permissions indicates the type of file. Notice that the SCSI hard drive files are all marked as block (b) files, and the COM port device files are marked as character (c) files.

To create a new device node you can use the `mknode` command. The format of the `mknode` command is

```
mknod [option] name type [major minor]
```

where `name` is the filename and `type` is the filetype (character or block). The `option` parameter has only one usable option. The `-m` option allows you to set the permissions of the file as it is created. You must be careful to select a unique major/minor device node number pair.

File System Management

Unlike some other operating systems, the UNIX kernel can support different types of file systems to read and write data to hard drives. Currently there are 15 different file system types available on UNIX systems. The kernel must be compiled with support for all types of file systems that the system will use. Table 3.4 lists the standard file systems that a UNIX system can use to read and write data.

TABLE 3.4 UNIX File Systems

File System	Description
affs	Amiga file system
ext	Linux Extended file system
ext2	Second extended file system
hpfs	OS/2 high performance file system
iso9660	ISO 9660 file system (CD-ROMs)
minix	MINIX file system
msdos	Microsoft FAT16
ncp	NetWare file system
nfs	Network file system

File System	Description
proc	Access to system information
smb	Samba SMB file system
sysv	Older UNIX file system
ufs	BSD file system
umsdos	UNIX-like file system that resides on top of MS-DOS
vfat	Windows 95 file system (FAT32)
xia	Similar to ext2, not used

Any hard drive that a UNIX server accesses must be formatted using one of the file system types listed in Table 3.4. Formatting a UNIX file system is similar to formatting an MS-DOS–type disk. The operating system must build the necessary file system information onto the disk before the disk can be used to store information. The command that Linux uses to format file systems is the mkfs command. The format of the mkfs command is

```
mkfs  [ -V ] [ -t fstype ] [ fs-options ] filesys [ blocks ]
```

where fstype is the type of file system to use and blocks is the number of blocks to use. The default file system type is ext2, and the default block count is all blocks available on the partition.

The Linux kernel interfaces with each file system using the Virtual File System (VFS). This provides a standard interface for the kernel to communicate with any type of file system. VFS caches information in memory as each file system is mounted and used.

The FreeBSD Operating System

The FreeBSD operating system evolved from the University of California at Berkeley's 4.4BSD lite operating system. This was specifically designed to be a port of the well-known Berkeley BSD 4.4 operating system for IBM-compatible computers. Over the years FreeBSD has survived both legal and technical battles. It has gained a reputation as one of the most stable operating systems around.

One of the nicest features of the FreeBSD operating system is its capability to use the network efficiently. It is well known for its excellent TCP/IP network support. Often, network programs running on a FreeBSD system outperform the same programs running on the same hardware using the Linux operating system—so much so that FreeBSD is the operating system of choice for many ISPs and Web sites, such as Yahoo! and Walnut Creek.

This section describes the two core components of the FreeBSD system, the kernel and its libraries.

The FreeBSD Kernel

The development of the FreeBSD system is tightly controlled by the FreeBSD Project, a group of developers who have joined together to control the advancement of FreeBSD. While they welcome kernel change requests, ultimately the Project team controls all kernel code additions and changes.

The FreeBSD kernel is released in three separate threads:

- The Release version
- The Stable version
- The Current version

All developmental work is done in the Current thread. As Current versions are deemed "useable by the general public," they are migrated into the Stable thread. As Stable versions are patched with bug fixes, they are migrated through the Release thread. Users wanting to install FreeBSD in a production environment should always use a Release version of the software.

At the time of this writing, the latest Release version of FreeBSD is version 4.0, and the latest Current version is 5.0. It is expected that the next Stable version will come from the 5.0 thread, and that the 4.0 version will have maintenance Release versions only.

In the past, adding new features to a FreeBSD server required recompiling a new kernel. This became a tedious process. Now the FreeBSD kernel supports loadable kernel modules. These modules are individual pieces of kernel code that can be inserted and removed from the running kernel code using special programs.

The *kldload* and *kldunload* programs are used to insert and remove module code. Any modules added to the running kernel code will not be present after the next boot of the operating system. Thus, any modules that are used must be added every time the FreeBSD system reboots. This is done within the system startup script.

The *kldstat* program can be used to list the kernel modules that are currently installed in a running kernel. Listing 3.6 shows a sample output from the kldstat program.

LISTING 3.6   A Sample Kldstat Output

```
shadrach# kldstat -v
Id Refs Address    Size    Name
 1    2 0xc0100000 25a190  kernel
        Contains modules:
                Id Name
                 1 rootbus
```

```
          2 fpu
          3 mfs
          4 ufs
          5 nfs
          6 msdos
          7 procfs
          8 cd9660
          9 if_tun
         10 if_sl
         11 if_ppp
         12 if_loop
         13 shell
         14 execgzip
         15 elf
         16 aout
 2    1 0xc0a36000 e000     linux.ko
        Contains modules:
          Id Name
         17 linuxelf
         18 linuxaout
shadrach#
```

Listing 3.6 shows the verbose output option of the kldstat program. All modules that were loaded into the running kernel are shown. Notice that support for various file systems is loaded into the kernel individually, along with support for SLIP, PPP, and loopback interfaces.

The FreeBSD Libraries

The UNIX system relies heavily on the C programming language. Most applications that run on UNIX systems are written in C. One method used to reduce the size of programs is to share common code between applications. Much like the Microsoft Windows DLL files, FreeBSD supports the use of common C libraries.

If you are familiar with DLL files in Windows, you probably have experienced the problem of one application updating a DLL and then another program that used the old version of the DLL breaking. This is not a problem in UNIX. All library files are checked into a library database. The library database can contain multiple entries for different versions of the same library file. This enables one application to add an updated library file without affecting the old library file.

The ldconfig program is used to configure the library database. Listing 3.7 shows a sample listing from the ldconfig program.

LISTING 3.7 A Sample Ldconfig Output

```
shadrach# ldconfig -r
/var/run/ld-elf.so.hints:
        search directories: /usr/lib:/usr/lib/compat:/usr/X11R6/lib:
➥/usr/local/lib
        0:-lcom_err.2 => /usr/lib/libcom_err.so.2
        1:-lscrypt.2 => /usr/lib/libscrypt.so.2
        2:-lcrypt.2 => /usr/lib/libcrypt.so.2
        3:-lm.2 => /usr/lib/libm.so.2
        4:-lmd.2 => /usr/lib/libmd.so.2
        5:-lmytinfo.2 => /usr/lib/libmytinfo.so.2
        6:-lncurses.3 => /usr/lib/libncurses.so.3
        7:-lradius.1 => /usr/lib/libradius.so.1
        8:-lskey.2 => /usr/lib/libskey.so.2
        9:-ltacplus.1 => /usr/lib/libtacplus.so.1
        10:-ltermcap.2 => /usr/lib/libtermcap.so.2
        11:-lalias.3 => /usr/lib/libalias.so.3
        12:-latm.2 => /usr/lib/libatm.so.2
        13:-lc.3 => /usr/lib/libc.so.3
        14:-lc_r.3 => /usr/lib/libc_r.so.3

        15:-lcalendar.2 => /usr/lib/libcalendar.so.2
        150:-laa.1 => /usr/local/lib/libaa.so.1
        151:-lmpeg.1 => /usr/local/lib/libmpeg.so.1
        152:-lpico.1 => /usr/local/lib/libpico.so.1
        153:-lsnmp.4 => /usr/local/lib/libsnmp.so.4
        154:-lc-client4.5 => /usr/local/lib/libc-client4.so.5
shadrach#
```

The output from the ldconfig command shows the individual C libraries loaded on the FreeBSD system and maps them by name to their actual location on the system. As shown in Listing 3.7, there were 154 separate libraries on the sample FreeBSD system.

The FreeBSD operating system also has the capability to run applications written for the Linux environment by using Linux-compatible libraries. This opens the FreeBSD system to a host of applications written specifically for the Linux environment. Often Linux applications run faster on a FreeBSD system using the Linux libraries.

The Linux Operating System

The other popular free UNIX implementation is the Linux operating system. Linux has gained increasing acceptance in the UNIX marketplace as a solid production UNIX operating system.

The Linux system consists of a core UNIX-like kernel and a host of libraries. This section describes the pieces of the Linux operating system.

The Linux Kernel

The development of the Linux kernel has taken on a very rapid pace. Linus Torvalds maintains strict control over the Linux kernel, although he accepts change requests from anyone, anywhere. There have been many advances in the Linux kernel design over the years, such as the addition of modules.

The kernel developers use a strict version control system. The format of a kernel release is

```
linux-a.b.c
```

where a is the major release number, b is the minor release number, and c is the patch number. Currently, a convention has been established in which odd-numbered minor releases are considered developmental releases and even-numbered minor releases are considered stable production releases.

At the time of this writing, the current stable production release of the Linux kernel is 2.2.15, and the current development release is 2.3.99. Although version 2.2.15 is the current kernel release, most Linux distributions have not released versions using this kernel.

To determine the kernel version your Linux system is using, you can use the uname command with the -a option. Listing 3.8 shows an example of this command using a Mandrake 6.0 Linux system.

3

SERVER
REQUIREMENTS
FOR QMAIL

LISTING 3.8   A Sample uname -a Output

```
1  [rich@shadrach rich]$ uname -a
2  Linux shadrach.smallorg.org 2.2.9-19mdk #1 Wed May 19 19:53:00 GMT 1999
➥  i586 unknown
3  [rich@shadrach rich]$
```

The output from the uname command is shown in line 2. The third field shows the specific Linux kernel version used. In this example, it is using the 2.2.9 kernel, which was compiled specifically for the Mandrake Linux distribution, thus the added -19mdk information.

It is possible to download newer versions of the kernel to install in a running Linux system. You must have the kernel source code files, which are usually available for download from the Linux kernel archives at http://www.kernel.org. Compiling and installing a new kernel is not for the beginner. Numerous steps are involved in the process. If you decide to upgrade your Linux kernel, please read all the documentation that comes with the kernel source code and any tips provided by your specific Linux distribution support group.

CAUTION

Installing a new Linux kernel falls under the category of "if it ain't broke, don't fix it." If your Linux server is not experiencing any problems, don't attempt to install a new kernel just because it is newer. Many Linux distributions are fine-tuned to work with a specific kernel; changing only the kernel can have unpredictable results.

The Linux Libraries

The Linux operating system also depends heavily on the C programming language. The kernel, many device drivers, and almost all the utilities were written using the C language. It is not surprising that most of the application programs written for the Linux platform were also written using the C programming language.

In UNIX, the `lib` prefix denotes library files. A library table keeps track of all the shared libraries registered on the system. The file `/etc/ld.so.conf` contains the list of libraries that are inserted into the library table. You can display the current library table on your Linux system by using the `ldconfig` command. Listing 3.9 shows a sample partial output from the `ldconfig` command on a Mandrake 6.0 Linux system. This is only a partial listing because, as shown in line 2, 534 different libraries are registered on this Linux system.

LISTING 3.9   A Sample `ldconfig` Partial Output

```
1   [rich@shadrach rich]$ /sbin/ldconfig -p
2   534 libs found in cache `/etc/ld.so.cache' (version 1.7.0)
3          libzvt.so.2 (libc6) => /usr/lib/libzvt.so.2
4          libzvt.so.2 (libc6) => /usr/lib/libzvt.so.2
5          libz.so.1 (libc6) => /usr/lib/libz.so.1
6          libz.so.1 (libc6) => /usr/lib/libz.so.1
7          libx11amp.so.0 (libc6) => /usr/X11R6/lib/libx11amp.so.0
8          libxml.so.0 (libc6) => /usr/lib/libxml.so.0
9          libxml.so.0 (libc6) => /usr/lib/libxml.so.0
10         libvgagl.so.1 (libc6) => /usr/lib/libvgagl.so.1
11         libvgagl.so.1 (libc5) => /usr/i486-linux-libc5/lib/libvgagl.so.1
12         libvgagl.so.1 (libc6) => /usr/lib/libvgagl.so.1
13         libvgagl.so (libc6) => /usr/lib/libvgagl.so
14         libvgagl.so (libc6) => /usr/lib/libvgagl.so
15         libvga.so.1 (libc6) => /usr/lib/libvga.so.1
16         libvga.so.1 (libc5) => /usr/i486-linux-libc5/lib/libvga.so.1
17         libvga.so.1 (libc6) => /usr/lib/libvga.so.1
18         libvga.so (libc6) => /usr/lib/libvga.so
19         libvga.so (libc6) => /usr/lib/libvga.so
```

```
20      libuulib.so.5 (libc6) => /usr/lib/libuulib.so.5
21      libuulib.so.5 (libc6) => /usr/lib/libuulib.so.5
22      libuulib.so (libc6) => /usr/lib/libuulib.so
23      libuulib.so (libc6) => /usr/lib/libuulib.so
```

Each Linux implementation requires that a version of the standard C library be installed. The standard C library contains many of the commonly used functions for the system. This is where Linux has had a checkered past. In the early days of Linux, the Linux C library was tightly coupled with the kernel. Changes in the kernel required C library changes and vice versa. The first version of the Linux C library was called libc1. This version was improved with versions libc2, libc3, and libc4. These libraries were used to create many Linux utilities and application programs during the early years of Linux.

After a while, Linux developers decided that the old C library method was not good. Not only was it too closely related to the Linux kernel, it also produced executable files in an older executable format called a.out. Most newer POSIX-type systems had already converted to Executable and Linking Format (ELF), which proved to be faster and more efficient. The next version of the C library—libc5—implemented the ELF format. Programs compiled using the libc5 library would not run on older Linux systems that still were using the a.out-style libraries. However, older programs compiled on the a.out-style would execute well on the new libc5 systems. This created the first round of confusion in the Linux application world.

At the same time that the libc5 library was being developed and used, the GNU Project developed its own library that was not tied to a specific kernel. The GNU Project's C library was called glibc. With the libc5 library working so well, no one really continued work on the glibc library.

After a period of dormancy, programmers revisited the glibc code. They thought it could be made better than the libc5 library. One advantage that glibc had was its independence from any particular operating system or kernel. Out of the effort of those programmers came the glibc 2.0 library.

Many Linux distributors decided to bundle the new glibc 2.0 code with their new Linux distributions. Unfortunately, many Linux distributors decided to keep the libc5 library with the new kernel. This quickly became confusing.

The Linux distributions that used the glibc 2.0 library also included the libc5 library for backward compatibility. Remember that Linux maintains a table of library files, so using two separate C libraries at the same time is possible. Because of this, many Linux applications continued to use the libc5 library for compatibility purposes.

Netscape's Communicator and Corel's WordPerfect are two applications that continued to be written using the libc5 library and can be used on almost every Linux distribution. Some

Linux application programmers decided to take advantage of features of the new glibc 2.0 library and released versions of their software for that platform. Star Division's StarOffice 5.0 and Oracle's Oracle8 database software are two applications that use the glibc 2.0 library. These applications will not run on Linux distributions that use the libc5 library exclusively.

It would be bad enough if the story ended there. Recently the GNU Project released the glibc 2.1 library. What complicated things is that some functions were changed from the glibc 2.0 library, so some applications written with the glibc 2.0 library (such as StarOffice 5.0) crash when they are run on a Linux system using the glibc 2.1 library.

Linux Libraries

If after reading this section you are concerned about your Linux system, don't be. For applications distributed in source code (such as all the mail server programs discussed in this book), compile the code using whichever C library your system uses; that code will run just fine. For applications distributed in binary format, just remember to use the version that is released for the C library on your Linux system (libc5, glibc 2.0, or glibc 2.1).

If you do not know which library your Linux distribution is using, you can find out by looking for the libraries in the /lib directory. Table 3.5 shows the different C libraries that might be present on a Linux system.

TABLE 3.5   A List of Linux C Libraries

Library	Description
libc.so	libc1 a.out library
libc.so.2	libc2 a.out library
libc.so.3	libc3 a.out library
libc.so.4	libc4 a.out library
libc.so.5	libc5 ELF library
libc.so.6	Symbolic link to a glibc library
libc-2.0.x.so	glibc 2.0 ELF library
libc-2.1.x.so	glibc 2.1 ELF library

The GNU Project

The GNU Project was created in 1984 to create a free UNIX-like operating system. It is responsible for maintaining open source versions of many common UNIX utilities. Without the GNU Project, the Linux operating system would not be very exciting. Most of the core pieces of the Linux operating system are products of the GNU Project. FreeBSD also uses many GNU utilities. This section describes three programs that are crucial to the operation of the mail server: the bash shell, the gcc compiler, and the make utility.

GNU Bash

The kernel requires some kind of macro processor to enable a user to execute programs on the system. In the UNIX world, that macro processor is called the *shell*. The most common shell in the UNIX environment is the Bourne shell, named after its creator, Stephen Bourne. The Bourne shell is a program that runs as a process on the system and has an interactive session that enables the user to enter commands at a command prompt. The command can be an executable program, an internal shell command, or a program file that contains shell commands (called a *script file*). The shell launches executable programs by creating a new process and running the program within that new process. This allows every program that runs from the shell to have its own process on the system.

The GNU Project developers knew that it was crucial to have a good open source shell to use with an open source UNIX-like operating system. The shell program they developed was called *bash*, for Bourne-Again SHell. The bash shell is compatible with the original Bourne shell (called *sh*). The bash shell also includes features from other shells that have been developed in the UNIX environment—the C shell (*csh*) and the Korn shell (*ksh*). Bash has become the default shell for Linux systems. The current version of bash at the time of this writing is version 2.03.

The shell a user uses after logging in to a Linux system is determined by the user's entry in the `/etc/passwd` file. A typical record in this file looks like this:

```
riley:x:504:506:Riley M.:/home/riley:/bin/bash
```

Colons are used to separate the fields in the record. The first field identifies the user login name. The second field is a placeholder for the user password. This particular Linux system uses shadow passwords, so the real password is encrypted and placed in a separate file. The third and fourth fields are the user ID and group ID for the user. The fifth field is the text identifier for the user. The sixth field identifies the user's default, or home, directory when he logs in to the system. The last field identifies the default shell for the user. This points to the location of the bash shell executable file on the server.

The bash shell has several different configuration files that can be used to modify the features of the shell as a user logs in. When bash is invoked as a shell from a login process, any commands present in the /etc/profile file are executed. This occurs for all users who specify the bash shell as the default login shell in the password file. Listing 3.10 shows the default /etc/profile file from a Mandrake 6.0 Linux system.

LISTING 3.10   A Sample /etc/profile File

```
1  # /etc/profile
2
3  # System wide environment and startup programs
4  # Functions and aliases go in /etc/bashrc
5
6  PATH="$PATH:/usr/X11R6/bin"
7  PS1="[\u@\h \W]\\$ "
8
9  # In bash2 we can't define a ulimit for user :-(
10 [ "$UID" = "0" ] && {
11 ulimit -c 1000000
12 }
13
14 if [ `id -gn` = `id -un` -a `id -u` -gt 14 ]; then
15     umask 002
16 else
17     umask 022
18 fi
19
20 USER=`id -un`
21 LOGNAME=$USER
22 MAIL="/var/spool/mail/$USER"
23
24 HOSTNAME=`/bin/hostname`
25 HISTSIZE=1000
26 HISTFILESIZE=1000
27 export PATH PS1 HOSTNAME HISTSIZE HISTFILESIZE USER LOGNAME MAIL
28
29 for i in /etc/profile.d/*.sh ; do
30     if [ -x $i ]; then
31         . $i
32     fi
33 done
34
35 unset i
```

The main thing the /etc/profile file does is create new environment variables for the shell to identify special characteristics for the session that can be used by application programs running in the shell. Line 22, the MAIL environment variable, is of special interest to the mail administrator. It points the user's mail program to the proper mailbox for the user.

After the common /etc/profile program is executed, bash looks for three more configuration files in the user's default (home) directory. If they exist, the .bash_profile, .bash_login, and .profile files are executed, in order. Each of these files should be located in the user's home directory, so these files can be specific for a particular user. One final configuration file is available for use: .bash_logout. This script file is executed when the user logs out of the interactive session. By using a combination of script files, the system administrator can fine-tune the bash shell for each user on the system.

GNU gcc

If you plan to install software programs that are distributed in source code, you must be able to compile the code to create an executable file. To do this, you need the proper compiler. All the programs described in this book are written in the C programming language. This requires that a C compiler be installed on your UNIX server. The most common C compiler package for Linux and FreeBSD is the GNU C compiler (gcc).

The gcc package has itself has had quite an interesting past. The GNU Project team developed gcc and released version 1 in early 1990. The GNU Project continued development of gcc, creating version 2.0 and continuing with improvements until version 2.8 was released in 1997. At the same time, another group of developers was working on a C++ compiler called *egcs* (pronounced "eggs"). After gcc 2.8, both projects were combined into the egcs Project, and egcs 1.0 was released. Egcs 1.0 combined both the C and C++ compilers into one package.

Unfortunately, the egcs Project was short-lived (getting only to version 1.1). Now both the gcc and egcs projects have been rolled into the gcc Project again. At the time of this writing, the current version of gcc is version 2.95. This version supports both C and C++ compilers. To complicate things even more, some Linux distributions still call this distribution egcs version 2.95. I hope this confusion will clear up soon.

To determine the version of gcc your UNIX distribution uses, you can use the --version option as follows:

```
[rich@shadrach rich]$ gcc --version
pgcc-2.91.66
[rich@shadrach rich]$
```

The sample Mandrake 6.1 Linux system shown is using gcc version 2.91 with patch level 66.

3

SERVER
REQUIREMENTS
FOR QMAIL

GNU Make

Large C and C++ projects often become complicated. There are several different source code files, each with several different header files. Compiling individual source files creates multiple object files that must be linked together in specific combinations to create executable files. Maintaining the source, object, and executable files is often a difficult job. To simplify this task, most C and C++ compilers use a make program. The job of the make program is to control the creation of executable files, based on changes made to the source code files or to variables in a standard make configuration file.

The GNU Project has a version of make that is compatible with the gcc compiler. At the time of this writing, the current version available is version 3.78.1.

The meat and potatoes of the make utility is the Makefile. The Makefile specifies how the make utility compiles the source code to create the executable program(s). A sample Makefile is shown in Listing 3.11.

LISTING 3.11   A Sample Makefile

```
1  # Makefile -- Make file for test program
2  #
3
4  # Edit the following for your installation
5
6  CC   =   gcc
7  #===================================
8
9  # Compiler and linker flags
10
11 CFLAGS  =    -O
12 LFLAGS  =    -O
13
14 # This program's object code files
15
16 OBJS     =    test.o
17
18 # File dependencies
19
20 all:    test
21
22 objs:   $(OBJS)
23
24 clean:
25      rm -f $(OBJS)
26      rm -f test
```

```
27
28 test: $(OBJS)
29     $(CC) -o $@ $(LFLAGS) $(OBJS) $(LIBS)
30
31 test.o:  test.c
32     $(CC) -c $(CFLAGS) -o $@ $<
```

Lines 6, 11, 12, and 16 show the use of variables within the Makefile. The user can change these values to the appropriate values for the system. Line 18 declares the make targets for the system. Each target can be run individually by specifying the target name as a parameter on the make command line. For example, to run the `clean` target, which removes any old object and executable files, you can enter

```
make clean
```

To create just the object files for the test program, you can enter

```
make objs
```

If you type only **make** at the command line, the `all` target will be executed, which builds the executable file `test`.

Summary

The qmail mail server package was written to run on a UNIX platform. The UNIX operating systems provide the necessary file and process control that qmail requires to handle multiple processes and files. The core of the UNIX operating system is the kernel. The kernel controls many facets of the operating system, including memory management, process management, device management, and file system management.

There are many different UNIX platforms that can be used by qmail. The FreeBSD and Linux UNIX distributions are both excellent UNIX implementations that are available for minimal cost. Both Linux and FreeBSD use many utilities developed by the GNU Project. Both operating systems use the GNU gcc compiler to compile C programs. With these operating systems, the mail administrator can easily turn a standard IBM-compatible computer into a full-featured email server.

DNS and qmail

IN THIS CHAPTER

One of the most important and misunderstood pieces of an email system is the use of host-names. It is crucial to ensure that hostnames are defined properly for mail systems to communicate. qmail is no different.

The *domain name system* (DNS) was developed to allow systems to communicate using a hierarchy of hostnames. DNS is also used to identify servers that provide special services for domains, such as email. This is where DNS becomes crucial for email servers.

Although knowledge of the DNS system isn't essential for installing and configuring qmail, it certainly helps when you are trying to troubleshoot mail problems. At some point in your career as a mail administrator, you will most likely meet a customer who is positive that he is sending his email message to the right address, but it still bounces back as undeliverable. It will be your job to prove that the address he used was incorrect.

This chapter describes the history and design of DNS. It also presents some common applications that can be used on a UNIX host to troubleshoot DNS problems. Finally, this chapter discusses two software packages that can be used to enable your UNIX host to become a DNS server.

History of Computer Names

Back in the old days when the Internet was small (just a few hundred computers), it wasn't too complicated to locate another computer. Each Internet computer had a database of hostnames and IP addresses. Internet hostnames could be anything the administrator wanted—Fred, Barney, Acct1, anything. There was a central clearinghouse for keeping track of new computer names and addresses. Once a week or so, a system administrator would download a new copy of the current database. Of course, this system did have its drawbacks. When someone brought a new computer online, he needed to search the database to make sure that someone hadn't already used the clever new hostname he wanted to use. It didn't take system administrators long to figure out that this method was on a collision course with progress. As the Internet grew, so did the database. As the database grew, so did the time it took to download and search it. It was also starting to get difficult to come up with a unique hostname. Something had to change, and it did.

Domain Names

The method that was agreed upon was the domain name system (DNS). The DNS uses a hierarchical distributed database to break up the hostnames database. That means that now no single computer has to maintain the entire database of Internet devices. The database is distributed among multiple computers, called *DNS servers*, on the Internet. For a client computer to locate another computer on the Internet, it only needs to find the nearest DNS server and query for the IP address of the remote computer it seeks. To implement this system, a new protocol was invented to pass the DNS information from the DNS server to the client, and software was created for DNS server computers to implement the new database system.

DNS Structure

The structure of a hierarchical database is similar to an organizational chart, with nodes connected in a tree-like manner (the hierarchical part). The top node is called the *root*. The root node does not explicitly show up in addresses, so it is called the *nameless node*. Multiple categories were created under the root level to divide the database into *domains*. Each domain contains DNS servers that are responsible for maintaining the database of computer names for that area of the database (the distributed part). Figure 4.1 shows a diagram of how DNS domains are distributed.

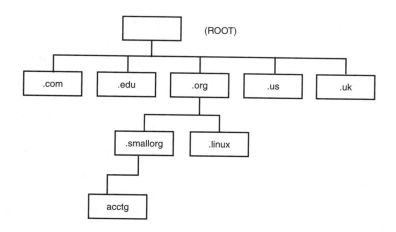

FIGURE 4.1

A diagram of the Internet domain name system.

The first (or top) level of distribution is divided into domains based on country codes. Additional top-level domains for specific United States organizations were created to prevent the .us domain from becoming overcrowded. The domain name is appended to the end of the computer hostname to form the unique Internet hostname for that computer. This is the popular hostname format with which we are now familiar. Table 4.1 shows how the top-level DNS domains are laid out.

TABLE 4.1   DNS Top-Level Domain Names

Name	Description
.com	U.S. commercial organizations
.edu	U.S. educational institutions
.gov	U.S. government organizations
.mil	U.S. military sites
.net	U.S. Internet providers
.org	U.S. non-profit organizations
.us	Other U.S. organizations
.ca	Canadian organizations
.de	German organizations
(Other country codes)	Other countries' organizations

As the Internet grows, each top-level domain is divided into subdomains, or *zones*. Each zone is an independent domain in itself, but it relies on its parent domain for connectivity to the database. A parent zone must grant permission for a child zone to exist and is responsible for the child zone's behavior (just like in real life). Each zone has at least two DNS servers that maintain the DNS database for the zone.

The original specifications stipulated that the DNS servers for a single zone must have separate connections to the Internet and be housed in separate locations for fault-tolerance purposes. Because of this stipulation, many organizations rely on other organizations to host their secondary and tertiary DNS servers.

A host within a zone adds its domain name to its hostname to form its unique Internet name. Thus, computer `fred` in the `smallorg.org` domain would be called `fred.smallorg.org`. It becomes a little confusing because a domain can contain hosts as well as zones.

For example, the `smallorg.org` domain can contain host `fred.smallorg.org`. It also can grant authority for zone `acctg.smallorg.org` to a subdomain, which in turn can contain another host `barney.acctg.smallorg.org`. Although this simplifies the database system, it makes finding hosts on the Internet more complicated. Figure 4.2 shows an example of a domain and an associated subdomain.

NOTE

In the past few years, Internet domain names have become a hot topic. In the past, a single corporation controlled all U.S. domain names in the .com, .net, and .org domains—the InterNIC Corporation. Recently, the Internet Corporation for Assigned

Names and Numbers (ICANN), a non-profit organization, was created to control this process. ICANN is now responsible for the management of all U.S. domain names. The purchase of a domain name can now be made from multiple vendors, not just one company. All domain names must be cleared by ICANN for use in U.S. domains.

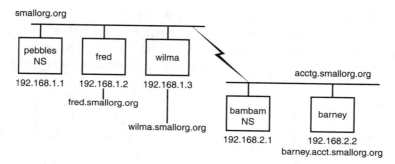

FIGURE 4.2

A sample domain and subdomain on the Internet.

DNS allows for three different scenarios to occur in finding an IP address using the DNS system:

1. A computer that wants to communicate with another computer in the same zone queries the local DNS server to find the address of the remote computer. The local DNS server should have the address of the remote computer in its local database and return the IP address.

2. A computer that wants to communicate with a computer in another zone queries the local DNS server in its zone. The local DNS server realizes the requested computer is in a different zone and queries a root-level DNS server for the answer. The root DNS server then walks the tree of DNS servers to find the local zone DNS server and gets an IP address for the remote computer. It then passes the address to the local DNS server, which in turn passes the information it receives to the requesting computer.

   Part of the information that is returned with the IP address of the remote computer is a *time to live* (TTL) value. This instructs the local DNS server that it can keep the IP address of the remote computer in a local name cache for an amount of time equal to the TTL value. This will speed up any subsequent name requests.

3. A computer that wants to communicate with the same remote computer in another zone queries the local DNS server in its zone. The local DNS server checks its name cache and, if the TTL value has not expired, the server sends the IP address of the remote computer to the requesting client computer. This is considered a non-authoritative response, because the local DNS server is assuming that the remote computer's IP address has not changed since it was last checked.

In all three instances, the local computer needs to know only the IP address of its local DNS server to find the IP address of any computer on the Internet. It is the job of the local DNS server to find the proper IP address for the given hostname. The local computer's life is now much simpler. Figure 4.3 shows a diagram of how these different functions operate.

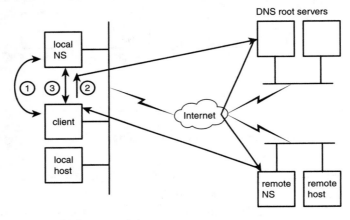

DNS name resolution:

1. local host-DNS record found in local NS database

2. remote host-DNS record found in remote NS database

3. remote host-DNS record found in local NS cache

FIGURE 4.3
A diagram of different DNS resolution methods.

As the DNS tree grows, new requirements are made on DNS servers. As mentioned, parent DNS servers are required to know the IP addresses of their child zone DNS servers to properly pass DNS queries on to them for resolution. The tricky part comes with the lower-level zone DNS servers. For them to properly process DNS queries, they have to be able to start their name searches somewhere in the DNS tree. When the Internet was in its infancy, most of the name searches were for local hostnames. The bulk of the DNS traffic was able to stay local to the zone DNS server or, at worst, its parent. However, with the increased popularity of the Internet and Web browsing, more DNS requests were made for remote hostnames. When a DNS server did not have the hostname in its local database, it would need to query a remote DNS server.

The most likely candidate for the remote DNS server is a top-level domain DNS server that has the knowledge to work its way down the tree until it finds the responsible zone DNS server for the remote host and returns the result to the local DNS server. This puts a great deal of stress on the root servers. Fortunately, there are quite a few of them, and they do a good job of distributing the load. The local DNS servers communicate with the top-level domain DNS servers using the DNS protocol, which is discussed later in this chapter.

DNS is a two-way street. Not only is it useful for finding the IP address of a computer based on its hostname, but it is also useful for finding the hostname of a computer based on its IP address. Many Internet Web and FTP sites restrict access based on a client computer's domain. When the connection request is made from a client, the host server passes the IP address of the client to the DNS server as a reverse DNS query. If the client's DNS zone database is configured correctly, the client's hostname should be returned to the server, which in turn can decide whether to grant access to the client.

NOTE

If your organization uses Dynamic Host Configuration Protocol (DHCP) to dynamically assign IP addresses to workstations, you may have to create DNS records for all possible DHCP addresses that can be assigned by the server. Often, a generic hostname can be assigned to each address, such as `station1.smallorg.org`.

DNS Database Records

Each DNS server is responsible for keeping track of the hostnames in its zone. To accomplish this, the DNS server must have a method of storing host information in a database that can be queried by remote machines. A DNS database is a text file that consists of resource records (RRs) that describe computers and functions in the zone. The Linux server must run a DNS server software package—usually *Named*, to communicate the DNS information from the database to remote DNS servers. The Named program is discussed in detail later in this chapter.

The DNS server's database first has to declare the zone that it is responsible for. Then, it must declare each host computer in its zone. Finally, the database can declare special information for the zone, such as email and name servers. Resource record formats were created to track all the information required for the DNS server. Table 4.2 shows some of the basic RRs that a DNS database could contain. DNS database design has become a hot topic lately with researchers who want to add more information to the database and also increase the security of the information that is there. New record types are constantly being added to the DNS database. The record types in Table 4.2 represent the core records needed to establish a zone in the DNS database.

TABLE 4.2   DNS Database Resource Record Types

Record Type	Description
SOA	Start of Authority
A	Internet address
NS	Name server
CNAME	Canonical name (nickname)
HINFO	Host information
MX	Mail server
PTR	Pointer

Each domain DNS server should contain resource records for the hosts in the domain. There should be one SOA record for the domain listed at the top of the database. Any other resource records for the domain can be added in any order after that. Figure 4.4 demonstrates how the DNS database would look for the sample network that was shown previously in Figure 4.2. The next section describes the DNS records in more detail.

Start of Authority Record (SOA)

Each database starts with an SOA record that defines the zone in which the database resides. The format for the SOA record is

```
domain name     [TTL] [class] SOA origin person (
                      serial number
                      refresh
                      retry
                      expire
                      minimum)
```

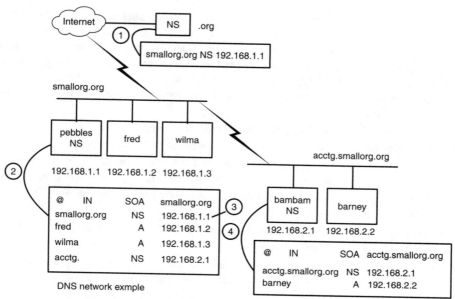

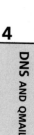

FIGURE 4.4

DNS records for the sample network.

In this format

> domain name is the name of the zone that is being defined (the @ sign can be used as a placeholder to signify the computer's default domain).

> TTL is how long (in seconds) that a requesting computer will keep any DNS information from this zone in its local name cache. This value is optional.

> class is the protocol being used (which in our case will always be class IN for Internet). This value is optional and will default to IN.

> origin is the name of the computer on which the master zone database is located. Be careful to include a trailing period (.) after the hostname, or your local domain name will be appended to the hostname (unless of course you want to use that feature).

4

DNS AND QMAIL

person is the email address of the person responsible for the zone. This is different, because the @ sign is already used to signify the default domain name, so it can't be used in the mail address. Instead, use a period (.) in place of the @ sign. For example, instead of using sysadm@smallorg.org, use sysadm.smallorg.org. If there are any periods . in the name, they must be escaped out by using a backslash (\). An example of this would be the address john.jones@smallorg.org, which would translate to john\
.jones.smallorg.org.

serial number is a unique number that identifies the version of the zone database file. This is often the date created plus a version count (such as 199908051).

refresh is how often (in seconds) a secondary DNS server should query a primary DNS server to check the SOA serial number. If the number changes from one check to the next, the secondary DNS server will request an update to its database. Specifying one hour (3600) is common for this value.

retry is the length of time (in seconds) a secondary DNS server should wait before it retries after a failed refresh attempt.

expire is how long (in seconds) a secondary DNS server can use the data retrieved from the primary DNS server without getting refreshed. This value should be large, such as 3600000 (about 42 days).

minimum is the time (in seconds) that should be used as the TTL in all RRs in this zone. Usually, 86400 (1 day) is a good value.

Internet Address Record (A)

Each host in the zone defined by the database should have a valid A record to define its hostname to the Internet. The format for the A record is

```
host    [TTL]    [class]    A    address
```

where

host is the fully qualified hostname for the computer (including the domain name).

address is the IP address of the computer.

Canonical Name (CNAME)

Besides a normal hostname, many computers also have a nickname. This is useful if you want to identify particular services without having to rename computers in your domain, such as www.smallorg.org. The CNAME record links nicknames with the real hostname. The format of the CNAME record is

```
nickname    [TTL]    [class]    CNAME    hostname
```

Name Server Record (NS)

Each zone should have at least two DNS servers. NS records are used to identify these servers to other DNS servers trying to resolve hostnames within the zone. The format of an NS record is

```
domain    [TTL]    [class]    NS    server
```

where

> domain is the domain name of the zone that the DNS server is responsible for. If it is blank, the NS record refers to the zone defined in the SOA record.

> server is the hostname of the DNS server. There should also be an associated A record to identify the IP address of the DNS server.

Host Information Record (HINFO)

Additional information about a computer can be made available to DNS servers by using the HINFO record. The format of the HINFO record is

```
host    [TTL]    [class]    HINFO    hardware    software
```

where

> host is the hostname of the computer to which the information applies.

> hardware is the type of hardware the computer is using.

> software is the operating system type and version of the computer.

Pointer Record (PTR)

In addition to an A record, each computer in the zone should also have a PTR record. This allows the DNS server to perform reverse queries from the IP address of the computer. Without this information, remote servers could not determine the domain on which your computer is located. The format of a PTR record is

```
IN-ADDR name    [TTL]    [class]    PTR    name
```

where

> IN-ADDR name is the reverse DNS name of the IP address. If that sounds confusing, it is. This name allows the DNS server to work backward from the IP address of the computer. The IN-ADDR.ARPA address is a special domain to support gateway location and Internet address to host mapping. Inverse queries are not necessary because the IP address is mapped to a fictitious hostname. The IN-ADDR name of a computer with IP address 192.168.0.1 would be 1.0.168.192.IN-ADDR.ARPA.

> name is the hostname of the computer, as found in the A record.

4

DNS AND QMAIL

Mail Server Record (MX)

Most important (at least as far as we mail administrators are concerned) are MX records. They instruct remote mail servers where to forward mail for your zone. The format of the MX record is

```
name    [TTL]    [class]    MX    preference    host
```

where

name is the zone name (or, if blank, the SOA zone). This can also be a hostname if you want to redirect mail for a particular host in your network.

preference is an integer signifying the order in which remote servers should try connecting if multiple mail servers are specified—0 being the highest preference and decreasing in preference for increasing numbers. This is used to create primary and secondary mail servers for a zone. When a remote mail server queries the DNS server for a mail server responsible for the zone, the entire list of servers and preferences is sent. The remote mail server should attempt to connect to the highest-priority mail server listed and, if that fails, continue down the list by preference.

host is the hostname of the mail server. There should also be an associated A record to identify the IP address of the mail server.

A Sample DNS Database for a Domain

If you allow your ISP to host your domain name and email, it will have records in its DNS database identifying your domain to the Internet. The SOA record will identify your domain name, but it will point to the ISP's host as the authoritative host. The NS records for your domain will point to your ISP's DNS servers, and your MX records will point to your ISP's mail servers. As far as the rest of the Internet is concerned, these computers are part of your network, even though they do not really exist on your network. Listing 4.1 shows a sample of how your ISP might define your zone in its DNS database.

LISTING 4.1   DNS Zone Database Entry

```
1  smallorg.org  IN  SOA   master.isp.net. postmaster.master.isp.net. (
2                                1999080501      ;unique serial number
3                                8H         ; refresh rate
4                                2H         ;retry period
5                                1W         ; expiration period
6                                1D)        ; minimum
7
8              NS    ns1.isp.net.    ;defines primary name server
9              NS    ns2.isp.net.    ; defines secondary name server
10
```

```
11              MX    10 mail1.isp.net.    ; defines primary mail server
12              MX    20 mail2.isp.net.    ; defines secondary mail server
13
14   www    CNAME    host1.isp.net.    ;defines your www server at the ISP
15   ftp    CNAME    host1.isp.net.    ; defines your FTP server at the ISP
16
17   host1.isp.net.   A    10.0.0.1
18
19   1.0.0.10.IN-ADDR.ARPA.    PTR    host1.isp.net.    ; pointer address for
➥reverse DNS
```

Lines 1–6 show the SOA record for your new domain. The ISP points your domain name
smallorg.org to the ISP server master.isp.net. Lines 8 and 9 define the primary and secondary DNS servers that will be used to resolve your hostnames (again, belonging to the ISP),
and lines 11 and 12 define the primary (mail1.isp.net) and secondary (mail2.isp.net) mail
servers that will receive and spool mail for your domain. Lines 14 and 15 define nicknames for
services in your domain. The hostname www.smallorg.org is a nickname that points to the ISP
server that hosts your Web pages. The address ftp.smallorg.org is also a nickname that
points to the same ISP server that also hosts your FTP site. This is a service that most ISPs
provide to customers who cannot afford to have a dedicated connection to the Internet, but who
want to provide Web and FTP services to their customers. Lines 17 and 19 provide the Internet
IP address information so that remote clients can connect to this server.

> **NOTE**
>
> Often, PTR records like the one shown in line 19 are placed in a separate database file
> on the server to help simplify the databases. With just one PTR record, as in this
> example, that is not a problem, but often there can be dozens or hundreds of them.

4

DNS AND QMAIL

When a DNS server has a valid database installed, it must be able to communicate with other
DNS servers to resolve hostname requests from clients and to respond to other DNS servers'
queries about hosts in its zone. The DNS protocol was invented to accomplish that.

DNS and Email

Computers must follow a set process to properly deliver email, and knowing how that process
works sometimes helps when troubleshooting email problems. When a remote client tries to

send an email message to prez@smallorg.org, several steps are taken before the message is
sent:

1. The local DNS server for the client must first determine to which computer in
   smallorg.org to send the email. It does this by looking for an MX record for the
   smallorg.org domain.

2. If the local DNS server does not contain any information in its local database or name
   cache, it must traverse the Internet, searching for an answer. The first stop would be one
   of the top-level domain DNS servers. That server would not have your MX record, but it
   would know how to get to a DNS server for the .org domain.

3. That server also would not have your information, but it would (or at least *should*) know
   the IP address of a DNS server for the smallorg.org domain and query it for an appropriate MX record. If one or more MX records exist, they are sent back up the chain until
   they get to the requesting client computer.

4. When the client has the address(es) in hand, it must then try to establish an SMTP
   connection (see Chapter 5, "SMTP and qmail") to the primary mail server for the
   smallorg.org domain.

5. If that connection fails, it will then try the secondary mail server address returned in the
   answer section, and so on until it either establishes a connection or runs out of servers to
   try. At this point, what to do next is up to the client's mail program. Most will try the
   same process again a few hours later, up to a set point when it will finally give up.

If your domain database is not configured correctly, the DNS search for your mail host will
fail, and the client will not be able to deliver the mail message. Remember that at no point in
the DNS process was the mail message sent. The purpose of this process is for the remote
client to find the IP address of a computer that will accept mail messages for the smallorg.org
domain. When it finds an address, then (hopefully) it will initiate an SMTP mail session.

Using DNS Client Programs

If you do not have a dedicated connection to the Internet, you should not use your UNIX
server as a DNS server for your domain. If someone tried sending email to you at three o'clock
in the morning, and your DNS server was not up and connected to the Internet, he might not be
able to resolve your domain name and send the message. Most ISPs provide a DNS server for
their clients that is continually connected to the Internet. The ISP's DNS server will direct the
remote client to the proper email server for your domain. Again, if your network is not directly
connected to the Internet, most likely the ISP will accept email messages and spool them to be
picked up later by your UNIX mail server when it is convenient.

If the UNIX server has a dedicated connection to the Internet, but you still want the ISP to host your DNS domain records, the UNIX server can be configured to use the ISP's DNS server to resolve remote hostnames. The following sections describe how to configure the UNIX server to do this.

Configuring DNS Client Files

Three files are needed to use your UNIX server as a DNS client to resolve hostnames. All three files are normally located in the /etc directory. They are resolv.conf, hosts, and host.conf.

Hostname Resolver File

The /etc/resolv.conf file is used to configure the DNS server to which you want to send your DNS queries. You can list up to three DNS servers. The second and third entries will be used as backups if no response is received from the first (primary) server. If you have a local DNS server in your network, you should use that as your primary, although it isn't required. If you access other computers in your local network by name, it would increase performance to specify the local DNS server, because it would have quick name resolution. If you use DNS just to access remote computers, there probably won't be much performance increase.

You can also specify a default domain name to use when looking up domain names. If your domain is smallorg.org, you can specify that as the default domain in which to search. Then, if you need the IP address for hostname fred.smallorg.org, you can specify fred, and Linux will automatically append smallorg.org to it.

Unfortunately, that can work against you. The DNS software will automatically append smallorg.org to everything it tries to resolve. If you try connecting to www.freebsd.org, it will first attempt to find www.freebsd.org.smallorg.org. When that fails, it will try www.freebsd.org. To avoid this situation, you can ensure that your domain names contain a trailing period. This prevents the DNS software from appending the search domain. Listing 4.2 shows a sample /etc/resolv.conf file used in a UNIX server.

LISTING 4.2   A Sample /etc/resolv.conf File

```
1    search smallorg.org
2    nameserver 10.0.0.1
3    nameserver 10.0.0.2
4    nameserver 10.0.0.3
```

Line 1 shows the search statement that defines the default domain to use in all DNS queries. Remember that this will slow down queries for hosts not in your domain, because the search text is appended to all queries. Lines 2–4 show the primary, secondary, and tertiary DNS servers that service this UNIX server. Most often they are the DNS servers assigned to you by your ISP, although you are free to try other DNS servers if you want (unless your ISP filters out DNS requests).

Hosts File

Another method of resolving hostnames is to use a local host database, much like what was previously done on the Internet. The /etc/hosts file contains a list of hostnames and related IP addresses. Listing 4.3 shows a sample /etc/hosts file for a UNIX server.

At the minimum, this file should contain your local hostname and IP address and the common loopback address 127.0.0.1 for internal communications on the UNIX server. If there are remote hosts that you access frequently, you can enter their IP addresses into the /etc/hosts file manually. Then, every time you access those hostnames, the server will have the addresses on hand and not need to perform a DNS lookup. This greatly improves the connection time.

LISTING 4.3   A Sample /etc/hosts File

```
1   127.0.0.1     localhost
2   192.168.0.1      shadrach.smallorg.org
3   10.0.0.1      mail1.isp.net
4   10.0.0.2      mail2.isp.net
5   10.0.0.3      fred.otherplace.com
```

Lines 1 and 2 show the IP addresses used for the local UNIX server. Lines 3–5 show IP addresses for commonly used computers on your network. This allows the server to access these sites by name more quickly than by using DNS.

> **NOTE**
>
> All UNIX computers include a special localhost hostname. This name always points to the special IP address 127.0.0.1, which is associated with a special network device called the *loopback device*. This name and address allow internal processes to communicate with other processes on the same system using network programming. Many programs are configured to use the localhost address. Changing localhost to point to anything else could change the behavior of these programs.

DNS Resolution File

The /etc/host.conf file specifies the methods that UNIX can use to resolve hostnames and the order in which to try the methods. Unfortunately, different UNIX distributions configure this file differently. Listing 4.4 shows a sample /etc/host.conf file for a FreeBSD server.

LISTING 4.4   A Sample `/etc/host.conf` File

```
# $FreeBSD: src/etc/host.conf,v 1.5.2.1 1999/08/29 14:18:44 peter Exp $
# First try the /etc/hosts file
hosts
# Now try the nameserver next.
bind
# If you have YP/NIS configured, uncomment the next line
# nis
```

The server will use the methods in the order in which they appear. In this example, the server first will look up the hostname in its `/etc/hosts` file. If it is not found, the server will then use DNS (`bind`). Finally, if the server is using an NIS database, that will be used.

DNS Utilities

Numerous utilities have been written for UNIX systems to help system administrators find DNS information for remote hosts and networks. The Internet Software Consortium has created the Berkeley Internet Name Domain (BIND) package for UNIX systems. This package includes three of my favorite and most-often-used utilities: *host*, *nslookup*, and *dig*. On most UNIX distributions, these programs are included with the software.

These utilities often come in handy when troubleshooting email problems on the Internet. Often, a customer will copy an email address incorrectly and his email will be rejected. Of course, he is 100% sure that he is using the proper address, and he can't understand why the message is rejected. With a little DNS work, you can determine if the host part of the email address is correct or a typo.

The Host Program

The host program does basic DNS name resolution. The format of the `host` command is as follows:

```
host [-l] [-v] [-w] [-r] [-d] [-t querytype] [-a] host [server]
```

By default, host will attempt to resolve the hostname `host` by using the default DNS server specified in the `/etc/resolv.conf` file. If `server` is added, host will attempt to use that instead of the default DNS server. By adding parameters to the command line, the output and behavior of host can be modified. These parameters are shown in Table 4.3.

TABLE 4.3   host Command Parameters

Parameter	Description
-l	Lists the complete domain information
-v	Uses verbose output format
-w	Makes host wait for a response
-r	Turns off recursion
-d	Turns on debugging
-t querytype	Specifies definite query type
-a	Retrieves all DNS records

The -l option can be used to find information about all the hosts listed in a domain. This is often used with the -t option to filter particular types of information (such as -t MX, which returns all the MX records for a domain). Unfortunately, in this day of security awareness, it is often difficult to use the -l option, because many DNS servers will refuse attempts to access all the host information contained in the database. If you are trying to get information from a slow DNS server (or a slow link to the network), you might want to try the -w parameter. This tells the host program to wait forever for a response to a query. By default, it will time out after about one minute.

-r tells the DNS server to return only information regarding the query that it has in its own local DNS database. The DNS server will not attempt to contact a remote DNS server to find the information. This is useful in determining if your DNS server is properly caching DNS answers.

First, try resolving a hostname using the -r parameter. If no one else has gone there, you should not get an answer from your DNS. Then try it without the -r parameter. You should get back the normal DNS information, because the local DNS server was allowed to contact a remote DNS server to retrieve the information. Next, try the host command again with the -r parameter. You should get the same information you received in the previous attempt. This means that the DNS server did indeed cache the results from the previous DNS query in its local name cache. If you do not receive any information, your local DNS server did not cache the previous response. You should have noticed a significant decrease in the time it took to respond with an answer from cache, compared to when it responded after doing the DNS query on the network.

By default, host attempts to produce its output in human-readable format. For example, a typical output is shown in Listing 4.5. If you use the -v option, the output changes to resemble the normal RR format found in the DNS database. This can be useful in trying to debug a DNS problem with the configuration of the DNS server.

LISTING 4.5   Sample host Command Output

```
1  $ host -t mx www.freebsd.org
2  www.freebsd.org is a nickname for freefall.freebsd.org
3  freefall.freebsd.org mail is handled (pri=10) by hub.freebsd.org
4  freefall.freebsd.org mail is handled (pri=10) by hub.FreeBSD.org
5  $
```

Line 1 shows the basic format for using the host command to find the mail servers for a domain. Lines 2–4 show the output from the command. First, line 2 shows that the DNS server was able to determine that www.freebsd.org is a nickname for the freefall.freebsd.org server. Then, lines 3 and 4 show that the hostname has two different mail server (MX) records of computers that can accept email for that host. Notice that the preferences of each mail server are also listed. In this example, both MX servers have the same priority. This is a good technique to use if you think your mail server is not delivering messages to a remote site properly.

The Nslookup Program

The nslookup program is an extremely versatile tool that can be used in a variety of troubleshooting situations. There are two modes under which nslookup can be run. In non-interactive mode, it behaves much like the host command, discussed previously. The interactive mode is where all the fun can be found. It can give more detailed information about remote computers and domains, because you can change options as you traverse the DNS database. The basic format of the nslookup command is

```
nslookup [-option ...] [host-to-find | -[server]]
```

If you enter the host-to-find parameter on the command line, nslookup operates in non-interactive mode and returns the result of the query similarly to the host command. If no arguments are given or the first argument is a hyphen (-), nslookup will enter interactive mode. If you want to use a different DNS server, you can specify it using the -server argument, where server is the IP address of the DNS server to use. Otherwise, nslookup will use the default DNS server listed in the /etc/resolv.conf file.

There are three ways to change option settings in the nslookup program. One way is to list them as options in the command line. Another way is to specify them on the interactive command line when nslookup starts by using the set command. The third way is to create a file in your $HOME directory called .nslookuprc and enter one option per line. A list of available options is shown in Table 4.4.

4

DNS AND QMAIL

TABLE 4.4   Nslookup Options

Option	Description
all	Prints current values of options
class	Sets the DNS class value (default is IN)
[no]debug	Turns on (or off) debugging mode (default is nodebug)
[no]d2	Turns on (or off) exhaustive debugging mode (default is nod2)
domain=name	Sets the default domain name to name
srchlist=name1/name2...	Changes the default domain name to name1 and the search list to name1, name2, and so on
[no]defname	Appends the default domain name to a single component lookup request
[no]search	Appends the domain names in the search list to the hostname (default is search)
port=value	Changes TCP/UDP port to value (default is 53)
querytype=value	Changes the type of information requested to type value (default is A)
type=value	Same as querytype
[no]recurse	Tells the name server to query other servers to obtain an answer (default is recurse)
retry=number	Sets the number of retries to number (default is 4)
root=host	Changes the name of the root server to host (default is ns.internic.net)
timeout=number	Changes initial timeout interval to wait for a reply to number seconds (default is 5)
[no]vc	Always uses a virtual circuit (default is novc)
[no]ignoretc	Ignores packet truncation errors (default is noignoretc)

Listing 4.6 shows a sample nslookup session used to get information for host www.linux.org. The default parameters return the IP address for the hostname. This example demonstrates changing the parameters to find the mail servers for the domain.

LISTING 4.6   A Sample Nslookup Session

```
1  $ nslookup
2  Default Server:  ns1.ispnet1.net
3  Address:  192.168.1.1
4
```

```
 5  > www.freebsd.org
 6  Server:  ns1.ispnet1.net
 7  Address:  192.168.1.1
 8
 9  Non-authoritative answer:
10  Name:     freefall.freebsd.org
11 Address:  204.216.27.21
12  Aliases:  www.freebsd.org
13
14  > set type=MX
15  > www.freebsd.org
16  Server:  ns1.ispnet1.net
17  Address:  192.168.1.1
18
19  Non-authoritative answer:
20  www.freebsd.org canonical name = freefall.freebsd.org
21  freefall.freebsd.org    preference = 10, mail exchanger = hub.freebsd.org
22
23  Authoritative answers can be found from:
24  freebsd.org        nameserver = ns1.root.com
25  freebsd.org        nameserver = who.cdrom.com
26  freebsd.org        nameserver = ns1.crl.com
27  freebsd.org        nameserver = ns2.crl.com
28  freebsd.org        nameserver = ns1.iafrica.com
29  freebsd.org        nameserver = ns2.iafrica.com
30  freebsd.org        nameserver = ns.gnome.co.uk
31  hub.freebsd.org internet address = 204.216.27.18
32  ns1.root.com    internet address = 209.102.106.178
33  who.cdrom.com   internet address = 204.216.27.3
34  ns1.crl.com     internet address = 165.113.1.36
35  ns2.crl.com     internet address = 165.113.61.37
36  ns1.iafrica.com internet address = 196.7.0.139
37  ns2.iafrica.com internet address = 196.7.142.133
38  ns.gnome.co.uk  internet address = 193.243.228.142
39  > exit
40  $
```

Line 5 shows the query for the hostname www.freebsd.org. Lines 6 and 7 show the DNS server used to process the query, and lines 9–12 show that the server contained a non-authoritative answer for the IP address. Obviously someone must have accessed this site before, and its IP address was still in the DNS server's local name cache.

In line 14, the option is set to return information on the mail servers in the domain. Lines 19–38 show the information returned by the DNS server. Lines 19–21 show the answer section of the DNS packet, which again indicates that the answer is non-authoritative, and lists the three mail servers responsible for the www.freebsd.org hostname. Lines 23–38 show the information in the authoritative and additional sections in the DNS packet. Lines 23–30 show that there are seven DNS servers that are authoritative for the freebsd.org domain and have the RR records for www.freebsd.org. Lines 31–38 show the additional information section, listing IP addresses for hostnames contained in the responses.

If you want to extend this example, you could change the default DNS server to one of the authoritative DNS servers listed (by using the server command) and retry the MX query to see if the information has changed at all from the information returned by the non-authoritative DNS server.

The Dig Program

The dig program uses a simple command-line format to query DNS servers regarding domain information. The format for the dig command is as follows:

```
dig [@server] domain [query-type] [query-class] [+query-option]
➥ [-dig-option] [%comment]
```

where

> server is an optional DNS server that you can specify. By default, dig will use the DNS server defined in the /etc/resolv.conf file. You can specify the server option by using either an IP address in numeric dot notation or a hostname. If you use a hostname for the server option, dig will use the default DNS server to resolve the hostname and then use that DNS server to find the information on the domain.

> query-type is the RR type information that you are requesting, such as the A, SOA, NS, and MX records. any can be used to return all information available about a domain.

> query-class is the network class of information you are requesting. The default is Internet (IN), which is the type of information we are looking for.

> +query-option is used to change an option value in the DNS packet or to change the format of the dig output. Many of these options shadow options available in the nslookup program. Table 4.5 shows the query options available.

TABLE 4.5   dig Command Query Options

Option	Description
[no]debug	Turns on (off) debugging
[no]d2	Turns on (off) extra debugging
[no]recurse	(Doesn't) use recursive lookups
retry=#	Sets number of retries
time=#	Sets timeout length
[no]ko	Keeps open option (implies vc)

Option	Description
[no]vc	(Doesn't) use virtual circuit
[no]defname	(Doesn't) use default domain name
[no]search	(Doesn't) use domain search list
domain=NAME	Sets default domain name to NAME
[no]ignore	(Doesn't) ignore truncation errors
[no]primary	(Doesn't) use primary server
[no]aaonly	Authoritative query only flag
[no]cmd	Echoes parsed arguments
[no]stats	Prints query statistics
[no]Header	Prints basic header
[no]header	Prints header flags
[no]ttlid	Prints TTLs
[no]cl	Prints class info
[no]qr	Prints outgoing query
[no]reply	Prints reply
[no]ques	Prints question section
[no]answer	Prints answer section
[no]author	Prints authoritative section
[no]addit	Prints additional section
pfdef	Sets to default print flags
pfmin	Sets to minimal print flags
pfset=#	Sets print flags to #
pfand=#	Bitwise AND prints flags with #
pfor=#	Bitwise OR prints flags with #

-dig-option is used to specify other options that affect the operation of dig. Table 4.6 shows some of the other options available to fine-tune the dig command and its output.

TABLE 4.6 -dig-option Options

Option	Description
-x	Specifies inverse address mapping in normal dot notation
-f	Reads a file for batch mode processing
-T	Time in seconds between batch mode command processing

TABLE 4.6   Continued

Option	Description
-p	Port number to use
-P	After a response, issues a `ping` command
-t	Specifies the type of query
-c	Specifies the class of query
-envsav	Specifies that the dig options should be saved to become the default dig environment

A sample dig session output is shown in Listing 4.7. As you can see, the dig program produces the same information as host and nslookup, but it shows more detail on how and where the answers came from.

LISTING 4.7   Sample Dig Output

```
$ dig www.freebsd.org

; <<>> DiG 8.2 <<>> www.freebsd.org
;; res options: init recurs defnam dnsrch
;; got answer:
;; ->>HEADER<<- opcode: QUERY, status: NOERROR, id: 4
;; flags: qr rd ra; QUERY: 1, ANSWER: 2, AUTHORITY: 7, ADDITIONAL: 7
;; QUERY SECTION:
;;      www.freebsd.org, type = A, class = IN

;; ANSWER SECTION:
www.freebsd.org.         13m15s IN CNAME  freefall.freebsd.org.
freefall.freebsd.org.    13m15s IN A      204.216.27.21

;; AUTHORITY SECTION:
freebsd.org.             16m11s IN NS     ns1.root.com.
freebsd.org.             16m11s IN NS     who.cdrom.com.
freebsd.org.             16m11s IN NS     ns1.crl.com.
freebsd.org.             16m11s IN NS     ns2.crl.com.
freebsd.org.             16m11s IN NS     ns1.iafrica.com.
freebsd.org.             16m11s IN NS     ns2.iafrica.com.
freebsd.org.             16m11s IN NS     ns.gnome.co.uk.

;; ADDITIONAL SECTION:
ns1.root.com.            2h20m56s IN A    209.102.106.178
who.cdrom.com.           43m15s IN A      204.216.27.3
ns1.crl.com.             2d23h43m15s IN A  165.113.1.36
```

```
ns2.crl.com.          2d23h43m15s IN A  165.113.61.37
ns1.iafrica.com.      1d22h40m59s IN A  196.7.0.139
ns2.iafrica.com.      1d22h40m59s IN A  196.7.142.133
ns.gnome.co.uk.       3h41m22s IN A   193.243.228.142

;; Total query time: 41 msec
;; FROM: shadrach.ispnet1.net to SERVER: default -- 207.133.66.242
;; WHEN: Fri May 26 16:12:06 2000
;; MSG SIZE  sent: 33  rcvd: 357

$
```

UNIX as a DNS Server

If you have a direct full-time connection to the Internet, you might want to host your own DNS server for your domain. You can do this with your UNIX server. You could also use your UNIX server as a local DNS server in name-caching mode. This would save some network time on DNS requests, in that your server will implement its local name cache and use the name cache to answer future DNS requests (within the TTL limit of the information).

This section describes two packages that can be used to provide DNS server capabilities to a UNIX host—BIND and dnscache.

The BIND Program

The Berkley Internet Name Domain (BIND) by the Internet Software Consortium, mentioned previously, also contains software for implementing a DNS server. The DNS server software program is called *named*. Many UNIX distributions contain the named program in a canned binary package. If you don't have a binary package or you want to use the latest version of BIND, you can download the source code from the Internet Software Consortium at ftp.isc.org. The current version at the time of this writing is BIND 8.2.2. You must have the GCC compiler installed on your UNIX server to be able to compile the new software.

Compiling BIND

The latest version of source code for the BIND package can always be downloaded as the file ftp://ftp.isc.org/isc/src/cur/bind-8/bind-src.tar.gz. At the time of this writing, this points to version 8.2.2, patch 5. The steps involved in compiling a new named program are as follows:

1. Unpack the file into a work directory by entering

   tar -zxvf bind-src.tar.gz -C /usr/local/src

2. Change to the newly created directory.

3. Enter `make clean`.

4. Enter `make depend`.

5. Enter `make` to produce the binaries.

6. Enter `make install` to place the binaries and configuration files in the appropriate directories.

After BIND has been installed by either compiling the source or installing a binary distribution, you can start configuring the named configuration files for the specific situation you want.

Using Named as a Workstation Cache Server

The easiest way to use the named program is as a way to cache DNS responses on your local server for future requests. First, you must configure the `/etc/named.conf` file for your local computer. Listing 4.8 shows what the `/etc/named.conf` file would look like if used as a caching DNS server.

LISTING 4.8   A Sample DNS `/etc/named.conf` File Used as a Caching DNS Server

```
1   options {
2           directory "/var/named";
3   };
4
5     zone "." {
6           type hint;
7           file "root.cache";
8
9   };
10
11
12    zone "localhost" {
13           type master;
14           file "pri/localhost";
15  };
16
17  zone "0.0.127.in-addr.arpa" {
18           type master;
19           file "pri/127.0.0";
20  };
```

Lines 1–3 define options that are used in the named program. Line 2 shows that the default directory for the configuration files will be in the `/var/named` directory. Lines 5–7 define the root domain definitions. As discussed previously, each DNS server must know the address of the root servers to be able to query the DNS tree. Line 7 indicates that the file that contains the root server addresses is /var/named/root.cache. This file can be produced with the dig command:

```
dig @f.root-servers.net . ns >> root.cache
```

Listing 4.9 shows a sample /var/named/root.cache file.

LISTING 4.9 A Sample DNS /var/named/root.cache File

```
1   ; <<>> DiG 8.2 <<>> @f.root-servers.net . ns
2   ; (1 server found)
3   ;; res options: init recurs defnam dnsrch
4   ;; got answer:
5   ;; ->>HEADER<<- opcode: QUERY, status: NOERROR, id: 10
6   ;; flags: qr aa rd; QUERY: 1, ANSWER: 13, AUTHORITY: 0, ADDITIONAL: 13
7   ;; QUERY SECTION:
8   ;;      ., type = NS, class = IN
9
10  ;; ANSWER SECTION:
11  .                       6D IN NS        G.ROOT-SERVERS.NET.
12  .                       6D IN NS        J.ROOT-SERVERS.NET.
13  .                       6D IN NS        K.ROOT-SERVERS.NET.
14  .                       6D IN NS        L.ROOT-SERVERS.NET.
15  .                       6D IN NS        M.ROOT-SERVERS.NET.
16  .                       6D IN NS        A.ROOT-SERVERS.NET.
17  .                       6D IN NS        H.ROOT-SERVERS.NET.
18  .                       6D IN NS        B.ROOT-SERVERS.NET.
19  .                       6D IN NS        C.ROOT-SERVERS.NET.
20  .                       6D IN NS        D.ROOT-SERVERS.NET.
21  .                       6D IN NS        E.ROOT-SERVERS.NET.
22  .                       6D IN NS        I.ROOT-SERVERS.NET.
23  .                       6D IN NS        F.ROOT-SERVERS.NET.
24
25  ;; ADDITIONAL SECTION:
26  G.ROOT-SERVERS.NET.     5w6d16h IN A    192.112.36.4
27  J.ROOT-SERVERS.NET.     5w6d16h IN A    198.41.0.10
28  K.ROOT-SERVERS.NET.     5w6d16h IN A    193.0.14.129
29  L.ROOT-SERVERS.NET.     5w6d16h IN A    198.32.64.12
30  M.ROOT-SERVERS.NET.     5w6d16h IN A    202.12.27.33
31  A.ROOT-SERVERS.NET.     5w6d16h IN A    198.41.0.4
32  H.ROOT-SERVERS.NET.     5w6d16h IN A    128.63.2.53
33  B.ROOT-SERVERS.NET.     5w6d16h IN A    128.9.0.107
34  C.ROOT-SERVERS.NET.     5w6d16h IN A    192.33.4.12
35  D.ROOT-SERVERS.NET.     5w6d16h IN A    128.8.10.90
36  E.ROOT-SERVERS.NET.     5w6d16h IN A    192.203.230.10
```

4

DNS AND QMAIL

LISTING 4.9   Continued

```
37 I.ROOT-SERVERS.NET.     5w6d16h IN A     192.36.148.17
38 F.ROOT-SERVERS.NET.     5w6d16h IN A     192.5.5.241
39
40 ;; Total query time: 10 msec
41 ;; FROM: power.rc.vix.com to SERVER: f.root-servers.net  192.5.5.241
42 ;; WHEN: Thu Jun  3 14:55:57 1999
43 ;; MSG SIZE  sent: 17  rcvd: 436
```

Lines 26–38 show the IP addresses of the root-level servers as of June 1999. You will have to update this file (every 5 weeks, 6 days, and 16 hours according to the TTL values) to make sure that your DNS server forwards DNS queries to the proper root-level servers.

Back in the /etc/named.conf file in Listing 4.8, you also defined two zones for which your DNS server will be responsible. Each zone must also have its own definition file. Lines 10–13 show the definition for the localhost zone. It is defined in /var/named/pri/localhost. Listing 4.10 shows an example of what this file would look like.

LISTING 4.10   A Sample /var/named/pri/localhost DNS File

```
1  ;localhost.
2  @            in    soa     localhost. postmaster.localhost. (
3                             1993050801      ;serial
4                             3600            ;refresh
5                             1800            ;retry
6                             604800          ;expiration
7                             3600 )          ;minimum
8
9                     ns      localhost.
10
11                    a       127.0.0.1
```

The localhost file defines the SOA for your server, stating that it is its own DNS name server (line 9), and gives the loopback address as its IP address (line 11). The last section in the /etc/named.conf file is the reverse lookup zone for your Linux server. Lines 17–19 in Listing 4.8 define the 0.0.127.in-addr.arpa zone and point to configuration file /var/named/pri/127.0.0. Listing 4.11 shows what this file would look like.

LISTING 4.11   A Sample /var/named/pri/127.0.0 DNS File

```
1  ; 0.0.127.in-addr.arpa
2  @            in    soa     localhost. postmaster.localhost. (
3                             1993050801      ;serial
```

```
4                              3600              ;refresh
5                              1800              ;retry
6                              604800            ;expiration
7                              3600 )            ;minimum
8
9                   ns         localhost.
10
11 1                ptr        localhost.
```

Line 11 defines the loopback address 127.0.0.1 as the localhost address.

The final piece of the puzzle is to change the /etc/resolv.conf file to point to the local Linux server. By specifying the loopback address (127.0.0.1) as the primary name server, Linux will "query itself" for DNS name resolutions. This completes the DNS configuration for the workstation. By running named as a background process, your Linux server will be able to respond to DNS queries and cache the responses in memory to answer future requests more quick.

Using Named as a Zone DNS Server

The final example will use your UNIX server as a full-blown DNS server for your domain. This will use the same named configuration files as in the previous example, but it will add two more zones to the /etc/named.conf file shown in Listing 4.8. The new zones will define your domain for the named program. Listing 4.12 shows the sections that will be added to the /etc/named.conf file.

LISTING 4.12   Additional /etc/named.conf Sections

```
1  zone smallorg.org {
2      type master
3      file "pri/smallorg.org";
4  };
5
6  zone 0.168.192.in-addr.arpa {
7      type master;
8      file "pri/192.168.0";
9  };
```

4

DNS AND QMAIL

Much like the other example, the zone sections define the type of zone DNS server this will be (master, or primary) and in what files the zone definitions will be found. Listing 4.13 shows a sample zone definition for the smallorg.org zone file.

LISTING 4.13 A Sample /etc/named/pri/smallorg.org DNS File

```
1   @       IN      SOA     master.smallorg.org. postmaster.smallorg.org. (
2                           199802151           ; serial, todays date + todays
▶serial #
3                           3600                ; refresh, seconds
4                           1800                ; retry, seconds
5                           604800              ; expire, seconds
6                           3600)               ; minimum, seconds
7
8                   NS      master              ; name server
9                   MX      10 mail.smallorg.org.      ; Primary mail server
10                  MX      20 mail.isp.net.    ; Secondary mail server
11
12  localhost       A       127.0.0.1
13  master          A       192.168.0.1
14  mail            A       192.168.0.2
```

Now you're halfway to hosting your domain. Next, you must create the DNS database file for your reverse domain address as listed in the /etc/named.conf file in Listing 4.12. Listing 4.14 shows what this file would look like.

LISTING 4.14 A Sample /etc/named/pri/192.168.0 DNS File

```
1   @       IN      SOA     master.smallorg.org. postmaster.smallorg.org. (
2                           199802151 ; Serial, todays date + todays serial
3                           3600      ; Refresh
4                           1800      ; Retry
5                           604800    ; Expire
6                           3600)     ; Minimum TTL
7                   NS      master
8
9   1               PTR     master.smallorg.org.
10  2               PTR     mail.smallorg.org.
```

These configuration files will allow your named program to respond properly to DNS queries for your domain. Of course, this assumes that you have properly registered your domain with the Network Information Center (NIC) and that the root DNS servers for the proper first-level domain (.org in this example) have pointers to the IP address of the Linux server that is serving as your DNS server.

The Dnscache Program

If creating lots of databases for the named program seems confusing, it is. Unfortunately, not much has been done over the years to remedy that problem. Dan Bernstein, the developer of qmail, has attempted to solve this problem by developing the dnscache package. The dnscache package contains utilities to replace the BIND DNS client and server utilities. The dnscache package server utilities allow for much simpler configuration of DNS servers, using easy command-line programs to add records to the DNS database. This section describes the dnscache server utilities.

Installing Dnscache

The dnscache package can be downloaded from Bernstein's Web site at `http://cr.yp.to/dnscache.html`. The current version at the time of this writing is version 1.00, which can be downloaded as file `dnscache-1.00.tar.gz`. When it is downloaded, follow these steps to compile and install it:

1. Unpack the distribution file into a working directory:

   ```
   tar -zxvf dnscache-1.00.tar.gz -C /usr/local/src
   ```

2. Change to the newly created source code directory.

3. Use the GNU `make` command to compile the source code.

4. Use the `make` command with the `setup` and `check` options to install the software:

   ```
   make setup check
   ```

This should install the program in the `/usr/local/bin` directory on your server.

> **NOTE**
>
> The dnscache package requires that Bernstein's daemontools package also be installed on the server. Installing and configuring the daemontools package is discussed in Chapter 16, "The Daemontool Utilities."

Using Dnscache as a Local Caching DNS Server

The dnscache package contains utilities to easily configure the UNIX server as a local DNS cache server. No DNS database records need to be created for dnscache.

There must be two new user IDs created on the system to run the dnscache programs:

- dnscache
- dnslog

Besides the two user IDs, dnscache also requires a directory to contain the supervise scripts to start dnscache and maintain a log file. Remember that dnscache requires the daemontools supervise programs to operate.

The dnscache-conf program creates the required supervise scripts for dnscache in the supervise directory. The format of the dnscache-conf command is

```
dnscache-conf dnscache dnslog /var/qmail/supervise/dnscache
```

The directory listed on the dnscache-conf command line identifies the location of the dnscache supervise scripts created by dnscache-conf. If you use the supervise program to control other qmail programs, it is common to create a supervise directory under /var/qmail (see Chapter 16). You can use this location to contain the dnscache supervise scripts, as shown in the example.

If the supervise directory has a svscan service watching it, the dnscache program should start automatically, along with the multilog log file generator. If it is not running, you can start it manually using the command

```
svscan /var/qmail/supervise &
```

After dnscache has been installed, you can change your name server in the /etc/resolv.conf file to point to localhost (127.0.0.1). This ensures that the dnscache program running on the local server will be used to resolve all IP address names.

As hostnames are requested, dnscache goes to the list of root DNS servers to resolve the name into the proper IP address. As new IP addresses are resolved, dnscache keeps them in a local name cache, decreasing the response time for future queries for the same name. This creates a standard local DNS cache system with practically no configuration required.

Using Tinydns as an External DNS Server

The tinydns program is part of the dnscache package. It can be used to allow the UNIX server to be an authoritative DNS server for a specified domain. Much like the dnscache program, you must create two new user IDs for the tinydns program and create the supervise scripts. These are the steps necessary to configure a tinydns server:

1. Create system user IDs tinydns and dnslog.
2. Run the tinydns-conf utility, using the supervise script directory and the IP address of the DNS server:

   ```
   tinydns-conf tinydns dnslog /var/qmail/supervise/tinydns 192.168.1.1
   ```

That's all that's needed to create a DNS server. Assuming that the svscan program is running on the supervise directory, the tinydns DNS server program should be running as a background process, listening for DNS queries. If you do not have the svscan program running already, you can start it with the command

```
svscan /var/qmail/supervise &
```

At this point, however, you should have a DNS server with no information in the DNS database—not too exciting. There are several utilities in the dnscache package that can be used to enter DNS records into the empty database automatically. Table 4.7 shows the utilities that can be used to manipulate the DNS database for tinydns.

TABLE 4.7 Tinydns DNS Database Commands

Command	Description
add-ns	Add a name server NS record
add-host	Add a host A record
add-alias	Add an alias CNAME record
add-mx	Add a mail server MX record
add-childdns	Add a subdomain NS record

Each of these commands is located in the `tinydns/root` directory. After each command, you must use the GNU `make` command to add the record to the database.

To create a new name server for a DNS domain, you would use the `add-ns` command:

```
cd /var/qmail/supervise/tinydns/root
./add-ns smallorg.org 192.168.1.1
./add-ns 1.168.192.in-addr.arpa 192.168.1.1
make
```

These commands create entries in the tinydns DNS database for the `smallorg.org` name server at IP address `192.168.1.1`. To define a domain mail server record, use these commands:

```
cd /var/qmail/supervise/tinydns/root
./add-mx smallorg.org 192.168.1.1
make
```

To define a hostname within the domain, use these commands:

```
cd /var/qmail/supervise/tinydns/root
./add-host www.smallorg.org 192.168.1.2
make
```

By using simple tinydns commands, the system administrator can build a complete DNS database without having to mess with the standard BIND database formats.

4

DNS AND QMAIL

CAUTION

One final word of caution. The examples in this chapter use fictitious IP addresses for example purposes. To host your own domain, you must have a valid IP address space on the Internet assigned by the Internet Assigned Numbers Authority (IANA) and use a valid IP address for your DNS server so that other Internet computers can connect to it. Also, your domain must be properly registered with ICANN before any DNS queries will work on your domain. If you choose to let your ISP host your domain, you can use the public IP address network of 192.168.0.0 to assign IP addresses to hosts on your network. However, these hosts cannot use a valid domain name in your domain.

Summary

This chapter discusses the domain name system (DNS) and how it relates to email. Each computer connected to the Internet has a unique hostname and a unique IP address. The DNS database system matches the hostnames and IP addresses. The database is distributed among many different servers on the Internet, so no one server has to maintain the list of all computers. You can find a remote computer's IP address by its hostname by sending a DNS query to a DNS server. That server has the capability to walk the DNS tree to find the database record that relates the hostname to the IP address, or vice versa. Many domains use their domain names as generic email addresses. Your email server must know how to use DNS to find a server responsible for receiving email messages for the domain. The BIND and dnscache packages provide utilities to allow UNIX servers to be either a DNS client or a DNS server. By using either package, you can connect to remote DNS servers to resolve hostnames, or you can host your own domain DNS records on your UNIX server.

SMTP and qmail

IN THIS CHAPTER

In Chapter 4, "DNS and qmail," you learned how to locate another computer on the Internet using hostnames and DNS servers. Now that you know where the other computer is, you might want to be able to actually do something with it. This chapter explains how to send a message to a user on the remote computer from your computer. The Simple Mail Transfer Protocol (SMTP) has been used since 1982 to relay email messages and attachments to many different types of computer systems. Its ease of use and portability made it the standard protocol used to transfer messages between computer systems on the Internet. To have an understanding of how email works, you should get to know SMTP.

For qmail servers that communicate directly with other qmail servers, Dan Bernstein has developed an alternative mail protocol, called Quick Mail Transfer Protocol (QMTP). This protocol is discussed at the end of this chapter.

The SMTP Protocol

SMTP was designed to work on many different types of transport media. The most common transport medium is the Internet, using a TCP/IP connection on port 25. Many Linux distributions will automatically install an SMTP package when the IP services are installed. A common troubleshooting technique to use to check if a remote server is running an SMTP server package is to Telnet to TCP port 25 and see if you get a response. You can test this out on your own UNIX server by Telneting to hostname `localhost` using port 25. Listing 5.1 shows a sample Telnet session to a FreeBSD server running the `qmail-smtpd` SMTP package.

LISTING 5.1   A Sample Telnet Session to Port 25

```
1  $ telnet localhost 25
2  Trying 127.0.0.1...
3  Connected to localhost.ispnet1.net.
4  Escape character is '^]'.
5  220 shadrach.ispnet1.net ESMTP
6  QUIT
7  221 shadrach.ispnet1.net
8  Connection closed by foreign host.
9  $
```

Line 1 shows the `telnet` command format using host `localhost` and TCP port 25. Line 5 shows a typical response if your UNIX server has an SMTP software package installed. The first number is a 3-digit response code. This code can be used for troubleshooting purposes if mail is not being transferred properly. Next, the hostname of the SMTP server and a description of the SMTP software package that the server is using are displayed. This server is using the qmail SMTP software package, using the `qmail-smtpd` program to accept incoming SMTP connections. Line 6 shows how you can close the Telnet connection by typing the word QUIT and pressing the Enter key. The SMTP server should send you a closing message and kill the TCP connection.

As you can tell from this example, SMTP uses simple ASCII text commands and returns 3-digit reply codes with optional ASCII text messages. SMTP is defined in Internet Request For Comment (RFC) document number 821, maintained by the Internet Engineering Task Force (IETF) and published on August 21, 1982. Several modifications have been made to SMTP over the years, but the basic protocol commands still remain in use.

Basic SMTP Client Commands

When a TCP session has been established and the SMTP server acknowledges the client by sending a welcome banner (as shown in Listing 5.1), it is the client's responsibility to control the connection between the two computers. The client accomplishes this by sending special commands to the server. The server should respond to each command appropriately.

RFC 821 defines the basic client commands that an SMTP server should recognize and respond to. Since then, there have been several extensions to SMTP that not all servers have used. This section documents the basic SMTP keywords that are defined in RFC 821. The section "Extended SMTP," later in this chapter, covers some of the new extensions that have been implemented by several SMTP software packages.

The basic format of an SMTP command is

```
command [parameters]
```

where command is a four-character SMTP command and parameters are optional qualifying data for the command. Table 5.1 shows the basic SMTP commands that are available. The following sections describe the commands in more detail.

TABLE 5.1 Basic SMTP Commands

Command	Description
HELO	Opening greeting from client
MAIL	Identifies sender of message
RCPT	Identifies recipient(s)
DATA	Identifies start of message
SEND	Sends message to terminal
SOML	Send Or MaiL
SAML	Send And MaiL
RSET	Resets SMTP connection

5

TABLE 5.1   Continued

Command	Description
VRFY	Verifies username on system
EXPN	Queries for lists and aliases
HELP	Requests list of commands
NOOP	No operation—does nothing
QUIT	Stops the SMTP session
TURN	Reverses the SMTP roles

HELO Command

This is not a typo. By definition, SMTP commands are four characters long, so the opening greeting by the client to the server is the HELO command. The format for this command is

```
HELO domain name
```

The purpose of the HELO command is for the client to identify itself to the SMTP server. Unfortunately, this method was devised in the early days of the Internet before mass hacker break-in attempts. As you can see, the client can be identified as whatever it wants to use in the text string. That being the case, most SMTP servers use this command just as a formality. If they really need to know the identity of the client, they will try to use a reverse DNS lookup of the client's IP address to determine the client's DNS name. In fact, for security reasons many SMTP servers will refuse to talk to hosts whose IP address does not resolve to a proper DNS hostname. By sending this command, the client indicates that it wants to initialize a new SMTP session with the server. By responding to this command, the server acknowledges the new connection and should be ready to receive further commands from the client.

People Clients Versus Host Clients

In SMTP you must remember to differentiate between people and hosts. When creating a new mail message, the email user is the client of his local host. Once the user sends his message, he is no longer the client in the SMTP process. His local host computer takes over the process of mailing the message and becomes the client, as far as SMTP is concerned. When the local host contacts the remote host to transfer the message using SMTP, it is now acting as the client in the SMTP process. The HELO command identifies the local hostname as the client, not the actual sender of the message. This terminology often gets confusing.

MAIL Command

The MAIL command is used to initiate a mail session with the server after the initial HELO command is sent. It identifies from whom the message is being sent. The format of the MAIL command is

```
MAIL reverse-path
```

The reverse-path argument not only identifies the sender, but it also identifies how to reach the sender with a return message. If the sender is a user on the client computer that initiated the SMTP session, the format for the MAIL command would look something like this:

```
MAIL FROM:rich@shadrach.smallorg.org
```

Notice how the FROM section denotes the proper email address for the sender of the message, including the full hostname of the client computer. This information should appear in the FROM section of the text of the email message (but more on that later). If the email message has been routed through several different systems between the original sender and the desired recipient, each system will add its routing information to the reverse-path section. This documents the path that the email message used to get to the server. Often, mail from clients on private networks has to traverse several mail relay points before getting to the Internet. The reverse-path information is often useful in troubleshooting email problems or in tracking down emailers who are purposely trying to hide their identities by bouncing their email messages off of several unknowing SMTP servers.

RCPT Command

The RCPT command defines the recipients of the message. There can be multiple recipients for the same message, and each recipient is normally listed in a separate RCPT command line. The format of the RCPT command is

```
RCPT forward-path
```

The forward-path argument defines where the email is ultimately destined. This is usually a fully qualified email address, but it could be just a username that is local to the SMTP server. For example, the following RCPT command

```
RCPT TO:haley
```

would send the message to user haley on the SMTP server computer that is processing the message. Messages can also be sent to users on other computer systems that are remote from the SMTP server to which the message is sent. For example, sending the following RCPT command

```
RCPT TO:riley@meshach.smallorg.org
```

to the SMTP server on computer shadrach.smallorg.org would cause shadrach.smallorg.org to make a decision. Because the user is not local to shadrach, it must decide what to do with the message. There are three possible actions that shadrach could take with the message. They are as follows:

- shadrach could forward the message to the destination computer and return an OK response to the client. In that case, shadrach would add its hostname to the <reverse-path> of the MAIL command line to indicate that it is part of the return path to route a message back to the original sender.

- shadrach could *not* forward the message and send a reply to the client, specifying that it was not able to deliver the message, but that it verified the address of meshach. smallorg.org to be correct. The client could then try to resend the message directly to meshach.smallorg.org.

- Finally, shadrach could *not* forward the message and send a reply to the client, specifying that this operation is not permitted from this server. It would be up to the system administrator at shadrach to figure out what happened and why.

In the early days of the Internet, it was common to run across computers that used the first scenario and blindly forwarded email messages across the world. Unfortunately, that technique became popular with email spammers. Spammers are people who do mass mailings across the Internet for fun or profit. They often use unsuspecting SMTP servers that blindly forward email messages in an attempt to disguise the origin of their mail messages. To combat this situation, most mail system administrators either have turned off mail forwarding completely or have at least limited email forwarding to hosts within their domains. Many ISPs allow their customers to relay email from their mail servers but restrict outside computers from that privilege.

In the case of multiple recipients, how to handle situations in which some of the recipients are not acknowledged is up to the client. Some clients will abort the entire message and return an error to the sending user. Some will continue sending the message to the recipients that are acknowledged and list the recipients that aren't acknowledged in a return message.

DATA Command

The DATA command is the meat-and-potatoes of the SMTP operation. After the MAIL and RCPT commands are hashed out, the DATA command is used to transfer the actual message. The format of the DATA command is

DATA

Anything after that is treated as the message to transfer. Usually, the SMTP server will add a timestamp and the return-path information to the head of the message. The client indicates the end of the message by sending a line with just a single period. The format for that line is

<CR><LF>.<CR><LF>

When the SMTP server receives this sequence, it knows that the transmission is done and that it should return a response code to the client, indicating whether the message is accepted.

There has been much work done on the format of actual DATA messages. Technically, there is no wrong way to send a message, although attempts are being made to standardize a method (see the "Message Formats" section, later in this chapter). Any combination of valid ASCII characters will be transferred to the recipients. Listing 5.2 shows a sample session sending a short mail message to a local user on an SMTP server.

LISTING 5.2   A Sample SMTP Session

```
1   $ telnet localhost 25
2   Trying 127.0.0.1...
3   Connected to localhost.ispnet1.net.
4   Escape character is '^]'.
5   220 shadrach.ispnet1.net ESMTP
6   HELO localhost
7   250 shadrach.ispnet1.net
8   MAIL FROM: rich@localhost
9   250 ok
10  RCPT TO:rich
11  250 ok
12  DATA
13  354 go ahead
14  This is a short test of the SMTP email system.
15  .
16  250 ok 959876575 qp 40419
17  QUIT
18  221 shadrach.ispnet1.net
19  Connection closed by foreign host.
20  you have mail
21  $ mail
22  Mail version 8.1 6/6/93.  Type ? for help.
23  "/var/mail/rich": 1 message 1 new
24  >N  1 rich@localhost         Thu Jun  1 11:22    8/339
25  & 1
26  Message 1:
27  From rich@localhost Thu Jun  1 11:22:55 2000
28
29  This is a short test of the SMTP email system.
30
31  & x
32  $
```

Listing 5.2 shows a typical SMTP exchange between two hosts. Line 12 shows the client entering the DATA command, and line 13 shows the response returned by the SMTP server. Lines 14 and 15 show the text message sent by the client. Line 15 is the terminating period that indicates the end of the message to the server. As you can see in lines 20–33, the SMTP server transferred the message to the local user's mailbox account exactly as the server received it. Also note how in line 27 the SMTP server included a timestamp and the return path information in the text of the message.

Much has been done to standardize the format of Internet mail messages. RFC 822 specifies a standard format for sending text mail messages between hosts. The section "Message Formats," later in this chapter, covers some of these features.

SEND Command

The SEND command is used to send a mail message directly to the terminal of a logged-in user. This command works only when the user is logged in, and it usually pops up as a message, much like the UNIX write command.

This command has a serious drawback. It is an easy way for an external user to determine who is logged into a computer system at any given time without having to log into the system. Hackers have exploited this "feature" by searching the Internet for unsuspecting victims' user IDs and when they are logged in. Because it is such a security threat, most SMTP software packages no longer implement this command.

SOML Command

SOML stands for *Send Or MaiL*. If the recipients are logged onto the computer system, it behaves like the preceding SEND command. If not, it behaves like the MAIL command and mails the message to the recipients' mailboxes. The capability of this command to be exploited has made it another victim of the Internet world, and often it is not implemented on newer SMTP server packages.

SAML Command

The SAML command stands for *Send And MaiL*. This command tries to cover both bases by sending a message to the terminal of a logged-in user *and* by placing the message in the user's mailbox. Again, the potential for abuse of this command has rendered it unsafe to implement.

RSET Command

The RSET command is short for *reset*. If the client somehow gets confused by responses from the server and thinks that the SMTP connection has gotten out of sync, it can issue the RSET command to return the connection to the HELO command state. Thus, any MAIL, RCPT, or DATA information entered will be lost. Often this is used as a last ditch effort when the client either has lost track of where it was in the command series or did not expect a particular response from the server.

VRFY Command

The VRFY command is short for *verify*. You can use the VRFY command to determine if an SMTP server can deliver mail to a particular recipient before entering the RCPT command mode. The format of this command is

VRFY username

When the command is received, the SMTP server will determine if the user is on the local server. If so, the server will return the full email address of the user. If not, the SMTP server will either return a negative response to the client or indicate that it is willing to forward any mail messages to the remote user, depending on whether the SMTP server will forward messages for the particular client.

The VRFY command can be a very valuable troubleshooting tool. Often a user types a username or hostname in an email message incorrectly and doesn't know why his mail message didn't get to where he wanted it to go. Of course, the first thing he will do is complain about the lousy mail system; then he will contact you—the mail administrator.

You can attempt to verify the email address in two ways. First, use the DNS host command to determine if the domain name is correct and has a mail server associated with it. Then, you can Telnet to port 25 of the mail server and use the VRFY command to determine if the username is correct. Listing 5.3 shows an example of using the VRFY command to check the validity of usernames.

LISTING 5.3   An Example of the VRFY Command

```
1  [riley@shadrach riley]$ telnet localhost 25
2  Trying 127.0.0.1...
3  Connected to localhost.
4  Escape character is '^]'.
5  220 shadrach.smallorg.org ESMTP Sendmail 8.9.3/8.9.3;
➥  Thu, 26 Aug 1999 19:20:16 -050
6  HELO localhost
7  250 shadrach.smallorg.org Hello localhost [127.0.0.1], pleased to meet you
8  VRFY rich
9  250 <rich@shadrach.smallorg.org>
10 VRFY prez@mechach.smallorg.org
11 252 <prez@mechach.smallorg.org>
12 VRFY jessica
13 550 jessica... User unknown
14 QUIT
15 221 shadrach.smallorg.org closing connection
16 Connection closed by foreign host.
17 [riley@shadrach riley]$
```

Lines 8–13 show the VRFY commands tried and the results. Line 8 shows an attempt to VRFY a local user, rich. The SMTP server's response in line 9 shows that the username is valid and returns the full email address to the client. Line 10 shows a different approach. On line 10, the client attempts to verify a username on a remote computer. The response in line 11 from shadrach shows a different result than in line 9. The section "Server Responses," later in this chapter, discusses the meaning of this code in greater detail but, briefly, shadrach is telling the client that it is willing to forward mail to the username prez at the remote computer meshach.smallorg.org. Line 12 shows an attempt to VRFY a non-existent username. In line 13, the response from the SMTP server is fairly self-explanatory.

Much like some of the others, this command is capable of being exploited by hackers. Because of this, many sites do not implement the VRFY command. This will seriously impede your ability to troubleshoot bad email addresses.

EXPN Command

EXPN is short for *expand*. This command queries the SMTP server for mail lists and aliases. Mail lists are handy ways of sending a mass mailing to a group of people who share one address. Chapter 15, "Supporting Mail Lists," looks at the topic of mail lists in depth. The format of the EXPN command is

```
EXPN mail-list
```

where mail-list is the name of the mail list or alias. The SMTP server will either return an error code if the client does not have privileges to see the list or return the complete mailing list, one email address per line.

HELP Command

The HELP command is used to return a list of SMTP commands that the SMTP server will understand. Most SMTP software packages will understand and process the basic RFC 821 commands listed here (except, of course, those that contain security issues). Differences occur with the extended SMTP options. Listing 5.4 shows the output from a HELP command issued to a Linux server running the sendmail SMTP package, version 8.9.3.

LISTING 5.4   SMTP HELP Command Output

```
1  [katie@shadrach katie]$ telnet localhost 25
2  Trying 127.0.0.1...
3  Connected to localhost.
4  Escape character is '^]'.
5  220 shadrach.smallorg.org ESMTP Sendmail 8.9.3/8.9.3;
   Thu, 26 Aug 1999 19:50:57 -050
6  HELO localhost
```

```
7   250 shadrach.smallorg.org Hello localhost [127.0.0.1], pleased to meet you
8   HELP
9   214-This is Sendmail version 8.9.3
10  214-Topics:
11  214-    HELO    EHLO    MAIL    RCPT    DATA
12  214-    RSET    NOOP    QUIT    HELP    VRFY
13  214-    EXPN    VERB    ETRN    DSN
14  214-For more info use "HELP <topic>".
15  214-To report bugs in the implementation send email to
16  214-    sendmail-bugs@sendmail.org.
17  214-For local information send email to Postmaster at your site.
18  214 End of HELP info
19  HELP RCPT
20  214-RCPT TO: <recipient> [ <parameters> ]
21  214-    Specifies the recipient.  Can be used any number of times.
22  214-    Parameters are ESMTP extensions.  See "HELP DSN" for details.
23  214 End of HELP info
24  HELP VRFY
25  214-VRFY <recipient>
26  214-    Verify an address.  If you want to see what it aliases
27  214-    to, use EXPN instead.
28  214 End of HELP info
29  QUIT
30  221 shadrach.smallorg.org closing connection
31  Connection closed by foreign host.
32  [katie@shadrach katie]$
```

As shown in Listing 5.4, there are two levels of help available. Sending the HELP command alone will cause the SMTP server to give a brief overview of all the available commands. Sending the HELP command with another SMTP command as an argument will cause the server to return a more detailed description of the command, including any required parameters.

NOOP Command

The NOOP command is short for *no operation*. This command has no effect on the SMTP server, other than for it to return a positive response code. This is often a useful command to send to test connectivity without actually starting the message transfer process.

QUIT Command

The QUIT command does what it says. It indicates that the client computer is finished with the current SMTP session and wants to close the connection. It is the responsibility of the SMTP server to respond to this command and to initiate the closing of the TCP connection. If the server receives a QUIT command in the middle of an email transaction, any data previously transferred should be deleted and not sent to any recipients.

TURN Command

For security reasons, the TURN command is not implemented on SMTP servers any longer. It is part of the RFC 821 standard because it was a great idea that, unfortunately, was exploited by hackers. The TURN command idea was modified in the extended SMTP RFCs and is discussed in the section "Extended SMTP." It is included here as a background reference for the extended SMTP version ETRN.

The purpose of the TURN command is to allow two-way mail transfer between two computers during one TCP connection. Normally, SMTP sends mail in only one direction for each connection. The client host is in control of the transmission medium and directs the actions of the server by the SMTP commands that are sent. Mail can be sent only from the client to the server. It would be desirable for a computer to make contact with an SMTP server and be able to send mail to the server *and* be able to receive any mail that the server had waiting to send back to the client.

As discussed previously, the server uses the domain name indicated by the HELO command text string to identify the client it is talking to. The idea of the TURN command is to allow the SMTP server to switch roles with the client and send any mail destined for the client's domain name to the client. The problem with this is the assumption by the SMTP server that the client is actually who it says it is. If a hacker connected to the SMTP server and identified himself as another computer domain, the server would unknowingly send all mail messages destined for that domain name to the hacker. Ouch!

Server Responses

For each command that the client sends to the SMTP server, the server must reply with a response message. As you can see from Listings 5.2 and 5.3, response messages are made up of two parts. The first part is a three-digit code that is used by the SMTP software to identify if the command was successful and, if not, why. The second part is a text string that helps humans understand the reply. Often, the text string is passed on by the SMTP software and displayed to the user as part of a response message.

A space usually separates the code from the text string. In the case of multiline responses (such as the HELP and EXPN commands in Listing 5.4), a dash (-) separates the code from the text on all but the last line, which conforms to the normal pattern of using a space. This tells the client host when to expect more lines from the server. There are four different categories of reply codes. The following sections explain them.

Error Response Codes

Table 5.2 shows the response codes for error conditions that could occur from various problems in the SMTP transaction.

TABLE 5.2   SMTP Error Response Codes

Code	Description
500	Syntax error, command not recognized
501	Syntax error in parameters
502	Command not implemented
503	Bad sequence of commands
504	Command parameter not implemented

SMTP error responses are not overly descriptive. They just give a general idea of what might have gone wrong in the SMTP process. When you are troubleshooting mail problems, it is helpful to be able to watch the actual SMTP transactions and watch for command errors if you are communicating with an unfamiliar SMTP server. Often 500, 502, and 504 errors occur when you are trying to implement extended SMTP commands with older SMTP software servers.

Informational Response Codes

The next category of response codes is *informational* codes. Informational codes are used to display additional information about a command. Table 5.3 shows these codes.

TABLE 5.3   SMTP Informational Response Codes

Code	Description
211	System status or system help
214	Help message

As shown in Listing 5.4, the 214 response code is used when displaying output from the HELP command. When there are multiple lines of output, a dash is used after the response code to signify that more lines are coming. The last line uses a space to separate the response code from the text.

Service Response Codes

Another response code category is the *service* codes. Service codes are used to mark the status of the SMTP service in the connection. Table 5.4 shows these codes.

TABLE 5.4   SMTP Service Response Codes

Code	Description
220	Service ready
221	Service closing transmission channel
421	Service not available

Each of these response codes will include the hostname of the SMTP server in the text string portion, as well as the text description. The 421 response code is a little misleading. Many mail administrators think that this response code is returned when there is no SMTP software available on the remote server. Although this can happen, usually this response code means that there is an SMTP server, but it is not accepting mail messages at the time. Sometimes this is the case if a server locks its file system to perform nightly data backups. The SMTP server would be unable to store mail messages on the locked file system, so the SMTP server shuts down temporarily while the backup is running. Trying to connect to the same server a little later would result in a successful transaction.

Action Response Codes

The last response code category covers replies to SMTP client actions. Table 5.5 shows the action codes used in an SMTP transaction.

TABLE 5.5   SMTP Action Response Codes

Code	Description
250	Requested mail action OK, completed
251	User not local, will forward to <forward-path>
354	Start mail input: end with <CRLF>.<CRLF>
450	Requested mail action not taken: mailbox unavailable
451	Requested action aborted: error in processing
452	Requested action not taken: insufficient system storage
550	Requested action not taken: mailbox unavailable
551	User not local: please try <forward-path>
552	Requested mail action aborted: exceeded storage allocation
553	Requested action not taken: mailbox name not allowed
554	Transaction failed

Action codes are a result of the SMTP server trying to perform a function requested by the client, such as MAIL, RCPT, and DATA commands. They return the status of the requested action so that the client will know what actions to take next in the SMTP process.

SMTP server response codes are often behind-the-scenes players in the SMTP world. Some email client packages will send any error response codes they receive back to the sender of the email. When this happens, it is easy to check the response codes against the code lists to determine what went wrong. Sometimes it is difficult to determine what went wrong with an email message that does not get processed properly. A return email message does not get routed back properly to the client, so no error text is sent to the user. Often the mail administrator has to resort to using network analyzers to watch the actual TCP packets on the LAN to see the response codes that are coming from the SMTP server. Remember that SMTP data packets are ASCII text, so they are easy to read and decode.

The SMTP Message Format

Listing 5.2, earlier in this chapter, shows a simple example of an SMTP session. The format of the message is extremely basic—just one line of text. The resulting email message is functional but not too exciting.

Today's email messages are much more complex, and users expect that level of complexity from their email service. Niceties such as Subject, CC:, and BCC: lines are the norm in email text. RFC 822 describes a standard email message format that most SMTP systems implement to somewhat standardize the look and feel of email. Simple one-line text messages have become unacceptable in the business world.

Basic RFC 822 Header Fields

RFC 822 specifies splitting the message into two separate parts. The first part is called the *header*. Its job is to identify the message. The second part is the body of the *message*. The header consists of data fields that can be used whenever additional information is needed in the message. The header fields should appear before the text body of the message and should be separated by one blank line. Header fields do not need to appear in any particular order, and the message can have multiple occurrences of any header field. Figure 5.1 shows how a basic RFC 822–compliant message looks.

Received Header Field

The format for the Received header field is as follows:

```
Received:
    from host name
    by host name
    via physical-path
    with protocol
    id message-id
    for final email destination
```

The Received header field is used to identify the SMTP servers that relayed the email message from the sender to the destination. Each server will add a new Received field to the email message, identifying itself. The subfields in the Received header field further identify the path, protocol, and computers that were used in transferring the email message.

RFC 822 compliant email message

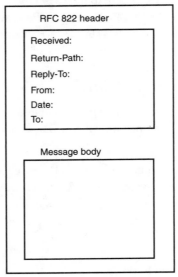

FIGURE 5.1

The RFC 822 message format.

Return-Path Header Field

The Return-Path header field format is as follows:

```
Return-Path: route
```

The last SMTP server in the relay chain adds the Return-Path field to the message. Its purpose is to identify the route taken to the destination server. If the message was sent directly to the destination server, there will be only one address in this field. Otherwise, this will list the path that was taken to transfer the message.

Reply-To Header Field

The Reply-To field shows the address where the message originated. This is extremely useful on messages that have been bounced around several times on private networks before making it to the Internet. The format of this field is

```
Reply-To: address
```

The Reply-To field is a subset of the full header field. It allows smaller SMTP packages to get by without having to implement a full-blown Authentic header field.

Resent Header Field

The Resent header field identifies an email message that for some reason was sent from the client again. The format for this field is

```
Resent-Reply-To: address
```

Each resent message will contain the same Resent-Reply-To header. It is usually impossible to determine if a message has been resent multiple times.

Authentic Header Fields

The Authentic header fields identify—*authenticize*—the sender of the email message. The formats of the Authentic fields are

```
From:    username
Sender:  username
```

The From field identifies the author of the original message. The From and Sender fields usually identify the same user, so only one is needed. If the sender of the email is not the original author, both can be identified for return mail purposes.

Resent-Authentic Header Fields

The Resent-Authentic header identifies the sender of an email message that for some reason had to be sent by the client again. The format for this is

```
Resent-From:   username
Resent-Sender: username
```

The Resent-From and Resent-Sender fields behave just like the From and Sender Authentic fields. They signify that the email message was re-sent from the client for some unknown reason.

Date Header Fields

The Date header fields are used to timestamp the message as the client sends it to the server. The format for the Date field is

```
Date:    date-time
Resent-Date:  date-time
```

The Date header field will pass the date information in the message header exactly as it is entered in the original message. This is useful for tracking the time of responses, especially multiple responses.

Destination Header Fields

The destination header fields identify email addresses that are the intended recipients of the mail message. These fields are purely informational. The SMTP server will not send a message to a user mailbox unless there has been a RCPT command issued for that user (see the "Basic SMTP Client Commands" section, earlier in this chapter). The formats for the destination fields are

```
To: address
Resent-To: address
cc: address
Resent-cc: address
bcc: address
Resent-bcc: address
```

The To, cc, and bcc fields have set a standard in the way email is processed. Most email packages now use this terminology to classify the recipients of a message. The To field indicates the main recipient of the message. The cc field, much like in a memo, indicates recipients that should receive a copy of the message. One item that email has made popular is the term *bcc*, or blind carbon copy. A blind carbon copy recipient will receive a copy of the message, but his address won't show up on the message for other people to see. There has been some debate in computer ethics circles over the ethics of such a tactic, but practically every email package in use today implements this feature.

Optional Header Fields

Optional header fields are those that further identify the message to the SMTP server but are not required for a message to be RFC 822–compatible. These fields are some of the niceties mentioned earlier that many email customers have come to expect. Some of the optional header fields are

```
Message-ID:  message-id
Resent-Message-ID:  message-id
In-Reply-To: message-id
References: message-id
Keywords: text-list
Subject: text
Comments:  text
Encrypted: word
```

The most useful and frequently used optional header field is the Subject field. Most email packages allow the sender to include a one-line subject that identifies the email message for the recipient. This text string is often used in the email client package when listing multiple email messages. Other optional header fields help further identify the email message. The Message-ID fields give it a unique identity that can be referred to in return messages. The Encrypted field indicates if the message has been encrypted for security purposes, and the Keyword field offers keywords that can be used when searching for specific content in multiple messages.

Using the RFC 822 Format in an SMTP Mail Transaction

A sample SMTP mail transaction using RFC 822 message formats is shown in Listing 5.5.

LISTING 5.5   A Sample SMTP RFC 822 Message Transaction

```
1  [rich@shadrach rich]$ telnet localhost 25
2  Trying 127.0.0.1...
3  Connected to localhost.
4  Escape character is '^]'.
5  250 shadrach.smallorg.org Hello localhost [127.0.0.1], pleased to meet you
6  MAIL FROM:rich@localhost
7  250 rich@localhost... Sender ok
8  RCPT TO:rich
9  250 rich... Recipient ok
10 DATA
11 354 Enter mail, end with "." on a line by itself
12 Return-Path:rich@localhost
13 received: from localhost by localhost with TCP/IP id 1 for Richard Blum
14 Reply-to:rich@localhost
15 From:rich
16 Date:Aug 27, 1999
17 To:rich
18 cc:jessica
19 cc:katie
20 bcc:barbara
21 bcc:haley
22 Message-ID:1
23 Subject:Test RFC 822 message
24
25 This is a test message sent from the local host to rich.
26 This message is a little larger, but in the right format.
27 .
28 250 PAA02866 Message accepted for delivery
29 QUIT
30 221 shadrach.smallorg.org closing connection
31 Connection closed by foreign host.
32 You have new mail in /var/spool/mail/rich
33 [rich@shadrach rich]$ mail
34 Mail version 8.1 6/6/93.  Type ? for help.
35 "/var/spool/mail/rich": 1 message 1 new
36 >N  1 rich@shadrach.smallo  Fri Aug 27 18:50   18/622    "Test RFC 822 message"
37 &1
38 Message 1:
39 From rich@smallorg.org  Fri Aug 27 18:50:21 1999
```

LISTING 5.5   Continued

```
40 From: rich@shadrach.smallorg.org
41 Reply-to: rich@shadrach.smallorg.org
42 Date: Aug 27, 1999
43 To: rich@shadrach.smallorg.org
44 cc: jessica@shadrach.smallorg.org
45 cc: katie@shadrach.smallorg.org
46 Subject: Test RFC 822 message
47
48 This is a test message sent from the local host to rich.
49 This message is a little larger, but in the right format.
50
51 &x
52 [rich@shadrach rich]$
```

This example is similar to the one in Listing 5.2, but notice the differences. Lines 12–23 show the RFC 822 header fields that were used for the message. Line 36 shows how the email reader package has used the RFC 822 Subject field as a short description of the message. Lines 39–46 show how the header fields were displayed by the email reader package in the message. One thing that stands out is the missing bcc fields. It makes sense that those fields do not show up in the email reader. Another obvious difference is the Date line. Line 28 in Listing 5.2 shows a complete date that was automatically added by the email package. Line 42 in Listing 5.5 shows the date as it was set by the RFC 822 message. This email reader package allowed the RFC 822 field to override its automatic field insertion.

MIME and Binary Data

You might have noticed that the DATA command is the only way to transfer messages to the SMTP server. You might also have noticed that the DATA command allows for only ASCII text lines to be entered. You are probably wondering how you can email those great digital pictures to all your relatives if SMTP mail sends only text messages. The answer is simple. The client's email program must convert the binary message data into an ASCII text message before it passes it on to the SMTP program. Then the recipient's email program must be able to convert the ASCII text back into the binary data that was originally sent. That is much easier said than done.

Several years before SMTP was invented, UNIX system administrators were sending binary data using ASCII text mail programs. The methods they used to convert binary data into ASCII text were called *uuencode* and *uudecode*. The *uu* stands for UNIX-to-UNIX, a protocol suite that was invented to help transfer data between UNIX computers using modems. When SMTP became popular, it was natural for UNIX system administrators to use these existing utilities for transferring binary data within an SMTP message across the Internet. Many older email packages still use this method for encoding binary data to send via SMTP. Unfortunately, many newer email packages don't include this capability.

> **NOTE**
>
> If you receive a binary file that used the uuencode coding method, and your email software can't decode it, don't worry. You can save the entire message as a text file and use a separate uudecode program to extract the binary file. Most UNIX distributions come with the uudecode utility, and many DOS and Windows versions of uudecode are available.

The reason many newer email packages don't use uuencode is that an Internet standard for encoding binary data has been created. RFCs 2045 and 2046 describe the multipurpose Internet mail extensions (MIME) format. MIME is more versatile than uuencode. It identifies the type of binary file that was converted and passes additional information about the file to the decoder. MIME enables binary data to be incorporated directly into a standard RFC 822 message. Five new header fields were defined to identify binary data types embedded in an RFC 822 message. Email packages that can handle MIME messages must be able to process these five new header types. All five header fields do not necessarily need to be present to properly define a MIME message. Figure 5.2 demonstrates how this fits together in a standard email message.

MIME-Version Header Field

The first additional header type identifies the version of MIME that the sender used to encode the message. Currently this is always 1.0.

Content-Transfer–Encoding Header Field

The Content-transfer–encoding header field identifies how the binary data embedded in the message is encoded into ASCII text. There are currently seven different ways to encode the binary data, but the most common is the base 64 type. This method encodes the binary data by mapping 6-bit blocks of data to 8-bit blocks of printable ASCII text.

Content-ID Header Field

The Content-ID header field is used to identify a MIME session with a unique identification code when using multiple contents.

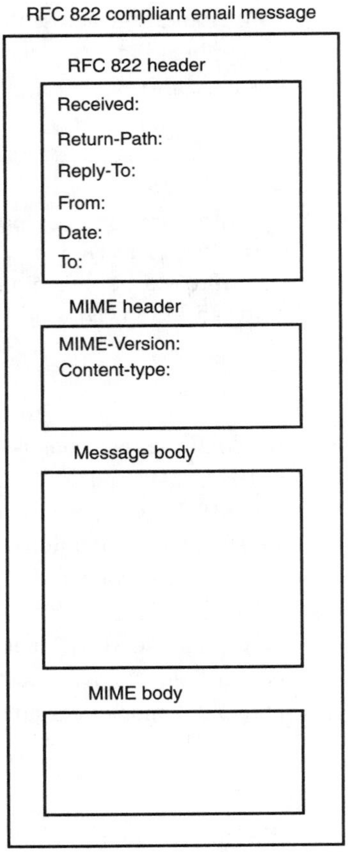

RFC 822 compliant email message

RFC 822 header

Received:
Return-Path:
Reply-To:
From:
Date:
To:

MIME header

MIME-Version:
Content-type:

Message body

MIME body

FIGURE 5.2
The MIME message header fields.

Content-Description Header Field

The Content-description header field is an ASCII text description of the data to help identify it in the text of the email message. This comes in handy when sending binary data such as word processing documents or graphic images that would otherwise be unidentifiable by their base 64 encoding.

Content-Type Header Field

The Content-type header field is where the action is. This field identifies the data that is enclosed in the MIME message. Currently there are seven basic classes of content-type identified by MIME. Each type has different subtypes that further define the type of data in the message.

The text content-type identifies data that is in ASCII format and should be able to be read as it is. There are two subtypes—plain, which signifies unformatted ASCII text, and enriched, which signifies formatting features similar to a Rich Text format. Many newer email packages can display the email message in Rich Text Format (RTF).

The message content-type allows the email package to send RFC 822 messages within a single RFC 822 message. The subtypes for this content-type are rfc822, which specifies a normal embedded RFC 822–formatted message, partial, which allows for breaking up long email messages into separate bodies, and external-body, which allows for a pointer to an object that is not within the email message.

The image content-type defines embedded binary data streams that represent graphic images. Currently, two subtypes are defined—jpeg and gif.

The video content-type defines embedded binary data streams that represent video data. The only subtype defined at this time is mpeg.

The audio content-type defines embedded binary data streams that represent audio data. Currently, its only subtype is basic, which defines a single-channel ISDN mu-law encoding at an 8kHz sample rate.

The application content-type is used to identify embedded binary data that represents application data, such as spreadsheets, word processor documents, and other applications. Currently, there are two formal subtypes defined—postscript and octet-stream. octet-stream is often used when embedding application-specific data, such as Microsoft Word documents and Microsoft Excel spreadsheets.

The multipart content-type identifies messages that contain different data content-types combined in one message. This is common in email packages that can present a message in a variety of ways, such as ASCII text, HTML, and audio formats. A boundary identifier separates each content-type, and each content-type is identified with its own content-type header field. The multipart content-type has four subtypes:

mixed   This subtype indicates that each of the parts is independent of the others and that all should be presented to the recipient in the order they were sent.

parallel   This subtype indicates that the parts are independent of one another and can be presented to the recipient in any order.

alternative   The use of this subtype indicates that each of the parts represents a different way of presenting the same data. The best method available for the recipient is used.

digest   This subtype indicates the same method as the mixed subtype, but specifies that the body of the message is always in RFC 822 format.

Listing 5.6 demonstrates the use of content-type definitions in a multipart email message.

LISTING 5.6   A Sample SMTP multipart MIME Message Session

```
1   $ telnet localhost 25
2   Trying 127.0.0.1...
3   Connected to localhost.
4   Escape character is '^]'.
5   220 shadrach.smallorg.org ESMTP
6   HELO localhost
7   250 shadrach.smallorg.org
8   MAIL FROM:rich@localhost
9   250 ok
10  RCPT TO:rich
11  250 ok
12  DATA
13  354 go ahead
14  From:"Rich Blum" <rich@localhost>
15  To:"rich"<rich@localhost>
16  Subject:Formatted text message test
17  MIME-Version: 1.0
18  Content-Type: multipart/alternative; boundary=bounds1
19
20  --bounds1
21  Content-Type: text/plain; charset=us-ascii
22
23  This is the plain text part of the message that can be read by simple
24  e-mail readers.
25
26  --bounds1
27  Context-Type: text/entriched
28
29  This is the <bold>rich text</bold> version of the <bigger>SAME</bigger>
➥message.
30
31  --bounds1--
32  .
33  250 ok 959882500 qp 84053
34  QUIT
35  221 shadrach.smallorg.org
36  Connection closed by foreign host.
38  $
```

Listing 5.6 shows a two-part MIME message. Line 18 gives the content-type definition for the entire message. The multipart/alternative type indicates that there are multiple content-types included in this message and that they are separated by the boundary identifier bounds1. The first content-type starts at line 21 and is a simple plain ASCII text message that can be read by virtually any email reader.

The second content-type starts at line 27 and is a fancier enriched text message that uses the standard Rich Text Format for the message. Because the MIME content-type specified for the message was `multipart/alternative`, it is at the discretion of the email reader which content-type version of the message to present.

Figure 5.3 shows how a Eudora reader would display the message. Notice how the plain ASCII text part of the message was discarded and the enriched text part was presented to the reader. In a normal email message, both parts would have the same message. I made them different here to show which version the email reader would use.

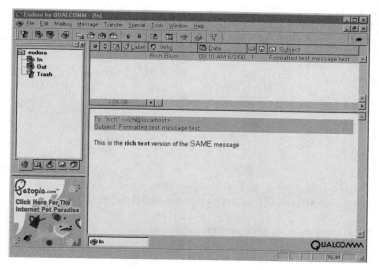

FIGURE 5.3
Using Eudora to read a MIME `multipart` *message.*

Extended SMTP

Since its invention in 1982, SMTP has performed well in transporting messages between computers across the Internet. As it got older, system administrators began to recognize its limitations. Instead of trying to replace a standard protocol that was in use all over the world, efforts were made to improve the basic SMTP protocol by keeping the original specifications and adding new features.

RFC 1869 was published in 1995 and defined a method of extending the capabilities of SMTP, calling it "SMTP Service Extensions."

Extended SMTP is implemented by replacing the original SMTP greeting (`HELO`) with a new greeting command—`EHLO`. When an SMTP server receives this command, it should realize that the client is capable of sending extended SMTP commands. Listing 5.7 shows a sample EHLO session and the commands that are available.

LISTING 5.7   Extended SMTP Commands

```
1  [katie@shadrach katie]$ telnet localhost 25
2  Trying 127.0.0.1...
3  Connected to localhost.
4  Escape character is '^]'.
5  220 shadrach.smallorg.org ESMTP Sendmail 8.9.3/8.9.3;
➥ Mon, 30 Aug 1999 16:36:48 -050
6  EHLO localhost
7  250-shadrach.smallorg.org Hello localhost [127.0.0.1], pleased to meet you
8  250-EXPN
9  250-VERB
10 250-8BITMIME
11 250-SIZE
12 250-DSN
13 250-ONEX
14 250-ETRN
15 250-XUSR
16 250 HELP
17 HELP DSN
18 214-MAIL FROM: <sender> [ RET={ FULL | HDRS} ] [ ENVID=<envid> ]
19 214-RCPT TO: <recipient> [ NOTIFY={NEVER,SUCCESS,FAILURE,DELAY} ]
20 214-                     [ ORCPT=<recipient> ]
21 214-    SMTP Delivery Status Notifications.
22 214-Descriptions:
23 214-    RET     Return either the full message or only headers.
24 214-    ENVID   Sender's "envelope identifier" for tracking.
25 214-    NOTIFY  When to send a DSN. Multiple options are OK, comma-
26 214-            delimited. NEVER must appear by itself.
27 214-    ORCPT   Original recipient.
28 214 End of HELP info
29 HELP ETRN
30 214-ETRN [ <hostname> | @<domain> | #<queuename> ]
31 214-    Run the queue for the specified <hostname>, or
32 214-    all hosts within a given <domain>, or a specially-named
33 214-    <queuename> (implementation-specific).
34 214 End of HELP info
35 QUIT
36 221 shadrach.smallorg.org closing connection
37 Connection closed by foreign host.
38 [katie@shadrach katie]$
```

Line 6 shows the new extended SMTP EHLO command used to connect to the SMTP server. Lines 7–16 show the server's response. Notice that the server indicates that more commands are available now that it is in extended mode. One of the new groups of commands is the Delivery Status Notification options. These options can be used on the MAIL and RCPT commands to indicate the delivery status of a particular email message for the client. One command that we are extremely interested in as mail administrators is the ETRN command.

The TURN SMTP command was mentioned earlier. This command is extremely useful but not very secure. To compensate, RFC 1985 defines a new method of implementing the TURN command that is more secure.

The ETRN command allows an SMTP client to issue a request for the SMTP server to initiate another SMTP connection with the client to transfer messages back to it. This differs from the original TURN command in that the ETRN command is just a request to start another SMTP session, not to transfer data on the existing session. This way, the SMTP server can then contact the client computer using the normal DNS hostname resolution methods. This does not rely on who the client computer says it is. If a hacker establishes an unauthorized SMTP connection and issues an ETRN command, the SMTP server will just start an SMTP connection with the real client and send any mail—no harm done.

The format for the ETRN command is

```
ETRN name
```

where name can be either an individual hostname or a domain name if you are requesting mail for an entire domain. The ETRN command is a valuable tool for the mail administrator. If you elect to have an ISP spool mail for your email server, you might use this method to notify the ISP when you are ready to receive your spooled mail.

Another extended SMTP command gaining popularity is the AUTH command. This command enables the SMTP client to properly identify itself with the SMTP server using a user ID and password or some other type of authentication technique. Once the client is positively identified to the server, it may be allowed to perform special functions that unauthenticated clients would not be allowed to do, such as using the server as a mail relay.

The QMTP Protocol

Bernstein has developed a replacement protocol for SMTP. The Quick Mail Transfer Protocol (QMTP) can be used between two mail servers that are both using qmail software. This section describes QMTP for both the client and the server machines.

QMTP Client Commands

Unlike SMTP, QMTP does not use a series of ASCII commands to control the mail transfer. Instead, it assumes that the client sends mail packages and the server receives mail packages.

A QMTP mail *package* consists of the message, the sender, and one or more recipients. The server must return a confirmation message in response to a completed package, but the client does not need to wait for the response before sending the next package. This technique greatly increases the data flow for a client sending multiple messages to a single remote server.

Using QMTP Netstrings

The QMTP package is formatted using what Bernstein terms *netstrings*. A netstring uses the following format:

```
[len]"|"[string]","
```

Each netstring is preceded by the ASCII encoding of its length. A sample string this is qmail would become the following netstring (in hexadecimal):

```
31 33 3a 74 68 69 73 20 69 73 20 71 6d 61 69 6c 2c
```

or in ASCII

```
1 3 | t h i s   i s   q m a i l ,
```

The first two bytes represent the length of the string—13. The third byte is the | character. The following 13 bytes are the text string this is qmail. The final byte is the comma character (,), indicating the end of the netstring.

QMTP Package Format

Each section of the QMTP package is encoded into netstring format. Figure 5.4 illustrates a QMTP package.

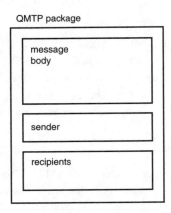

FIGURE 5.4
The QMTP package format.

The Message section is encoded as a single netstring. There are two methods that indicate end-of-line markers:

- A UNIX-style single line feed (0a)
- A DOS-style carriage return/line feed (0d 0a)

QMTP hosts must be able to recognize and handle either method. This prevents problems with DOS and UNIX QMTP servers and clients.

The Sender and Recipient sections are encoded as separate netstring values. Each recipient on the remote host can be included in a single Recipient netstring.

Server Responses

The QMTP server listens for QMTP connections using TCP port 209. After the server receives a complete QMTP package, it must send a response. The response must be encoded as a netstring. The response is a string consisting of a one-character response code followed by readable response text.

The one-character response code must be one of the following three characters:

K—Message received OK and accepted for delivery.

Z—Temporary failure

D—Permanent failure

If the client receives a Z response, it may attempt to resubmit the package. If the client receives a D response, it should return an error message to the local MTA system, indicating the permanent delivery error.

The QMTP server must be able to queue packages, because the client can begin sending a package before receiving the response from the previous package. At the end of the package transmission, the server must respond with a QMTP response for each package received.

Summary

The Simple Mail Transfer Protocol (SMTP) allows computers to transfer messages from a user on one computer to a user (or multiple users) on another computer using a standard method. SMTP is defined in RFC 821 and defines a standard set of commands that are used to identify the mail sender and recipients and transfer the message.

The actual message can be in any form, but a standard format has been set forth in RFC 822. This format provides for two sections—the message header and the message body. The message header contains fields that identify important parts of the message, such as the sender, recipients, subject, and comments.

Binary data must be encoded into an ASCII text stream before it can be sent via SMTP. An Internet standard has been implemented for encoding and transferring binary data within a standard RFC 822 message. RFCs 2045 and 2046 describe new RFC 822 header fields that help identify binary data encoding and its purpose. The Quick Mail Transfer Protocol (QMTP) can be used between two qmail servers to increase the delivery speeds between the servers. At this time, QMTP can be used only between two qmail servers.

Installing and Configuring qmail

IN THIS PART

Installing qmail

IN THIS CHAPTER

The previous chapters provided background information regarding qmail and email in general. This chapter begins the specific qmail installation process by describing how to download and install the qmail software package.

At the time of this writing, the current version of qmail is version 1.03. Unfortunately, most Linux distributions do not include a prepackaged binary distribution of qmail; thus, it must be downloaded from the qmail Web site to install. However, FreeBSD does include a binary distribution that can be installed from the FreeBSD installation CD. Both downloading from the Internet and installing from a FreeBSD binary distribution are described in this chapter, along with descriptions of the qmail directory structure and the qmail executable programs that are installed.

Downloading and Compiling the qmail Source Code

If your UNIX system does not have a binary distribution of the qmail software package (most don't), you must download the qmail source code and compile it on your system. The qmail source code distribution is available from the qmail Web site at `http://www.qmail.org`. By clicking on the `download qmail 1.03` link, the latest version will automatically start to download. The size of the qmail version 1.03 distribution is about 220KB. The source code distribution is packaged as a compressed tar file. Once the file is downloaded, it can be uncompressed and untarred into a working directory.

It has become common practice among UNIX administrators to use the `/usr/local/src` directory structure for a work area when downloading and compiling new software. To work in this area, you must be logged in as the root user. The command used to extract the source code into the qmail working directory would be

```
tar -zxvf qmail-1.03.tar.gz -C /usr/local/src
```

This command produces a `/usr/local/src/qmail-1.03` directory that contains the source code distribution and related installation documentation.

Precompilation Steps

Before the source code can be compiled, there are a few steps that must be done to prepare qmail and the UNIX system for installing and running qmail. The qmail directory, userids, and configuration parameters must all be set according to the specific qmail installation desired before you can begin to compile the qmail program. The steps to be taken are described in the following sections and are as follows:

1. Create the operational directory
2. Modify the program parameters

3. Create the userids and groupids

4. Fix the qmail DNS problem

Creating the qmail Operational Directory

The qmail directory location is important in that it contains all of the qmail operational elements. The binary executables, the configuration files, and the qmail mail queue directories are all located under the qmail directory.

By default, the qmail source code distribution sets the qmail directory to /var/qmail. If you want to change this to a different location, you must edit the conf-qmail file located in the /usr/local/qmail-1.03 directory (or whatever working qmail directory you selected) before compiling qmail. The file is a text file whose first line contains the location of the qmail directory.

Once the conf-qmail file is set to the qmail directory location, you must manually create the new qmail directory. This can be accomplished using this command:

```
mkdir /var/qmail
```

(or whatever qmail directory you selected) while logged in as the root user.

If you are preparing a qmail server for a large organization or ISP, you will need to determine the amount of disk space that will be needed for your mail environment. There are two disk requirements of the qmail mail environment that must be considered:

- Messages waiting in the mail queue for delivery
- Messages in the user's mailbox

qmail stores all messages waiting to be processed in a mail queue directory, which by default is located at /var/qmail/queue (see Chapter 2, "qmail Services"). While qmail deletes messages from the queue as soon as they are delivered, on a high-volume mail server this directory can still get rather large. Also, messages that fail on the initial delivery attempt are stored in the mail queue for another delivery attempt. With high volumes of mail, there could easily be many messages waiting in the mail queue for delivery. In an organization that uses a lot of mail attachments such as spreadsheets and word processing documents, these messages could get large.

The second directory the mail administrator must examine is the one used by qmail to store messages intended for local mail users. With qmail, each user's mailbox can be either in his local home directory or in the system mail directory (see Chapter 8, "Using qmail"). If all users' mailboxes are located in the system mail directory, that directory could become full quickly. As discussed in Chapter 1, "Email Services," the method you select for users to access their mailboxes (either POP3 or IMAP) also affects the number of mail messages located in each user's mailbox. The IMAP protocol allows users to store mail in separate folders in their home directories as well as the system mailbox directory.

Most Linux distributions locate the system mail directory at /var/spool/mail, while FreeBSD uses /var/mail. Both systems share the same common higher-level directory as the qmail mail queue—the /var directory.

> **NOTE**
>
> Since both the qmail mail queue and qmail user mailboxes can be configured to reside on the /var directory, often it is beneficial to set aside an entire disk just for the /var directory. It also contains other subdirectories, making it advisable to do this during initial installation of the operating system. Similarly, if you decide to use qmail's method of storing messages in the user $HOME directories, ensure that the /home partition is large enough.

On FreeBSD system installations, the disk partitioner program automatically creates a separate disk partition for the /var filesystem. However, if you are planning to create a dedicated email server, the partition created is often too small. Make sure that you either increase the size of the /var partition or, better yet, move it to a separate disk altogether. In either case, you must make sure that your /var filesystem has enough disk space to support the email storage requirements for your organization.

Modifying qmail Configuration Parameters

As demonstrated in the previous section, there are special conf files that specify parameters used in the qmail configuration. The conf-qmail file is just one of several such files that can be modified. The conf files are located in the source code directory that was created when untarring the qmail distribution package. Listing 6.1 is a list of all the conf files that are used in the qmail installation.

LISTING 6.1   qmail conf Files

```
$ ls -al conf-*
-rw-r--r--  1 root  daemon  280 Jun 15  1998 conf-break
-rw-r--r--  1 root  daemon   47 Jun 15  1998 conf-cc
-rw-r--r--  1 root  daemon  215 Jun 15  1998 conf-groups
-rw-r--r--  1 root  daemon   62 Jun 15  1998 conf-ld
-rw-r--r--  1 root  daemon  189 Jun 15  1998 conf-patrn
-rw-r--r--  1 root  daemon  521 Jun 15  1998 conf-qmail
-rw-r--r--  1 root  daemon  168 Jun 15  1998 conf-spawn
-rw-r--r--  1 root  daemon   42 Jun 15  1998 conf-split
-rw-r--r--  1 root  daemon  347 Jun 15  1998 conf-users
```

The following sections describe the individual conf files and how they affect the qmail installation.

conf-break File

The `conf-break` file specifies the character delimiter for user-defined mail usernames. By default this value is set to a dash (-).

This character is used by qmail to allow a local user to create his own separate mail address. By adding a dash and other text to the end of the username, a user can create alternative mail addresses. For example, user `rich` could create a mail address called `rich-list`, which could contain a list of other userids—both local and remote. This list would be completely controlled by the userid `rich`.

By changing the value of the `conf-break` file, the mail administrator can change the desired break character from a dash to something else.

> **NOTE**
>
> Chapter 7, "Changing qmail Operational Parameters," describes user-defined mail addresses in more detail.

conf-cc File

The `conf-cc` file is used to specify the compiler command and command line options that will be used to compile the qmail `.c` source code files. By default this is set to the value `cc -02`.

This command uses the local UNIX C compiler, along with the `-02` option that includes code optimization if possible. You should not have to change this parameter if your UNIX system uses the GNU C compiler.

conf-groups

The `conf-groups` file specifies the groups that qmail uses to contain the usernames it creates. There are two separate groups that must be created. By default these groups are named `qmail` and `nofiles`.

The `qmail` group contains usernames that are for controlling the qmail system. The `nofiles` group is used for qmail processes that are not allowed access to any files on the system. This increases the security of the qmail system. If a hacker compromises any of the `qmail` userids, he still does not have access to anything on the UNIX system.

conf-ld

The `conf-ld` file specifies the command that links qmail `.o` object files. By default this is set to `cc -s`.

This command uses the local UNIX C compiler with the -s option, which is used for linking object files. You should not have to change this file for normal UNIX systems using the GNU C compiler.

conf-patrn

The conf-patrn file specifies the default mask settings for qmail files. The default value for this parameter is 002.

conf-qmail

The conf-qmail file specifies the location of the qmail directory. By default this value is set to /var/qmail.

All of the qmail binary, configuration, and mail queues are located under this directory.

conf-spawn

The conf-spawn file is used to specify the maximum number of simultaneous qmail-local and qmail-remote sessions that can be running on the system. The default value for this parameter is 120.

As described in Chapter 2, one feature of qmail is the capability to process multiple mail deliveries simultaneously. The actual number of sessions that can occur is controlled by an entry in the qmail control configuration files (see Chapter 7). This parameter sets the maximum number that can be set in the control file. This number can never be greater than 255.

Remember that although qmail can support up to 255 simultaneous qmail sessions, this may not necessarily be a good thing. You should take into consideration the UNIX system's processor, memory, and other running applications before setting this parameter too high. Having a couple hundred qmail sessions running may affect performance of other applications on the UNIX server.

conf-split

The conf-split file specifies the number of subdirectories that the qmail mail queue info, local, mess, and remote subdirectories are subdivided into. The default value for this parameter is 23.

On qmail servers with a large volume of mail, the OS file access speed in the qmail queue can become a limiting factor in mail delivery speed. Accessing files in directories with over 1000 files can become overwhelming for some systems. To help offset this problem, qmail provides the conf-split value. This value is used to divide the queued messages between multiple subdirectories in the queue, thus reducing the number of files per directory in the queue.

Each queue directory is subdivided into directories numbered from 0 to (conf-split - 1). As each message is received in the mail queue, it is placed in the appropriate subdirectory based on the following equation:

$$dir = \mathrm{msg} \ \% \ \mathrm{conf\text{-}split}$$

where msg is the inode number assigned to the message file (see Chapter 2 for a description of how qmail assigns filenames to queued messages). dir is the subdirectory under the main queue directory where the message is placed. This directory name is just a number. For large qmail servers, conf-split values as high as 3,000 have been recommended.

conf-users

The conf-users file is used to specify the unique usernames that qmail requires to be present on the UNIX system. Each username is used for a separate function within qmail. Table 6.1 shows the default usernames and their purposes.

TABLE 6.1 Default qmail Usernames

Username	Description
alias	The qmail alias user account
qmaild	The qmail daemon user account
qmaill	The qmail log user account
root	The owner of the qmail binary files
qmailp	The qmail password user account
qmailq	The qmail queue user account
qmailr	The qmail remote user account
qmails	The qmail send user account

The usernames shown in Table 6.1 are the default usernames that qmail will look for on the UNIX system. You can change these to any usernames you want. Each username should be listed on a separate line. Remember that whatever usernames are defined in the conf-users file must be present as valid users on the UNIX system for qmail to install and operate properly. Also, the conf-groups file has the two groups that qmail uses to contain usernames.

Creating qmail Userids and Groupids

As mentioned before, qmail uses several unique usernames and group names to control security in the mail system. Each of the group names and usernames defined in the conf-groups and conf-users files must be created on the UNIX system before compiling and installing qmail.

As shown earlier, there are two new group names that must be added to the UNIX system for qmail:

- nofiles
- qmail

These two groups contain the usernames that are used for qmail. The default usernames were shown in Table 6.1. The UNIX system assigns groupid and userid numbers to the individual group names and usernames. It is not important what numbers are assigned. The important thing is that each of the specific group names and usernames is created on the system.

Each UNIX system has its own method for installing new userids and groupids. The qmail source code distribution includes a sample script file that can be used to automatically create the qmail groupids and userids for various UNIX systems.

The INSTALL.ids file contains several different script files that can be used for installing the new userids and groupids on the UNIX system. Linux systems can use the groupadd and useradd Linux commands to create the new groups and userids. Listing 6.2 shows the script file that can be used.

LISTING 6.2   Linux Script for Adding qmail Groups and Userids

```
groupadd nofiles
useradd -g nofiles -d /var/qmail/alias alias
useradd -g nofiles -d /var/qmail qmaild
useradd -g nofiles -d /var/qmail qmaill
useradd -g nofiles -d /var/qmail qmailp
groupadd qmail
useradd -g qmail -d /var/qmail qmailq
useradd -g qmail -d /var/qmail qmailr
useradd -g qmail -d /var/qmail qmails
```

The script file creates the new qmail groups and assigns the new qmail userids for the particular group. The useradd command is used to create the new userids. The -d parameter is used to specify a default home directory for each individual userid.

> **CAUTION**
>
> When creating new usernames, remember to be logged in as the root user. If useradd is not in your path, you may have to use the full pathname (usually /usr/sbin/useradd) to run it.

For FreeBSD systems, the pw command is used for all userid and groupid operations. The parameters used on the pw command line specify whether a new groupid or userid is being created. Listing 6.3 shows a script file that can be used on FreeBSD systems for creating the qmail groups and userids.

LISTING 6.3   FreeBSD Script for Adding qmail Groups and Userids

```
pw groupadd nofiles
pw useradd alias -g nofiles -d /var/qmail/alias -s /nonexistent
pw useradd qmaild -g nofiles -d /var/qmail -s /nonexistent
pw useradd qmaill -g nofiles -d /var/qmail -s /nonexistent
pw useradd qmailp -g nofiles -d /var/qmail -s /nonexistent
pw groupadd qmail
pw useradd qmailq -g qmail -d /var/qmail -s /nonexistent
pw useradd qmailr -g qmail -d /var/qmail -s /nonexistent
pw useradd qmails -g qmail -d /var/qmail -s /nonexistent
```

Similar to the Linux useradd command, the FreeBSD pw useradd command uses command-line parameters to specify the default group and home directory of the new userid. The -s parameter is used to specify a default UNIX shell to assign to the username. Since no one should log into the UNIX system with these usernames, a shell of /nonexistent is used.

Fixing the qmail DNS Problem

As mentioned in Chapter 4, "DNS and qmail," there is one annoying bug to version 1.03 of qmail. Using the default source code, the qmail program cannot handle DNS response packets larger than 512 bytes. This prevents qmail from determining the mail host for a domain, making delivery of any messages to that domain impossible.

Unfortunately, many large ISP organizations send large TCP packets defining all of the possible mail servers that can accept mail for their domains. As written, qmail will not be able to process these response packets and thus cannot deliver mail messages to these sites.

The bug appears in the dns.c program code in qmail. The DNS packet size maximum is set at 512 bytes. Christopher Davis, a qmail user, has created a patch file that fixes this problem in the dns.c code and has made it available on the Internet. A link to his site is on the qmail home Web page.

An easier (although not as elegant) way to fix this problem has been suggested by other qmail users. You can manually change the maximum DNS packet size value directly in the dns.c source code before compiling. The constant used to define the packet size is PACKETSZ. Line 24 of the dns.c code file should look like this:

```
static union { HEADER hdr; unsigned char buf[PACKETSZ]; } response;
```

By changing PACKETSZ to the value 65536 in the dns.c code before compiling, you can prevent qmail choking on large DNS packets.

Compiling qmail

Once all of the items identified in the previous section have been checked and set according to your particular qmail installation, you can begin the process of compiling the qmail software package. The compiling process is the simplest step in the qmail installation process.

To compile the qmail software, from the `/usr/local/qmail-1.03` directory, type this command:

```
make setup check
```

This command uses the prebuilt makefile from the qmail software distribution. The makefile `setup` section calls for both the `it` and `man` sections to be built. The `it` section builds all of the qmail binary files, while the `man` section builds all of the qmail man page files. After the binary files are built, the qmail directories are created, the binary files are copied to their proper location, and the installation is checked for completion.

Using the FreeBSD qmail Package Installer

The FreeBSD UNIX system contains a binary distribution of the qmail package. As described in Chapter 3, "Server Requirements for qmail," the FreeBSD operating system uses a concept called packages to install binary distributions of software.

The FreeBSD package installs all the files and programs required by qmail, including any patches. The package is preconfigured for optimal installation on a FreeBSD system, including the installation directories chosen.

To display the FreeBSD software package distributions, you must use the `sysinstall` program, which is located in the `/stand` directory. Figure 6.1 shows the `sysinstall` main menu screen that is displayed.

FIGURE 6.1

The FreeBSD sysinstall *main menu screen.*

From the main menu you can select the Configure option. This displays the Configuration menu. From the Configuration menu you can select the Packages option.

The Packages option produces a menu that allows you to select where the package files are to be located. If you have the FreeBSD installation CD set, you can select the CD-ROM option. If your FreeBSD system is connected to the Internet, you can select the FTP option, which connects the system to the FreeBSD FTP site and downloads any new packages.

After you select the package location, the Package Selection menu shown in Figure 6.2 appears.

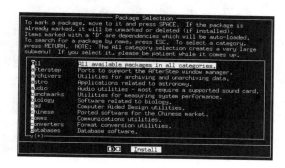

FIGURE 6.2

The sysinstall *Package Selection menu.*

All of the packages available for the FreeBSD system are divided into categories to make searching easier. The qmail software distribution is in the mail package. If you scroll to the mail package listing and press Enter, the Electronic Mail Packages and Utilities menu appears.

Scrolling down the Mail Packages list, you will find the qmail-1.03 listing. Pressing the space-bar when on this line selects the qmail-1.03 package for installation.

The qmail-1.03 package creates the appropriate qmail directories for using qmail on a FreeBSD system. It uses the qmail recommended default location of /var/qmail. The package also automatically creates the default qmail group names and usernames required.

Using the FreeBSD qmail Port Installer

Another method for distributing applications on the FreeBSD system is to use the Port method. FreeBSD ports allow software developers to package the application source code along with any patches that are necessary for the application to compile, install, and run properly on a FreeBSD system.

When you first install FreeBSD, it asks if you want to install the Ports files. These files provide information for the system administrator to select the applications that he wants to install from the Ports collection. Skeleton information for the Ports makefile on how and where to get the source code to compile is also included.

FreeBSD ports can be found on the FreeBSD CD-ROM sets or from the FreeBSD Internet site. You can install additional ports by selecting the Ports option on the `sysinstall` distributions menu as shown in Figure 6.3.

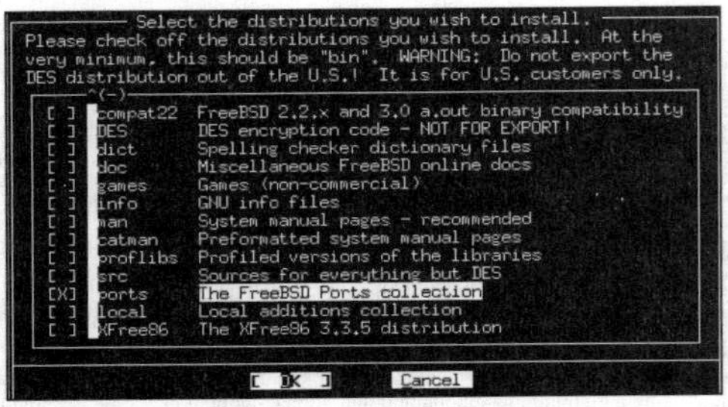

FIGURE 6.3
Selecting the FreeBSD Ports option.

Once the Ports option has been selected, another menu screen will appear, asking where the Ports skeleton files are located. Select the method that you will use to install the ports. Once the method is selected, all ports will be loaded from the selected medium.

After selecting the medium to load the port files, they are downloaded to the `/usr/ports` directory. Like FreeBSD packages, the ports are divided into categories to help in finding specific ports. The qmail software port is located in the `mail` subdirectory in the `qmail` directory.

The core of the port system is the makefile. The makefile tells the compiler how to get, compile, and install the software package, including any patches necessary. If your FreeBSD system is connected to the Internet, you can use the FTP Port option to download the latest version of the software distribution. The makefile includes addresses that can be used to download the software. Listing 6.4 shows the code from the makefile that is used to search for the qmail software source code.

LISTING 6.4   qmail Port Makefile Lines for FTP Download

```
# Version required:    1.03
# Date created:        25 May 1998
# Whom:                Mario S F Ferreira <lioux@gns.com.br> et al.
#
```

```
# $FreeBSD: ports/mail/qmail/Makefile,v 1.12 1999/10/07 03:01:45 cpiazza Exp $
#

DISTNAME=        qmail-1.03
CATEGORIES=      mail
MASTER_SITES=    ftp://ftp.net.ohio-state.edu/pub/networking/mail/qmail/ \
                 ftp://ftp.ntnu.no/pub/unix/mail/qmail/ \
                 ftp://ftp.mira.net.au/unix/mail/qmail/ \
                 ftp://ftp.id.wustl.edu/pub/qmail/ \
                 ftp://mirror.uk.uu.net/pub/qmail/ \
                 ftp://ftp.jp.qmail.org/qmail/ \
                 http://ftp.rifkin.technion.ac.il/pub/qmail/ \
                 http://koobera.math.uic.edu/www/software/ \
                 http://pobox.com/~djb/software/

# Patch necessary to cope with non-RFC >512 dns entries
# Since AOL has been using those, the problem has skyrocketed from minor to
# groundzero. qmail being RFC compliant need to be "fixed" to work with those
PATCH_SITES=     http://www.ckdhr.com/ckd/
PATCHFILES=      qmail-103.patch
PATCH_DIST_STRIP+=   -p1

MAINTAINER=      lioux@gns.com.br

# A normal qmail installation puts everything into /var/qmail/.
# If you want to install to /usr/local/, then "/usr/local/qmail" is
# suggested instead of "/usr/local", but both will work.
PREFIX=          /var/qmail
```

As can be seen from the partial makefile in Listing 6.4, there are several places from which the port can attempt to download the qmail source code. Also, as can be seen in the listing, the FreeBSD port provides for all of the necessary qmail configuration options. The PREFIX constant defines the default location of the qmail directory. This can be changed to the location where you want qmail installed on your FreeBSD system.

Installing software from a FreeBSD port is very simple. There are only three steps necessary:

1. Change the directory to the port location: /usr/ports/mail/qmail
2. Run the GNU make command: make
3. Run the make command using the install option: make install

When the make command is run, the source code will be automatically downloaded from the FTP site and compiled. As with the package method, the port automatically creates the /var/qmail directory and all of the default qmail group names and usernames.

The qmail Directory Structure

Once the compiling and installing processes are complete, qmail should be installed in the subdirectory that was set in the conf-qmail file. Table 6.2 shows the subdirectories that are created in the /var/qmail directory for qmail.

TABLE 6.2   qmail Directory Structure

Directory	Description
alias	Contains qmail alias files
bin	Contains all qmail executable files
boot	Contains scripts for starting qmail in various mail environments
control	Contains all qmail configuration control files
doc	Contains the qmail documentation files
man	Contains the qmail man pages
queue	Contains the qmail mail queue directories
users	Contains any qmail user database files created for qmail-lspawn

The qmail Programs

The qmail installation process creates many new binary executable programs that are used in qmail. These files contain the core qmail programs, along with various helper utility files that can be used with the qmail system. All of the qmail executable programs are located in the /var/qmail/bin directory. This section describes the programs that are created and installed when qmail is compiled.

The qmail Core System Programs

The qmail core system programs are used for the main operation of the qmail system. The core programs are used directly in processing messages coming into the mail server and messages sent out from the mail server. These programs are either run as background processes or spawned from other qmail processes.

The qmail-clean Program

The qmail-clean program is used to remove unsent messages from the mail queue that appear to have failed in delivery. qmail uses a multistate system of identifying messages in the mail queue. Each message traverses several states while it is being processed. If at any time the mail server crashes, the qmail-send program can detect the last successful state of the message and continue processing the message. If qmail-send is unable to process the message, due to either server errors or the message being undeliverable, the qmail-clean program is called to remove the message from the mail queue.

The qmail-inject Program

The qmail-inject program is used to insert new messages into the qmail mail queue. The format of the qmail-inject command is

```
qmail-inject -[nNaAhH] [ -fsender] [recip ... ]
```

where *sender* is the envelope sender address that will be passed to qmail-queue, and *recip* is the recipient(s) of the message. Table 6.3 describes the options for qmail-inject.

TABLE 6.3   qmail-inject Options

Option	Description
-a	Send the message to all recipients listed on the command line
-A	Send the message to all recipients listed. If no recipients are listed, send the message to all recipients in the message header
-h	Send the message to all recipients in the message header
-H	Send the message to all recipients in the message header and all recipients listed on the command line

The qmail-local Program

The qmail-local program is used by qmail to deliver a message to a local user on the mail system. The format of the qmail-local command is

```
qmail-local [-nN] user homedir local dash ext domain sender defaultdelivery
```

where *user* is the local username, *homedir* is the home directory of the user, *local* and *domain* are combined to create the email address of the user, *dash* and *ext* are used to identify any .qmail configuration files used by the user, *sender* is the message envelope sender, and *defaultdelivery* is any local delivery instructions necessary to deliver the mail message.

The qmail-lspawn Program

The qmail-lspawn program is used to schedule delivery of messages on the local mail system. The format of the qmail-lspawn command is

```
qmail-lspawn defaultdelivery
```

where defaultdelivery is used to identify the commands necessary to deliver the message on the local mail system.

The `qmail-pop3d` Program

The `qmail-pop3d` program is qmail's version of a POP3 server program that allows remote clients to connect to the qmail mail server using the POP3 protocol and read messages in their mailboxes. This program will work only with qmail's Maildir mailbox format (see Chapter 9, "Using the Maildir Mailbox Format").

The `qmail-popup` Program

The `qmail-popup` program is used in conjunction with the `qmail-pop3d` program. The `qmail-popup` program validates the POP userid and password of the POP3 connection before invoking the `qmail-pop3d` program. `qmail-popup` can use either the USER-PASS plain text authentication or the APOP encrypted authentication methods.

The `qmail-qmtpd` Program

The `qmail-qmtpd` program is used to accept QMTP connections from remote clients (see Chapter 5, "SMTP and qmail"). Once a connection is accepted, any messages received are passed to the `qmail-queue` program to insert into the qmail mail queue.

The `qmail-queue` Program

The `qmail-queue` program handles messages from the `qmail-inject` and `qmail-smtpd` programs and moves them to a mail queue for delivery. While `qmail-queue` processes the message, it scans the sender and recipient addresses. The mail message is passed to the `qmail-queue` program on descriptor 0, while the sender and recipient information is passed on descriptor 1. `qmail-queue` expects the sender and recipient information to be presented in a particular format:

- The sender address is preceded by an F character and terminated by a NULL character.
- Each recipient address is preceded by a T character and terminated by a NULL character.
- The end of the recipient list is indicated by an extra NULL character.

Per RFC822 rules, the `qmail-queue` program always adds the appropriate Received: header line to the mail message header.

The `qmail-remote` Program

The `qmail-remote` program is used to deliver mail messages destined for remote mail hosts. The format of the `qmail-remote` command is

```
qmail-remote host sender recip [recip ...]
```

Where *host* is the hostname of the remote mail server, *sender* is the envelope sender address, and *recip* is the username(s) that should receive the message on the remote host. `qmail-remote` uses the SMTP protocol to transfer the mail message to the remote mail host.

The `qmail-rspawn` Program

The `qmail-rspawn` program is called by the `qmail-send` program when a message is determined to be for a user on a remote mail server. `qmail-rspawn` attempts to schedule the message for delivery by the `qmail-remote` program, then asynchronously invokes `qmail-remote`. One job of `qmail-rspawn` is to determine the destination mail servers for each of the recipients of the message. `qmail-remote` is called once for each remote destination host.

The `qmail-send` Program

Once a message has been successfully placed in the mail queue, the `qmail-send` program is used to process it. `qmail-send` checks the status of each message in the mail queue. Messages that have failed on a previous mail attempt are identified, and it is determined if they are in a temporary or permanent delivery failure status. Messages in a temporary delivery failure status are tried again. Messages in a permanent delivery failure status are passed to `qmail-clean` for deletion. Messages that have not been sent are forwarded for sending.

`qmail-send` uses the `qmail-lspawn` and `qmail-rspawn` programs. Any message with a recipient address determined to be local to the mail server is passed to `qmail-lspawn`. Any message with a recipient address determined to be on a remote mail server is passed to `qmail-rspawn`. Once the message is passed to either of those two programs, `qmail-send`'s job is done.

The `qmail-smtpd` Program

The `qmail-smtpd` program listens to the network for connections from remote mail servers. It accepts mail messages using the Simple Mail Transfer Protocol (SMTP) and passes them to the `qmail-queue` program to be inserted into the qmail mail queue. The `qmail-smtpd` program supports the Extended Simple Mail Transfer Protocol (ESMTP) as described in Chapter 5.

The `sendmail` Program

Although it sounds like a contradiction in terms, qmail includes an executable program called `sendmail`. The purpose for this executable is to replace the standard `sendmail` program provided by nearly every UNIX system available.

The `sendmail` program became so popular that most MUA programs use it to forward outgoing mail messages. By passing the message and the recipient address(es) to the `sendmail` program, MUA programs are able to include MTA functionality without having to provide MTA code.

To trick the MUA programs, qmail includes a wrapper of the `qmail-inject` program that mimics the `sendmail` program MTA functionality for injecting messages into the qmail mail queue for delivery. By calling the wrapper program `sendmail`, qmail was able to completely fool the MUA programs into thinking they really were passing the messages off to the `sendmail` program.

The `splogger` Program

The `splogger` program is used to insert entries into the system logger. The system logger is used to record system and application messages generated on the UNIX system.

The qmail Mail Helper Utility Programs

The qmail mail utility programs are used within the qmail system to send and deliver messages. These programs are often used from user `.qmail` files that modify the default behavior of qmail delivery for that user (described in detail in Chapter 8).

The `bouncesaying` Program

The `bouncesaying` program is used in the local qmail users' `.qmail` file (described in detail in Chapter 8). The format of the `bouncesaying` program is

```
bouncesaying error [program [arg ...] ]
```

The `bouncesaying` program sends the message to the *program* program (with any necessary command-line parameters *arg*). If *program* exits with an exit code of `0`, the text indicated by *error* is printed and the message is bounced. If *program* is not indicated, `bouncesaying` returns this message:

```
bouncesaying 'This address no longer accepts mail.'
```

The `condredirect` Program

The `condredirect` program is also used in the local qmail users' `.qmail` file. The format of `condredirect` is

```
condredirect newaddress program [arg ...]
```

The `condredirect` program forwards each message to the program *program* (along with any command-line parameters *arg*). If *program* exits with a `0` exit code, `condredirect` forwards the message to *newaddress*. If *program* exits with exit code `111`, `condredirect` forces the message to be retried later. Any other exit code generated by `program` causes `condredirect` to do nothing, and the rest of the `.qmail` file is processed.

The `except` Program

The `except` program is often used in conjunction with the `bouncesaying` and `condredirect` programs. The format of the `except` program is

```
except program [arg ...]
```

where *program* is a program that is normally passed to by `bouncesaying` or `condredirect`. The purpose of the `except` program is to change the exit code of the program. If the program exits with a code of `0`, `except` will exit with a code of `100`. If the program exits with a code of

111, except will also exit with an exit code of 111. Any other exit code from the program results in an exit code of 0 from except.

The forward Program

The forward program is used to forward messages to an alternate mail address. The format of the forward command is

```
forward address ...
```

The preline Program

The preline program is used to process messages before forwarding them to other programs. The format of the preline command is

```
preline [-dfr] command
```

where *command* is the program that preline passes the message to. By default the preline program adds three fields to the message header. The From:, Return-Path:, and Delivered-To: lines are added with the appropriate information. Table 6.4 shows the preline command options that can be used to modify the default behavior of preline.

TABLE 6.4   The preline Command Options

Option	Description
-d	Do not insert the Delivered-To header field.
-f	Do not insert the From header field.
-r	Do not insert the Return-Path header field.

The qbiff Program

The qbiff program is used to write a message to the terminal of the user when a message is received. This command is used in the user's local .qmail file, which is described in detail in Chapter 8.

The qreceipt Program

The qreceipt program is used to respond to messages that ask for a delivery notification status. The format of the qreceipt command is

```
qreceipt address
```

where *address* is the email address that will trigger a return notice message if it appears in the Notice-Requested-Upon-Delivery-To: header field.

By placing the qreceipt command in the user's .qmail file, qmail will return a notice message to the message sender.

The `maildirwatch` Program

The `maildirwatch` program is used to monitor a user's mail directory and report any new messages that arrive. The `maildir` program uses the `MAILDIR` environment variable to identify the `maildir` directory to monitor.

This program uses the qmail `maildir` mailbox format and is not compatible with the standard UNIX `mbox` format (see Chapter 9).

The qmail Administrator Utility Programs

The qmail administrator utility programs are used for assisting the mail administrator in administering the qmail server. These files are used to take statistics of the qmail server, get operating parameters from the qmail system, and set operating parameters.

The `qmail-getpw` Program

The `qmail-getpw` program is used to find information regarding a local email userid. The format of the `qmail-getpw` command is

```
qmail-getpw username
```

where *username* is an email address on the local mail server. The `qmail-getpw` program returns the information on the local mail user, as shown in Table 6.5.

TABLE 6.5   `qmail-getpw` Display Information

Field	Description
user	UNIX username of the mail user
uid	UNIX userid of the mail user
gid	UNIX groupid that the username belongs to
homedir	UNIX home directory of the user
dash	Separator character used to identify locally owned user mailboxes
ext	Extension used to identify locally owned user mailboxes

> **NOTE**
>
> The output from the `qmail-getpw` command is a series of NUL-terminated ASCII strings. The output is intended for use within other programs and does not display properly if you try the command on the system console.

The `qmail-newmrh` Program

The qmail-newmrh program is used to create a database file from the /var/qmail/control/morercpthosts file (see Chapter 7). The qmail-smtpd program can use this database to efficiently parse hostnames and determine addresses for which to accept incoming mail.

The `qmail-qstat` Program

The qmail-qstat program is used by the mail administrator to produce a report on the number of messages waiting in the various qmail message states in the mail queue (see Chapter 2). Listing 6.5 shows a sample output from the qmail-qstat program.

LISTING 6.5 Sample qmail-qstat Output

```
shadrach# /var/qmail/bin/qmail-qstat
messages in queue: 0
messages in queue but not yet preprocessed: 0
shadrach#
```

The `qmail-qread` Program

The qmail-qread program is used by the mail administrator to produce a report showing the current messages in the mail queues. The qmail-qread command provides a detailed description of each message, including the date the message was placed in the queue, the size of the message, the message sender, and all recipients waiting for delivery.

The `qmail-showctl` Program

The qmail-showctl program is used by the mail administrator to analyze and display the current configuration of qmail, based on the qmail configuration files (described in Chapter 7). Listing 6.6 shows a sample output from a qmail-showctl command.

LISTING 6.6 Sample qmail-showctl Command Output

```
shadrach# qmail-showctl
qmail home directory: /var/qmail.
user-ext delimiter: -.
paternalism (in decimal): 2.
silent concurrency limit: 120.
subdirectory split: 23.
user ids: 81, 82, 83, 0, 84, 85, 86, 87.
group ids: 81, 82.
badmailfrom: (Default.) Any MAIL FROM is allowed.
bouncefrom: (Default.) Bounce user name is MAILER-DAEMON.
bouncehost: (Default.) Bounce host name is shadrach.ispnet1.net.
```

LISTING 6.6   Continued

```
concurrencylocal: (Default.) Local concurrency is 10.
concurrencyremote: (Default.) Remote concurrency is 20.
databytes: (Default.) SMTP DATA limit is 0 bytes.
defaultdomain: (Default.) Default domain name is shadrach.ispnet1.net.
defaulthost: (Default.) Default host name is shadrach.ispnet1.net.
doublebouncehost: (Default.) 2B recipient host: shadrach.ispnet1.net.
doublebounceto: (Default.) 2B recipient user: postmaster.
envnoathost: (Default.) Presumed domain name is shadrach.ispnet1.net.
helohost: (Default.) SMTP client HELO host name is shadrach.ispnet1.net.
idhost: (Default.) Message-ID host name is shadrach.ispnet1.net.
localiphost: (Default.) Local IP address becomes shadrach.ispnet1.net.
locals:
Messages for shadrach.ispnet1.net are delivered locally.
me: My name is shadrach.ispnet1.net.
percenthack: (Default.) The percent hack is not allowed.
plusdomain: (Default.) Plus domain name is shadrach.ispnet1.net.
qmqpservers: (Default.) No QMQP servers.
queuelifetime: (Default.) Message lifetime in the queue is 604800 seconds.
rcpthosts:
SMTP clients may send messages to recipients at shadrach.ispnet1.net.
SMTP clients may send messages to recipients at test.isp.
morercpthosts: (Default.) No effect.
morercpthosts.cdb: (Default.) No effect.
smtpgreeting: (Default.) SMTP greeting: 220 shadrach.ispnet1.net.
smtproutes: (Default.) No artificial SMTP routes.
timeoutconnect: (Default.) SMTP client connection timeout is 60 seconds.
timeoutremote: (Default.) SMTP client data timeout is 1200 seconds.
timeoutsmtpd: (Default.) SMTP server data timeout is 1200 seconds.
virtualdomains:
Virtual domain: test.isp:jessica
shadrach#
```

The `qmail-tcpok` Program

The qmail-tcpok program is used by the mail administrator to clear qmail-remote's TCP
timeout table. If qmail-remote fails on an SMTP connection attempt with a remote mail host,
it records the IP address of the remote host in the TCP timeout table. If the SMTP connection
fails a second time, the table entry is marked and qmail will not attempt to redeliver the message for one hour.

By resetting this table, qmail-remote will not make any assumptions about failing destination
addresses and attempt a normal SMTP delivery.

The `qmail-tcpto` Program

The `qmail-tcpto` program is used by the mail administrator to print the current TCP timeout table values.

The `qmail-pw2u` Program

The `qmail-pw2u` program is one of the two programs used by the mail administrator to create a qmail username database from the UNIX password file. The user database can then be used by qmail to identify qmail users. The format of the `qmail-pw2u` command is

```
qmail-pw2u [-/ohHuUC] [-char]
```

`qmail-pw2u` uses the standard UNIX password file as its input and produces an output that can be used by the `qmail-newu` program. The standard UNIX password file format is

```
user:password:uid:gid:gecos:home:shell
```

Usually the output from `qmail-pw2u` is saved in the file `/var/qmail/users/assign`. Table 6.6 shows the command-line options available to use with `qmail-pw2u`.

TABLE 6.6 qmail-pw2u Command-Line Options

Option	Description
-/	Uses home/.qmail-/ to locate user-defined mailboxes
-o	Skips user if home does not exist (default)
-h	Stops if home does not exist
-H	Does not check if home exists
-u	Allows uppercase letters in user
-U	Skips user if there are any uppercase letters in user (default)
-cchar	Uses char as the user-defined mailbox extension
-C	Disables the user-defined mailbox extension

The `qmail-newu` Program

The `qmail-newu` program is the second part of the qmail user-creation system, with `qmail-pw2u`. The `qmail-newu` program reads the `/var/qmail/users/assign` file and creates a binary database file `/var/qmail/users/cdb`, which is used by `qmail-lspawn` to determine the locations of local mail system users and the locations of their home directories.

> **NOTE**
>
> Both the `qmail-pw2u` and `qmail-newu` programs are described in detail in Chapter 7.

Summary

This chapter discusses the steps required to download and install the qmail software package. Since most of the current Linux distributions do not include a binary distribution of qmail, you will have to download the source code from the qmail Web site and compile it to create the binary executable files. The FreeBSD system does include both a binary package and a source code port for the qmail software. Either method can be used on the FreeBSD system to install qmail.

Before compiling the source code, you should look over the configuration files necessary to define the qmail installation. One important part is the location of the `qmail` directory on the UNIX system. All of the qmail binary files, configuration files, and mail queues are located under the `qmail` directory. For large organizations it is advisable to use a separate disk drive to contain the `/var` directory. This allows all of the qmail mail queues and user mailboxes to be located on a separate disk that has enough space available to support the organization.

There is a wealth of executable programs that qmail uses to operate. All of these files are located in the `bin` directory under the default `qmail` directory. While qmail uses several different executable files to process mail delivery, there are dozens of other executable files available for the qmail mail administrator and for normal mail users to help them control the behavior of qmail in processing individual mailboxes. The following chapters describe how to use these executables to control and fine-tune the qmail system.

Changing qmail Operational Parameters

IN THIS CHAPTER

The previous chapter discussed how to download, compile, and install the qmail software package. Once the qmail software is installed, it must be configured to support the desired email configuration for the mail server. This is one of the areas where qmail separates itself from other mail packages.

The qmail configuration system is different in that it uses multiple configuration files to define the mail server configuration. The main configuration is done using qmail control files. A separate control file is used to define each qmail feature. If a control file exists, its content defines the value of the configuration variable.

Besides configuration control files, qmail also has files that control the local mail delivery system. qmail uses a `users` directory that can contain a table of special usernames that qmail maps to local users on the mail server. Besides a user table, qmail may also include many different alias tables, allowing users as well as the mail administrator to define mail aliases. Much like the control file system, qmail uses separate alias files for each alias defined in the system. This chapter describes all of the configuration, user, and alias name files that are used in a qmail installation.

Control Files

The control files are the center of the qmail configuration. The qmail control files do what they say—they control the operation and behavior of qmail. They are located in the `control` directory under the main `qmail` directory. In a default qmail installation this would be located at

`/var/qmail/control`

Unlike most MTA server software that places most (if not all) server parameters in a central configuration file, qmail does things a little differently. Separate files are used to control the core executable qmail programs. Each control file contains a value that defines a different variable within a qmail executable program. This section lists and describes the different control files that are used in qmail.

Control File Structure and Permissions

The qmail control files are ASCII text files that define qmail parameters. Most control files require a single text value, which can be entered on one line. Some control files can contain multiple values. In this case, each value is entered on a separate line, each line terminated with a standard UNIX linefeed (LF) character.

qmail automatically assigns default values when a control file is not present to define a parameter specifically. The presence of a control file indicates that the qmail administrator wants to change the default value of a parameter.

Changing qmail Operational Parameters

CHAPTER 7

163

7

CHANGING QMAIL
OPERATIONAL
PARAMETERS

The UNIX echo command is often used to create the qmail control file. An example of this is as follows:

```
echo "shadrach.ispnet1.net - Welcome to our SMTP server" > smtpgreeting
```

This command sets the value of the smtpgreeting control file to the ASCII text string listed in the echo command. After creating the control file, you should always check the permissions that were set for the file. This can be done using the long listing option of the ls command:

```
$ ls -l smtpgreeting
-rw-r--r-- 1 root  qmail  50 Feb 24 16:18 smtpgreeting
```

The permissions show that the example file is readable and writeable by the file owner (root) and is read-only for the group (qmail) and all other users. This permission scheme allows the root user to set control files, while other users can read but not alter the control file. This is the recommended setting for all qmail control files.

To set the proper permissions for the control files, you can use the chmod program. The chmod program uses either the text value of the permissions, such as rw, or it can use a numerical version of the permissions by assigning each position a binary value. Using the numerical method, the chmod command to set the permissions as shown in the example would be

```
chmod 644 /var/qmail/control/smtpgreeting
```

qmail Program Control Files

One or more control files control most of the qmail core programs. Table 7.1 shows the qmail core programs and the associated control files used for each one.

TABLE 7.1 qmail Control Files

qmail Program	Control File(s)
qmail-smtpd	badmailfrom
	databytes
	localiphost
	morercpthosts
	rcpthosts
	smtpgreeting
	timeoutsmtpd
qmail-qmqpc	qmqpservers
qmail-inject	defaultdomain
	defaulthost

Table 7.1 Continued

qmail Program	Control File(s)
	idhost
	plusdomain
qmail-send	bouncefrom
	bouncehost
	concurrencylocal
	concurrencyremote
	doublebouncehost
	doublebounceto
	envnoathost
	locals
	me
	percenthack
	queuelifetime
	virtualdomains
qmail-remote	helohost
	smtproutes
	timeoutconnect
	timeoutremote

These are the control files that are used by qmail to configure operational parameters of the system. Not all qmail programs use (or need) control files.

The following sections describe the control files as they are used with the qmail programs.

badmailfrom

The badmailfrom control file is used to tell the qmail server which remote addresses it should refuse to receive messages from. Each address should be listed on a separate line. Domain names can be used to indicate all senders at a particular domain. If a badmailfrom file is not present in the control file directory, no addresses are blocked from the mail server.

The badmailfrom control file is a direct result of Internet email spam. *Spam* is unsolicited email that is used mainly for advertisement purposes on the Internet. Email lists are sold to companies that use spam (called *spammers*), who in turn send spam email messages to every address in the list.

The `badmailfrom` list contains the ASCII text of the list of addresses you want barred from sending email messages to your local qmail users. An example of a `badmailfrom` listing would be

```
nuisance@advert.corp1.com
@mail.hq.corp.com
@evildomain.net
```

The first example shows restricts a specific username at a specific hostname—`nuisance@advert.corp1.com`. Any other user at the `advert.corp1.com` mail server would be able to send mail to the local qmail server. The second example restricts all users on a remote server, and the third example restricts mail from an entire domain. Addresses can be added and deleted from the `badmailfrom` file without having to restart qmail.

Listing 7.1 shows a sample SMTP connection from a host whose domain is in the `badmailfrom` file.

LISTING 7.1   Sample `badmailfrom` Host Session

```
1  $ telnet localhost 25
2  Trying 127.0.0.1...
3  Connected to localhost.ispnet1.net.
4  Escape character is '^]'.
5  220 shadrach.ispnet1.net ESMTP
6  helo evildomain.net
7  250 shadrach.ispnet1.net
8  mail from: <badguy@evildomain.net>
9  250 ok
10 rcpt to: <rich@ispnet1.net>
11 553 sorry, your envelope sender is in my badmailfrom list (#5.7.1)
12 quit
13 221 shadrach.ispnet1.net
14 Connection closed by foreign host.
15 $
```

Line 1 shows a sample Telnet session to the SMTP port of the local qmail server. Line 5 shows the standard SMTP greeting banner produced from qmail. In line 6, the client starts the SMTP session by issuing the HELO command. The domain name of the offending email host is used to identify the remote SMTP client. Line 7 indicates that qmail accepted the SMTP session start. In line 8, the remote SMTP client identifies the sender of the mail message that it wants to transmit. In line 10, the recipient of the mail message is indicated to be a local user on the qmail server. In line 11 qmail responds with a negative SMTP response (code 553), indicating that it will not allow the offending message sender access to local email recipients.

bouncefrom

The `bouncefrom` control file is used to define a username that appears on messages that are bounced back to the original sender. Most often this consists of messages that suffer a permanent delivery failure from qmail.

The default value for `bouncefrom` is the generic username `MAILER-DAEMON`. This does not represent a normal UNIX username. It is often a fictitious username that is aliased to point to a real username on the mail system.

If you want the bounced messages to appear to come from a different username, you can place that name in the `bouncefrom` control file using the following command:

```
echo postmaster > /var/qmail/control/bouncefrom
```

Once the `bouncefrom` control file exists, qmail will use the username in the file as the default bounced message sender.

bouncehost

The `bouncehost` control file is related to the `bouncefrom` file in that it specifies the default hostname that appears on messages that are bounced back to the original sender. Again, this is most common with messages that have suffered a permanent delivery failure from qmail.

The default value for `bouncehost` is the hostname defined in the `me` control file. If the `me` control file does not exist, then qmail uses the hostname `bouncehost`.

The combination of `bouncefrom` and `bouncehost` defines the sender email address of all messages that are bounced by qmail for any reason. The format of the sender address is

```
bouncefrom@bouncehost
```

Using the default values, this address becomes `MAILER-DAEMON@hostname`, where `hostname` is the local mail server hostname. The `MAILER-DAEMON` username is often used as an alias pointing to the real username of the mail administrator of the system. Listing 7.2 shows the format of a bounced message in qmail.

LISTING 7.2   Sample Bounced Message

```
1  $ mail
2  Mail version 8.1 6/6/93.  Type ? for help.
3  "/var/mail/rich": 1 message 1 new
4  >N  1 MAILER-DAEMON@shadra   Thu Feb 26 11:47   28/981    "failure notice"
5  &1
6  Message 1:
7  From MAILER-DAEMON Thu Feb 26 11:47:48 2000
```

```
 8  Date: 26 Feb 2000 16:47:48 -0000
 9  From: MAILER-DAEMON@shadrach.ispnet1.net
10  To: rich@shadrach.ispnet1.net
11  Subject: failure notice
12
13  Hi. This is the qmail-send program at shadrach.ispnet1.net.
14  I'm afraid I wasn't able to deliver your message to the following addresses.
15  This is a permanent error; I've given up. Sorry it didn't work out.
16
17  <baduser@shadrach.ispnet1.net>:
18  Sorry, no mailbox here by that name. (#5.1.1)
19
20  --- Below this line is a copy of the message.
21
22  Return-Path: <rich@shadrach.ispnet1.net>
23  Received: (qmail 13411 invoked by uid 1001); 26 Feb 2000 16:47:47 -0000
24  Date: 26 Feb 2000 16:47:47 -0000
25  Message-ID: <20000224164747.13410.qmail@shadrach.ispnet1.net>
26  From: rich@shadrach.ispnet1.net
27  To: baduser@shadrach.ispnet1.net
28  Subject: test message
29
30  This is a test message sent to a non-existant user.
31
32  & d
33  & q
34  $
```

Line 4 shows a sample bounced message header line from the `mail` program. It indicates the message was sent from the `MAILER-DAEMON` username on the local host. Lines 7 through 20 contain a canned bounced message notification from qmail. The original message is contained in the bounced message, as shown in lines 21 through 31.

concurrencylocal

The `concurrencylocal` control file defines the number of simultaneous local delivery processes that qmail can run. One feature of qmail is its capability to process multiple message deliveries simultaneously. This feature can come in extremely handy when hosting large mailing lists that must process several hundred email deliveries.

The default value for this parameter is `10`—which allows for up to 10 local mail delivery processes to run simultaneously. The maximum value for this control file is set by the `conf-spawn` compile parameter. By default this value is set to `120`, as described in Chapter 6, "Installing qmail." The maximum value is `255`.

concurrencyremote

The `concurrencyremote` control file is similar to the `concurrencylocal` control file defined above. It defines the number of simultaneous remote delivery processes that qmail can run.

The default value for this parameter is `20`—which allows for up to 20 remote mail delivery processes to run simultaneously. The maximum value that can be set in this control file is also set by the `conf-spawn` compile parameter. By default this value is set to `120`, as described in Chapter 6.

Although it is possible to have up to 255 different local and remote mail delivery processes running, this may not necessarily be a good idea. Each running process requires memory and disk space to operate. The mail server can become overloaded if too many mail processes are running simultaneously. It is the job of the mail administrator to regulate the number of mail processes running and not overload the mail server.

defaultdomain

The `defaultdomain` control file is used to augment any email addresses in the message that are not recognized as being in proper `user@host.domain` format. By default, `qmail-inject` adds `defaultdomain` to the host address if it does not see any dots in the host address. If the `defaultdomain` file does not exist, it is set to the value used in the `me` control file—the hostname of the local mail server.

`defaultdomain` is most often used when sending mail messages to local users on the same mail server. If user `rich` on host `shadrach.ispnet1.net` sends a message to local user `jessica@shadrach`, qmail will automatically assume that the recipient should be `jessica@shadrach.ispnet1.net` and use that address as the recipient address.

If the `QMAILDEFAULTDOMAIN` environment variable is set, it will override the `defaultdomain` control file value.

defaulthost

The `defaulthost` control file is used to define the hostname that is used to augment any email addresses in the message that do not have a hostname in the address. By default `qmail-inject` adds the value of `defaulthost` to the username part of the address. If the `defaulthost` control file does not exist, the string `"defaulthost"` is used.

The `defaulthost` control file is most often used when sending mail messages to local users on the same mail server, much like the `defaultdomain` control file. For example, if user `rich` on host `shadrach.ispnet1.net` sends a message to local user `jessica`, qmail will automatically augment the recipient address to be `jessica@shadrach.ispnet1.net`. This allows the `qmail-send` function to identify local addresses easier and quicker.

This feature is also used when the mail server is acting as a domain mail server. Often an organization wants to have its email address be just its domain name and not include the hostname. The `defaulthost` value will also be augmented on outgoing messages, so a message from rich@shadrach.ispnet1.net may actually say rich@ispnet1.net.

If the `QMAILDEFAULTHOST` environment variable is set, it will override the `defaulthost` control file value.

databytes

The `databytes` control file is used to define the maximum number of bytes allowed in an email message received by `qmail-smtpd`. The default value for this parameter is 0, which indicates no limit to the message size. To specify a maximum message size, create the `databytes` control file with the text value of the message size desired. For example, the command

```
echo 1000000 > /var/qmail/control/databytes
```

would restrict incoming messages to 1MB or less. Any message larger than the set size would receive a permanent delivery failure error message. Listing 7.3 shows a sample error message generated from a message that was too large for the `databytes` size.

LISTING 7.3 Sample Large Message Session

```
1  $ telnet localhost 25
2  Trying 127.0.0.1...
3  Connected to localhost.ispnet1.net.
4  Escape character is '^]'.
5  220 shadrach.ispnet1.net ESMTP
6  helo test.net
7  250 shadrach.ispnet1.net
8  MAIL FROM: <katie@test.net>
9  250 ok
10 RCPT TO: <rich>
11 250 ok
12 DATA
13 354 go ahead
14 This is a test of a message that is too large for the databytes limit.
15 This is the end of the message size test.
16 .
17 552 sorry, that message size exceeds my databytes limit (#5.3.4)
18 QUIT
19 221 shadrach.ispnet1.net
20 Connection closed by foreign host.
21 $
```

Line 17 shows the error message returned to a remote client that sent a message that was larger than the `databytes` control file setting.

7
CHANGING QMAIL OPERATIONAL PARAMETERS

doublebouncehost

The doublebouncehost control file is used to specify the hostname to use for messages that suffer a double bounce. A *double bounce* occurs when a bounced message notification also bounces. qmail will attempt to send another notification of the double bounce to a different email address (often set to the mail administrator).

The doublebouncehost value is used in conjunction with the doublebounceto value, described next, to create a valid email address where qmail-send can forward double-bounced messages. If this control file does not exist, qmail uses the hostname value that appears in the me control file. If the me control file does not exist, qmail uses the value doublebouncehost, which most likely will fail on its delivery attempt.

doublebounceto

The doublebounceto control file is used to specify the username to use for messages that suffer a double bounce. As described above, a double bounce occurs when a bounced message notification also bounces.

By default qmail will use the username postmaster in conjunction with the doublebouncehost hostname to forward the double bounce notification message. If the double bounce message also bounces, qmail-send gives up and does not try to forward the bounce notification any more.

envnoathost

The envnoathost control file is used by qmail-send to specify the hostname for mail message recipients that do not specify a hostname. By default, if this control file is not present, qmail-send will use the value defined in the me control file, which should be the local server hostname. If the me control file does not exist, qmail-send will use the string envnoathost, which most likely will produce an error message on the delivery attempt.

This control file allows qmail-send to change the local recipient addresses into the proper user@host format using a predetermined hostname format for the host.

helohost

The helohost control file is used to specify the hostname used in qmail-remote SMTP sessions with remote mail servers. The SMTP HELO command is used to identify the SMTP client to the remote SMTP server (see Chapter 5, "SMTP and qmail").

If the helohost control file is not present, qmail-remote uses the value specified in the me control file. If the me control file is not present, qmail-remote will refuse to run.

idhost

The `idhost` control file is used to specify the hostname that is used to produce Message-ID: header fields in messages. By default `qmail-inject` will use the hostname specified in the `me` control file in the Message-ID: field. A sample of the `qmail-inject`–generated Message ID: field can be seen on line 25 in Listing 7.2. qmail generates a unique RFC 822 Message-ID: field for all messages sent via `qmail-inject` that do not already contain a Message-ID: field. qmail uses the hostname specified in the `idhost` control file if you do not want to use the hostname specified in the `me` control file.

If neither the `idhost` nor the `me` control file is present, `qmail-inject` uses a hostname of `idhost`. Also, `qmail-inject` checks for the presence of the `QMAILIDHOST` environment variable. If this variable exists, it will override the values present in both the `idhost` and `me` control files.

localiphost

The `localiphost` control file is used to specify the local hostname for mail messages that use the dotted decimal IP address notation of the local IP address.

It is the responsibility of `qmail-smtpd` to recognize the local IP address of the qmail server in mail messages and replace that address with the text hostname address specified in `localiphost`. If the `localiphost` control file is not present, `qmail-smtpd` will use the value specified in the `me` control file.

Using the actual IP address of the mail server as the hostname in an address is perfectly legal in RFC822 formatted messages, but its use with DNS servers is frowned on. The format of this type of address looks like this:

```
user@[a.b.c.d]
```

where *user* is the username of the message recipient, and *a.b.c.d* is the IP address of the recipient's mail server. Note that when using this format you must know the IP address of the mail server able to accept mail messages for the username. The DNS method of specifying hostnames has become more popular because DNS databases can be created to allow multiple hosts to accept messages for a domain (see Chapter 4, "DNS and qmail").

locals

The `locals` control file is used to specify mail addresses that qmail should consider to be local addresses to the mail server. `qmail-send` will process any message whose recipient address appears in the `locals` control file as a local message by forwarding it to the `qmail-lspawn` process. Also, note that any hostname NOT found in the `locals` control file is assumed to be a remote host (even if it is the local mail server hostname).

If the `locals` control file does not exist, `qmail-send` assumes that the hostname defined in the `me` control file is the only local mail host available. If the `me` control file does not exist, `qmail-send` will refuse to run.

me

The me control file is the most important control file in qmail. qmail will not run if the me control file is not present.

The me control file is used to specify the hostname of the local mail server. The value defined is used as the default value for many of the other control files if they are not present.

The me control file is usually created from running the config script in the qmail configuration subdirectory. The config script automatically determines the DNS name of the mail server and creates the proper control files (me, locals, and rcpthosts). If for some reason your mail server cannot connect to the DNS server (such as on a dial-up line), you can run the config-fast script manually, specifying the hostname of the mail server:

```
/var/qmail/configure/config-fast shadrach.ispnet1.net
```

morercpthosts

The morercpthosts control file is used to specify additional host and domain names that the qmail server will accept messages for. The main control file that is used to specify hosts to receive messages for is the rcpthosts file (discussed later).

The qmail documentation recommends placing no more than about 50 hostnames in the rcpthosts file. Any additional hosts that the mail server needs to receive messages for should be placed in the morercpthosts file.

The morercpthosts file is not used directly by qmail. The qmail-newmrh program is used to process hostnames in the morercpthosts file to create a binary database file based on the addresses listed in morercphosts. After running the qmail-newmrh program, qmail produces the morercpthosts.cdb file, which contains the binary database. qmail-smtpd uses the morercpthosts.cdb file to search the addresses listed in the morercpthosts file.

percenthack

The percenthack control file is used to specify a list of domains where usernames that contain a percent sign (%) in the address are converted to DNS-style domain names. The older UNIX-to-UNIX Copy (UUCP) email protocol used the percent sign to separate the username and the hostname in an email address (user%hostname).

The qmail-send program uses the percenthack control file to determine when to convert %-style address to DNS-style addresses. For example, if the domain test.net is present in the percenthack file, an address in the form barbara%corp1.net@test.net will be converted to the mail address barbara@corp1.net.

plusdomain

The plusdomain control file is used to specify a domain name to any address that ends with a plus sign (+). By default the domain name present in the me control file is added to any email address that ends with a plus sign. If the me control file is not present, qmail-inject adds the string plusdomain to the end of the email address.

qmqpservers

The qmqpservers control file is used to specify the address(es) of Quick Mail Queuing Protocol (QMQP) servers used by the qmail-qmqpc program. The qmail-qmqpc program is usually used to send messages from a workstation to a central mail server using the qmail QMQP protocol instead of storing the message in the local qmail mail queue. Often a symbolic link is created to replace qmail-queue with qmail-qmqpc so that all messages are automatically forwarded to the QMQP server.

> **NOTE**
>
> The QMQP protocol is a qmail-specific protocol. It can be used only between two qmail servers. It is described in Chapter 5.

queuelifetime

The queuelifetime control file is used to specify the number of seconds that a message can stay in the mail queue before it is removed. The default value for this parameter is 604800 seconds, or one week. After the queuelifetime value expires, qmail-send attempts to deliver the message one final time. If the message is still undeliverable, it is removed from the mail queue.

rcpthosts

The rcpthosts control file is another important file that should be present in the qmail configuration. The rcpthosts file defines the hosts and domains for which qmail-smtpd will accept messages. Any message destined for a recipient on a host or domain not listed in the rcpthosts file will be rejected.

> **CAUTION**
>
> Make sure that there is a rcpthosts control file configured with at least the local hostname configured. If no rcpthosts file is present, qmail-smtpd will accept messages destined for ANY recipient, even those on remote hosts. This process is called *relaying* and, while limited relaying is not bad, relaying all recipients can be catastrophic. Internet spam experts look for mail servers that use relaying and use them to transfer their spam messages to thousands of unsuspecting victims.

If the environment variable RELAYCLIENT is present, qmail-smtpd will ignore the rcpthosts file (if any) and appends the value of the RELAYCLIENT environment variable to the end of each recipient address.

smtpgreeting

The smtpgreeting control file is used to specify the SMTP greeting banner that qmail-smtpd uses to initiate an SMTP connection with a remote client. By default qmail-smtpd uses the hostname present in the me control file. If no me control file is present qmail-smtpd will refuse to run.

Any string can be used for the SMTP greeting banner. It has become somewhat of a standard to start the greeting with the hostname of the mail server. To change the greeting banner, you can use the following commands:

```
cd /var/qmail/control
echo "shadrach.ispnet1.net - Welcome to our mail server" > smtpgreeting
```

Listing 7.4 shows how this greeting banner appears on SMTP connections.

LISTING 7.4 Sample SMTP Greeting Banner Session

```
1  # echo "shadrach.ispnet1.net - Welcome to our mail server" > /var/qmail/
➥  control/smtpgreeting
2  #chmod 644 /var/qmail/control/smtpgreeting
3  # telnet localhost 25
4  Trying 127.0.0.1...
5  Connected to localhost.ispnet1.net.
6  Escape character is '^]'.
7  220 shadrach.ispnet1.net - Welcome to our mail server ESMTP
8  QUIT
9  221 shadrach.ispnet1.net - Welcome to our mail server
10 Connection closed by foreign host.
11 #
```

In Listing 7.4, line 1 shows the echo command being used to create the SMTP greeting banner. Line 2 shows setting the proper permissions required for a qmail control file (you wouldn't want users changing your SMTP greeting, would you?). Lines 7 and 9 show the new SMTP greeting banner in action on the mail server.

smtproutes

The smtproutes control file is used to specify static SMTP routes that can be used to deliver mail to specific destinations. The format of an smtproute line is

```
host:relay
```

where *host* can be a hostname or domain name that should be redirected to a specific mail host defined by *relay*. Listing 7.5 shows a few sample smtproutes entries.

LISTING 7.5 Sample smtproutes Entries

```
1   ispnet2.net:meshach.ispnet2.net
2   .testisp.net:
3   :firewall.isp2.net:1000
```

In Listing 7.5, line 1 shows a sample entry that redirects any messages destined for ispnet2.net to the specific mail server meshach.ispnet2.net. This prevents qmail from doing any DNS MX record searching on the ispnet2.net domain address. Line 2 shows an example of forcing qmail to perform a DNS MX record check. By not specifying a relay host, qmail will attempt a DNS lookup to determine the mail servers for any address that ends in .testisp.net.

Line 3 shows still another special smtproutes format. By not specifying the first parameter, any message that was not covered in either of the first two lines will be automatically forwarded to the special mail server firewall.isp2.net. Also shown is how to specify an alternate TCP port (1000) instead of the standard SMTP TCP port 25. This technique is often used when relaying email through a firewall device to the Internet.

CAUTION

The smtproutes control file allows for many specific SMTP routes to be defined for qmail. Care should be taken when listing the addresses: qmail processes the addresses in the order that they appear in the smtproutes file. Often a misplaced address can alter the desired behavior of the qmail server. This is a great source for mail loops.

timeoutconnect

The timeoutconnect control file is used to specify the number of seconds that qmail-remote will wait for the remote SMTP server to accept a new SMTP connection before disconnecting. The default value for this parameter is 60 seconds (one minute). This parameter can be used when connecting to a remote SMTP server across a slow Internet link.

timeoutremote

The timeoutremote control file is used to specify the number of seconds that qmail-remote will wait for each response from the remote SMTP server. By default qmail-remote will wait 1200 seconds (20 minutes) for a response from the remote SMTP server before disconnecting the session and logging a temporary delivery failure.

timeoutsmtpd

The `timeoutsmtpd` control file is used to specify the number of seconds that `qmail-smtpd` will wait to receive a buffer of data from the remote SMTP client. The default value for this parameter is 1200 seconds (20 minutes). If no data is received by `qmail-smtpd` by the end of the `timeoutsmtpd` period, the SMTP connection with the remote server will be terminated.

virtualdomains

The `virtualdomains` control file is an important control file for ISPs. It allows the qmail server to accept mail for users or domains other than for the local mail server and hold those messages in a special location for the local mail server to collect at a later time.

The `virtualdomains` control file consists of entries of virtual users or domains that the mail administrator wants the qmail server to accept messages for. Each user or domain is listed on a separate line in the file. There are two formats that can be used to enter data in the file. The first is for defining virtual users, and uses the form

`user@domain:prepend`

Using this format, `qmail-send` watches for message recipients with the address `user@domain`. When a message destined for `user@domain` is received, `qmail-send` converts the address to `prepend-user@domain` and passes the message to `qmail-lspawn` for local delivery.

The second format is used for defining virtual domains:

domain`:prepend`

Using this format, `qmail-send` watches for any message recipient address that contains the given *domain* in the address. When an address contains this *domain*, it is converted to `prepend-`*address*, where *address* is the original address of the recipient. *domain* may also represent a wildcard value, such as `.ispnet1.net`. This allows qmail to receive mail for any host machine within this domain.

If this sounds confusing, it is. Here's an example to help clear this up. If the following line is added to the `virtualdomain` control file

`mycorp5.com:mymail`

`qmail-send` will scan all recipient addresses for anything that is addressed to `mycorp5.com`. If a message is received for `prez@mycorp5.com`, `qmail-send` converts the recipient address to `mymail-prez@shadrach.ispnet1.net` and passes it to `qmail-lspawn` for processing to the local user mymail.

This example shows only half of the process required to accept messages for a virtual domain. In this process the message is captured and redirected to the local mail server. In the second half of the process, the local mail server must know where to store messages prepended with the `mymail` tag so that the `mycorp5.com` local office mail server can connect and retrieve it at a later time. Chapter 11, "Using qmail as an ISP Mail Server," describes the virtual domain process in detail.

qmail Environment Variables

Besides the control files, qmail also sets and uses UNIX environment variables to modify its behavior. Many of them are duplicates of control file parameters and override the control file value if present.

The qmail programs cannot set environment variables by themselves. They need another program to do this for them. This is most often accomplished using the tcpwrapper or tcpserver program. Both methods can set environment variables on-the-fly as the qmail programs are started.

> **NOTE**
>
> The use of the tcpserver program to set environment variables is described in detail in Chapter 10, "The ucspi-tcp Program."

Table 7.2 shows the environment variables that can be used by qmail.

TABLE 7.2   qmail Environment Variables

Variable	Description
DATABYTES	Overrides control file value
DEFAULT	Extension portion of the `.qmail-default` file
DTLINE	Address used in the Delivered-To: header field
EXT	Address extension
EXT2	Part of the address following the first dash in the extension
EXT3	Part of the address following the second dash in the extension
EXT4	Part of the address following the third dash in the extension
HOME	Home directory of the user
HOST	Hostname part of the address
HOST2	Part of the hostname preceding the last dot
HOST3	Part of the hostname preceding the second-to-last dot
HOST4	Part of the hostname preceding the third-to-last dot
LOCAL	Local part of the address

TABLE 7.2 Continued

Variable	Description
MAILHOST	Hostname used in the From: message header field
MAILNAME	Name used in the From: header field
MAILUSER	Username used in the From: header field
NAME	Name used in the From: header field
NEWSENDER	Sender address of forwarded messages
QMAILDEFAULTDOMAIN	Overrides `defaultdomain` control file
QMAILDEFAULTHOST	Overrides `defaulthost` control file
QMAILHOST	Hostname used in the From: header field
QMAILIDHOST	Overrides `idhost` control file
QMAILINJECT	Specifies `qmail-inject` options
QMAILMFTFILE	Specifies file containing list of addresses for Mail-Followup_to: creation
QMAILNAME	Name used in From: header field
QMAILPLUSDOMAIN	Overrides `plusdomain` control file
QMAILSHOST	Hostname specified in sender envelope
QMAILSUSER	Username specified in sender envelope
QMAILUSER	Username used in From: header field
RECIPIENT	Recipient address in the sender envelope
RELAYCLIENT	Overrides `rcpthosts` control file and appends value to all recipient addresses
RPLINE	Return-Path: header field
SENDER	Message sender address
UFLINE	UUCP-style From: header field
USER	Username used in the From: header field

Alias Files

qmail has the capability to support local mail aliases. Mail aliases allow the mail administrator to create special mail accounts that do not exist as system users. Instead, mail destined for an alias username is redirected by qmail to another user, usually locally to the mail host. Figure 7.1 demonstrates how qmail uses aliases.

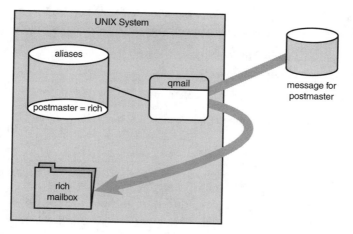

FIGURE 7.1

qmail Alias Redirection.

As shown in Figure 7.1, when qmail receives a message with a recipient that is an alias, it will redirect the message to the username associated with the alias. There are two types of aliases that qmail supports—system aliases and user aliases. The following sections describe these aliases.

System Aliases

qmail uses a slightly different method of tracking alias usernames than most other MTA programs. The /var/qmail/alias directory is used to contain files that represent aliases. Instead of having one file that maps all alias names, separate files are created, with each file representing one system alias name.

Each alias file is identified by a special filename. The format of an alias filename is

.qmail-*alias*

where *alias* is the alias name that will be recognized by qmail. Thus, to create an alias of postmaster, you must create a file called /var/qmail/alias/.qmail-postmaster. When this file is created, qmail accepts messages destined for the postmaster recipient and forwards them to the username listed in the file.

To create a mail alias for the MAILER-DAEMON username, which is the default name used for bounced messages, you can use the command

```
echo rich > /var/qmail/alias/.qmail-mailer-daemon
```

This will redirect all messages sent to either the MAILER-DAEMON or mailer-daemon username to the username rich. Notice that qmail converts uppercase usernames to lowercase.

Also, if the alias name contains dots (such as r.k.blum), you must use colons (:) to replace any dots in the alias name. For example

```
echo rich > /var/qmail/alias/.qmail-r:k:blum
```

would create an alias for the username r.k.blum or R.K.Blum, forwarding all messages to the username rich.

> **CAUTION**
>
> By default qmail does not accept mail addressed to the root user. To allow qmail to accept messages destined for the root user, you must create an alias for the root username as /var/qmail/alias/.qmail-root. The alias will cause qmail to redirect any messages for the root user to the supplied system user (usually the mail administrator).

As with other qmail configuration files, be sure that alias files are created with the proper permissions set, namely chmod 644. This prevents unauthorized users from changing system-wide aliases.

The mail administrator can create simple multiuser mailing lists by adding several usernames to the alias file. qmail will deliver a message addressed to the alias to each of the usernames listed. Each username must be listed on a separate line in the file.

User-Created Aliases

qmail also allows a user to create his own aliases that can be used to forward messages. Each user has complete control over any aliases that he creates. User-controlled aliases are contained in the user's home directory and have the same format as system aliases:

```
$HOME/.qmail-alias
```

where alias is the alias name created by the user. The alias becomes an extension of the normal system username. Each user alias is preceded by the normal username in the mail address. Thus, the mail address format for a user created alias is

```
user-alias@hostname
```

where user is the normal username for the user, alias is the user created alias name, and hostname is the standard local mail server domain name.

For example, if user katie wants to create an alias mail user named friends, she just creates a file in her home directory called .qmail-friends. This will allow qmail to accept messages destined for the username katie-friends and forward the messages to all usernames listed in Katie's /home/katie/.qmail-friends file. Katie has control of the usernames contained in the .qmail-friends file, and thus she controls how the alias is processed.

As with system-wide aliases, the user-controlled alias file can contain several usernames, each listed on a separate line. This allows individual users to create simple multiuser mailing lists without pestering the mail administrator.

> **NOTE**
>
> Actually, .qmail files can contain more than just mail addresses. They can also contain programs and script files that process the mail messages. More on this in Chapter 8, "Using qmail."

There is a special user file named $HOME/.qmail-default that is used as a catch-all to process user/alias matches that occur without a corresponding .qmail file. With this format, each qmail system user can create an unlimited number of mail aliases without any intervention from the mail administrator. Again, all of the alias names will be preceded by the system username of the owning user. Chapter 8 describes the format of the .qmail file in more detail.

qmail User Files

Besides aliases, qmail allows for creating a separate user table that can map qmail names to system usernames. Although these are similar to aliases, qmail uses a separate method of handling qmail usernames. Figure 7.2 shows how qmail maps qmail usernames to system usernames.

The qmail user database files are found in the /var/qmail/users directory. This section describes the qmail user files and programs that are used to create qmail users.

qmail Mail user Tables

The users directory contains two files:

- assign
- cdb

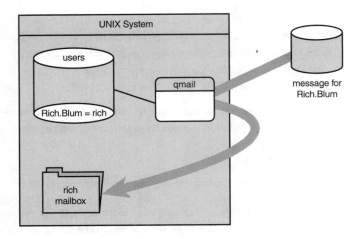

FIGURE 7.2

qmail usernames versus UNIX system names.

The `assign` file is an ASCII text file that maps qmail usernames to the UNIX system user-names that will receive messages destined to them. One mapping is performed per line. A line with a single period (.) indicates the end of the assign file. The `cdb` file is a binary database file that is created from the original text `assign` file using the `qmail-newu` program (discussed in the next section).

There are two forms that are used for mapping usernames in the `assign` file. The first is for a direct one-to-one assignment of a qmail address to a username. This format is

`=address:user:uid:gid:directory:dash:extension:`

Using this form, the mail administrator can directly map a qmail address to a particular user-name on the UNIX system. The `address` is the qmail mail address that will be used. `user`, `uid`, `gid`, and `directory` are the standard UNIX username, user ID, group ID, and home directory, respectively, that the address will be mapped to. The last two parameters, `dash` and `extension`, are used in combination to specify the `$HOME/.qmail` file that will be used to control the message delivery.

The second form used in the `assign` file is for wildcard address assignments. The format for this is

`+address:user:uid:gid:directory:dash:extension:`

Using this form, the mail administrator can use a wildcard format to map several possible mail usernames to a particular username on the UNIX system. The `address` in this form relates to the first part of an email address that matches the text `address`. Any other text following

Changing qmail Operational Parameters

CHAPTER 7

183

7

CHANGING QMAIL
OPERATIONAL
PARAMETERS

address will be ignored when matching. All of the other parameters used are the same as for the direct assignment.

The following is an example of the two types of entries in an `assign` file:

```
=postmaster:jessica:1001:1001:/home/jessica:::
+info-:jessica:1001:1001:/home/jessica:-::
```

In the first example, qmail will accept any message destined for the local user `postmaster`. Any messages received will be processed as if they were addressed to the system username `jessica`. The messages will be processed according to any processing instructions in Jessica's `/home/jessica/.qmail` file (described in detail in Chapter 8).

In the second example, qmail will accept any message destined for a local username that begins with the text `info-`. Again, the messages will be processed as if they were addressed to the system username `jessica`. Jessica can then include `.qmail` files to handle specific matches in her home directory. For instance, any messages sent to `info-dogs` will be processed by the instructions in the `/home/jessica/.qmail-dogs` file. As with the user alias files, the special file `.qmail-default` can be used as a catch-all to process any potential matches from the `assign` file.

The `assign` file is often used to map special usernames to system usernames. It has become a common practice on the Internet to use full names as email addresses. Unfortunately, it is not possible to create UNIX system names that match full usernames. This is where the `users` file could be used. Listing 7.6 shows a sample `assign` file that maps full usernames to system usernames.

LISTING 7.6   Sample qmail Assign File

```
=rich.blum:rich:1001:1001:/home/rich:::
=haley.snell:haley:1002:1002:/home/haley:::
=riley.mullen:riley:1003:1003:/home/riley:::
=matt.woenker:matt:1004:1004:/home/matt:::
=chris.woenker:chris:1005:1005:/home/chris:::
=frank.williams:frank:1006:1006:/home/frank:::
=melanie.williams:melanie:1007:1001:/home/melanie:::
```

As you can tell from Listing 7.6, mapping full usernames to system names is a simple but lengthy process.

If you are administering a mail server with thousands of users, manually creating the `assign` file for each user could become tedious. Fortunately, qmail helps make this chore more manageable. The next section describes a utility that helps create a basic qmail users `assign` file from the system `/etc/passwd` file.

qmail Admin Programs

The qmail qmail-pw2u utility can be used to automatically generate assign files for all system users contained in the /etc/passwd file. The command for doing this is

```
cat /etc/passwd | /var/qmail/bin/qmail-pw2u > /var/qmail/users/assign
```

The qmail-pw2u program will extract all of the non-root userids from the /etc/passwd file and create lines in the assign file for them. Listing 7.7 shows a sample assign file created from a standard FreeBSD /etc/passwd file.

LISTING 7.7   Sample qmail-pw2u–Generated File

```
=uucp:uucp:66:66:/var/spool/uucppublic:::
+uucp-:uucp:66:66:/var/spool/uucppublic:-::
+:alias:81:81:/var/qmail/alias:-::
=alias:alias:81:81:/var/qmail/alias:::
+alias-:alias:81:81:/var/qmail/alias:-::
=rich:rich:1001:1001:/home/rich:::
+rich-:rich:1001:1001:/home/rich:-::
=katie:katie:1002:1002:/home/katie:::
+katie-:katie:1002:1002:/home/katie:-::
=jessica:jessica:1003:1003:/home/jessica:::
+jessica-:jessica:1003:1003:/home/jessica:-::
.
```

Notice that qmail-pw2u creates two lines for each username in the /etc/passwd file. The first line is a direct assignment of the system username. The second line is a wildcard match of the assigned username with a dash. This creates the standard qmail username mapping that is used on the qmail system. Each system user can then create personal aliases using the user-alias format and then create $HOME/.qmail-alias files to control the processing of messages sent to those addresses. After the assign file has been generated by qmail-pw2u, the mail administrator can manually alter any fields, such as changing the original system username to the full username.

Note the third line in Listing 7.7. It is set to map any possible address to the qmail alias system username. The qmail-pw2u program includes this line to prevent any system user that is not listed in the assign table from receiving messages. Instead, any address not matching an entry in the assign table will instead be forwarded to the qmail aliases table. If no alias exists, the message will bounce.

Once the assign file has been generated and modified by the mail administrator, the qmail-newu program must be run to create the cdb database file. The cdb database file is used by qmail-lspawn to quickly recognize local usernames in the qmail users table.

> **CAUTION**
>
> By default qmail will automatically recognize system usernames as well as extensions of system usernames for aliases without the users database. The qmail users database is most useful for mapping special qmail names to system usernames.
>
> If you are using the `qmail-pw2u` program, remember that any time the `/etc/passwd` file changes, the `qmail-pw2u` and `qmail-newu` utilities should be run to update the `assign` and `cdb` database files. Otherwise, new system users will not be able to receive messages.

Besides the `assign` table, the `qmail-newu` program also recognizes a few other user tables. The `include` table is used to add to the `assign` file. The `exclude` table is used to skip users in the `/etc/passwd` file. The `mailnames` table is used to provide alternative mailnames to users, and the `append` table is used to include other usernames besides the `/etc/passwd` usernames.

Summary

There are many parts to configuring the qmail system. qmail differs from most MTA packages in that it uses several different configuration files rather than one large file. The qmail control files are located in the `/var/qmail/control` directory and control the basic behavior of the qmail system. Host and domain names that qmail will receive messages for must be configured in the proper control files before qmail will accept messages for them.

Virtual domains can be created on the qmail server, allowing an ISP to receive and spool messages destined for a remote mail server that may not be connected to the Internet all the time. The qmail system also uses mail aliases and special usernames that are configurable by the mail administrator. The qmail aliases can be found in the `/var/qmail/aliases` directory. Each alias is assigned a separate file. The alias file contains the true email address, usually that of a local system username. The qmail users system can also use a binary database to map qmail usernames to UNIX system usernames. This allows qmail to accept messages for alternate usernames and quickly map them to the proper UNIX system username.

Using qmail

IN THIS CHAPTER

Chapter 7, "Changing qmail Operational Parameters," described the configuration files used for qmail. Now that you have a basic understanding of the different configuration files, it is time to get the qmail server running using a simple configuration.

If you have been following along in the previous chapters, qmail should be installed and ready to run. The following can be used as a last-minute checklist to help you determine if all of the qmail pieces are installed and ready to go:

1. All of the qmail usernames and group names should be configured.

2. The /var/qmail directory should be created.

3. The qmail program files should be in /var/qmail/bin.

If all of the above steps have been accomplished, you are ready to test the qmail installation and use it as the MTA process for your mail server. This chapter describes basic qmail server setup and configuration. Later chapters will describe more detailed configurations for more specific qmail installations. There are several steps necessary to configure the qmail server. The basic steps involved in this process are

- Create the basic qmail control files
- Create necessary qmail aliases
- Determine the local mail delivery method
- Start and test qmail

After completing the steps involved in the installation, we must then set up the operational parameter files that enable us to process messages:

- Set up the qmail boot script file
- Change the MUA program interface
- Set up qmail SMTP capability
- Establish user configuration files

Create the Basic qmail Control Files

Chapter 7, "Changing qmail Operational Parameters," described the 28 different control files that qmail can use. Don't worry about having to set values for each and every one of them. There is only one control file that is absolutely necessary for qmail to operate. The me control file must be present for qmail to determine what hostname to accept mail for. Without it, qmail will refuse to start. For a basic qmail configuration, you can allow the other control files to use their default values. Many of the other control files obtain their default values from the me control file.

The me control file contains the fully qualified domain name for the local mail server. If your qmail server is connected to the Internet, you can use the config program located in the /var/qmail/configure directory to create the me control file automatically. You can run the config program by typing this command:

```
./config
```

The config program is located in the directory where you unpacked the qmail source code. If you installed qmail from a FreeBSD package, the config program will be located in the /var/qmail/configure directory.

The config program attempts to perform a DNS lookup on the hostname of the qmail server. If it is successful, it will create the me control file with the appropriate hostname information.

Unfortunately, many qmail servers do not have the luxury of being connected to the Internet when they are configured. If your qmail server is not connected to the Internet or you are not using a valid DNS name for your mail server, you must manually create the me control file using the following command:

```
echo hostname > /var/qmail/control/me
```

where *hostname* is the fully qualified host name of the qmail server. Remember that you must be logged in as the root user to perform this command. Also remember that permissions must be set to the 644 mode for all control files.

Although the me control file is all that is absolutely required, it is a good idea to create a couple of other control files. The `locals` and `rcpthosts` control files are also used to identify hosts for which qmail will accept messages. For this basic installation, you can just copy the me control file to both the `locals` and `rcpthosts` files.

> **CAUTION**
>
> If no `rcpthosts` control file is present, qmail will accept messages for any user, including users on remote hosts, and attempt to relay the message to the proper host. This feature has been exploited by Internet mass mail spammers and should be disabled. To disable open relaying, create a `rcpthosts` control file using the value of the me control file.

Create Necessary qmail Aliases

By default qmail will not accept mail messages destined for the `root` user. This is used as a security precaution, so that no malicious messages can be sent directly to the `root` user to cause security problems on the mail server.

8

USING QMAIL

Unfortunately, many UNIX systems send log reports to the root user account. If you need to receive messages for the root user, you must configure a qmail alias for that account. This can be done in one simple command:

```
echo user > /var/qmail/aliases/.qmail-root
```

where *user* is the username to which you want to forward any message sent to the root user. A good idea is to use the username of the system administrator. (Your system administrator does have his own account, doesn't he?)

Two other necessary mail aliases are postmaster and MAILER-DAEMON. These addresses are often used in mail message administration. Bounced messages are sent from the MAILER-DAEMON account, and sometimes an ill-informed user might respond to them. Also, the postmaster username has become commonly used as a point of contact for Web and FTP sites. These two aliases can be forwarded to the mail administrator's user account the same way as the root account was aliased. Remember to include the .qmail part of the alias file-name for each new alias account.

Determining the Local Mail Delivery Method

The qmail-lspawn program is responsible for forwarding messages destined for local mail users. One of the more confusing aspects of qmail is that there are three different methods that qmail can use to deliver messages destined for users on the local mail server. You must select and configure one of the following three methods for qmail to be able to deliver mail to local system users:

- The existing local mail method
- The $HOME/Mailbox method
- The $HOME/Maildir method

> **NOTE**
>
> qmail uses a startup script to start the qmail program. The startup script starts the qmail-lspawn and qmail-rspawn programs, as well as the qmail-send and qmail-clean programs. By default the startup script is located in the file /var/qmail/rc. The qmail software installation provides several templates that can be used for creating the qmail startup script. The rc script templates are located in the /var/qmail/boot directory. Only one script can be used for the system, and it is copied to the /var/qmail/rc file.

This section compares the three different local mail delivery methods and shows how to configure qmail to use each of them. The method that you choose to support your mail server may depend on several factors, both technical and political.

Use Existing Local Mail Method

Every UNIX implementation contains at least one program that can perform local mail delivery to users on the system. You can configure qmail to use the local mail delivery program to forward mail to users on the local mail system. Figure 8.1 demonstrates how this delivery system works.

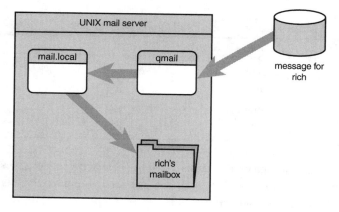

FIGURE 8.1

qmail using the local mail delivery program.

qmail uses the `preline` program to forward messages to the local mail delivery program. The `preline` program processes messages before sending them to the local mail delivery program. By default, `preline` adds From, Return-Path:, and Delivered-To: header fields to each message.

To complicate things further, there are three different local mail delivery programs that are in use on UNIX platforms. You must know the proper local mail delivery program that your UNIX system is using to select the right qmail startup script. The three programs are

- mail.local, which is used by BSD 4.4 UNIX systems such as FreeBSD.
- binmail (which uses a program called mail). There are two different versions of the binmail program—for both V7 and SRV4 systems. Linux systems use the V7 version of binmail.
- procmail, which can be installed as an option on both Linux and FreeBSD systems.

> **NOTE**
>
> The binmail program name is really a misnomer. The actual program used is called mail. It gets its name from its normal location—/bin/mail.

Although qmail can use any of these local mail programs, it uses a different script file to implement each. Once you determine the local mail delivery program your UNIX system uses, you can select the proper startup script. Table 8.1 shows the script files as they are related to the local mail delivery systems.

TABLE 8.1   qmail Script Files and Local Mail Delivery Programs

Script	Mail Delivery System
binm1	mail.local
binm2	SRV4 binmail
binm3	V7 binmail
proc	procmail

You may notice that each of the qmail scripts listed in Table 8.1 also has a version with a +df after it. These versions are for using the qmail dot-forward program, which is described in Chapter 14, "Migrating from Sendmail to qmail."

Listing 8.1 shows a sample startup script template used on a FreeBSD system.

LISTING 8.1   Sample qmail Startup Script for mail.local

```
#!/bin/sh

# Using splogger to send the log through syslog.
# Using binmail to deliver messages to /var/spool/mail/$USER by default.
# Using BSD 4.4 binmail interface: /usr/libexec/mail.local -r

exec env - PATH="/var/qmail/bin:$PATH" \
qmail-start \
'|preline -f /usr/libexec/mail.local -r "${SENDER:-MAILER-DAEMON}"
➥ -d "$USER"' \
splogger qmail&
```

The qmail startup script uses the qmail-start program to initialize the qmail core programs and to start the necessary background processes for qmail. The format of the qmail-start program is

```
qmail-start [ defaultdelivery [ logger arg ...  ] ]
```

As shown in Listing 8.1, the startup script used for the FreeBSD UNIX system uses the `preline` command with the `mail.local` mail delivery program as the `qmail-start` `defaultdelivery` parameter. The logger parameter is replaced with the qmail `splogger` program.

To use the `binm1` startup script, copy it to the `/var/qmail/rc` script file:

```
cp /var/qmail/boot/binm1 /var/qmail/rc
```

Use $HOME/Mailbox Method

The standard UNIX mail local delivery programs listed above all use a common system to store messages for users. All mail messages are stored in a common mail directory. The common mail directory is usually located in one of two places: `/var/spool/mail` or `/var/mail`.

Most Linux systems store mail in the `/var/spool/mail` directory, while FreeBSD systems use the `/var/mail` directory.

Each user has a separate file in the common mail directory that contains all of the messages sent to that user. The filename is the same as the username. Each user has access only to his own mail file within the mail directory. As new messages are received by the MTA for users, they are appended to the appropriate user's mail file in the mail directory.

There are a few problems that have been identified with the standard UNIX mailbox system. By placing all user mailboxes in a single directory, the mail system is vulnerable to both security and disk access speed problems. By creating a common mail directory that every user must have access to, the standard UNIX mailbox system opens a security can of worms. Because the mailbox must be user writeable, the mailbox directory must be writeable by everyone, a possible security problem. Programs that read mail must carefully check permissions to allow the owner of a mailbox access but refuse users trying to access mailboxes owned by other users.

With one mailbox file for every user, systems that support thousands of users have lots of mailbox files. This creates quite a large mailbox directory. It has been proven that large directories slow down disk access speeds. It is much better to have many directories with a few files than a few directories with a lot of files.

To solve the problems identified with the standard UNIX mailbox system, qmail uses two alternative mailbox systems. The first moves users' mailboxes to their home directories. Figure 8.2 demonstrates how this system works.

When user mailboxes are moved to their home directories, security and disk problems are remedied. Each user's mailbox is created as a file Mailbox in his home directory. While this solves some problems, it creates another.

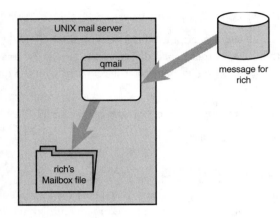

FIGURE 8.2

The qmail Mailbox mailbox format.

Most MUA software has been written to use the standard UNIX mailbox format. By moving users' mailboxes to their home directories, qmail creates a problem for MUA programs. MUA programs do not know that the mailboxes have been moved. To solve this problem, some qmail users have written patches for some of the more common MUA programs to allow them to access the new user mailboxes. Sometimes a mail user can change the MAIL environment variable to reflect the new location of his mailbox.

```
MAIL=$HOME/Mailbox ; export MAIL
```

Another solution is to create symbolic links to the new user mailboxes from where the standard UNIX mailboxes are normally located. This solution works for most of the common MUA programs and is easy to implement.

To ensure that no mail is lost in this process, the following steps should be performed with the mail MTA program disabled and with no users logged into the system:

1. As the root user, move each user mailbox found in the standard UNIX system mailbox area to the user's home directory, renaming it Mailbox:

   ```
   mv /var/mail/barbara /home/barbara/Mailbox
   ```

2. Create a link from the standard UNIX mailbox location to the new mailbox location:

   ```
   ln -s /home/barbara/Mailbox /var/mail/barbara
   ```

After performing these steps for each system user, you must create the qmail startup script that uses the qmail Mailbox format. The Mailbox template script is located at /var/qmail/boot/ home. Again, if you are using the qmail dot-forward program, you must use the home+df script. The proper startup script template must be copied to the /var/qmail/rc file. Listing 8.2 shows the qmail startup script used to support the qmail Mailbox method of storing messages.

LISTING 8.2   Sample qmail Startup Script for the Mailbox Format

```
#!/bin/sh

# Using splogger to send the log through syslog.
# Using qmail-local to deliver messages to ~/Mailbox by default.

exec env - PATH="/var/qmail/bin:$PATH" \
qmail-start ./Mailbox splogger qmail&
```

Again, the qmail startup script uses the `qmail-start` program to initialize and start the qmail core programs. This time the `defaultdelivery` parameter is set the value of `./Mailbox`. This value is passed to the `qmail-lspawn` program to set the default message delivery method for `qmail-local` to the Mailbox format.

Use `$HOME/Maildir` Method

The third mailbox system that qmail uses is the Maildir system. The Maildir system takes the qmail Mailbox one step further. Not only is each user's mailbox moved to his home directory, the standard UNIX mailbox format is changed.

One problem identified with the standard UNIX mailbox system is that it is highly vulnerable to data corruption. Because the mailbox contains all of the user's mail messages, corrupting the mailbox could have catastrophic results. The qmail Maildir system changes the method used for storing user messages. Much like other qmail files, user messages are stored as separate files within a specially formatted user mailbox directory. This ensures that even if one message becomes corrupt, the rest of the messages are safe within the mailbox directory. Figure 8.3 shows how the qmail Maildir format works. The qmail Maildir system is described in more detail in Chapter 9, "Using the Maildir Mailbox Format."

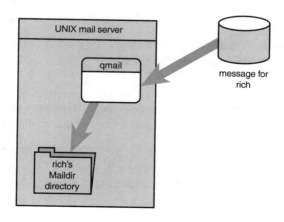

FIGURE 8.3
The qmail Maildir system.

If you decide to use the Maildir format, you must copy the appropriate startup script template to the `/var/qmail/rc` file. The Maildir startup script is located in the `/var/qmail/boot/maildir` file. Listing 8.3 shows the Maildir startup script.

LISTING 8.3   Sample qmail Startup Script for the Maildir Format

```
#!/bin/sh

# Using splogger to send the log through syslog.
# Using qmail-local to deliver messages to Maildir format by default

exec env - PATH="@PREFIX@/qmail/bin:$PATH" \
qmail-start ./Maildir/ splogger qmail &
```

As normal, the startup script uses the `qmail-start` program to initialize and run the qmail core programs.

> **NOTE**
>
> Be sure to include the trailing / on the `/Maildir/` parameter, or qmail will just create a Mailbox-type mailbox but use the filename `Maildir` instead. The trailing / is what triggers qmail to use the Maildir format.

Starting and Testing qmail

After the appropriate startup script is copied to the `/var/qmail/rc` file, you can test the qmail configuration. One nice feature of qmail is that if there is another MTA program currently running on the mail server, it does not need to be disabled to test qmail. You can continue to use the existing mail service to process messages while you test your qmail configuration.

First, you must start qmail. To start the qmail process, you must be logged in as the `root` user and run the qmail startup script using this command:

```
csh -cf '/var/qmail/rc &'
```

This command uses a new C shell to run the normal qmail startup script. The & tells the C shell to run the startup script in Background mode, thus returning the terminal to the shell prompt.

To determine if qmail started properly, you can look at the running processes on the mail server using the `ps` command. To see the qmail processes you must use the a option to display other users' processes. A sample output from the `ps` command is shown in Listing 8.4.

LISTING 8.4   Sample ps Command Output

```
1  shadrach# ps a
2    PID  TT  STAT      TIME COMMAND
3  25337  p0  Ss  0:00.14 -sh (sh)
4  25376  p0  S   0:00.12 -su (csh)
5  25380  p0  S   0:00.07 qmail-send
6  25381  p0  S   0:00.02 splogger qmail
7  25382  p0  S   0:00.01 qmail-lspawn |preline -f /usr/libexec/mail.local -r "
8  25383  p0  S   0:00.01 qmail-rspawn
9  25384  p0  S   0:00.01 qmail-clean
10 25385  p0  R+  0:00.00 ps -a
11 25260  v0  Is+0:00.03 /usr/libexec/getty Pc ttyv0
12 25195  v1  Is+0:00.03 /usr/libexec/getty Pc ttyv1
13   260  v2  Is+0:00.03 /usr/libexec/getty Pc ttyv2
14   261  v3  Is+0:00.03 /usr/libexec/getty Pc ttyv3
15   262  v4  Is+0:00.03 /usr/libexec/getty Pc ttyv4
16   263  v5  Is+0:00.03 /usr/libexec/getty Pc ttyv5
17   264  v6  Is+0:00.03 /usr/libexec/getty Pc ttyv6
18   265  v7  Is+0:00.03 /usr/libexec/getty Pc ttyv7
19 shadrach#
```

8

USING QMAIL

In Listing 8.4, line 1 shows the ps command using the a option to display the qmail processes. Lines 5 through 9 show the qmail processes that are started by the qmail-start process. Line 7 shows that the test qmail system is configured to use the mail.local program for local message delivery. This line should reflect the local message delivery method that you chose to implement. If not, make sure that you copied the proper template file from the /var/qmail/boot directory to the /var/qmail/rc file.

Another method to use to determine if qmail started properly is to check the qmail log file. Chapter 13, "qmail Server Administration," describes the format of the qmail log file. The qmail log file is located in the /var/log directory, and is called maillog. For now, if qmail starts properly, you should see a single entry such as this:

```
Mar 2 18:13:40 shadrach qmail: 952031620.674666 status: local 0/10 remote 0/20
```

This log file entry indicates that qmail is running successfully. The status indicates that qmail is configured to process up to 10 concurrent local mail deliveries and up to 20 concurrent remote mail deliveries. These numbers should reflect your particular qmail configuration.

Testing qmail Local Delivery

You can test qmail's mail delivery processes by sending a message directly to the qmail-inject program. The qmail-inject program was described in Chapter 2, "qmail Services."

Its job is to receive messages from MUA programs and place them in the qmail mail queue for processing. For now, we can bypass the MUA programs and send a message directly to the `qmail-inject` program as a test.

The `qmail-inject` program is expecting to receive a message in the proper RFC822 message format. It will parse the RFC822 header fields to determine the message recipients. To perform a test, all that needs to be done is to create a simple RFC822 formatted message and pipe it to the `qmail-inject` program.

First, create a text file with the following text:

```
To: user
From: user
Subject: This is a test message

This is a test message for qmail.
```

Replace the *user* parameter with your username. Next, you can pipe the test file to the `qmail-inject` program for delivery. Listing 8.5 shows this process.

LISTING 8.5   Sample Local qmail Delivery Test

```
1  $ cat test | /var/qmail/bin/qmail-inject
2  $
3  you have mail
4  $ mail
5  Mail version 8.1 6/6/93.  Type ? for help.
6  "/var/mail/rich": 1 message 1 new
7  >N  1 rich@shadrach.ispnet   Thu Mar 2 16:27  12/432 "This is a test messag"
8  &1
9  Message 1:
10 From rich@shadrach.ispnet1.net Thu Mar  2 16:27:56 2000
11 Date: 2 Mar 2000 21:27:56 -0000
12 To: rich@shadrach.ispnet1.net
13 From: rich@shadrach.ispnet1.net
14 Subject: This is a test message
15
16 This is a test message for qmail.
17
18 &d
19 &q
20 $
```

In Listing 8.5, line 1 shows the command that can be used to send the test message directly to the `qmail-inject` program. As the sample qmail installation is using the local mail delivery program, the system recognizes the new message in the user's mailbox and notifies the user of the new message in line 3. In line 4 the user uses the local `mail` program to display the message.

Testing qmail Remote Delivery

Next, you should test qmail's capability to send a message to a user on a remote mail system. This test requires that you know a mail address on a remote mail system. You can modify the test text message file to send the message to a remote email address:

```
To: katie@meshach.ispnet2.net
```

Again, the command used to send the test text message to the `qmail-inject` program is

```
cat test | /var/qmail/bin/qmail-inject
```

Listing 8.6 shows the result of the qmail remote delivery test performed on the sample mail system.

LISTING 8.6   Sample qmail Remote Delivery Test

```
FreeBSD 3.4-RELEASE (GENERIC) #0: Mon Dec 20 06:54:39 GMT 1999

Welcome to FreeBSD!

You have new mail.
$ mail
Mail version 8.1 6/6/93.  Type ? for help.
"/var/mail/katie": 1 message 1 new
>N  1 rich@shadrach.ispnet  Fri Mar 03 19:52   15/615   "This is a test message"
&1
Message 1:
From rich@shadrach.ispnet1.net Fri Mar 03 19:52:06 2000
Date: 3 Mar 2000 19:49:54 -0000
To: katie@meshach.ispnet2.net
From: rich@shadrach.ispnet1.net
Subject: This is a test message

This is a test message for qmail.

& d
& q
$
```

As can be seen in Listing 8.6, the message was successfully sent from the qmail test mail server to the remote mail server. The qmail remote delivery process worked.

Testing qmail Alias Username Delivery

After you have determined that the local and remote qmail delivery functions are operating properly, it is time to test some of qmail's more esoteric capabilities. The first test is to make sure that the qmail system alias files are configured properly. This can be done by sending the test message to a locally configured alias name.

First, change the To: line in the test message to a configured alias:

```
To: postmaster
```

Then, as before, send the test message to the `qmail-inject` program:

```
cat test | /var/qmail/bin/qmail-inject
```

After sending the message, the user name that the `postmaster` alias is pointing to should receive the message. Be careful though; if the alias points to your username, you must make sure you get the right message. If the attempt failed and the message bounced, you will also get a message, but it will be from `MAILER_DAEMON` indicating that the message bounced.

Testing qmail Bounced Messages Delivery

Speaking of bounced messages, it is a good idea to force a bounced message to test if that function works. The easiest way to do this is to send a message to a non-existent username. Change the test message To: line to

```
To: baduser
```

Then send the test message to the `qmail-inject` program as shown previously. Listing 8.7 shows the message that is returned.

LISTING 8.7   Sample qmail Bounced Message

```
1  $ cat test | /var/qmail/bin/qmail-inject
2  $
3  you have mail
4  $ mail
5  Mail version 8.1 6/6/93.  Type ? for help.
6  "/var/mail/rich": 1 message 1 new
7  >N  1 MAILER-DAEMON@shadra  Fri Mar  3 18:01   28/969    "failure notice"
8  &1
9  Message 1:
10 From MAILER-DAEMON Fri Mar  3 18:01:26 2000
11 Date: 3 Mar 2000 23:01:26 -0000
12 From: MAILER-DAEMON@shadrach.ispnet1.net
13 To: rich@shadrach.ispnet1.net
```

```
14 Subject: failure notice
15
16 Hi. This is the qmail-send program at shadrach.ispnet1.net.
17 I'm afraid I wasn't able to deliver your message to the following.
18 addresses. This is a permanent error; I've given up. Sorry it didn't
➥ work out.
19
20 <baduser@shadrach.ispnet1.net>:
21 Sorry, no mailbox here by that name. (#5.1.1)
22
23 --- Below this line is a copy of the message.
24
25 Return-Path: <rich@shadrach.ispnet1.net>
26 Received: (qmail 26335 invoked by uid 1001); 3 Mar 2000 23:01:25 -0000
27 Date: 3 Mar 2000 23:01:25 -0000
28 Message-ID: <20000303150125.26334.qmail@shadrach.ispnet1.net>
29 To: baduser@shadrach.ispnet1.net
30 From: rich@shadrach.ispnet1.net
31 Subject: This is a test message
32
33 This is a test message for qmail.
34
35 &
```

In Listing 8.7, lines 10 through 23 show the canned bounced mail message generated by qmail.
Line 21 specifically identifies the error message received by the host, defining why the message bounced. Besides the bounced message header, the original message is attached at the end
of the message.

Setting Up the qmail Boot Script File

Once you decide that the qmail configuration is working, you need to make sure that qmail
will start when the mail server is booted. Different UNIX systems use different methods of
starting programs at boot time. This section describes the steps necessary to ensure that qmail
will start on a Linux or FreeBSD system. Other UNIX systems should be able to use one of
the two different methods.

Starting qmail on FreeBSD Systems

As described in Chapter 3, "Server Requirements for qmail," the FreeBSD UNIX system uses
a single script file to load programs at boot time. The /etc/rc script file is run by the init
process when the system is booted. Within the /etc/rc script is the following section:

```
# for each valid dir in $local_startup, search for init scripts matching *.sh
if [ "X${local_startup}" != X"NO" ]; then
        echo -n 'Local package initialization:'
        for dir in ${local_startup}; do
                [ -d ${dir} ] && for script in ${dir}/*.sh; do
                        [ -x ${script} ] && \
                                (set -T ; trap 'exit 1' 2 ; ${script} start)
                done
        done
        echo .
fi
```

This section runs any scripts that are located in the directories pointed to by the variable `$local_startup`. This variable is defined in the `/etc/defaults/rc.conf` file. One of the directories defined is the `/usr/local/etc/rc.d` directory. This is where FreeBSD expects to find the qmail startup script. Also, notice in the `/etc/rc` script that FreeBSD expects that the scripts end with a `.sh` tag. The qmail startup script is not in this format, and something needs to be changed for it to work properly.

If you install qmail from the FreeBSD installation package or port, it automatically creates a link from the qmail startup script set at `/var/qmail/rc` to a file `/usr/local/etc/rc.d/qmail.sh`. This link allows FreeBSD to run the qmail normal startup script located at `/var/qmail/rc` without having to modify any of the FreeBSD `rc` files. This method is the easiest and cleanest way to do this, so we will copy it.

If you installed qmail from the source code download file, you must manually create this link. You can do this using this command:

```
ln -s /var/qmail/rc /usr/local/etc/rc.d/qmail.sh
```

Remember to be logged in as the `root` user to run this command. This should produce a linked file in the `/usr/local/etc/rc.d` directory that looks like the following:

```
lrwxr-xr-x  1 root  wheel  13 Jan 31 10:48 qmail.sh -> /var/qmail/rc
```

The next time the FreeBSD system is started, qmail should load automatically. Again, you can determine this by observing the running processes using the FreeBSD `ps` command, as described earlier in the "Testing Mail Delivery" section.

Starting qmail on Linux Systems

As described in Chapter 3, Linux systems use a slightly different method of starting programs at boot time. The Linux system uses a series of startup scripts that are located in the `/etc/rc.d` directory. Each init run level uses a different set of startup scripts, located in directories `/etc/rc.d/rcx.d`, where x is the run level. This allows Linux to start different programs according to the system's run level. The startup scripts located in the `rcx.d` directories are links to the actual scripts files located in a central script directory `/etc/rc.d/init.d`.

Under this scenario, you must create a new qmail startup script that follows the standard Linux startup script format. Listing 8.8 shows a sample of a qmail startup script for Linux.

LISTING 8.8   Sample Linux qmail Startup Script

```
#!/bin/sh

PATH=/var/qmail/bin
export PATH

#Check that qmail is loaded
[ -f /var/qmail/bin/qmail-start ] || exit 0

case "$1" in
  start)
        echo -n "Starting qmail..."
        daemon /var/qmail/rc

    stop)
        echo -n "Stopping qmail..."
        killall qmail-send

    restart)
        $0 stop
        $0 start

    *)
        echo -n "Usage: $0 {start|stop|restart}"
        exit 1
esac

exit 0
```

The startup script shown in Listing 8.8 can be placed in the `/etc/rc.d/init.d` directory as the file `qmail`. This file can then be linked into the appropriate `rc.d` subdirectories for the run levels at which qmail should be started:

```
ln -s /etc/rc.d/init.d/qmail /etc/rc.d/rc3.d/S81qmail
ln -s /etc/rc.d/init.d/qmail /etc/rc.d/rc5.d/S81qmail
```

The example places the qmail startup scripts in the run levels 3 and 5 directories and places them next to where the original `sendmail` startup scripts would normally load.

8

USING QMAIL

Changing the MUA Program Interface

As discussed in Chapter 6, "Installing qmail," the qmail program includes an executable file that replaces the standard `sendmail` program that almost all UNIX distributions use as the MTA interface. To use qmail as your mail server, you must replace the existing `sendmail` program with qmail's `sendmail` wrapper program.

The qmail `sendmail` wrapper program is just a frontend to the normal `qmail-inject` program. It is written to accept parameters similar to the standard `sendmail` program, so it is 100% compatible with MUA programs that are written to use `sendmail` as the MTA. The qmail `sendmail` program is located in the `/var/qmail/bin` directory.

The original `sendmail` program location depends on your UNIX distribution. You must replace all of the occurrences of the `sendmail` program that are appropriate for your UNIX distribution. The two most common locations are

```
/usr/lib/sendmail
/usr/sbin/sendmail
```

To replace the existing `sendmail` programs with qmail's sendmail wrapper program, you must first move the existing programs to a different filename (in case you ever want to remove qmail and go back to `sendmail`):

```
mv /usr/sbin/sendmail /usr/sbin/sendmail.org
```

> **NOTE**
>
> The original `sendmail` program uses the UNIX `setuid` bit to allow users to run the `sendmail` program as the `root` user. For security purposes, you might want to remove this from the `sendmail` program that you copied. You can use the chmod program to do this using the command
>
> ```
> chmod 0 /usr/sbin/sendmail.org
> ```

Once the original `sendmail` programs are moved, you can create a link from the original `sendmail` file location to the qmail sendmail wrapper program:

```
ln -s /var/qmail/bin/sendmail /usr/sbin/sendmail
```

To test the qmail `sendmail` wrapper program, you can use a common MUA program to send a mail message to a local user. The standard UNIX `mail` program would work just fine. Listing 8.9 shows an example of testing the qmail `sendmail` wrapper program.

LISTING 8.9   Sample qmail `sendmail` Wrapper Test

```
$ mail rich
Subject: Test message
This is a test message
.
EOT
$ mail
Mail version 8.1 6/6/93.  Type ? for help.
"/var/mail/rich": 1 message 1 new
>N  1 rich@shadrach.ispnet  Mon Mar  6 12:57   12/411    "Test message"
&1
Message 1:
From rich@shadrach.ispnet1.net Mon Mar  6 12:57:27 2000
Date: 6 Mar 2000 17:57:26 -0000
From: rich@shadrach.ispnet1.net
To: rich@shadrach.ispnet1.net
Subject: Test message

This is a test message

& d
& q
$
```

Setting Up qmail SMTP Capability

After creating the qmail startup script and replacing the UNIX `sendmail` program, you are almost done installing qmail. I said *almost* because there is still one more important piece of qmail that needs to be configured.

The standard qmail startup script runs the programs necessary to process mail messages that are placed in the qmail mail queue. The `sendmail` wrapper program allows local MUA programs to forward messages to the `qmail-inject` program to place them into the qmail mail queue. The only piece missing is the method used to accept mail messages from remote hosts to put in the mail queue.

As described in Chapter 2, the `qmail-smtpd` program is used to accept mail messages from remote mail hosts using the SMTP mail protocol. The following sections describe how to configure the `qmail-smtpd` program to accept SMTP connections from remote mail servers.

Using `qmail-smtpd`

Unlike the other qmail core programs, `qmail-smtpd` is not run as a background process. Instead, `qmail-smtpd` uses a background process that is already running.

The UNIX *inetd* process is a program that runs in background waiting for remote clients to request new IP connections with the mail server. Once a connection is established, inetd determines which application the connection is destined for and passes off the connection to the application. qmail-smtpd can be configured to be an inetd application. When the inetd program receives an SMTP connection request from a remote mail server, it can pass the new connection directly to the qmail-smtpd program.

To configure inetd to know about qmail-smtpd, you must add a line to the /etc/inetd.conf configuration file. The inetd.conf configuration file is divided by IP port names as described in the /etc/services file. The keyword used for the SMTP service is smtp (very clever). The line added to the /etc/inetd.conf file should look like this:

```
smtp    stream  tcp     nowait  qmaild  /var/qmail/bin/tcp-env tcp-env
➥ /var/qmail/bin/qmail-smtpd
```

Because qmail needs to know about the network connection that is passed to it by inetd, a helper program is used. The tcp-env program is a qmail utility that converts the network information received from the inetd program to UNIX environment variables. When the qmail-smtpd program runs, it can check the appropriate environment variables to obtain the network information about the remote mail client.

To allow inetd to recognize the new configuration, you must send it an HUP signal. This can be done by determining the inetd process ID (PID) and using the UNIX kill program with the -HUP command line option. First, to find the PID of the inetd program, you can use the ps command with the ax command-line option:

```
$ ps ax | grep inetd
  184  ??  Is     0:00.48 inetd -wW
```

As shown in this example, the PID for the inetd process would be 184. To restart the inetd process, you can issue this command:

```
kill -HUP 184
```

This forces the inetd process to reread the /etc/inetd.conf file, which should now pass any SMTP connections to the qmail-smtpd program. You can test this by Telneting to port 25 of the mail server, as shown in Listing 8.10.

LISTING 8.10   Sample SMTP Connection to the qmail Server

```
$ telnet localhost 25
Trying 127.0.0.1...
Connected to localhost.ispnet1.net.
Escape character is '^]'.
220 shadrach.ispnet1.net ESMTP
QUIT
```

```
221 shadrach.ispnet1.net
Connection closed by foreign host.
$
```

If the /etc/inetd.conf file is configured properly for qmail-smtpd, you should get the qmail smtpgreeting banner when you Telnet to the SMTP port. If there is no smtpgreeting control file, qmail defaults to the contents of the me control file (as shown in Listing 8.10). To exit the SMTP session, you can type **QUIT**.

Using the tcpwrapper Program

Using just the UNIX inetd program to pass SMTP network connections to the qmail-smtpd program works fine, but it has its limitations. The inetd program passes all connections that are destined for the SMTP IP port to qmail-smtpd. There is no capability to filter known trouble sites, nor is there a way to log incoming connection attempts into a log file.

To solve these problems, some users have made use of another UNIX network software package on top of inetd. The tcpwrapper program is used as a middleman between inetd and other network packages. It can accept a network connection from the inetd program and perform basic security checks and logging functions before forwarding the connection to the final destination program.

The tcpwrapper program is installed by default on Linux systems. On FreeBSD systems it is not loaded by default, but it can be installed using either the package or the port installation method. Once tcpwrapper is installed, you can modify the inetd configuration line for the SMTP port as follows:

```
smtp    stream  tcp     nowait  qmaild  /usr/local/libexec/tcpd
➥ /var/qmail/bin/tcp-env  /var/qmail/bin/qmail-smtpd
```

Remember that this statement needs to be on one line in the /etc/inetd.conf file. The actual tcpwrapper executable program is called tcpd. The above inetd configuration line passes the SMTP connection to the tcpd program, using the tcp-env program as a command-line parameter. After sending an HUP signal to the inetd process as described previously, the tcpwrapper program should be running as the middleman for qmail-smtpd.

The tcpd program utilizes a configuration file to allow filtering of incoming IP connections. The hosts.allow file is used to list IP addresses that are either specifically allowed or denied connectivity to the server for certain applications. Individual records in the hosts.allow file specify addresses to be allowed or denied. This can be used to block SMTP access to sites that are known to abuse the mail system (spammers).

On Linux systems the hosts.allow file is located in the /etc directory. For FreeBSD systems it is placed in the /usr/local/etc directory. The format of a record in the hosts.allow file is

8

USING QMAIL

```
daemon: address: operators shell commands
```

daemon is the filename of the network program called by `tcpd`. *address* is a list of IP addresses and domain names (including wildcards). The *operators* parameter specifies action operators for `tcpd`, such as `allow` and `deny`. Finally, additional *shell commands* can be entered on the command line to specify commands that are run when the connection is established.

Using tcpwrapper to Allow Selective Relaying

As a real-life example, tcpwrapper is used with qmail for allowing selective relaying. As mentioned previously, it is not a wise practice to allow open relaying on the mail server. Unfortunately, many sites require local users to forward outbound mail messages through the mail server to the Internet. The `tcpd` program can be used to allow only certain IP addresses the capability to relay messages through `qmail-smtpd`, while continuing to block any outside IP addresses (such as spammers).

The trick to this setup is the behavior of `qmail-smtpd`. By default, if a `rcpthosts` control file exists, `qmail-smtpd` refuses all mail relaying. However, there is a caveat to this rule. If the UNIX environment variable `RELAYCLIENT` exists, `qmail-smtpd` will ignore the rcpthosts control file and use the relay client specified in the environment variable.

The idea is to set the `RELAYCLIENT` environment variable to nothing for connections from local clients, tricking `qmail-smtpd` into sending the message to the intended recipient. However, if a connection is established from a remote host, the `RELAYCLIENT` environment variable is not set, and the `rcpthosts` control file applies, blocking any relay attempts.

The inetd program does not provide a method to set UNIX environment variables when a connection is established. However, the `tcpd` program does, so it can be used for this application. If all of the local mail clients that require relaying are on the same subnet, the `tcpd` configuration requires only one line in the `hosts.allow` file:

```
tcp-env: 192.168.: setenv = RELAYCLIENT
```

This configuration record specifies the tcp-env program (to which `tcpd` will pass the connection). Next it specifies the IP addresses that the record applies to. If all of the clients are on the same subnet, you can use your subnet wildcard address (`192.168.` in this example). If multiple subnets are required, you can enter each subnet on a separate `hosts.allow` record. Finally, a shell command is listed that sets the `RELAYCLIENT` environment variable using the `setenv` command but does not assign a value to it.

This configuration allows any host in the `192.168.` subnet to relay messages through the mail server but blocks attempts from a host on any other network from using the mail server as a mail relay.

User Configuration Files

Besides the system configuration files, qmail supports individual user configuration files. By default, a user does not need to have any special configuration files to receive mail messages from qmail. However, by specifying commands in the qmail user configuration file, the user can take advantage of various qmail utilities and features. A qmail user configuration file is identified by the filename .qmail and is located in the user's home directory. User-configurable alias names are identified by the filename .qmail-alias, where alias is the name of the user-defined alias. This section describes the user configuration file and the features that can be configured.

Format of the .qmail File

The .qmail file is most often used to forward incoming messages either to a qmail utility or to another email address. Each line in the .qmail file represents a single program or email address to process. The first character of the line identifies the type of action qmail must take with the message. Table 8.2 shows the available delivery options.

TABLE 8.2   qmail Delivery Options

Character	Delivery Option
#	Comment
		Send message to program
/ or .	Send message to user's mailbox
&	Forward message to address
alphanumeric	Forward message to address

Each of the delivery types listed in Table 8.2 can be used multiple times in the .qmail file. Often multiple delivery types are identified within the .qmail file (but still one per line).

The vertical bar (|) is used to forward a received message to another program for processing. Most often this is the qmail preline program which formats the message before passing it off to another program.

Using the / or . character allows the user to redirect incoming messages to a different mailbox than what was specified in the /var/qmail/rc file. This allows each individual user to deviate from the default local mail delivery method chosen by the mail administrator.

If the user wants to use the qmail Maildir mailbox format, he could include a line in his .qmail file, such as

./Mydir/

8

USING QMAIL

where *Mydir* is the name of the Maildir-formatted mailbox directory in the user's home directory. Notice the ending / character. This is important. Placing the / character at the end of the directory name tells qmail that this will be a Maildir-formatted mailbox. Chapter 9 describes the Maildir mailbox in more detail.

If the user wants to use the qmail Mailbox mailbox format, he could include a line in his .qmail file, such as

```
./Mailbox
```

where *Mailbox* is the name of the Mailbox-formatted mailbox file in the user's home directory. Again, it is important not to have a trailing / here, or qmail will think that it is a Maildir-formatted mailbox.

The & and alphanumeric characters define addresses to which qmail will attempt to forward the message. The address must be in proper domain name format. No spaces, comments, or <> symbols can be used. Remember that if the user wants to receive a copy of the message, he must include a command for his local mailbox as well as the list of email addresses.

User Alias Files

The last use for user .qmail files is for creating user-defined mail aliases. This is done by extending the .qmail filename with the name of the desired alias. The new .qmail file contains any mail forwarding commands that are necessary for the messages received with that alias name, just like the original .qmail file.

For example, if user chris wants to create a new mailing list called chris-football, he can create a .qmail file called

```
.qmail-football
```

in his home directory. Inside the .qmail-football file, Chris can place the list of all of the email addresses that should be part of the mailing list. Each recipient will receive a copy of any message sent to the chris-football mail name.

Summary

This chapter describes how to run a basic qmail server. The minimum control file necessary for qmail to start is the me control file. It is good practice to also include locals and rcpthosts control files. After setting up the control file, you must select the qmail startup script. There is a wealth of startup script templates available in the /var/qmail/boot directory. The startup script used depends on the type of local mail delivery you want. qmail can use the standard UNIX local mail delivery system and is also capable of using its own two mailbox formats instead. qmail provides for a new Mailbox format that moves user mailboxes to their home directories. Also, qmail provides another mailbox system called Maildir, which stores mail messages using a method that is less prone to message corruption than the standard UNIX mailbox method.

Once the startup script is determined, qmail can be started and tested. Several different methods of testing qmail's mailing capabilities were described. You can test qmail by sending a message to the `qmail-inject` program without disabling the existing mail system on the UNIX server.

After the qmail system is tested you can set up qmail's remote message capability. The `qmail-smtpd` program is used to receive messages from remote mail hosts using the SMTP protocol. After the qmail system is set up and running, individual qmail users can configure their own `.qmail` configuration files to personalize their mail delivery and create personal aliases that can be used by remote users.

8

USING QMAIL

Using the Maildir Mailbox Format

IN THIS CHAPTER

The previous chapter described how to start a basic qmail mail server. When configuring the qmail server, one of the options available to the mail administrator is how to store messages for local users. Of the three methods available, the most unique and possibly the most confusing is the Maildir method. This chapter describes the qmail Maildir mailbox format in more detail and demonstrates how to use it on a production mail server.

Standard UNIX Mailboxes

UNIX systems have been using email for a long time. All UNIX systems include a local mail delivery program to deliver simple text messages between users on the local server. The first local mail delivery program was called *binmail*—because of its normal location on the system at /bin/mail. BSD UNIX systems use a similar program called *mail.local* (not too imaginative either).

The binmail and mail.local programs use a specific format for storing messages destined for local users on the mail server. Over the years there has been much discussion and research on the reliability and efficiency of this mailbox format.

The purpose of the qmail Maildir mailbox format is to provide a reliable and efficient replacement for the standard UNIX mailbox format. To understand why the Maildir format was created, it is best to first understand the original UNIX mailbox format and its pitfalls. This section describes the standard UNIX mailbox format.

Local Message Storage

The first UNIX mail messaging systems required a method to store messages for users. It was decided that the simplest method was to have a common mail directory with individual user files that for the messages destined for each local user. Figure 9.1 illustrates this method.

Mailbox Message Format

Within the user's mail file, messages are saved according to a strict format. The start of each message needs to be identified, so a message header line was created. The message header line uses this format:

```
From sender date
```

where *sender* is the complete email address of the sender of the message and *date* is the complete date the message was received in the UNIX ctime() format (the same format used by the UNIX date command).

After the message header line, the complete text of the message is stored. The message would be in RFC822 format (see Chapter 5, "SMTP and qmail"). A blank line is inserted at the end of the normal message text. A blank line followed by a From header line signifies the start of another message in the mailbox. Thus, new messages are appended to previous messages in the mailbox.

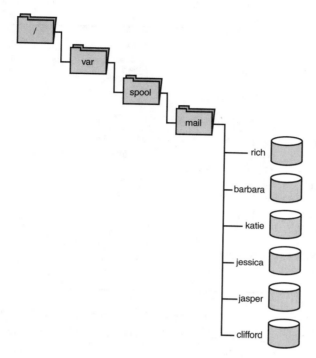

FIGURE 9.1
The standard UNIX mailbox layout.

It is the responsibility of the local mail delivery program to create the From message header line before inserting the message in the mailbox. It is important to remember that the message header line From statement does not use a colon after the word *From*. This is to differentiate it from the normal RFC822 mail FROM: header field in the message. Listing 9.1 shows an example of a sample user mailbox containing two messages.

LISTING 9.1   A Sample UNIX User Mailbox

```
$ cat rich
From rich  Fri Mar 10 17:15:08 2000
Return-Path: <rich>
Received: (from rich@localhost)
        by shadrach.ispnet1.net (8.8.7/8.8.7) id RAA07208
        for rich; Fri, 10 Mar 2000 17:15:07 -0500
Date: Fri, 10 Mar 2000 17:15:07 -0500
From: rich@shadrach.ispnet1.net
Message-Id: <200003102215.RAA07208@shadrach.ispnet1.net>
To: rich@shadrach.ispnet1.net
```

LISTING 9.1   Continued

```
Subject: Test message 1

This is the first test message.

From rich  Fri Mar 10 17:15:20 2000
Return-Path: <rich>
Received: (from rich@localhost)
        by shadrach.ispnet1.net (8.8.7/8.8.7) id RAA07213
        for rich; Fri, 10 Mar 2000 17:15:20 -0500
Date: Fri, 10 Mar 2000 17:15:20 -0500
From: rich@shadrach.ispnet1.net
Message-Id: <200003102215.RAA07213@shadrach.ispnet1.net>
To: rich@shadrach.ispnet1.net
Subject: Test message 2

This is the second test message.

$
```

As shown in Listing 9.1, each message is identified by a separate From line identifying the sender and date of the message. The full RFC822 header and body of the message are stored in the mailbox file after the message header line.

Problems with the Standard UNIX Mailbox Format

There has been much research and debate on the standard UNIX mailbox format. It has been shown that for mail servers with lots (thousands) of users, disk access speeds begin to deteriorate as it takes longer for the UNIX operating system to access files within a directory with lots of other files.

Along with disk access speeds, the reliability of the standard UNIX mailbox format has been questioned. By using a system in which new messages are appended to a file containing old messages, errors could have catastrophic effects.

If the mail server crashes while a message is being written to a user mailbox, the entire mailbox is at risk of becoming corrupted. If the local mail delivery program fails to create the From header line properly, the message will not be recognized as a new message by MUA programs and will instead be read as part of the preceding message. This not only corrupts the new message, it also corrupts the previous message. If a fatal error occurs when a message is being written to a user's mailbox, the entire mailbox file could be at risk of corruption, thus losing all of the user's messages.

Local Message Retrieval

Using the standard UNIX mailbox format requires Mail User Agent (MUA) programs to also use a standard method to extract messages from the mailbox. Any MUA program that is required to display messages from the user mailbox must be able to interpret the standard UNIX mailbox format to differentiate messages stored for the user.

If the MUA program displays a list of all the messages along with their Subject: header fields, it must read the entire mailbox contents when it starts up. Figure 9.2 demonstrates an MUA program reading messages contained in a user's mailbox.

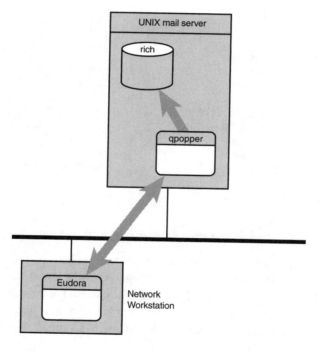

FIGURE 9.2

Using an MUA program to read mail messages.

Listing 9.2 shows a sample output from the standard UNIX mail program reading the mailbox messages shown in Listing 9.1.

9

USING THE MAILDIR MAILBOX FORMAT

LISTING 9.2   A Sample Mail Program Output

```
$ mail
Mail version 8.1 6/6/93.  Type ? for help.
"/var/spool/mail/rich": 2 messages 2 new
>N  1 rich@shadrach.ispnet   Fri Mar 10 17:15   13/385   "Test message 1"
 N  2 rich@shadrach.ispnet   Fri Mar 10 17:15   13/386   "Test message 2"
& 1
Message 1:
From rich  Fri Mar 10 17:15:08 2000
Date: Fri, 10 Mar 2000 17:15:07 -0500
From: rich@shadrach.ispnet1.net
To: rich@shadrach.ispnet1.net
Subject: Test message 1

This is the first test message.

& 2
Message 2:
From rich  Fri Mar 10 17:15:20 2000
Date: Fri, 10 Mar 2000 17:15:20 -0500
From: rich@shadrach.ispnet1.net
To: rich@shadrach.ispnet1.net
Subject: Test message 2

This is the second test message.

&
```

As can be seen in the first part of Listing 9.2, the mail program lists the messages and the beginning of the Subject: header field for each message. After the messages are listed, the user is presented with a command-line prompt from which he can list the messages individually. Notice how the first line of each message contains the mailbox header line. It has become a part of the message, even though the sender or the sending MTA program did not generate it.

Another disadvantage of the UNIX mailbox format is that if a user is using an MUA program to read messages at the same time the local mail delivery program is storing new messages, file access could possibly become an issue. This might prevent new messages from being written or, worse, corrupt the entire mailbox file.

The Maildir Mailbox Format

To compensate for the possible problems with the standard UNIX mailbox format, Dan Bernstein, the creator of qmail, designed a new mailbox system that could be more reliable.

The new mailbox system stores messages individually in a separate mailbox directory for each user. This solves the file access, disk access speed, and incomplete message problems possible with standard UNIX mailboxes.

Normally each user's mailbox directory is located in his home directory to simplify security issues. Figure 9.3 demonstrates the normal Maildir directory format.

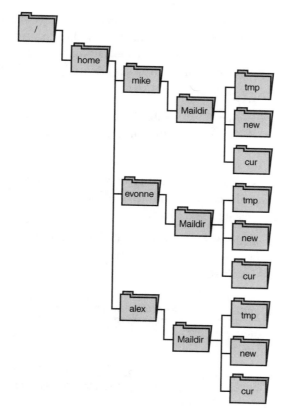

FIGURE 9.3

The qmail Maildir mailbox format.

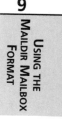

As can be seen in Figure 9.3, the Maildir mailbox is a directory divided into three separate subdirectories—tmp, new, and cur. Each message is stored as a separate file within one of the three Maildir subdirectories.

The qmail-local local mail delivery program can be configured to store messages using the Maildir mailbox format. As discussed in Chapter 2, "qmail Services," the qmail-local program is called by the qmail-lspawn program when a message is determined to be destined for a user on the local mail system. By specifying the mailbox type for the `qmail-lspawn` program, you can control the mailbox delivery method used by `qmail-local`.

The following sections describe storing and retrieving messages from a Maildir mailbox.

Local Message Storage

Unlike the standard UNIX mailbox message storage method, Maildir uses a complicated system to ensure that any messages received by qmail are created properly and stored in the Maildir mail directory. The three subdirectories in the Maildir directory are used to manipulate the messages so that qmail knows exactly what state the messages are in. The following sections describe the Maildir directories and how messages are manipulated in them.

The Maildir new Directory

The new directory is used for storing messages that have not been read by the user. Each message stored in this directory is given a unique filename, using this naming convention:

`time.pid.host`

where *time* is the number of seconds since 00:00 January 1, 1970, *pid* is the process ID of the receiving program, and *host* is the complete hostname of the receiving mail server. This ensures a unique filename for each message received.

Messages stored in the new subdirectory are stored in the same format in which they were received by qmail. No additional header lines are added to the message. Listing 9.3 demonstrates a sample user's new Maildir subdirectory.

LISTING 9.3   A Sample Maildir new Subdirectory and Messages

```
$ cd /home/rich/Maildir/new
$ ls -l
total 2
-rw-------  1 rich  rich  347 Mar 15 09:32 953130728.64111.meshach.ispnet1.net
-rw-------  1 rich  rich  348 Mar 15 09:32 953130741.64117.meshach.ispnet1.net
$ cat 953130728.64111.meshach.ispnet1.net
Return-Path: <rich@meshach.ispnet1.net>
Delivered-To: rich@meshach.ispnet1.net
Received: (qmail 64108 invoked by uid 1001); 15 Mar 2000 14:32:07 -0000
Date: 15 Mar 2000 14:32:07 -0000
Message-ID: <20000315143207.64107.qmail@meshach.ispnet1.net>
From: rich@meshach.ispnet1.net
To: rich@meshach.ispnet1.net
Subject: Test message 1

This is the first test message.
$
```

As can be seen in Listing 9.3, there are two messages in this user's new mailbox. Each message is shown as a separate file, each with a unique filename based on the `time` and `pid` numbers. By using the UNIX `cat` command, you can display the message that is contained in the message file. As also can be seen in Listing 9.3, the message is stored in standard RFC822 format, complete with the message header and body. No additional header fields or lines have been added by qmail to store the message.

The Maildir `cur` directory

The `cur` directory is used for storing messages that have been read using some type of MUA program. Once the user has read the message, it is moved to the `cur` directory using a new filename. The format of the new filename is

```
time.pid.host:info
```

The *time*, *pid*, and *host* parameters are the same as those used for the message in the new directory. The additional *info* parameter is used to help identify the status of the message for MUA programs.

The *info* parameter consists of flags that are used by most mail readers. Each flag identifies the status of the message. The flag consists of two parts, each part separated by a comma. The first part is a number, which identifies the type of flags used:

- 1 for experimental message flags
- 2 for standard message flags

For the purposes of a production qmail server, the standard flags should always be used.

Table 9.1 shows the possible flags that can be used for standard messages stored in the `cur` directory.

TABLE 9.1   Standard Message Flags Used for `info`

Flag	Description
R	Replied
S	Seen
F	User-defined flag

Each message can have any number of flags set, including none. Multiple flags should be listed in alphabetical order. Listing 9.4 shows an example of a `cur` directory with multiple messages.

LISTING 9.4   Sample Maildir/cur Subdirectory

```
$ cd /home/rich/Maildir/cur
$ ls -l
total 2
-rw-------  1 rich  rich  347 Mar 15 09:32 953130728.64111.meshach.dfas.mil:2,
-rw-------  1 rich  rich  348 Mar 15 09:32 953130741.64117.meshach.dfas.mil:2,
$ cat 953130728.64111.meshach.dfas.mil:2,
Return-Path: <rich@meshach.dfas.mil>
Delivered-To: rich@meshach.dfas.mil
Received: (qmail 64108 invoked by uid 1001); 15 Mar 2000 14:32:07 -0000
Date: 15 Mar 2000 14:32:07 -0000
Message-ID: <20000315143207.64107.qmail@meshach.dfas.mil>
From: rich@meshach.dfas.mil
To: rich@meshach.dfas.mil
Subject: Test message 1

This is the first test message.
$
```

As can be seen in Listing 9.4, there are two messages stored in this user's mailbox. They are both identified as being read, and they are now located in the cur directory. As seen from the UNIX ls command, both messages retain the same filenames as when they were in the new subdirectory (as shown previously, in Listing 9.3) except for the additional info section. Both messages are tagged as being type 2 messages (as expected), with no additional mail flags set. This may seem surprising; we would expect at least the S flag to be set, since the message has been seen. It is the responsibility of the MUA program to set the message flags properly. These messages were read from an MUA program that uses the Post Office Protocol (discussed later). This protocol was designed to be simple and does not accommodate message flag setting.

The Maildir tmp Directory

The tmp directory is used for creating new messages in the user's mailbox. Its use is similar to the pid directory used in the qmail mail queue directory (described in Chapter 2). qmail uses the tmp directory to create the initial file that holds the incoming new message to ensure that the message is safely written.

When qmail receives a message destined for a local user, the qmail-local program follows six steps to safely store the message in the user's mailbox. These steps are

1. Change to the user's Maildir directory.

2. Use the UNIX stat() command to determine if the file tmp/time.pid.host exists.

3. If the filename exists, wait two seconds and try again using the updated time parameter. After a set number of attempts, qmail-local gives up and returns an error.

4. The file `tmp/time.pid.host` is created.

5. The message received is written to the newly created file.

6. The file is linked to the file `new/time.pid.host`. This links the message to a file in the new directory with the same filename. Before the `tmp` file is created, a 24-hour timer is set. If the timer expires, if `qmail-local` returns an error, or if there is a successful link, the `tmp/time.pid.host` file is deleted.

These six steps ensure that each message is written safely to the user's Maildir directory.

Local Message Retrieval

Since the Maildir method uses a special format to store messages, any MUA or MDA programs that need to retrieve messages from the Maildir directory must understand the Maildir message format. Unfortunately, there is a limited number of MUA and MDA programs available that can read messages stored in the Maildir format.

The Maildir message reader must be able to distinguish between messages in the new directory and messages in the cur directory. Any message read from the new directory must be transferred to the cur directory. Also, as mentioned in the previous section, when the message is transferred, its name must also be appended with the status flags for the message.

The messages stored will be in the same format as the original RFC822-formatted message. No additional text will be present. Listing 9.5 shows a sample POP3 session that reads a message from a Maildir-formatted mailbox.

LISTING 9.5   A Sample Message from a Maildir Mailbox

```
1  $ telnet localhost 110
2  Trying 127.0.0.1...
3  Connected to localhost.
4  Escape character is '^]'.
5  +OK <64454.953155453@meshach.ispnet1.net>
6  USER rich
7  +OK
8  PASS guitar
9  +OK
10 LIST
11 +OK
12 1 347
13 2 348
14 .
15 RETR 1
16 +OK
17 Return-Path: <rich@meshach.ispnet1.net>
```

LISTING 9.5   Continued

```
18 Delivered-To: rich@ispnet1.net
19 Received: (qmail 64108 invoked by uid 1001); 15 Mar 2000 14:32:07 -0000
20 Date: 15 Mar 2000 14:32:07 -0000
21 Message-ID: <20000315143207.64107.qmail@meshach.ispnet1.net>
22 From: rich@meshach.ispnet1.net
23 To: rich@meshach.ispnet1.net
24 Subject: Test message 1
25
26 This is the first test message.
27
28 .
29 QUIT
30 +OK
31 Connection closed by foreign host.
32 $
```

In Listing 9.5, line 1 shows an example of how to use the Telnet program to manually connect to the POP3 server software running on the local mail server. Line 5 shows the greeting banner displayed by the POP3 server. In lines 6 through 9, the user is authenticated using a plain text username and password. Line 10 shows the POP3 command used to list all the messages that are in the user's mailbox. Lines 12 through 14 are the response from the server. There are two messages that are in the user's mailbox. In line 15 the user requests the first message. The message is then displayed in lines 17 through 28. Notice that this differs from the message that was stored in the standard UNIX mailbox shown in Listing 9.2. The standard From header line is not inserted into the message by the local mail program.

Besides reading messages in the new and cur directories, the MDA is also expected to scan the contents of the tmp directory. Any message left in the tmp directory over 36 hours is considered a delivery failure and should be deleted by the MDA program.

qmail Maildir Utilities

The Maildir mailbox format requires special software to read and write messages, and qmail includes utilities to help the mail administrator deal with new mailboxes. The following sections describe the qmail utilities that can be used to administer a mail server that utilizes the Maildir mailbox format.

maildirmake

To start off, any user that will use the Maildir mailbox format must have a properly configured Maildir mailbox. Usually each user's Maildir mailbox is located in his home directory. If the qmail system is configured for all users to use the Maildir mailbox format, then each user's

Maildir mailbox must be named the same as the Maildir mailbox configured in the `/var/qmail/rc` script file. Most often this directory is called `Maildir`.

To create a Maildir mailbox, either the user or the mail administrator must run the qmail `maildirmake` command. The `maildirmake` command does what it says—it creates a new Maildir formatted mailbox for the user. The format for the `maildirmake` command is

```
maildirmake directory
```

The *directory* parameter defines the location of the new Maildir mailbox. If you are creating a user's mailbox, be sure that you change the owner of the `Maildir`, `new`, `cur`, and `tmp` directories to the appropriate username, or the user will not be able to receive his messages.

maildir2mbox

The `maildir2mbox` command is used for converting Maildir mailboxes back to the standard UNIX mailbox format. The `maildir2mbox` command requires three environment variables to be set before it will convert the mailbox. Table 9.2 lists the UNIX environment variables required.

TABLE 9.2   `maildir2mbox` Environment Variables

Variable	Description
MAILDIR	Location of the user's Maildir mailbox.
MAIL	Location of the user's standard UNIX mailbox.
MAILTMP	Location of a temporary file to which the user has write access.

Each of the UNIX environment variables must be set for the `maildir2mbox` program to work properly. When the `maildir2mbox` program begins transferring messages, the mailbox pointed to by the `MAIL` environment variable will be locked, so no messages can be received while Maildir messages are being converted. Also, a message in the Maildir mailbox will not be removed until `maildir2mbox` knows that it has successfully written the entire message to the new mailbox file. Listing 9.6 shows an example of using the `maildir2mbox` command to convert an existing Maildir-formatted mailbox.

LISTING 9.6   A Sample `maildir2mbox` Session

```
1  $ MAILDIR=/home/jessica/Maildir ; export MAILDIR
2  $ MAIL=/home/jessica/mbox ; export MAIL
3  $ MAILTMP=/home/jessica/tmp ; export MAILTMP
4  $ /var/qmail/bin/maildir2mbox
5  you have mail
```

9

USING THE
MAILDIR MAILBOX
FORMAT

LISTING 9.6 Continued

```
6  $ mail
7  Mail version 8.1 6/6/93.  Type ? for help.
8  "/home/jessica/mbox": 2 messages 2 new
9  >N 1 jessica@shadrach.isp  Wed Mar 15 22:05  12/438    "Test message 1"
10  N 2 jessica@shadrach.isp  Wed Mar 15 22:05  12/439    "Test message 2"
11 & q
12 Held 2 messages in /home/jessica/mbox
13 you have mail
14 $ cat mbox
15 From jessica@shadrach.ispnet1.net Wed Mar 15 22:05:45 2000
16 Return-Path: <jessica@shadrach.ispnet1.net>
17 Delivered-To: jessica@shadrach.ispnet1.net
18 Received: (qmail 45141 invoked by uid 1003); 15 Mar 2000 22:05:44 -0000
19 Date: 15 Mar 2000 22:05:44 -0000
20 Message-ID: <20000315220544.45140.qmail@shadrach.ispnet1.net>
21 From: jessica@shadrach.ispnet1.net
22 To: jessica@shadrach.ispnet1.net
23 Subject: Test message 1
24 Status: O
25
26 This is the first test message
27
28 From jessica@shadrach.ispnet1.net Wed Mar 15 22:05:56 2000
29 Return-Path: <jessica@shadrach.ispnet1.net>
30 Delivered-To: jessica@shadrach.ispnet1.net
31 Received: (qmail 45147 invoked by uid 1003); 15 Mar 2000 22:05:56 -0000
32 Date: 15 Mar 2000 22:05:56 -0000
33 Message-ID: <20000315220556.45146.qmail@shadrach.ispnet1.net>
34 From: jessica@shadrach.ispnet1.net
35 To: jessica@shadrach.ispnet1.net
36 Subject: Test message 2
37 Status: O
38
39 This is the second test message
40
41 $
```

In Listing 9.6, lines 1 through 3 demonstrate setting the necessary UNIX environment variables for the three maildir2mbox variables. It is best to set the MAIL environment variable to the user's local mbox file rather than the system /var/mail/jessica file to avoid file-locking problems with the running MTA program. Most MUA programs will recognize this file as an alternative mailbox location (as shown in line 8). This is evident by the message displayed in line 5 after the mailbox was created. You can use the UNIX mail command to verify that the messages were moved to the user's standard UNIX mailbox. Alternatively, you can list the contents of the new mailbox as shown in line 14 and displayed in lines 15 through 40. As you can see, both messages were properly converted to the standard UNIX mailbox format, complete with the additional From message header line added.

maildirwatch

When the user decides to use a Maildir-formatted mailbox, the standard UNIX mail notification method as shown in line 5 in Listing 9.6 will no longer work. To compensate for this, qmail includes the `maildirwatch` utility.

The `maildirwatch` utility is intended to run on a separate console window. When run, `maildirwatch` clears the terminal screen and waits for new messages to be received. As new messages are sent to the user's Maildir mailbox, the `maildirwatch` program displays a short synopsis of the message that has been received. Figure 9.4 shows an example of the `maildirwatch` program running in a separate Telnet window using the VT-100 emulation protocol.

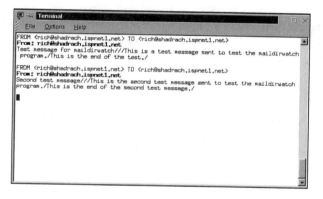

FIGURE 9.4
A sample `maildirwatch` *session display.*

As can be seen in Figure 9.4, the `maildirwatch` program displays a short synopsis of each incoming message, including the date, sender, Subject: field, and the first part of the message body.

Using Maildir Mailboxes

If you decide to utilize the Maildir mailbox format, you must configure qmail to deliver messages to the new mailboxes properly. There are two methods to do this.

If you just want to test out the new Maildir mailbox format, you can configure the qmail system to use normal UNIX mailboxes, but configure individual users to use the Maildir mailboxes. If you are feeling confident about the Maildir system, you can configure the entire qmail system to use the Maildir mailboxes by default. The following sections describe how to configure qmail for these two scenarios.

Individual Users

If you want to test using the Maildir mailbox format, you can configure individual users to use Maildir mailboxes while keeping the standard UNIX mailboxes for everyone else on the mail server. This is done using the standard `.qmail` file, located in the user's home directory.

To enable the Maildir mailbox format for a user, in his `.qmail` file, enter

```
./Maildir/
```

where *Maildir* is the name of the `Maildir` directory in his home directory. Remember to create the `Maildir` directory using the qmail `maildirmake` program described earlier.

When qmail prepares to deliver a message to a local user, it scans the user's `.qmail` file. If there is a line that begins with either a period (.) or a forward slash (/), qmail assumes that it points to an alternative mailbox. If the line ends with a forward slash, it assumes that the alternative mailbox will use the Maildir format.

System-Wide

If you decide that you want to deploy the qmail Maildir mailbox format for all your mail users, you can create a qmail startup script that includes the `./Maildir/` parameter for the `qmail-lspawn` command. In the qmail source code distribution, the `/var/qmail/boot/maildir` script file is included to accomplish this. This script file includes these lines:

```
exec env - PATH="@PREFIX@/qmail/bin:$PATH" \
qmail-start ./Maildir/ splogger qmail &
```

You can copy the `maildir` startup script template to the qmail `rc` file with the following command:

```
cp /var/qmail/boot/maildir /var/qmail/rc
```

If qmail is running on the system, you must stop and restart it. If your particular UNIX distribution does not support start and stop scripts, you can use the commands

```
killall qmail-send
csh -cf '/var/qmail/rc &'
```

These commands stop the currently running qmail programs and restart qmail using the new `rc` startup script.

Again, remember that all users must have Maildir mailboxes in their home directories. Once qmail has been restarted, it should deliver new messages to the users' Maildir mailboxes.

Using an MUA Program to Read Maildir Mailboxes

As mentioned previously, if you decide to use the qmail Maildir mailbox format, you must also ensure that the MUA program your users are using has the capability to read Maildir-formatted mailboxes. Several qmail users have modified popular MUA programs to recognize Maildir mailboxes. Dan Bernstein has included one MUA program with the qmail distribution. That is the qmail-pop3d program. The qmail-pop3d program is a POP3 server that allows remote network clients to use popular MUA programs to connect to the qmail mail server to read their mailboxes. This section describes the software required to run the qmail-pop3d program, as well as how to use the qmail-pop3d program as a POP3 server.

The `qmail-pop3d` Program

The qmail-pop3d program is the POP3 server software that allows remote clients to read messages in their Maildir-formatted mailboxes. Other programs are required to establish the network connection and authenticate the remote client. There are three phases to initiating a POP3 connection. Figure 9.5 demonstrates the connection phases for a POP3 client.

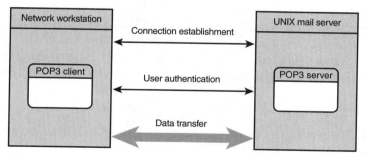

FIGURE 9.5

The three phases of a POP3 connection.

As shown in Figure 9.5, the three phases are

1. Establish the network connection
2. Authenticate the remote client
3. Communicate with the remote client using the POP3 protocol

Each of these phases is handled by a different software package on the mail server. Each software program is responsible for passing to the next phase the POP3 connections that successfully complete the phase. The following sections describe the three phases of the POP3 server in detail.

Establishing the Network Connection

The qmail software package includes a separate program that is used to establish the POP3 connection with remote clients. The qmail-popup program accepts POP3 connection attempts from the UNIX inetd program. The format of the qmail-popup command is

```
qmail-popup hostname program
```

The *hostname* parameter is used to identify the hostname of the local mail server. The *program* parameter is used to identify the program to which qmail-popup passes the POP3 connection after it is established.

The qmail-popup program does not run continuously as a background process. Instead, it relies on the UNIX inetd program to pass POP3 connection attempts to it. For this method to work, the inetd configuration file must be configured to recognize POP3 connections. The pertinent line in the /etc/inetd.conf file should look similar to the following:

```
pop3    stream  tcp     nowait  root    /var/qmail/bin/qmail-popup
➥ qmail-popup meshach.ispnet1.net /usr/local/bin/checkpassword
➥ /var/qmail/bin/qmail-pop3d Maildir
```

The above statement should appear as a single line in the /etc/inetd.conf configuration file. This line indicates that if the inetd program receives a POP3 connection attempt, it should pass the request to the qmail-popup program along with the local hostname and the program that will process successful POP3 connections. The program that is passed is the checkpassword program and its parameters, which is discussed in the following section. After inserting the POP3 line in the /etc/inetd.conf file, you should send a SIGHUP signal to the inetd process so it can reread the configuration file with the new information.

As mentioned, the next program that must process the POP3 connection should be an authentication program. In the previous example, the checkpassword program is used to authenticate the user.

Authenticating the Remote Client

Once the POP3 network connection is established, the POP3 server must be able to authenticate the identity of the remote client. This allows the server to know which user mailbox the connected client should access.

The POP3 protocol supports several different methods of authentication. The qmail-pop3d program itself does not authenticate the POP3 connection. It requires a separate program to authenticate the connection. Different programs can be used to support the different POP3 authentication methods. The most common program is the UNIX checkpassword program. This program supports the text username/password authentication method.

The `checkpassword` program was written by Dan Bernstein to provide an interface for any root application to be able to verify a username and password pair from the system `/etc/passwd` database. The current version of `checkpassword` can be downloaded from several Internet sources, such as Dan Bernstein's site at `http://cr.yp.to/software/checkpassword-0.81.tar.gz`.

To install `checkpassword` from the source code download, you should perform the following steps:

1. Download the source code from the Web site.
2. Unpack the source code into a working directory.
   ```
   mkdir /usr/local/checkpassword
   tar -zxvf checkpassword-0.81.tar.gz -C /usr/local/checkpassword
   ```
3. Run the GNU `make` program in the working directory to compile and install the program.
   ```
   cd /usr/local/checkpassword/checkpassword-0.81
   make
   make setup check
   ```

Besides the source code download, FreeBSD supports the `checkpassword` program as a software port. To install `checkpassword` from the FreeBSD software port, you should perform the following steps:

1. Change to the `checkpassword` port directory in the security area:
   ```
   cd /usr/ports/security/checkpassword
   ```
2. Run the GNU `make install` command to install the software port:
   ```
   make install
   ```

The `checkpassword` program should be successfully installed. If you installed from the source code download, it will be located in the `/bin` directory. If you installed from the FreeBSD port, it will be located in the `/usr/local/bin` directory.

To test the `checkpassword` program, you can simulate a POP3 connection to the `qmail-popup` program and pass the connection to the `checkpassword` program for verification. Listing 9.7 shows an example of this.

LISTING 9.7   A Sample `checkpassword` Test

```
1  meshach# /var/qmail/bin/qmail-popup localhost checkpassword pwd
2  +OK <66838.953325790@localhost>
3  user rich
4  +OK
5  pass guitar
6  /usr/rich
7  meshach#
```

9

USING THE
MAILDIR MAILBOX
FORMAT

In Listing 9.7, line 1 shows an example of how to run the qmail-popup program manually. The qmail-popup program must be run by the root user. It uses the localhost as the hostname and the checkpassword program as the next program to call. The pwd program is used as the parameter for checkpassword so that checkpassword will return the home directory of the user for a successful authentication.

Line 2 shows the greeting banner generated by qmail-popup. The POP3 USER and PASS commands are issued in lines 3 and 5 to attempt to authenticate the user. Line 6 indicates the home directory of the user returned by checkpassword, showing that the authentication was successful, and checkpassword is ready for use.

Now that the POP3 connection can be authenticated, the next phase is to communicate messages with the remote client. The next section describes the steps required in this phase.

Communicating with the Remote Client

After the remote client is successfully authenticated, the qmail-pop3d program takes control of the connection. Its job is to enable the remote client to read and delete any messages in the user's Maildir mailbox.

The POP3 protocol specifies commands that can be used to transfer messages. The remote client sends each command as an ASCII text string followed by a carriage return. The POP3 server must respond to all POP3 commands with either +OK or -ERR. Listing 9.8 shows a sample POP3 connection with a remote client.

LISTING 9.8   A Sample POP3 Connection from a Client

```
$ telnet localhost 110
Trying 127.0.0.1...
Connected to localhost.
Escape character is '^]'.
+OK <66861.953326496@meshach.dfas.mil>
USER rich
+OK
PASS guitar
+OK
LIST
+OK
1 355
2 356
.
RETR 1
+OK
Return-Path: <rich@meshach.ispnet1.net>
Delivered-To: rich@meshach.ispnet1.net
```

```
Received: (qmail 66849 invoked by uid 1001); 17 Mar 2000 20:54:38 -0000
Date: 17 Mar 2000 20:54:38 -0000
Message-ID: <20000317205438.66848.qmail@meshach.ispnet1.net>
From: rich@meshach.ispnet1.net
To: rich@meshach.ispnet1.net
Subject: This is the first test message

This is test message 1.


.
DELE 1
+OK
LIST
+OK
2 356

.
QUIT
+OK
Connection closed by foreign host.
$
```

Each POP3 command sent from the client must get a response from the host before another command can be sent. The following sections briefly describe the basic POP3 client commands that can be sent to the qmail-pop3d POP3 server.

Authenticate User

The USER/PASS command combination is used to authenticate a UNIX username and password pair. The username must be found in the system /etc/passwd directory. The POP3 server will compare the password supplied by the remote client with the password in the system database. If they match, the connection is considered authenticated, and the client can continue issuing other POP3 commands.

> **CAUTION**
>
> The POP3 USER/PASS authentication method transmits UNIX usernames and passwords across the network in plain ASCII text format. This makes the user account susceptible to network monitoring. Do not use the USER/PASS authentication method if your users are connecting to the mail server across untrusted networks.

List Mailbox Status

The STAT command is used to obtain a short description of the user's mailbox from the POP3 server. The server response to the STAT command is in this format:

+OK *nn mm*

The *nn* parameter indicates the total number of unread messages in the user's mailbox. The *mm* parameter indicates the total number of bytes in the unread messages.

List Mailbox Messages

The LIST command is used to obtain a more descriptive listing of the unread messages in the user's mailbox. The server response to the LIST command should include all the unread messages numbered, along with each message's size in bytes.

Listing 9.8, previously, demonstrates using the LIST command. The server response is shown in the three lines following the LIST command. This indicates two unread messages in the user's mailbox.

The LIST command can also be issued with a specific message number as a parameter. In that situation, the server will respond with the information for only the message indicated.

Retrieve a Mailbox Message

The RETR command is used to obtain the text of a particular message. The RETR command has one parameter—the number of the message to return. The server response to the RETR command should be the text of the full message, including any message headers.

Listing 9.8 also demonstrates using the RETR command. The remote client requested message 1 from the mailbox. The server responded with the text of the message in its entirety. A line with a single period (.) indicates the end of the message.

Delete a Mailbox Message

The DELE command is used to remove a message from the user's mailbox. The DELE command has one parameter—the number of the message that should be deleted. The server response to the DELE command should be either OK or ERR, depending on the result of the deletion attempt. Actually, messages deleted using the DELE command are only marked for deletion. Actual message deletion does not take place until the QUIT command is executed.

> **CAUTION**
>
> The RETR and DELE commands use message numbers as parameters. The message numbers stay constant *within* a POP3 session, but they can change *between* POP3 sessions. Do not issue a DELE command for a message number received in a previous session, or you may be unpleasantly surprised.

The No Operation Command

The NOOP command does what is says—nothing. It is often used to check if the POP3 connection is still active. The server response to the NOOP command should always be +OK.

Reset the POP3 Session

The RSET command is used to reset the POP3 session to the state just after the authentication. All previously entered commands are ignored. One important feature of the RSET command is than all messages marked for deletion using the DELE command will be unmarked.

Quit the POP3 session

The QUIT command is used to terminate the POP3 session. When the server receives a QUIT command, it will delete any messages marked for deletion from the user's mailbox and terminate the POP3 session. If the POP3 session should terminate before the client issues a QUIT command, any messages marked for deletion are restored and not deleted.

List the Message Subjects

The TOP command is used to obtain a brief synopsis of messages available in the mailbox. The server will return the RFC822 header fields for a message, along with a designated number of lines from the body of the message. The TOP command has two parameters that are both required. The format of the TOP command is

TOP *msg* *n*

Where *msg* is the message number from a LIST listing and *n* is an integer representing the number of lines from the message body that will be displayed. Email clients often use this command to obtain Subject header fields of messages to display in a list of messages without having to download the entire text of the messages. Listing 9.9 shows an example of the TOP command being used.

LISTING 9.9   A Sample POP3 Session Using the TOP Command

```
$ telnet localhost 110
Trying 127.0.0.1...
Connected to localhost.
Escape character is '^]'.
+OK <66903.953329307@meshach.ispnet1.net>
USER rich
+OK
PASS guitar
+OK
LIST
+OK
1 356
.
```

LISTING 9.9   Continued

```
TOP 1 0
+OK
Return-Path: <rich@meshach.ispnet1.net>
Delivered-To: rich@meshach.ispnet1.net
Received: (qmail 66855 invoked by uid 1001); 17 Mar 2000 20:54:51 -0000
Date: 17 Mar 2000 20:54:50 -0000
Message-ID: <20000317205450.66854.qmail@meshach.ispnet1.net>
From: rich@meshach.ispnet1.net
To: rich@meshach.ispnet1.net
Subject: This is the second test message


.
TOP 1 100
+OK
Return-Path: <rich@meshach.ispnet1.net>
Delivered-To: rich@meshach.ispnet1.net
Received: (qmail 66855 invoked by uid 1001); 17 Mar 2000 20:54:51 -0000
Date: 17 Mar 2000 20:54:50 -0000
Message-ID: <20000317205450.66854.qmail@meshach.ispnet1.net>
From: rich@meshach.ispnet1.net
To: rich@meshach.ispnet1.net
Subject: This is the second test message

This is test message 2.

.
QUIT
+OK
Connection closed by foreign host.
$
```

List Unique Message IDs

The UIDL command is used to display the unique identifier for each message in the user's mailbox. As mentioned in the DELE section, messages are sequentially numbered for each POP3 session. If any messages are deleted, the remaining messages are renumbered. This system makes it impossible for an MUA client to identify a message between POP3 sessions.

To solve this problem, the POP3 server assigns a unique identifier to each message. These identifiers can be displayed with the UIDL command. Although messages may be renumbered between POP3 sessions, the UIDL number will always remain the same. This enables MUA programs to track individual messages and determine what messages have been seen. This is demonstrated in Listing 9.10.

LISTING 9.10   A Sample POP3 Session Using UIDL Numbers

```
$ telnet localhost 110
Trying 127.0.0.1...
Connected to localhost.
Escape character is '^]'.
+OK <66933.953329811@meshach.ispnet1.net>
USER rich
+OK
PASS guitar
+OK
LIST
+OK
1 355
2 357
3 355
.
UIDL
+OK
1 953329773.66916.meshach.ispnet1.net
2 953329790.66922.meshach.ispnet1.net
3 953329804.66931.meshach.ispnet1.net
.
DELE 2
+OK
QUIT
+OK
Connection closed by foreign host.
$
```

As can be seen in Listing 9.10, each of the three messages in the user's inbox is assigned a unique UIDL identifier. At the end of the session, the user deletes the second message in the mailbox but keeps the first and third messages. Listing 9.11 shows a second POP3 session with the same username.

LISTING 9.11   Sample POP3 UIDL Session After Deletion

```
$ telnet localhost 110
Trying 127.0.0.1...
Connected to localhost.
Escape character is '^]'.
+OK <66936.953329838@meshach.ispnet1.net>
USER rich
+OK
PASS prlnjg
+OK
LIST
```

LISTING 9.11   Continued

```
+OK
1 355
2 355
.
UIDL
+OK
1 953329773.66916.meshach.ispnet1.net
2 953329804.66931.meshach.ispnet1.net
.
QUIT
+OK
Connection closed by foreign host.
$
```

In Listing 9.11, there are only two messages remaining in the user's mailbox, because the second message was deleted in Listing 9.10. By using the LIST command, it appears that the messages have been renumbered by the POP3 server (message 3 is now message 2). However, by using the UIDL command, the client can observe the unique UIDL identifiers and determine that the original first and third messages are still remaining in the user's mailbox, and the original second message was the message deleted.

Summary

The standard UNIX mailbox format has been in use for many years. There has been much talk about its reliability and efficiency, but not much had been done about it. The qmail program provides an alternative mailbox format from the standard UNIX mailbox. The Maildir mailbox format allows each user to have his own directory where individual messages are stored as separate files. This method helps increase access speed and message reliability.

The Maildir mailbox format uses three subdirectories to store messages. The tmp directory creates the new message as a unique filename. After the message has been successfully written, it is moved to the new directory. Messages that have been read are moved from the new directory to the cur directory.

This system requires any MUA program that needs to retrieve messages to understand the Maildir format. The qmail program package includes a POP3 server program that is capable of reading Maildir mailboxes. The qmail-pop3d program can be used to serve remote POP3 clients to allow remote network users to access their mailboxes. The qmail-pop3d program requires the qmail-popup program, as well as another userid authentication program.

The most commonly used authentication program is the checkpassword program, which is also available from the qmail Web site. Once qmail-pop3d is installed, remote network clients can access their messages using an MUA program and the POP3 mail protocol.

The ucspi-tcp Program

IN THIS CHAPTER

The previous chapter discussed Maildir, an alternative qmail method for mailboxes. This chapter discusses ucspi-tcp, an alternative method for network connections. The ucspi-tcp program was developed by Dan Bernstein to improve on the standard UNIX inetd package used for accepting network connections and passing them off to the appropriate application program. The ucspi-tcp program can be used with any network application. In our case, we will use it to improve network performance for the `qmail-smtpd` and `qmail-send` programs.

This chapter first describes the inetd program, its format, and its deficiencies. Then the chapter describes the ucspi-tcp program, how to install it, and how it can be used as an alternative to inetd with the qmail SMTP server program.

The UNIX inetd Program

One of the fundamental features of UNIX systems is the capability to communicate across TCP/IP networks with other hosts and clients. For the UNIX system to act as a TCP/IP server device, programs must be able to listen to any connection attempt from network clients. This can be resource consuming if the server is supporting many network applications. Each application would have to run in background mode listening for network connections.

To solve this problem, the *inetd* program was created. The inetd program is a single network program that listens for any network connection requests from remote clients. If a connection request is identified, a specific application is called by inetd and the connection is passed off to the application. Figure 10.1 demonstrates how the inetd program is used.

By using a single program to listen for all network connections, system resources are not used needlessly, running multiple applications. Not only does this save system resources, it also creates a single place for all network configurations to be made.

Using the inetd Program

There are two different versions of the inetd program, used in different flavors of UNIX. Both versions use two configuration files as well as command-line parameters to control the operation of the program.

Unfortunately, the two programs have different command-line formats. The BSD version of inetd uses this format:

```
inetd [-d] [-l] [-w] [-W] [-c maximum] [-C rate] [-a address] [-p filename]
➡ [-R rate] [configuration file]
```

FreeBSD and other variations of BSD UNIX use this format. The command-line parameters used for this version of inetd are described in Table 10.1.

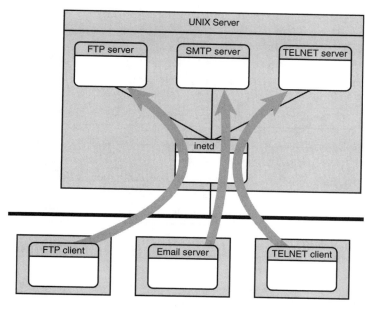

FIGURE 10.1

The UNIX inetd program.

TABLE 10.1   BSD inetd Program Command-Line Parameters

Parameter	Description
-d	Turns on debugging.
-l	Turns on logging.
-w	Turns on TCP wrapping for external services.
-W	Tuns on TCP wrapping for internal services.
-c maximum	Specifies the maximum number of services that can be invoked.
-C rate	Specifies the maximum number of times a service can be invoked from a single IP address.
-a address	Specifies a specific IP address to which to bind.
-p filename	Specifies an alternative file to store the process ID.
-R rate	Specifies the maximum number of times a service can be invoked in one minute. The default is 256.
configuration file	Specifies an alternative configuration file.

In contrast, the UNIX System V version of inetd uses this format:

```
inetd [-d] [-q queuelength] [configuration file]
```

Linux and other System V–based versions of UNIX use this format. The command-line parameters for this version of inetd are described in Table 10.2.

TABLE 10.2   UNIX System V inetd Program Command-Line Parameters

Parameter	Description
-d	Debug mode.
-q queuelength	Sets size of socket listen queue to queuelength. The default is 128.
configuration file	Defines an alternative configuration file.

In both instances, the system boot scripts start the inetd program. For Linux systems, the inetd program startup script is located in the /etc/init.d/inet file and is started by the /etc/rc.d/rc3.d/S50inet and /etc/rc.d/rc5.d/S50inet files (which are linked to the /etc/init.d/inet script). For FreeBSD systems, the inetd program is started directly from the /etc/rc startup script. The pertinent inetd lines in the /etc/rc script are

```
echo -n starting standard daemons:
if [ "X${inetd_enable}" != X"NO" ]; then
        echo -n ' inetd';      inetd ${inetd_flags}
fi
```

There are two environment variables that are used for the FreeBSD inetd startup script—
${inetd enable} and ${inetd flags}. These variables are set in the
/etc/defaults/rc.conf file as

```
inetd_enable="YES"          # Run the network daemon dispatcher (or NO).
inetd_flags="-wW"           # Optional flags to inetd.
```

The inetd Configuration Files

When the inetd program runs, it reads two separate configuration files to determine how it operates. The /etc/services configuration file is used to define TCP and UDP network ports that the UNIX server will communicate on. Listing 10.1 is a partial listing of an /etc/services file from a FreeBSD server.

LISTING 10.1   A Partial /etc/services File

```
ftp-data        20/tcp      #File Transfer [Default Data]
ftp-data        20/udp      #File Transfer [Default Data]
ftp             21/tcp      #File Transfer [Control]
```

```
ftp            21/udp      #File Transfer [Control]
ssh            22/tcp      #Secure Shell Login
ssh            22/udp      #Secure Shell Login
telnet         23/tcp
telnet         23/udp
#              24/tcp      any private mail system
#              24/udp      any private mail system
smtp           25/tcp      mail          #Simple Mail Transfer
smtp           25/udp      mail          #Simple Mail Transfer
nsw-fe         27/tcp      #NSW User System FE
nsw-fe         27/udp      #NSW User System FE
msg-icp        29/tcp      #MSG ICP
msg-icp        29/udp      #MSG ICP
msg-auth       31/tcp      #MSG Authentication
msg-auth       31/udp      #MSG Authentication
dsp            33/tcp      #Display Support Protocol
dsp            33/udp      #Display Support Protocol
#              35/tcp      any private printer server
#              35/udp      any private printer server
time           37/tcp      timserver
time           37/udp      timserver
rap            38/tcp      #Route Access Protocol
rap            38/udp      #Route Access Protocol
rlp            39/tcp      resource      #Resource Location Protocol
rlp            39/udp      resource      #Resource Location Protocol
graphics       41/tcp
graphics       41/udp
nameserver     42/tcp      name          #Host Name Server
nameserver     42/udp      name          #Host Name Server
```

Notice that most protocols reserve a port for both the TCP and UDP protocols. Although the SMTP port is reserved for both protocols, modern SMTP programs (including qmail-smtpd) use the TCP protocol to communicate with remote servers.

The core of the inetd program is the inetd.conf configuration file. This file defines what network ports inetd will listen for connections on and what programs it should pass accepted connections to. The inetd.conf file is located in the /etc directory. Listing 10.2 shows a simplified listing of a /etc/inetd.conf file for a FreeBSD server.

LISTING 10.2   A Partial /etc/inetd.conf File

```
ftp      stream   tcp   nowait   root   /usr/libexec/ftpd       ftpd -l
telnet   stream   tcp   nowait   root   /usr/libexec/telnetd    telnetd
shell    stream   tcp   nowait   root   /usr/libexec/rshd       rshd
login    stream   tcp   nowait   root   /usr/libexec/rlogind    rlogind
```

10

THE UCSPI-TCP
PROGRAM

LISTING 10.2   Continued

```
finger   stream tcp    nowait/3/10 nobody /usr/libexec/fingerd fingerd -s
#exec    stream tcp    nowait   root    /usr/libexec/rexecd      rexecd
#uucpd   stream tcp    nowait   root    /usr/libexec/uucpd       uucpd
#nntp    stream tcp    nowait   usenet  /usr/libexec/nntpd       nntpd
comsat   dgram  udp    wait     tty:tty /usr/libexec/comsat      comsat
ntalk    dgram  udp    wait     tty:tty /usr/libexec/ntalkd      ntalkd
#tftp    dgram  udp    wait     nobody  /usr/libexec/tftpd       tftpd /tftpboot
#bootps  dgram  udp    wait     root    /usr/libexec/bootpd      bootpd
pop3     stream tcp    nowait   root    /usr/local/libexec/popper  popper -s
#imap4   stream tcp    nowait   root    /usr/local/libexec/imapd          imapd
smtp     stream tcp    nowait   qmaild  /var/qmail/bin/tcp-env   tcp-env
➥ /var/qmail/bin/qmail-smtpd
```

Each line in the inetd.conf file represents a protocol that inetd must monitor for connections. Lines that begin with a pound sign (#) are commented out from the configuration and are not active. The format of an inetd.conf file line is

```
[service name] [socket type] [protocol] [wait/nowait] [user] [program]
➥[arguments]
```

The service name should match an entry in the /etc/services file. It defines the TCP or UDP port that inetd should monitor. The next three parameters describe the type of network connection required for the application. Each application should specify the socket type, protocol, and wait parameters required to communicate with the application. The user parameter specifies the username that will be used to run the application when a connection is established on the port.

The program parameter is used to map a particular application to the network port. For qmail, this can be a little confusing.

Instead of the SMTP connection being passed to the qmail-smtpd program, the tcp-env program is first used to establish the network connection and create UNIX environment variables for the qmail-smtpd program. As can be seen from Listing 10.2, inetd maps the tcp-env program to the SMTP network port. Any connection request for the SMTP protocol to the server will be passed off to the tcp-env program. As also can be seen from the listing, the tcp-env program then passes the connection to the qmail-smtpd program.

Problems with the inetd Program

The inet program has proven to be a very versatile program and is used in almost every UNIX distribution. Over the years there has been much debate and research on how to improve servicing network connection requests with the inetd program, but not much has been done. Some of the problems identified with the inetd program are as follows:

- Difficulty handling large bursts of connection requests (a fact exploited by hackers).
- Refuses new connections for 10 minutes if too many connection requests are detected.
- Hogs as much system memory as needed to support new connection attempts (also exploited).

Over the past few years, several programs have been developed to replace inetd and resolve these problems. The ucspi-tcp package is one such program.

The ucspi-tcp Package

Dan Bernstein developed the ucspi-tcp package as a replacement for the inetd program running on any UNIX system. The ucspi-tcp package contains two main programs, tcpserver and tcp-client. These programs use the UNIX Client-Server Program Interface (UCSPI) (also developed by Bernstein) to communicate TCP packets to the network (thus the name ucspi-tcp) from any application program (including shell scripts).

The UCSPI format defines a method by which programs communicate data. As described by Bernstein, the UCSPI format has three main benefits over standard network programming:

- The UCSPI interface is independent of the underlying communications medium.
- UCSPI allows shell script programs to take advantage of networking.
- UCSPI programs set up UNIX environment variables defining network information that can be used by programs and users.

UCSPI utilizes programs called *tools* to establish communications between application programs. The application programs must be UCSPI aware to send and receive data through the tool programs for communication. There are two types of UCSPI tools—client tools and server tools. These are shown in Figure 10.2.

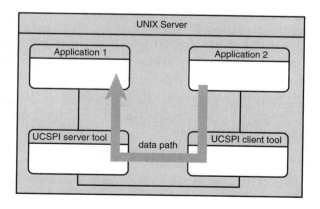

FIGURE 10.2
The UCSPI tool process.

The UCSPI server tool listens to the desired communications medium for requests from clients. When a request is received from a client, the tool creates the appropriate UNIX environment variables for defining the connection and passes the connection to the application program defined to the tool.

The UCSPI client tool allows programs (including script files) to access the desired communications medium using the UCSPI interface, rather than dealing with network programming (which shell script files cannot do).

Both client and server UCSPI tools conform to the same command-line format:

```
toolname [options] address application
```

The `address` parameter defines a protocol-specific remote address. For UCSPI clients, the `address` parameter defines the address of the host system the tool is running on. For UCSPI server tools, the `address` parameter defines the host address that the remote clients should connect to.

The `application` parameter specifies the UCSPI-aware application that will use the tool to transfer data through the communications medium. For server tools it is the application name that the received connection will be passed to for further processing.

The optional `options` parameters define options that can control the behavior of the UCSPI tool. Table 10.3 lists common options that are used in both UCSPI client and server tools.

TABLE 10.3   Common UCSPI Tool Options

Option	Description
-v	Print all available messages to stderr.
-q	Do not print any messages to stderr.
-Q	Print only error messages to stderr (default).

The options shown in Table 10.3 define how the tool will communicate messages (especially error messages) to the user. Often the -v option is desirable for debugging applications but is not used during production operations.

The ucspi-tcp package contains both a UCSPI client and a UCSPI server tool. The server tool is called tcpserver, while the client tool is called tcpclient.

Installing the ucspi-tcp Package

To be able to use the ucspi-tcp program, you must first install it on your UNIX system. Most UNIX distributions do not come with the ucspi-tcp program, so you must download the source code and compile it. FreeBSD does include a port for the ucspi-tcp program, so installation is a little easier. This section covers both methods of compiling and installing the ucspi-tcp program.

Downloading the ucspi-tcp Source Code

Bernstein has provided the source code for the ucspi-tcp package as a compressed tar file. At the time of this writing, the current version of ucspi-tcp is version 0.88. It can be obtained from Bernstein's Web site at `http://cr.yp.to/ucspi-tcp/ucspi-tcp-0.88.tar.gz`.

When the source code has been downloaded, you can untar it into a working directory. A common place for source code working directories is the `/usr/local/src` directory. To untar the source code into its own directory, use the following command:

```
tar -zxvf ucspi-tcp-0.88.tar.gz -C /usr/local/src
```

This creates the directory `/usr/local/src/ucspi-tcp-0.88` and untars the bundled source code into that directory.

> **NOTE**
>
> Remember, you must be the root user to create files in the `/usr/local` directory.

After the source code is untarred, you can use the GNU `make` program to compile the source code. The command to create the new programs from the source code is `make`.

This is not a difficult step. Next, place the executable programs created by the source code in a location where you can easily run them from boot scripts. A common location for executable programs is the `/usr/local/bin` directory. ucspi-tcp will automatically install the executable programs in this directory if you re-run the GNU make program using the `setup` and `check` options:

```
make setup check
```

This command copies the executable programs to the `/usr/local/bin` directory and checks to ensure that the installation was successful. Once this has been completed, the ucspi-tcp package has been successfully installed on your UNIX system.

Using the FreeBSD ucspi-tcp Port

If you are using a FreeBSD UNIX distribution, you can take advantage of the FreeBSD port of the ucspi-tcp program. The ucspi-tcp port is located in the `/usr/ports/sysutils/ucspi-tcp` directory.

10

THE UCSPI-TCP PROGRAM

At the time of this writing, the current release version of FreeBSD is version 3.4. This includes version 0.84 of the ucspi-tcp program. You should probably go to the Dan Bernstein's ucspi-tcp Web site (http://cr.yp.to/ucspi-tcp.html) to see what changes have been made to ucspi-tcp from the current 0.88 version. If you decide to use the newer version, you can follow the download and compiling instructions in the previous section. If you decide that the 0.84 version satisfies your requirements, you can install ucspi-tcp directly from the FreeBSD port.

To install a port, you must first be logged in as root and then change to the port installation directory:

```
cd /usr/ports/sysutils/ucspi-tcp
```

From the port directory, you can use the GNU make program to create the executable programs and install them into the directories appropriate for FreeBSD:

```
make
make install
```

The first make command creates the binary executable programs for the ucspi-tcp package, and the second make command moves the binary executable programs to their appropriate directories for the FreeBSD system. On FreeBSD 3.4 this is the /usr/local/bin directory.

Listing 10.3 shows the files that are created for the ucspi-tcp package. The next sections describe these programs in detail.

LISTING 10.3   ucspi-tcp Program Files

```
$ cd /usr/local/bin
$ ls -l
total 1879
-rwxr-xr-x  1 root  wheel   4280 Mar 20 13:04 addcr
-rwxr-xr-x  1 root  wheel   8704 Mar 20 13:04 argv0
-rwxr-xr-x  1 root  wheel    157 Mar 20 13:04 date@
-rwxr-xr-x  1 root  wheel   4440 Mar 20 13:04 delcr
-rwxr-xr-x  1 root  wheel    203 Mar 20 13:04 finger@
-rwxr-xr-x  1 root  wheel  12312 Mar 20 13:04 fixcrio
-rwxr-xr-x  1 root  wheel    287 Mar 20 13:04 http@
-rwxr-xr-x  1 root  wheel    149 Mar 20 13:04 mconnect
-rwxr-xr-x  1 root  wheel   8296 Mar 20 13:04 mconnect-io
-rwxr-xr-x  1 root  wheel  24696 Mar 20 13:04 rblsmtpd
-rwxr-xr-x  1 root  wheel  12744 Mar 20 13:04 recordio
-rwxr-xr-x  1 root  wheel    143 Mar 20 13:04 tcpcat
-rwxr-xr-x  1 root  wheel  30144 Mar 20 13:04 tcpclient
-rwxr-xr-x  1 root  wheel  13528 Mar 20 13:04 tcprules
-rwxr-xr-x  1 root  wheel  11304 Mar 20 13:04 tcprulescheck
-rwxr-xr-x  1 root  wheel  35088 Mar 20 13:04 tcpserver
-rwxr-xr-x  1 root  wheel    157 Mar 20 13:04 who@
$
```

The ucspi-tcp Programs

As can be seen in Listing 10.3, there are many programs included in the ucspi-tcp package. tcpserver is the main program used to replace the inetd program functionality. Besides this program, Bernstein has included other useful utilities and several sample UCSPI-aware client programs as examples. The sample programs are the files that end with the @ sign. The next sections describe some of the utilities included in the ucspi-tcp package.

The Tcpserver Program

The ucspi-tcp tcpserver program is used to replace the UNIX inetd program. It accepts incoming TCP connections from remote clients and passes them to an application program defined in the command-line parameters. The tcpserver program provides the following benefits over inetd:

- It can record all input and output from the server in a file.
- It can provide access control features to deny or allow connections from select clients.
- It contains concurrency limits to prevent overloading the UNIX system.

The tcpserver program provides access control by utilizing a hash database of rules configured by the administrator. This method has been proven to work faster than other types of access control systems, such as the tcpwrapper program described in Chapter 8, "Using qmail."

The format of the tcpserver command line is

```
tcpserver options host port application
```

The host and port parameters define the hostname and port number of the local server that the application will run on. The host parameter can be localhost to define the local server, an IP address of the host, or the full domain name of the host. The port parameter can be a numerical value or the name of a TCP port as defined in the /etc/services file on the server.

The application parameter defines the application that the connection will be passed to after it is established. Any command-line parameters needed for the application should also be included on the tcpserver command line.

The options parameter defines the behavior of the tcpserver program. There are three types of options that can be used. General options are the options defined for use on UCSPI tools as shown in Table 10.3. These options control how the tool displays messages. Connection options define how the tool will handle incoming connection requests. Data gathering options define how the tool obtains information to use in the UNIX environment variables passed to the application program. Table 10.4 shows the connection options that can be used in tcpserver.

TABLE 10.4   Tcpserver Connection Options

Option	Description
-b *n*	Allows a backlog of *n* connection requests.
-B banner	Write banner to the network connection after the connection has been established.
-c *n*	Do not accept more than *n* simultaneous connections.
-d	Delay sending data to remote hosts when host is responding slowly.
-D	Never delay in sending data to remote hosts.
-g *gid*	Change the active group ID to *gid* after preparing to receive connections.
-l	Print the local port number to stdout.
-o	Do not change IP options in the connection packets.
-O	Delete IP options to route packets (default).
-u *uid*	Change the active user ID to *uid* after preparing to receive connections.
-U	Equivalent to -g $GID -u $UID.
-x *db*	Use the rules in the hash database *db* to accept or deny remote clients.
-X	Allow connections if the database specified by the -x options does not exist.

The data gathering options that can be used with the tcpserver program are shown in Table 10.5.

TABLE 10.5   Tcpserver Data Gathering Options

Option	Description
-h	Look up remote hostname using DNS (default).
-H	Do not look up remote hostname using DNS. You must use this option for port 53.
-l localname	Do not look up the local server hostname using DNS; use localname instead.
-p	Paranoid. Look up the remote host IP address using reverse DNS and compare it to the hostname. If they do not match, remove the environment variable $TCPREMOTEHOST.
-P	Not paranoid. Do not look up the remote host IP address using reverse DNS (default).

Option	Description
-r	Attempt to obtain $TCPREMOTEINFO from the remote host (default).
-R	Do not attempt to obtain $TCPREMOTEINFO data from the remote host. You must use this option for ports 53 and 113.
-t *n*	Stop trying to get $TCPREMOTEINFO data after *n* seconds (default is 26).

As shown in Table 10.5, there are several UNIX environment variables for which tcpserver attempts to receive data. These environment variables help the application program process information regarding the network connection. Table 10.6 shows the environment variables used.

TABLE 10.6   Tcpserver UNIX Environment Variables

Variable	Description
$PROTO	The protocol used (default is TCP).
$TCPLOCALIP	The IP address of the local host in dotted decimal notation.
$TCPLOCALPORT	The local TCP port number in decimal.
$TCPLOCALHOST	The DNS lookup value of the local host.
$TCPREMOTEIP	The IP address of the remote client.
$TCPREMOTEPORT	The TCP port number of the remote client in decimal.
$TCPREMOTEHOST	The DNS lookup value of the remote host.
$TCPREMOTEINFO	An information string provided by the remote client using the IDENT, TAP, RFC931, or RFC1413 protocol.

When tcpserver accepts a connection from a remote client, it attempts to provide the environment variables listed in Table 10.6 to the application. When it cannot receive information for a particular variable, it does not set the variable.

The Tcpclient Program

The tcpclient program is used to create a network connection with a remote server and pass the connection to an application program. The format of the tcpclient program is

```
tcpclient options host port application
```

The *host* and *port* parameters are used to define the hostname of the remote server and the TCP port number to connect to. The *application* parameter specifies the application that the connection will be passed to after it is established. Any command-line parameters that are required by the application program should also be included in the tcpclient command line.

The *options* parameter is used to modify the behavior of the tcpclient program. As with the tcpserver program, there are three types of options that can be used. General options are those defined for use on UCSPI tools, as shown previously in Table 10.3. These options control how tcpclient displays messages. Connection options define how the tool will handle the connection attempt with the remote host. Data gathering options define how tcpclient obtains information to use in the UNIX environment variables passed to the application program. Table 10.7 shows the connection options that can be used in tcpclient.

TABLE 10.7 Tcpclient Connection Options

Option	Description
-T *x+y*	Times out the connection attempt after *x* seconds for the first attempt and *y* seconds for any retry attempts. The +*y* may be omitted to avoid retry attempts.
-i *localip*	Uses *localip* as the IP address of the local side of the connection.
-p *localport*	Uses *localport* as the TCP port number of the local side of the connection.
-d	Delays sending data to remote hosts when the host is responding slowly.
-D	Never delays in sending data to remote hosts.

The data gathering options that can be used with the tcpclient program are the same as for the tcpserver program shown in Table 10.5. Also similar to the tcpserver program, the tcpclient program sets UNIX environment variables once the connection is established. All of the environment variables shown in Table 10.6 are also used by tcpclient. Again, just like the tcpserver program, tcpclient does not set an environment variable if it cannot obtain the information from the remote server for the variable. The application program that the connection is passed to can utilize all of the environment variables set by tcpclient.

The Tcprules Program

One of the most versatile features of the tcpserver program is the capability to create rules that can restrict connections to application programs. The mail administrator can create rules to specifically allow or deny access from individual email addresses, IP addresses, or entire network addresses.

The rules are created in a text file, one rule per line. After the text file is completed, it is converted to a hash database using the cdb database format. This enables the tcpserver program to quickly process rules on-the-fly as remote clients request connections to the server.

As each connection request is received, it is checked against the tcpserver rules database. Figure 10.3 demonstrates how this works.

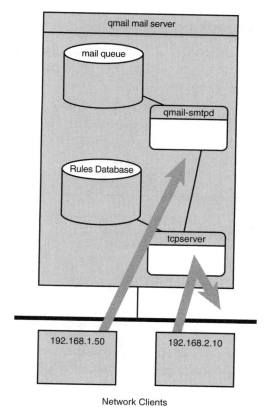

FIGURE 10.3

The tcpserver rules database.

Creating Rules

Rules are created in the format

```
address:action,variable
```

In this format, the `address` parameter is the source address for the connection packet, `action` indicates the handling for that packet, and `variable` includes any additional identifiers required for the action. The following sections describe the rules format in more detail.

Connection Source Address

The `address` parameter is used to match addresses of incoming connection attempts. The `address` parameter can be in any one of several different formats. Each format is based on the UCSPI environment variables shown in Table 10.6. Different combinations of the environment variables can be used to create a valid address. Table 10.8 lists the different address formats that tcpserver can recognize.

TABLE 10.8   Tcpserver Rule Address Formats

Address	Example
$TCPREMOTEINFO@$TCPREMOTEIP	rich@[192.168.1.10]
$TCPREMOTEINFO@=$TCPREMOTEHOST	rich@ispnet1.net
$TCPREMOTEIP	192.168.1.10
=$TCPREMOTEHOST	meshach.ispnet1.net
partial $TCPREMOTEIP	192.168.
partial $TCPREMOTEHOST	ispnet1.net
empty	Any address

Connection Request Handling

The `action` parameter is used to specify the action tcpserver should take when a connection request matching the address is received. There are two actions that can be taken:

- `allow`
- `deny`

Action Variables

Besides the action, additional comma-delimited environment variables can be added to the `action` parameter. This allows tcpserver to set environment variables as specific remote client connections are requested. This feature can be used to support special functions for qmail, such as selective relaying.

Building the Tcpserver Rules Database

The best way to describe tcpserver rules is to show a few examples. Table 10.9 shows several examples of possible tcpserver rules that could be used.

TABLE 10.9   Sample Tcpserver Rules

Rule	Description
`192.168.0.1:deny`	Block any connection from address `192.168.0.1`.
`192.168.2.:deny`	Block any connection from any client on the `192.168.2.0` network.
`192.168.1.:allow`	Accept any connection from any client on the `192.168.1.0` network.
`192.168.3.1-10:allow`	Accept connections from hosts `192.168.3.1` to `192.168.3.10`.
`:deny`	Block all connection attempts by default (usually used with `allow` rules).
`prez@whitehouse.gov:allow`	Allow the address `prez@whitehouse.gov` to connect.
`192.168.:allow,RELAYCLIENT=" "`	Accept any connection from any client on the `192.168.0.0` network and set the environment variable `RELAYCLIENT` to an empty string.

Once the text rule file is created, you must create the cdb database file that tcpserver will use. This is done with the tcprules program.

The format of the tcprules program is

```
tcprules database tmpfile
```

where *database* is the name of the cdb format rule file you want created, and *tmpfile* is the name of a temporary file that tcprules can create. The tcprules program reads rules from standard input. To parse rules from a text file, use the following command:

```
cat rules.txt | tcprules database tmpfile
```

where *rules.txt* is the text file containing the rules. Listing 10.4 demonstrates converting a sample text rule file to the tcpserver rules database using the tcprules program.

LISTING 10.4   Sample Tcpserver Rules

```
1   $ cat rules.txt
2   192.168.:allow,RELAYCLIENT=""
3   192.168.1.10:deny
192.168.2.:deny
5   :deny
6   $ cat rules.txt | tcprules rules.cdb rules.tmp
7   $ ls -al rules*
8   -rw-r--r--  1 rich   rich  2168 Mar 27 16:53 rules.cdb
9   -rw-r--r--  1 rich   rich    64 Mar 27 16:52 rules.txt
10 $
```

10

In Listing 10.4, lines 2–5 show an example of a rule text file. Line 2 allows any client on the 192.168 network to connect to the server and also sets the RELAYCLIENT environment variable to an empty string. Lines 3 and 4 are used to deny access from specific IP addresses. Line 3 denies access from the specific client 192.168.1.10, and line 4 denies access from any host on the 192.168.2.0 network. Line 5 is an important entry in the rule database. It denies access to any other IP address not mentioned in the database. This helps restrict unauthorized use of the TCP service. For some services (such as SMTP) this rule may be impractical, but for others (such as FTP) it could be very useful.

Activating the Rules Database

Once the rules database is created, you must tell tcpserver how to access it. This is accomplished using the -x parameter. A sample tcpserver command line using a rules database would look like this:

```
tcpserver -v -p -x /etc/tcp.smtp.cdb 0 smtp /var/qmail/bin/qmail-smtpd
```

In this example, tcpserver will use the rules database located in the file /etc/tcp.smtp.cdb. This is a common naming standard used for tcpserver rules. The first part of the filename signifies that the rules apply to the TCP protocol. The second part of the filename signifies that the rules are specifically for the SMTP protocol (although they will apply to any protocol used by the indicated clients). Finally, the third part signifies that the file is in the CDB database format.

Checking the Rules Database

After creating a rule, you can test to see if it works the way you intended. The tcprulescheck program is included in the ucspi-tcp package to allow the mail administrator to check rules before putting them on the system.

The tcprulescheck program uses two UNIX environment variables to check the rules. The TCPREMOTEIP and TCPREMOTEHOST variables should contain the values that you want to check against the rules created. You can set these variables to different values and run tcprulescheck to see the outcome. Listing 10.5 shows some examples testing various IP addresses and hostnames using tcprulescheck.

LISTING 10.5   Sample Tcprulescheck Sessions

```
1   $ cat rules.txt
2   192.168.:allow,RELAYCLIENT=""
3   192.168.1.10:deny
4   192.168.2.:deny
5   :deny
6   $ tcprulescheck rules.cdb
7   rule :
```

```
 8 deny connection
 9 $ TCPREMOTEIP=192.168.1.50 ; export TCPREMOTEIP
10 $ tcprulescheck rules.cdb
11 rule 192.168.:
12 set environment variable RELAYCLIENT=
13 allow connection
14 $ TCPREMOTEIP=192.168.1.10 ; export TCPREMOTEIP
15 $ tcprulescheck rules.cdb
16 rule 192.168.1.10:
17 deny connection
18 $ TCPREMOTEIP=192.168.2.50 ; export TCPREMOTEIP
19 $ tcprulescheck rules.cdb
20 rule 192.168.2.:
21 deny connection
22 $ TCPREMOTEIP=168.192.10.10 ; export TCPREMOTEIP
23 $ tcprulescheck rules.cdb
24 rule :
25 deny connection
31 $
```

Listing 10.5 demonstrates several different tests using the rules created in the sample rule data-base in Listing 10.4. To refresh your memory, the text rules are listed in lines 2 through 5. Line 6 shows the testing of the default behavior of the rule. As you can see in lines 7 and 8, the default behavior of this rule set is to deny a connection attempt.

In line 9, the UNIX environment variable TCPREMOTEIP is set to a test IP address representing a valid IP address on the local network. Again, tcprulescheck is run and lines 11–13 show the result. In line 11, tcprulescheck displays the matching rule for the IP address. The rule includes setting the environment variable RELAYCLIENT to an empty string, and tcprulescheck notifies us of this activity. Line 13 displays the connection status, which indicates that the local network IP address would be allowed connectivity to the TCP service.

Lines 14–25 test the connection blocking rules that are configured in the rule set. In line 14 the TCPREMOTEIP environment variable is set to an IP address that is specifically blocked in the rule set. Lines 16 and 17 show that tcprulescheck indicates that the address would be blocked from establishing a connection.

In line 18, the TCPREMOTEIP environment variable is set to an IP address from a subnet that is specifically blocked in the rule set. Again, lines 20 and 21 show that the address would be properly blocked from establishing a connection.

Finally, line 22 shows an example of using a remote IP address on a different network. The rule set defaults to block any connection attempt not defined in the rule set, so the attempt should be blocked. Lines 24 and 25 show that it is.

Rejecting Spam Mail

The rblsmtpd program is used to combat the ever-increasing problem of spam mail. Spam mail is unwanted, unsolicited advertisements that are sent from advertisers to any email address they can get their hands on. There has been much discussion about how to control spam mail on the Internet. One solution is the Realtime Blackhole List (RBL).

The RBL is a database of known email abusers. When an address has been verified to be sending spam mail, the address is added to the RBL database. RBL-aware programs can query the database to determine if an incoming message is being sent from a known spammer. If so, the program can reject the message. At the time of this writing, the database is maintained on server `rbl.maps.vix.com`. You can find out more about the RBL by visiting Web site `http://maps.vix.com/rbl/`.

The rblsmtpd program can query the RBL database server to determine if a username or hostname has been blacklisted on the Internet. If it has, rblsmtpd will deny the SMTP connection attempt. The format of the rblsmtpd command is

```
rblsmtpd options program
```

The `program` parameter is used to specify the application program that the connection will be passed to if the RBL database does not block the connection. For a qmail server this would be the `qmail-smtpd` program.

The `options` parameter is used to specify various options that modify the behavior of the rblsmtpd program. Table 10.10 shows the options that are available.

TABLE 10.10   Rblsmtpd Options

Option	Description
-a address	Use address as a source of the anti-RBL database.
-b	Use a 553 return error code if an address is listed in the RBL.
-B	Use a 451 return error code if an address is listed in the RBL (default).
-c	Block the connection if the RBL lookup fails.
-r address	Use address as a source of the RBL database.
-t n	Use a timeout of n seconds.

The -a and -r options can be used multiple times, defining more than one database to check. The anti-RBL database does what it says. It is a database of good email source addresses. If you want to limit your email to only specific hosts, this is one way to do it. The -r option can be used to define your own RBL database of specific spammers that have not yet been caught by the official RBL database.

Testing the SMTP Server

The mconnect program is used to establish an interactive SMTP connection with a remote mail server. This can come in handy when trying to troubleshoot email problems with either your own or another mail server. The mconnect program allows the mail administrator to establish a manual SMTP connection with any SMTP server for testing purposes.

The format of the mconnect command is

```
mconnect host
```

where *host* is the name or IP address of the remote SMTP server. Once the connection is established, you can enter SMTP commands and view the responses from the remote host. Listing 10.6 shows a sample mconnect session with the local qmail-smtpd SMTP server.

LISTING 10.6   Sample Mconnect Session

```
1  $ mconnect localhost
2  220 meshach.ispnet1.net ESMTP
3  HELO meshach.ispnet1.net
4  250 meshach.ispnet1.net
5  MAIL FROM: <rich>
6  250 ok
7  RCPT TO: <rich>
8  250 ok
9  DATA
10 354 go ahead
11 From: rich@meshach.ispnet1.net
12 To: rich@meshach.ispnet1.net
13 Subject: Testing the mconnect program
14
15 This is a test of a sample mconnect session.
16 This is the end of the test.
17 .
18 250 ok 954270188 qp 84241
19 QUIT
20 221 meshach.ispnet1.net
21 $
```

Line 1 shows the mconnect program being used to establish a connection with the SMTP server on the local host. Line 2 shows the SMTP greeting banner produced from the qmail-smtpd program running on the local host. Lines 3–17 show a sample SMTP email session with the local host. Line 18 shows the response to the email session. When the SMTP session is terminated, the mconnect program halts and returns to the command prompt.

10

Sample ucspi-tcp Client Programs

As mentioned previously in the section "The ucspi-tcp Package," programs can be written to take advantage of the UCSPI interface. The ucspi-tcp package includes some simple examples to demonstrate that feature. After reviewing the sample ucspi-tcp programs, you might be tempted to try creating a few useful utilities using ucspi-tcp yourself. This section discusses the sample programs.

Retrieving the Date and Time

The date@ program demonstrates using the tcpclient program to connect to a remote host's well-known daytime port and retrieving the current date and time. The date@ program is a script file that uses the tcpclient program. Its contents are

```
#!/bin/sh
# WARNING: This file was auto-generated. Do not edit!
/usr/local/bin/tcpclient -RH10 -- "${1-0}" 13 sh -c 'exec /usr/local/bin/delcr
➥   < &6' | cat -v
```

The date@ program displays the message that is returned from the remote host. The message is the normal output of the UNIX date command on the remote host. The output is sent to the ucspi-tcp delcr utility to remove the ending carriage return, and then it is listed to the terminal using the standard UNIX cat command. A sample date@ session is

```
$date@ 192.168.1.10
Tue March 28 19:24:30 2000
```

Retrieving System User Information

The finger@ command also uses the tcpclient program to connect to a remote host's well-known finger port to retrieve information regarding a local user. Again, it is a standard UNIX shell script that uses the tcpclient program:

```
#!/bin/sh
# WARNING: This file was auto-generated. Do not edit!
echo "${2-}" | /usr/local/bin/tcpclient -RH10 -- "${1-0}" 79 sh -c '
➥   /usr/local/bin/addcr >&7 exec /usr/local/bin/delcr <&6 ' | cat -v
```

CAUTION

With Internet security being what it is these days, many if not most UNIX hosts on the Internet have the finger function disabled. It would be a wise choice to disable this function on your mail server.

The output from a normal finger@ session is shown in Listing 10.7.

LISTING 10.7   Sample finger@ Session

```
$ finger@ localhost rich
Login: rich                      Name: Rich Blum
Directory: /usr/rich             Shell: /bin/sh
On since Tue Mar 28 16:12 (EST) on ttyp0 (messages off) from 192.168.1.10
No Mail.
No Plan.
$
```

Retrieve a Web Page

The http@ program allows you to connect to the HTTP port of a remote computer and retrieve the main HTML page from the site. This utility comes in handy when you need to test connectivity to HTTP servers. The format of this script is

```
#!/bin/sh
# WARNING: This file was auto-generated. Do not edit!
echo "GET /${2-} HTTP/1.0 Host: ${1-0}:${3-80}" | /usr/local/bin/tcpclient
➥ -RH10 -- "${1-0}" "${3-80}" sh -c ' /usr/local/bin/addcr >&7
➥ exec /usr/local/bin/delcr <&6' | awk '/^$/ { body=1; next }
➥ { if (body) print }'
```

The http@ program again uses the tcpclient program as well as the addcr and delcr programs. The addcr program is another ucspi-tcp utility that adds a carriage return to the text that is sent to the remote host. The output from a sample http@ session is shown in Listing 10.8.

LISTING 10.8   Sample http@ Session

```
$ http@ 192.168.1.1
<!DOCTYPE HTML PUBLIC "-//W3C//DTD HTML 3.2 Final//EN">
<HTML>
 <HEAD>
  <TITLE>Test Page for Apache Installation</TITLE>
 </HEAD>
<!-- Background white, links blue (unvisited), navy (visited), red (active) -->
 <BODY
  BGCOLOR="#FFFFFF"
  TEXT="#000000"
  LINK="#0000FF"
  VLINK="#000080"
  ALINK="#FF0000"
 >
  <H1 ALIGN="CENTER">It Worked!</H1>
  <P>
  If you can see this, it means that the installation of the
  <A
```

LISTING 10.8 Continued

```
 HREF="http://www.apache.org/"
>Apache</A>
software on this system was successful. You may now add content to
this directory and replace this page.
</P>
<HR WIDTH="50%" SIZE="8">
<BLOCKQUOTE>
 If you are seeing this instead of the content you expected, please
 <STRONG>contact the administrator of the site involved.</STRONG>  If
 you send mail about this to the authors of the Apache software, who almost
 certainly have nothing to do with this site, your message will be
 <STRONG><BIG>ignored</BIG></STRONG>.
</BLOCKQUOTE>
<HR WIDTH="50%" SIZE="8">
<P>
The Apache
<A
 HREF="manual/index.html"
>documentation</A>
has been included with this distribution.
</P>
<P>
You are free to use the image below on an Apache-powered web
server.  Thanks for using Apache!
</P>
<P ALIGN="CENTER">
 <a href="http://www.apache.org/"><IMG SRC="/icons/apache_gif" ALT="[ Powered
by Apache ]"></a>
</P>
</BODY>
</HTML>
$
```

Retrieving a List of Logged-On Users

The who@ program is used to obtain a listing of logged-in users from a remote host. This uses
the well-known who port. The format of the who@ script is

```
#!/bin/sh
# WARNING: This file was auto-generated. Do not edit!
/usr/local/bin/tcpclient -RH10 -- "${1-0}" 11 sh -c 'exec /usr/local/bin/delcr
➥ <&6' | cat -v
```

> **CAUTION**
>
> The who network function is another dangerous feature to activate on a host connected to the Internet. Using the who function, any user on the Internet can obtain a listing of all usernames logged into the system. Do not activate the who feature unless you are in a controlled network environment.

Using the ucspi-tcp Package with qmail

The part of qmail that uses the UNIX inetd program is the qmail-smtpd program. This program must be called when the mail server receives an SMTP connection attempt. Bernstein strongly recommends using his tcpserver program instead of inetd to spawn the qmail-smtpd program.

To use the tcpserver program to accept SMTP connections, you must create a boot script to start it automatically when the mail server boots. The command line that can be used in the script for the qmail-smtpd program would be

```
/usr/local/bin/tcpserver -p -x /etc/tcp.smtp.cdb -u qmailuid -g qmailgid
➥ 0 smtp /var/qmail/bin/qmail-smtpd
```

Here is a rundown of the command line:

-p—Allows tcpserver to accept connections without having to look up the remote host address using DNS.

-x—Allows tcpserver to use a rules database to control connections.

-u—Allows tcpserver to run as the qmaild userid (replace qmailuid with the user ID of the qmaild user).

-g—Allows tcpserver to run as the qmaild groupid (replace qmailgid with the group ID of the nofiles group).

0—Indicates that tcpserver is on the local host.

qmail-smtpd—The application that the SMTP connection will be passed off to.

Once the qmail-smtpd boot script is created, it must be run from a system boot script. On FreeBSD systems this can be the /etc/rc script. On Linux systems this can be in the /etc/rc.d/init.d directory and linked to the /etc/rc3.d and /etc/rc5.d directories.

Next you must create the rules database that the tcpserver command line calls for. In this example the rules database is called /etc/tcp.smtp.cdb. This is a common format used with the tcpserver program. It indicates what the rules database is used for (SMTP connections) as well as the fact that it must be a cdb-formatted database.

First, you must decide on the rules you need to support your mail environment. If you want all clients on your local network to be able to relay mail through your qmail server, you must include the RELAYCLIENT environment variable in the rule line. Also, you will need to include the local host address in case any MUA programs running on the mail server attempt to relay mail through the SMTP process. You will not want to configure the default operation to deny connections, because you will want remote servers to be able to connect to the SMTP port to transfer mail messages. Listing 10.9 shows a sample rules database that can be used for a qmail server.

LISTING 10.9   Sample Rules Database for qmail-smtpd

```
127.:allow,RELAYCLIENT=" "
192.168.:allow,RELAYCLIENT=" "
```

These two entries allow local network clients as well as the localhost to connect to the SMTP server and relay mail through the server. Other network addresses will be able to connect to the SMTP server, but they will not be allowed to use the server to relay mail. After the text rules database is created, it must be put in the cdb database format. The tcprules program can do that:

```
cat /etc/tcp.smtp | tcprules /etc/tcp.smtp.cdb /tmp/rules.tmp
chmod 644 /etc/tcp.smtp.cdb
```

Be sure that you are logged in as the root user to create the /etc/tcp.smtp.cdb file. Also remember to use the chmod program to restrict access to this file. The rules file can be rebuilt at any time without having to stop and restart the tcpserver program.

After the rules database is created, you can either restart the mail server or manually start the qmail-smtpd boot script. You should now see the tcpserver program running as a background process, using the UNIX ps command. You can also use the ucspi-tcp mconnect program to attempt a connection with the localhost to ensure that qmail-smtpd is working.

Summary

The ucspi-tcp package was created by Dan Bernstein to help alleviate problems associated with the UNIX inetd program. The main program in the package is tcpserver. The tcpserver program uses the UNIX Client-Server Program Interface (UCSPI) developed by Bernstein to link application programs with an underlying communications medium (such as a network). The tcpserver program can be used to monitor the network for connection attempts for a particular TCP port and pass the connections to the application program.

One nice feature of tcpserver is its capability to incorporate a rules database that can control access from remote hosts. Individual hosts as well as entire subnetworks can be configured in the rules database to be specifically denied or allowed connectivity to the server. Also, the rules database can be used to set UNIX environment variables and pass them to the application program as well.

These features make tcpserver ideal for use with the qmail `qmail-smtpd` program, which is used to allow remote mail servers to connect to the qmail server using the SMTP protocol.

Using qmail as an ISP Mail Server

IN THIS CHAPTER

With the explosion of the Internet, providing email accounts has become a big business. Many home users want personal email accounts that they can access from their home PCs. Business users are also getting on the email bandwagon. Providing email services for employees in small and medium-size companies has become a big part of the business world. This has created a rush of Internet service providers (ISPs) that can provide email services to various types of customers at the same time.

This chapter describes how to use the qmail email package to set up a commercial-quality ISP mail server on a UNIX platform. This mail server can service both individual email customers who dial in to a single email account and small and medium-size corporate email customers that have local mail servers that dial in to the ISP to retrieve mail for an entire corporate domain.

Features of an ISP Mail Server

Before describing the specifics of creating an ISP mail server, it may be helpful to understand the features and functions required of an ISP mail server. ISP mail servers have more requirements than a standard office mail server would have.

Most small and medium-size offices do not have dedicated connections to the Internet, and they rely on a remote host to accept and store incoming email messages for their domains. The local mail server for the office can then contact the Internet host via a dial-up modem at regular intervals and see if there are any incoming messages to download.

The ISP mail servers must be able to accept mail for these dial-up domains. In fact, if the ISP is servicing more than one customer, it must be able to accept messages for several dial-up domains. The mail must be kept isolated based on the domain so that the individual domain mail servers can contact the ISP mail server to retrieve the correct mail. Servicing multiple domains on a single mail server is called *hosting virtual domains*.

Another requirement for an ISP mail server is mail relaying. Most dial-up connections to the ISP are not able to process outgoing email messages directly to the Internet destination. Instead, the mail clients rely on a "smart" mail server that they can send all their outgoing messages to for delivery to the Internet. This smart mail server is most often the ISP mail server. To accomplish this, the ISP mail server must allow message relaying.

Relaying messages was once a common SMTP function. The SMTP protocol provides a means for clients to send messages intended to remote Internet users to a common mail server, which in turn could resend the message via SMTP to the appropriate destination mail server. With the increase of spam mail, mail relaying has become an ugly subject. It is not politically correct on the Internet to forward mail recklessly from any mail server to any other mail server. Instead, some degree of intelligence is required to forward email messages selectively. This is called *selective relaying*.

Using qmail as an ISP Mail Server
CHAPTER 11

269

11

USING QMAIL AS
AN ISP MAIL
SERVER

Virtual Domains

Using virtual domains on a mail server is becoming a common practice for ISPs. Many ISPs support email for small and medium-size organizations and businesses using this technique. Figure 11.1 demonstrates how this works.

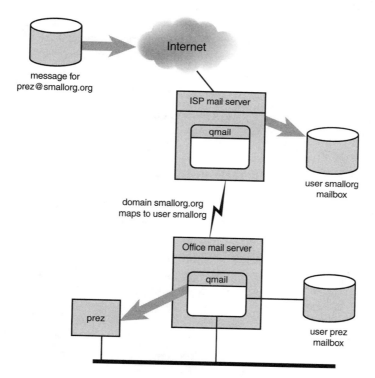

FIGURE 11.1
Using virtual domains for email.

The main idea behind virtual domains is the ability to store mail messages for another mail server locally on the ISP server, then retrieve them when the proper mail server for the domain is ready for them.

Using virtual domains requires two parts. The ISP must use a method on its mail server to accept messages destined for the domain and place them where they can be retrieved later. This usually involves forwarding all messages for a particular domain to a single user account on the UNIX system.

The second part requires the office mail server responsible for the actual domain to be able to connect to the ISP mail server and retrieve the messages. Once the messages are retrieved from the ISP, the office mail server must be able to parse the message header fields to determine the correct recipient and deliver the message to that user's mailbox. There are many software packages (including qmail) that can accomplish this function.

Selective Relaying

Mail relaying has become a complicated issue on the Internet. In the early days of the Internet, mail relaying was a common courtesy extended to other mail servers on the network. If a mail server attempted to deliver a message to your mail server for a user on a different mail server, you accepted the message and forwarded it to the appropriate remote mail server for the user. Unfortunately, with the popularity of the Internet came abuse of the Internet and email systems.

Spammers are constantly looking for ways to send out massive quantities of email to unsuspecting users. Of key importance to the spammer is the ability to hide the originating email address of the message (otherwise someone might be able to track them down and complain).

Enter mail relaying. By using some SMTP trickery, a spammer can bounce his email messages off an Internet mail relay using a phony originating mail address. The current SMTP protocol does not allow for validating the mail address of an incoming message, so the mail relay forwards the message to the recipient, using the phony originating address. Figure 11.2 demonstrates this principle.

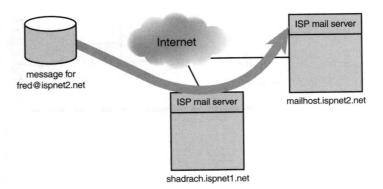

FIGURE 11.2

Using an open mail relay for spamming.

There has been much discussion on how to control spamming on the Internet. The most obvious methods involve improving the SMTP protocol to validate information sent in the MAIL FROM headers. This would ensure that spammers could not doctor the mail address.

The new SMTP protocol extensions have made many improvements to the security of Internet email. However, many (if not most) Internet mail servers are using software that does not take advantage of the new SMTP extensions.

To compensate for this, most email software packages provide a method of screening SMTP connection attempts. There are two basic approaches to relaying on the Internet. The first and most obvious is for the MTA mail program to refuse all relayed messages and accept only messages that are destined for users on the local mail server. This is the safest and easiest solution.

Unfortunately, most ISPs have users who dial into the ISP and use some type of MUA program on their PCs to receive mail. These programs must also be able to send messages to remote users on the Internet. The method that almost all MUA programs use to send messages is by forwarding the messages via SMTP to a smart host. The smart host is assumed to be able to relay the message to the appropriate destination mail server. This is the problem.

If you are a conscientious mail administrator and have disabled relaying on your mail server, none of your customers will be able to use your mail server to send messages to the Internet. That would not be good for business. To compensate for this, selective relaying uses the best of both worlds.

Figure 11.3 demonstrates the principle of selective relaying. By allowing the MTA mail program to check a local database, it can determine on a case-by-case basis what messages to relay and what messages to refuse.

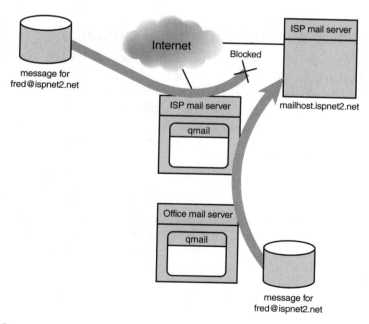

FIGURE 11.3

Using selective relaying on a mail server.

By placing all of the local IP addresses that are assigned to your customers in the relaying database, the MTA program can allow those addresses to use it as a smart host and forward any messages destined for remote Internet users. However, any message coming from an IP address not in the database and destined for a remote user will be refused.

Configuring Virtual Domains

The qmail email package allows for hosting multiple virtual domains on the ISP mail server. There are two methods that can be used to host a virtual domain using the qmail mail server.

The first method involves placing all mail destined for a particular domain in a single user account. It is then the responsibility of the real domain mail server to connect as the user account and retrieve the messages.

The second method involves the older UNIX-to-UNIX copy (UUCP) protocol. qmail can be used to send messages destined for a virtual domain directly to the UUCP queue of a remote UUCP host. The remote host can then connect at its leisure to retrieve the waiting messages, or the mail server can schedule regular connection times.

The following sections describe both methods used to configure virtual domains using the qmail software.

Configuring DNS Records for Virtual Domains

Before anything can be done with the qmail software, the proper DNS records must be added to inform remote Internet hosts where to send messages for the domain. The first step in hosting a virtual domain is to obtain a domain. As stated in Chapter 4, "DNS and qmail," each Internet domain must be registered with the Internet Corporation for Assigned Names and Numbers (ICANN). This enables Internet hosts to identify the organization. For the purposes of this example, we will use the fictitious domain smallorg.org. Figure 11.4 shows a diagram of how the domain will interact with the Internet.

When smallorg.org is registered with ICANN, it must specify two DNS servers that will support the domain. If the ISP site also supports DNS servers, you will want to include the ISP server as one of the DNS servers for the smallorg.org domain. Once the DNS server is identified as being an authoritative server for the smallorg.org domain, the DNS server must be configured with the appropriate DNS records. For the purposes of the Internet, the smallorg.org domain exists on the ISP mail server.

As shown in Chapter 4, there are several records that must be configured on the DNS server for the domain to be defined on the Internet. Listing 11.1 shows an example of what the DNS records for the smallorg.org domain might look like.

Using qmail as an ISP Mail Server

CHAPTER 11

273

11

USING QMAIL AS
AN ISP MAIL
SERVER

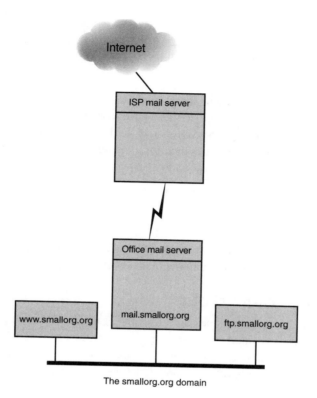

The smallorg.org domain

FIGURE 11.4

Sample domain smallorg.org *connected to the ISP.*

LISTING 11.1   Sample smallorg.org DNS Definition

```
1   smallorg.org.  IN  SOA  host1.ispnet1.net. postmaster.host1.ispnet1.net.  (
2               2000033001   ;unique serial number
3               8H          ; refresh rate
4           2H         ;retry period
5           1W         ; expiration period
6           1D)        ; minimum
7
8       NS    host1.ispnet1.net.    ;defines primary name server
9       NS    ns1.ispnet2.net.    ; defines secondary name server
10
11      MX    10 host1.ispnet1.net.    ; defines primary mail server
12
13  host1.isp.net.    A    10.0.0.1
14
15  1.0.0.10.IN-ADDR.ARPA.  PTR  host1.isp.net.  ;pointer addr for reverse DNS
```

As shown in Listing 11.1, lines 1–6 define the Start of Authority (SOA) record for the smallorg.org domain. The originating part of the SOA record points to the master DNS server for the domain, which for a virtual domain will be the ISP's DNS server. Lines 8 and 9 define the DNS servers for the domain.

Line 11 is important. It defines who will accept mail messages for the domain. You must ensure that the proper MX record for the domain is used, or messages from remote Internet users will not be delivered properly. The MX record for the domain must point to the ISP mail server. This ensures that any messages destined for the domain will be sent to the ISP mail server (which will be configured to accept them later).

Lines 13 and 15 define the Internet address of the ISP host that is being used to host the virtual domain. This allows other Internet mail servers to connect to the ISP mail server to transfer messages.

Once the DNS MX record properly points to the ISP mail server hosting the virtual domain, it is up to the mail administrator to configure the mail server to accept the incoming messages.

Using a Single User Account

The simplest method of storing mail messages for another domain is to use a single UNIX account dedicated to the domain. Any messages received by the qmail server destined for any user on the domain are forwarded to the local UNIX user on the qmail server. Each domain hosted by the qmail server will have a separate UNIX user account. Figure 11.5 demonstrates this technique.

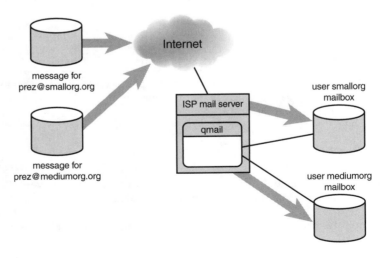

FIGURE 11.5

Hosting multiple virtual domains using UNIX accounts.

The following sections describe the steps necessary to configure the qmail mail server to accept and store messages for the virtual domains.

Create the UNIX Account

To allow the remote domain mail server to connect to the ISP mail server, you must create a normal user account. This can be done in several different ways, depending on the UNIX distribution you are using.

On FreeBSD UNIX systems, you can use the `pw` command with the `useradd` parameter:

```
pw useradd smallorg -c "Mail account for smallorg.org" -d /home/smallorg
```

This command creates the system userid `smallorg`, as well as a group `smallorg`. It assigns a home directory to the `smallorg` userid, but it is not created. You will have to do this yourself:

```
mkdir /home/smallorg
chown smallorg.smallorg /home/smallorg
```

On Linux systems, you can use the `adduser` command to accomplish all of these steps at once:

```
adduser -c "Mail account for smallorg.org" -d /home/smallorg smallorg
```

This command creates the userid `smallorg`, the group `smallorg`, and the home directory `/home/smallorg` with the proper permissions.

Remember to assign a password to the new system account:

```
passwd smallorg
```

> **CAUTION**
>
> It is extremely dangerous to edit the UNIX password and group files manually with the vi or other editor. Any mistakes could result in a corrupted password file and a UNIX system that does not allow anyone (including the `root` user) to log in. This would be bad—very bad.

Configure qmail for the Virtual Domain

The next step is to configure qmail so that it accepts messages destined for users in the remote domain. The file responsible for controlling what addresses qmail accepts mail for is the `rcpthosts` control file. This file lists all hosts and domains for which qmail will accept mail. By default, it should contain the hostname of the local mail server.

Any other domains that you need to host on the ISP mail server need to be added to the `rcpthosts` file. Each domain should be listed on a separate line. Listing 11.2 demonstrates a sample `rcpthosts` file for an ISP that hosts several domains.

LISTING 11.2   Sample `rcpthosts` File for Hosting Virtual Domains

```
shadrach.ispnet1.net
ispnet1.net
smallorg.org
largeorg.org
neworg.org
```

The `rcpthosts` file is located in the `/var/qmail/control` directory and can be edited with any standard UNIX editor, such as vi. By default, the first entry should be the hostname of the local mail server. In the example shown in Listing 11.2, not only does this mail server accept mail for itself, it also accepts mail for four other domains, including its own. Each domain must now be assigned a separate place for qmail to forward the messages so that the proper domain mail server can retrieve them when it connects to the ISP mail server.

The second qmail control file that must be configured is the `virtualdomains` file. The `virtualdomains` file controls to what account messages received for a particular domain go. Each domain is defined on a separate line in the file. The format of a domain record is

domain:*account*

where *domain* is the domain name and *account* is the mail account to which messages will be forwarded.

The mail account can be one of two things. It can be either a standard UNIX system account (as we created in the previous step) or it can be a configured qmail alias name. While it is possible to forward domain messages to a qmail alias, the purpose of this exercise is to allow a remote host to connect to the UNIX host and retrieve messages, so it will be easier to forward the messages to a system account (such as the one we created).

Listing 11.3 shows an example of a `virtualdomains` file that can be used to map domains to accounts on the UNIX mail server.

LISTING 11.3   Sample `virtualdomains` Control File

```
smallorg.org:smallorg
largeorg.org:largeorg
neworg.org:fred
```

In Listing 11.3, mail destined for any user at the `smallorg.org` domain will be forwarded to the `smallorg` UNIX system account as we intended. The next step is to have the `smallorg` account inform qmail what it wants to do with the messages.

Configure Message Delivery

This step is where things can get a little tricky for the mail administrator. So far, qmail has recognized that it can accept messages destined for the smallorg.org domain, and it knows to forward those messages to the smallorg system account. The trick is how they are forwarded.

qmail forwards the messages as if they were qmail user alias accounts under the system account name. For example, if a message is received for the user jessica@smallorg.org, qmail will forward the message to the qmail account smallorg-jessica.

Note the format that qmail uses to forward the message. This resembles the standard method of user-defined aliases described in Chapter 8, "Using qmail."

You can now take advantage of this fact and set up separate .qmail files for any userids that you need to receive messages for. Alternatively, you can set up a standard .qmail-default file to handle all of the messages for the smallorg.org domain.

The .qmail files are created in the user's home directory and direct qmail how to deliver the mail message when it is received. It can specify a program or, in this case, it can specify a local username that the message can be delivered to.

To allow all of the messages for the smallorg.org domain to be delivered to the smallorg system account, you can create the .qmail-default file using this command:

```
echo ./Maildir/ > /home/smallorg/.qmail-default
```

Now all messages received for the smallorg.org domain will be stored in the smallorg user mailbox until retrieved by the remote domain mail server.

Using Limited Local Mail Support for a Virtual Domain

Some ISPs allow an organization to have several mail accounts on the ISP mail server while supporting the bulk of its accounts on the remote domain mail server. This is done to allow special users to connect to the ISP mail server from home or another remote location using a dial-in modem. This can be accomplished easily using the qmail virtual domain configuration.

First, system accounts must be created to support the individual dial-in customers:

```
adduser -c "smallorg.org president" -d /home/soprez soprez
adduser -c "smallorg.org vp" -d /home/sovp sovp
```

Next you set up the .qmail files in the smallorg home directory to handle the messages that are destined for the special users and have them forwarded to the new accounts. For this example, we will assume that the president of smallorg.org will use the email address prez@smallorg.org, and the vice president of smallorg.org will use the email address vp@smallorg.org.

```
echo soprez > /home/smallorg/.qmail-prez
echo sovp > /home/smallorg/.qmail-vp
```

Remember to retain the .qmail-default file, or no other messages will be received. Now any message destined for the president will go to the soprez system account, and the vice president's mail will go to the sovp system account. The two can connect to the ISP mail server using a modem and a POP3 MUA package to retrieve their mail from anywhere they want. The other email accounts will still be forwarded to the smallorg system account to be picked up by the domain mail server for processing. This demonstrates the best of both worlds.

> **NOTE**
>
> When you configure an account from a virtual domain to be hosted on the local mail server, remember that users must always connect to the ISP mail server to retrieve mail messages. In a dial-up network environment, this may not be a good solution.

Using UUCP

The UUCP protocol was designed in the early days of UNIX as a means to transfer both mail and files between UNIX machines using slow speed modems. Since then, the FTP and SMTP protocols have all but replaced the UUCP protocol. However, with the explosion of Internet email, UUCP is making a small comeback.

Many small and medium-size businesses and organizations cannot afford a full-time connection to the Internet, but they still want basic email services. A simple and tested method is to use the old UUCP communications method to transfer mail to another UNIX host that can send and receive mail with the Internet. UUCP connections often are considerably cheaper than using a PPP connection with SMTP. As the ISP provider, you may open up a whole new category of customers by supporting UUCP. Figure 11.6 demonstrates how an office UNIX mail server can connect to the ISP via UUCP.

The most common UUCP implementation for UNIX is the Taylor UUCP package. Most Linux distributions include the Taylor UUCP package as a binary distribution. The FreeBSD UNIX distribution installs Taylor UUCP by default.

The Taylor UUCP package controls UUCP connections using several configuration files. The configuration files are located in the /etc/uucp directory. These files are shown in Table 11.1.

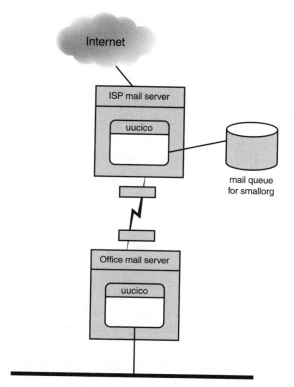

FIGURE 11.6

Using UUCP to connect to the ISP mail server.

TABLE 11.1 Taylor UUCP Configuration Files

File	Description
config	Defines the local UUCP system
sys	Defines the remote UUCP systems
port	Defines the dial ports used for UUCP connectivity
dial	Defines the modem dial commands used to dial remote systems

Once the remote UUCP system is defined in the Taylor UUCP configuration files, qmail can use the uux program to forward messages received by the virtual domain to the UUCP mail queue for delivery.

You will need to create a UNIX system account for the remote UUCP host to use when connecting to the ISP host. For this example, we can use the username `smallorg` and the UUCP host site name `smallhost`.

First, you must add a line to the `virtualdomains` control file to accept messages for the `smallorg.org` domain and forward them to the `smallorg` username:

```
smallorg.org:smallorg
```

Also, the `smallorg.org` domain must be added to the `rcpthosts` control file so that qmail knows to accept messages for the `smallorg.org` domain.

Next, the `smallorg` user must have a `.qmail` file to control how messages will be processed. For UUCP, you can pass the messages to the uux program to send via the rmail program contained in UUCP to the remote UUCP host. The `.qmail-default` file should contain the following line:

```
|preline -df /usr/bin/uux - -r -g0 smallhost!rmail
```

This command uses the uux program to forward the message to the `smallhost` UUCP host and executes the `rmail` command for it to be delivered locally on the `smallhost` host. The next time the remote domain mail server connects to the ISP mail server, any messages in the UUCP mail queue will be transferred and processed by the domain mail server.

Retrieving Mail from a Virtual Domain

Once the domain messages have been either stored in a single account or placed in the UUCP mail queue, the domain mail server must be able to connect to the ISP mail server to retrieve the messages and forward them to the appropriate users. This section describes how the domain mail server could retrieve messages from the ISP.

Retrieving Domain Mail from a Single User Account

The method of forwarding all messages for a domain to a single system account is simple and efficient. However, the remote domain mail server must be able to retrieve the messages from the single account and parse them out to the appropriate users on the domain mail server. It is a good idea for the ISP to understand how this process works.

The messages in the system account are stored as normal messages in the user's mailbox. Listing 11.4 shows an example of a mailbox that contains several messages sent to a domain hosted by the mail server using the account `smallorg`.

LISTING 11.4   Sample Mailbox for a Virtual Domain Account

```
1  $ cat /var/mail/smallorg
2  From rich Thu Mar 30 17:04:36 2000
3  Return-Path: <rich>
4  Delivered-To: smallorg@shadrach.ispnet1.net
5  Received: (qmail 5177 invoked by uid 1003); 30 Mar 2000 22:04:36 -0000
6  Delivered-To: smallorg-fred@smallorg.org
7  Received: (qmail 5174 invoked from network); 30 Mar 2000 22:04:09 -0000
8  Received: from localhost.ispnet1.net (HELO ispnet1.net) (127.0.0.1)
9    by localhost.ispnet1.net with SMTP; 30 Mar 2000 22:04:09 -0000
10 To: fred@smallorg.org
11 From: rich@shadrach.ispnet1.net
12 Subject: A test
13 Status: RO
14
15 This is a test of the virtual domain system
16 This is the end of the test.
17
18 From rich Thu Mar 30 17:05:55 2000
19 Return-Path: <rich>
20 Delivered-To: smallorg@shadrach.ispnet1.net
21 Received: (qmail 5192 invoked by uid 1003); 30 Mar 2000 22:05:55 -0000
22 Delivered-To: smallorg-prez@smallorg.org
23 Received: (qmail 5189 invoked from network); 30 Mar 2000 22:05:18 -0000
24 Received: from localhost.ispnet1.net (HELO ispnet1.net) (127.0.0.1)
25    by localhost.ispnet1.net with SMTP; 30 Mar 2000 22:05:18 -0000
26 To: prez@smallorg.org
27 From: rich@shadrach.ispnet1.net
28 Subject: You have mail
29 Status: RO
30
31 This is to confirm that your virtual domain is working on the qmail server.
32 This is the end of the test.
33
34 $
```

Listing 11.4 shows the contents of the /var/mail/smallorg mailbox. Lines 2–16 are the text of one mail message received for the smallorg.org domain, and lines 18–32 are the text of another message received for the domain. Notice that in lines 4 and 20 qmail did its job properly and delivered both messages to the user smallorg.

When the remote domain mail server retrieves the messages for the smallorg user, it must parse the messages and look specifically for the original message headers (shown in lines 10 and 26) to determine the real destination for the messages.

If the remote organization is also using qmail, this is an easy job. The next chapter discusses how to configure a qmail mail server for an office that will connect to the ISP, retrieve messages from a single user account, and parse them to the proper destination on the qmail server.

There are also other products available that can accomplish this. If the remote organization is using Microsoft Windows 95, 98, NT, or 2000 technology for its mail server, it can use the Deerfield mdaemon mail server product (http://www.mdaemon.com). This package runs in a standard Microsoft Windows environment and can support hundreds of users from a single ISP mail account.

If the remote organization is using a UNIX environment but doesn't use qmail, the fetchmail program is a great resource to use to retrieve messages. The fetchmail program is included with the FreeBSD packages as well as with most Linux distributions.

The fetchmail program is extremely versatile in being able to retrieve mail messages from remote mail servers. For this, the fetchmail program will be configured to retrieve messages from a single mailbox on the ISP mail server using the POP3 protocol.

Once fetchmail retrieves the mail messages from the ISP mail server, it must be able to parse the RFC822 header fields to determine the local user for whom the message is intended. This feature can be configured in the fetchmail configuration file.

Fetchmail uses a configuration file to define how it will retrieve the messages and how it will attempt to deliver them. The location of the configuration file is $HOME/.fetchmailrc. In this scenario, the root user will use a fetchmail configuration file that will log into the ISP mail server using the POP3 protocol with the ISP-assigned userid and password. Also, each local user who will receive mail from the Internet must be defined in the root user's .fetchmailrc file. Any mail that is retrieved by fetchmail that is not destined for a defined local user will be stored in the mailbox of the userid running the fetchmail program (in this case the root user). Listing 11.5 shows a sample .fetchmailrc file that can be used for this scenario.

LISTING 11.5   Sample $HOME/.fetchmailrc Configuration File

```
1  poll host1.ispnet1.net with proto POP3
2    localdomains smallorg.org
3    no envelope
4    no dns
5    user "smallorg" with password "freebie" is
6        rich
7        barbara
8        katie
9        jessica
10       haley
11       riley
```

Using qmail as an ISP Mail Server

CHAPTER 11

283

11

USING QMAIL AS
AN ISP MAIL
SERVER

```
12      chris
13      matthew
14      prez
15  here
```

In Listing 11.5, line 1 defines the ISP mail server that fetchmail will connect with to retrieve the domain mail. Line 1 also indicates to use the POP3 protocol for the connection. Lines 2–4 define options that will be used for the connection. Line 2 indicates what domain fetchmail will look for as the local domain address in message headers. Thus, it will recognize the address prez@smallorg.org as the local mail server user prez. Line 3 indicates not to use the X-Envelope-To: header field to parse the recipient address. These header fields are often added by MTAs as the mail passes from one site to another. They can be confusing to fetchmail. Line 4 indicates not to use DNS to confirm the identity of the sending host. Line 5 identifies the ISP mailbox userid and password that fetchmail will use to connect to the ISP mail server. These should be provided by the ISP.

Lines 6 through 14 list all of the local users on the mail server that can receive mail. Every local user that will receive mail needs to be included in this list. Fetchmail will parse the RFC822 message header fields and look for these usernames. If one is found, fetchmail forwards the message to that local user. If the destination user does not match any of the local usernames listed, fetchmail delivers the message to the userid that ran fetchmail. It is the job of the mail administrator to add new local users to the list. Line 15 indicates that the local usernames are located on the local host that fetchmail is running on.

Once the .fetchmailrc file is created and stored in the $HOME directory of the userid that will run fetchmail, the program can be run. Listing 11.6 shows an example of the output from a sample fetchmail session.

LISTING 11.6 Sample Fetchmail Session

```
$ fetchmail
2 messages for smallorg at host1.ispnet1.net (1156 octets).
reading message 1 of 2 (562 octets)  flushed
reading message 2 of 2 (594 octets)  flushed
$
```

When fetchmail finishes, the messages retrieved from the ISP mail server should be properly delivered to the proper domain mail server users.

Retrieving Domain Mail from a UUCP Account

If the ISP mail server is storing incoming messages for a virtual domain in a UUCP mail queue, the remote domain mail server must connect to the ISP mail server using the UUCP protocol. Again, the Taylor UUCP software package is an excellent UNIX UUCP package to use to connect with a remote UUCP host.

The domain mail server must be configured to dial the ISP UUCP host on a regular basis to transfer mail. If the domain mail server is also running qmail, you can configure qmail to forward all outbound messages to the ISP UUCP mail queue. This is similar to the description in the "Retrieving Domain Mail from a Single User Account" section of this chapter. The only difference is that, instead of a single virtual domain being forwarded to the UUCP username, all mail for any domain will be forwarded. This can be accomplished using an empty address parameter for the virtual domain record:

```
:isphost
```

This `virtualdomains` control file line forwards all messages to the `isphost` username. The `isphost` username should then contain a `.qmail-default` file that controls the processing of the messages. Again, this should be similar to the ISP's UUCP message processing method described previously.

Configuring Selective Relaying

Another important feature that the ISP must support is the capability for customers to use the ISP mail server to forward outbound messages to the Internet. The standard small office mail server will not have a full-time connection to the Internet, so it will not be able to send messages to remote users.

Instead, the small office mail server must place any outgoing messages in a message queue to send to the ISP mail server the next time a connection is made. It is the responsibility of the ISP mail server to forward those messages to the appropriate remote mail servers.

While forwarding messages from customers is required, the ISP needs to block forwarding attempts by other Internet hosts at the same time. This is where it gets tricky. The mail administrator must configure the mail system to reject mail relaying requests from some clients while allowing other clients to relay messages.

The `qmail-smtpd` program is used to receive messages from remote mail servers using the SMTP protocol. The `rcpthosts` control file controls the addresses for which `qmail-smtpd` will receive messages. If a remote host attempts to send a message for a user on a host not defined in the `rcpthosts` file, `qmail-smtpd` will reject the message.

There is one exception to this rule. If the UNIX environment variable `RELAYCLIENT` is set, `qmail-smtpd` ignores the values in the `rcpthosts` file and forwards all messages to the remote address specified by the `RELAYCLIENT` variable.

Using qmail as an ISP Mail Server

CHAPTER 11

285

11

USING QMAIL AS
AN ISP MAIL
SERVER

With this feature, the mail administrator can trick `qmail-smtpd` into relaying messages. If the `RELAYCLIENT` environment variable is set to an empty string, `qmail-smtpd` will attempt to forward the message to its appropriate remote mail server automatically. The trick is to set the `RELAYCLIENT` variable to an empty string only for certain IP addresses.

The following section describes two methods that can be used to set the `RELAYCLIENT` UNIX environment variable for certain IP addresses, thus implementing selective relaying on a qmail mail server.

Setting Environment Variables Using the Tcpwrappers Program

Tcpwrappers is a common UNIX program that is used as a middleman, along with the inetd program. As mentioned in Chapter 10, "The ucspi-tcp Program," the inetd program is used by almost all UNIX distributions to monitor network connection attempts and call application programs when connection attempts from remote clients are detected.

The tcpwrappers program provides additional functionality to the inetd program, in that it allows

- The creation of a database of IP addresses to allow or deny
- Additional logging capabilities for connections
- Verification of hostnames and IP addresses via DNS

If you are using the inetd program to monitor the network for SMTP connections, you can use the tcpwrappers program to provide selective relaying functionality to the `qmail-smtpd` program. The following sections describe how this is done.

Installing Tcpwrappers

Almost all Linux distributions include the tcpwrappers program by default. The FreeBSD UNIX distribution includes tcpwrappers as a software port. It can be installed using the standard FreeBSD port installation method:

1. Go to the tcpwrappers port directory:

   ```
   cd /usr/ports/security/tcp_wrappers
   ```

2. Run the GNU make program to compile and install tcpwrappers:

   ```
   make
   make install
   ```

That is all that is required to install tcpwrappers on a FreeBSD system. The tcpwrappers program tcpd is installed in the `/usr/local/libexec` directory.

Configuring Tcpwrappers

To implement selective relaying using the tcpwrappers program, you must set up an access control database for tcpwrappers. The tcpd program uses a standard host access text file as the access control database. The format of a host access text file is

```
daemon_list : client_list [ : shell_command ]
```

The `daemon_list` field defines the UNIX application program that the access rule should match against. Remember that the `tcp-env` program always precedes the `qmail-smtpd` program, so that is the entry that must be made in the access control database.

The `client_list` field defines the addresses that should be matched for the access rule. Addresses can be defined using hostnames, IP addresses, or wildcard patterns.

The `shell_command` field is where you can enter the shell command to set the `RELAYCLIENT` environment variable to trigger the `qmail-smtpd` relay function.

The access control database is contained in a file called `hosts.allow`. The location of this file varies, depending on the UNIX distribution. Linux systems often place this file in the `/etc` directory. FreeBSD systems place it in the `/usr/local/etc` directory. The following shows a sample `hosts.allow` access control database file:

```
tcp-env: 192.168.: setenv = RELAYCLIENT
tcp-env: localhost: setenv = RELAYCLIENT
```

The first line demonstrates setting the `RELAYCLIENT` environment variable for any connection originating from the `192.168` network. The second line demonstrates setting the `RELAYCLIENT` environment variable for any connection originating from the local mail server. This may be required for some MUA programs to work properly. After the `hosts.allow` file is created, you must let the inetd program know about the tcpwrapper. The next section describes this process.

Configuring /etc/inetd.conf

The inetd program must be configured to pass connection attempts to the tcpwrapper program. This is done in the `/etc/inetd.conf` configuration file. Adding the tcpwrapper program makes for a messy configuration line, but it works.

The line for the qmail `tcp-env` program in `/etc/inetd.conf` should look like this:

```
smtp    stream tcp    nowait qmaild /usr/local/libexec/tcpd
➥ /var/qmail/bin/tcp-env  /var/qmail/bin/qmail-smtpd
```

Remember that this must all be entered on a single line in the `/etc/inetd.conf` file. The inetd protocol tag should be set to `smtp` for all SMTP connections. The program that inetd passes the connection to now becomes the tcpwrapper tcpd program. This example is from a FreeBSD system. The location of the tcpd program for other UNIX systems may (and probably will) vary.

Setting Environment Variables Using the Tcpserver Program

The tcpserver program was introduced in Chapter 10. It is a replacement for the inetd program that was developed by Dan Bernstein. It provides improved network performance and control over the inetd program. Installing the tcpserver program was covered in detail in Chapter 10, so it will not be discussed here.

The tcpserver program uses an access control database similar to the tcpwrappers program. One improvement made by Bernstein is that tcpserver uses a hashed cdb database that can be accessed by tcpserver much quicker than a text file. This improves the time required for the server to determine if the connection should be accepted or not.

The mail administrator must first create a text version of the database and use the tcprules program to create the hashed cdb database. The format of the text database file is

address:action

where *address* is used to match incoming addresses from the network, and *action* is a defined tcprule action.

The formats of the *address* and *action* fields were described in Table 10.8 and demonstrated in Table 10.9, both in Chapter 10. As shown in Table 10.9, you can set the RELAYCLIENT environment variable for selected IP addresses within the tcpserver access control database. The following shows an example of an access control database:

```
192.168.:allow,RELAYCLIENT=""
192.168.1.10:deny
```

The first rule sets the RELAYCLIENT environment variable to an empty string for any connection originating from the 192.168.0.0 network. This allows relaying from any client within that network. The second rule denies a SMTP connection from the IP address 192.168.1.10. A connection originating from any other IP address will be allowed to connect via SMTP to transfer messages but will be blocked from relaying messages to another remote mail server.

Once the text access control database has been configured, you must create the hashed cdb database using the tcprules program:

```
tcprules database tmpfile
```

The tcprules program accepts input from UNIX standard input. To convert a text access control database file to a hashed cdb database file, you must send the text file to the tcprules program:

```
cat /etc/tcp.smtp.txt | tcprules /etc/tcp.smtp.cdb /etc/tcp.smtp.tmp
```

There is no set location for the tcpserver access control database. The tcpserver program uses the -x parameter to determine the location of the database. A standard has been adopted by Bernstein to use the filename

```
/etc/tcp.protocol.format
```

where *protocol* is the TCP protocol the rules were created for and *format* is the format of the database (either text or hashed).

When the database has been created, the `tcpserver` command can be inserted into the system boot scripts as described in Chapter 10. The format for the `tcpserver` command should be

```
tcpserver -v -p -x /etc/tcp.smtp.cdb 0 smtp /var/qmail/bin/qmail-smtpd
```

Rebooting the mail server causes qmail to start with selective relaying enabled.

Summary

The qmail mail server program is a very robust MTA program that can be used to support a large Internet email environment. Many ISPs use qmail to support thousands of email clients. Individual home users as well as small and medium-size corporate users can have mail received by qmail on the ISP mail server.

Two necessary functions for an ISP are support of virtual domains and selective relaying. A virtual domain allows the ISP to receive messages destined for users on a remote domain and store them in a location from which they can be retrieved later by the remote domain mail server. Many small companies do not have dedicated Internet service. Without a dedicated Internet host, remote mail servers don't know when or how to contact the corporate mail server for delivery. With virtual domains, the ISP host stays connected to the Internet all the time to accept messages for the small corporation's domain from remote hosts and store them, either in a single user account or a UUCP mail queue. The corporate domain mail server can then connect to the ISP at its leisure and download any messages.

Selective relaying allows an ISP to support remote customers. Most remote ISP customers are unable to send outbound email messages directly to the destination mail server. Instead, they require a smart host that can forward the message to the proper destination. Unfortunately, it is unwise to allow the ISP mail server to forward messages for everyone, because that can be abused by spammers. The qmail mail package allows for selective relaying, in which the ISP mail server allows selected remote clients to use the mail server as a smart host but blocks other remote hosts.

Using qmail as an Office Mail Server

IN THIS CHAPTER

The previous chapter described how qmail could be used as a fully functional commercial ISP mail server. qmail can also be configured to serve as the domain mail server, servicing local customers and connecting to the remote ISP to forward and retrieve mail messages. This chapter describes the methods that can be used to connect the office mail server to the ISP mail server.

Once the connection is made to the ISP, a method must be used to retrieve mail messages from the ISP and forward them to the proper users. The serialmail program is a Dan Bernstein creation that can be used to accomplish this. Serialmail is described in this chapter.

Requirements for an Office Mail Server

As mentioned in the Chapter 11, "Using qmail as an ISP Mail Server," corporate use of the Internet has exploded. Many large organizations have invested thousands of dollars incorporating commercial email systems to enable their employees to send and receive messages across the Internet. Unfortunately, most small and medium-size organizations do not have the resources to purchase or support large-scale commercial email systems.

This is where the multitude of free UNIX distributions save the day. Using the qmail email package, along with a freely available UNIX distribution such as FreeBSD or Linux, any small organization can efficiently and inexpensively provide Internet email capabilities to its employees.

As mentioned in Chapter 4, "DNS and qmail," the small organization must first register an Internet domain name with the Internet Corporation for Assigned Names and Numbers (ICANN). Once the organization has a domain name, it can hire an ISP to host the domain on the Internet, including receiving mail messages. The next step is for the local mail server to connect with the ISP on a regular basis to retrieve messages and to forward messages waiting to be sent out to the Internet.

There are four different scenarios for how the office mail server can connect with the ISP mail server to transfer mail. They are

- Full-time Internet connection
- Dial-up Internet connection
- Dial-on-demand Internet connection
- UUCP connection

Each scenario requires a different configuration for qmail. The following sections describe how the connections are established.

After those descriptions, the remainder of the chapter describes the Sendmail program, used to help qmail communicate with the ISP to retrieve messages.

Full-Time Internet Connection

With Internet communications improving, it is now possible for small and medium-size organizations to afford a full-time connection to the Internet. Often this is via an ISDN or DSL modem connection, although many cable TV systems are offering cable modem connectivity to the Internet. Figure 12.1 demonstrates a full-time connection to the ISP for the office mail server.

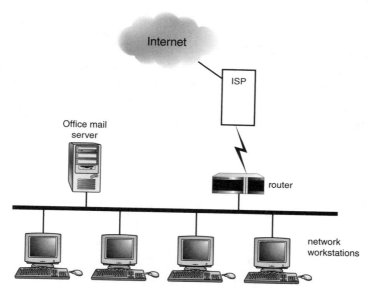

FIGURE 12.1

Full-time Internet connectivity to the ISP.

There are many pros and cons regarding full-time connectivity to the Internet. Each corporate situation is unique, so it is impossible to recommend a generic solution. It is the job of the network administrator to weigh the pros and cons for the organization to determine which (if any) full-time connectivity solution is best.

Both Linux and FreeBSD support direct ISDN connectivity. Both systems support plug-in PC ISDN cards as well as external ISDN terminal adapters (modems). A primary rate ISDN connection in the United States supports two B channels. Each B channel can handle 64kbp/s of data. If two-channel service is purchased, the organization can use 128kbp/s of full-time connectivity to the ISP. This is usually more than enough bandwidth to support email and simple Web browsing for small and even medium-size organizations.

The `isdn4linux` and `isdn4bsd` programs are designed to configure and run ISDN modems from a Linux or FreeBSD system. They make connecting the mail server to the Internet via ISDN simple.

> **CAUTION**
>
> Remember that if your mail server is connected full time to the Internet, it may be susceptible to hacker attacks. Extra caution needs to be exercised for mail servers that are directly connected to the Internet. While both Linux and FreeBSD can use firewall software to deter intruders, nothing is perfect. Always closely monitor system logs for improper activity.

Dial-Up Internet Connection

For organizations not wanting a full-time Internet connection, there is the capability to dial into the ISP using the Point-to-Point Protocol (PPP) to transfer IP packets with the ISP mail server. This service is often considerably cheaper than a full-time connection, and for simple email service is more than adequate. Figure 12.2 demonstrates a dial-up connection to the ISP.

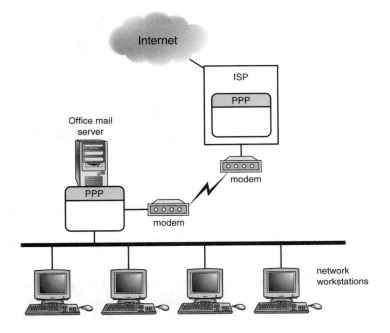

FIGURE 12.2

Dial-up connectivity to the ISP.

Both Linux and FreeBSD support PPP as a kernel function. The pppd program is used to supplement the kernel PPP functionality to provide PPP support.

FreeBSD installs the pppd program by default. All Linux distributions include it as a binary distribution. Once the pppd program is installed, it can be configured to connect to the ISP mail server via a dial-up modem at predetermined intervals. The following sections describe configuring the pppd program to connect with the ISP mail server.

Configuring the Pppd Program

The pppd program uses a standard modem to connect with the remote ISP mail server. The format of the pppd program is

```
pppd <tty line> <speed> [options]
```

where `<tty line>` is the COM port to which your modem is connected and `<speed>` is the speed at which you want to connect to the modem. The art of using the pppd program is in choosing the proper options for the client and server commands. Here are some of the options available to use pppd as a client:

> `connect`—Allows the pppd program to use an executable or shell script to set up the serial link before the pppd program will attempt to connect.
>
> `crtscts`—Uses RTS/CTS hardware flow control on the serial line.
>
> `defaultroute`—Adds a default route to the kernel routing table, pointing to the remote IP address of the PPP server. The route table entry is deleted when the PPP session is terminated. This allows the server to know to send IP traffic destined for other network devices out the PPP connection.
>
> `lock`—Creates a UUCP-style lock file to indicate that the modem is in use.
>
> `mru` and `mtu`—Allow the client to attempt to set the Maximum Receive Unit (MRU) and Maximum Transmit Unit (MTU) sizes during the PPP negotiation phase. It is still up to the PPP server to agree to the new sizes. Often this is used on slower modem connections to reduce the PPP packet size.
>
> `modem`—Allows the UNIX system to use the modem control lines. With this option, the pppd program will wait for the CD (*carrier detect*) modem signal when opening the modem line and will drop the DTR (*data terminal ready*) signal to the COM port briefly when the PPP connection is terminated, thus forcing the modem to disconnect with the remote modem.
>
> `Connect`—Establishes the modem connection with the remote ISP. Usually this option uses the chat program to dial the modem to establish the connection.

Configuring the Chat Program

The chat program is part of the pppd distribution and is used to simplify the `connect` string for pppd. The chat program can use a simple script file and communicate with the modem to initiate the connection with the PPP server. The chat script uses text strings that it can send to the remote server in response to text strings received. It tries to match the text strings in a chat session—one response for each string received. Listing 12.1 shows an example of a sample chat script for pppd.

LISTING 12.1   Sample Chat Script `isp.chat`

```
1    ""
2    ATDT5551234
3    CONNECT
4    ""
5    "ogin:"
6    rich
7    "word:"
8    guitar
9    "$"
10   "exec /usr/sbin/pppd silent modem crtscts proxyarp 10.0.0.100:10.0.0.2"
```

Line 2 shows the command that pppd will send to the modem to dial the ISP phone number.
Line 3 shows what text string pppd should wait for to establish that a connection has been
made to the PPP server. Line 4 indicates that when the chat program receives a connection
notice from the modem, it should send a single carriage return. Line 5 shows what text string
to wait for from the server. If the server is allowing terminal logins from this modem line, it
should issue a welcome banner with a login prompt. In line 6, pppd sends the userid to the PPP
server, and in line 8 it sends the password. When pppd gets a command prompt from the PPP
server (as shown in line 9), it then issues the host pppd command on the PPP server. The correct program and parameters used in this command line are unique to your ISP and should be
provided by the ISP. Most provide simple batch files for clients to use.

Once a successful chat script has been created, it can be used in the pppd configuration to dial
the ISP mail server when the pppd program is executed. The `connect` pppd option calls the
chat script using the following format:

```
pppd ttyS1 38400 connect '/usr/sbin/chat -v -f /home/rich/isp.chat' modem
➥ crtscts defaultroute
```

The `connect` option uses the chat program in its script to connect to the PPP server. The previous command line will automatically call the PPP server and start the pppd program on the
server. The `-v` option used in the chat program allows for extremely verbose output to the
`/var/log/messages` file. Use this for testing purposes, then remove it when you have all the
bugs worked out. Listing 12.2 shows the lines that the pppd and chat programs place in the
message log during a client PPP session.

LISTING 12.2   Lines from `/var/log/message` for Pppd and Chat

```
1    Sep 22 06:56:56 shadrach pppd[663]: pppd 2.3.5 started by root, uid 0
2    Sep 22 06:56:56 shadrach kernel: registered device ppp0
3    Sep 22 06:56:57 shadrach chat[664]: send (ATZS7=100^M)
4    Sep 22 06:56:57 shadrach chat[664]: expect (OK)
5    Sep 22 06:56:57 shadrach chat[664]: ATZS7=100^M^M
```

```
 6  Sep 22 06:56:57 shadrach chat[664]: OK
 7  Sep 22 06:56:57 shadrach chat[664]:  -- got it
 8  Sep 22 06:56:57 shadrach chat[664]: send (ATDT5551234^M)
 9  Sep 22 06:56:58 shadrach chat[664]: expect (CONNECT)
10  Sep 22 06:56:58 shadrach chat[664]: ^M
11  Sep 22 06:57:18 shadrach chat[664]: ATDT5551234^M^M
12  Sep 22 06:57:18 shadrach chat[664]: CONNECT
13  Sep 22 06:57:18 shadrach chat[664]:  -- got it
14  Sep 22 06:57:18 shadrach chat[664]: send (^M)
15  Sep 22 06:57:18 shadrach chat[664]: expect (ogin:)
16  Sep 22 06:57:18 shadrach chat[664]:  28800/V42BIS^M
17  Sep 22 06:57:19 shadrach chat[664]: ^M
18  Sep 22 06:57:19 shadrach chat[664]: ^MRed Hat Linux release 5.2 (Apollo)
19  Sep 22 06:57:19 shadrach chat[664]: ^MKernel 2.0.36 on an i486
20  Sep 22 06:57:19 shadrach chat[664]: ^M
21  Sep 22 06:57:19 shadrach chat[664]: ^M^M
22  Sep 22 06:57:19 shadrach chat[664]: mail1.isp.net login:
23  Sep 22 06:57:19 shadrach chat[664]:  -- got it
24  Sep 22 06:57:19 shadrach chat[664]: send (rich^M)
25  Sep 22 06:57:19 shadrach chat[664]: expect (word:)
26  Sep 22 06:57:19 shadrach chat[664]:  rich^M
27  Sep 22 06:57:19 shadrach chat[664]: Password:
28  Sep 22 06:57:19 shadrach chat[664]:  -- got it
29  Sep 22 06:57:19 shadrach chat[664]: send (guitar^M)
30  Sep 22 06:57:20 shadrach chat[664]: expect (rich]$)
31  Sep 22 06:57:20 shadrach chat[664]:  ^M
32  Sep 22 06:57:20 shadrach chat[664]: Last login: Tue Sep 21 20:45:47^M
33  Sep 22 06:57:21 shadrach chat[664]: [rich@mail1 rich]$
34  Sep 22 06:57:21 shadrach chat[664]:  -- got it
35  Sep 22 06:57:21 shadrach chat[664]: send (exec /usr/sbin/pppd passive
➥ silent modem crtscts^M)
36  Sep 22 06:57:22 shadrach pppd[663]: Serial connection established.
37  Sep 22 06:57:23 shadrach pppd[663]: Using interface ppp0
38  Sep 22 06:57:23 shadrach pppd[663]: Connect: ppp0 <--> /dev/ttyS1
39  Sep 22 06:57:27 shadrach pppd[663]: local  IP address 10.0.0.100
40  Sep 22 06:57:27 shadrach pppd[663]: remote IP address 10.0.0.2
```

Using the chat script and the pppd client commands establishes a PPP session with the ISP mail server. The next step is to create a method to establish the connection with the ISP on a regular basis.

Setting Up Pppd Dial Intervals

Now that you have a working pppd script, you must create a system for it to connect to the ISP mail server at a regular interval to send and retrieve mail messages. The UNIX cron program is just the answer.

The cron program has been in use for many years. Paul Vixie developed the version of cron that is commonly used on Linux and FreeBSD systems. The program reads a configuration file of commands and times that the commands should be executed. When the specified times are reached, the commands are executed. Each UNIX user can have his own cron configuration file.

To access the cron configuration file, use the crontab program. To list the contents of crontab, use the -1 parameter. To edit the contents, use the -e parameter. This brings up crontab using the vi editor.

Crontab entries use the following format:

```
min hour daym month dayw program
```

The first five placeholders represent the time(s) that the `program` parameter should be run. Table 12.1 shows the time values represented by the placeholders.

TABLE 12.1   Crontab Time Placeholders

Placeholder	Description
min	The minute of the day
hour	The hour of the day
daym	The day of the month
month	The month
dayw	The day of the week

Wildcards and ranges are allowed in defining the times the program should run. For example, using the * wildcard character defines all values for the placeholder. Ranges such as 1–5 or 1,4,5 define specific values the program should be run. The entry

```
0,15,30,45 * * * * /home/rich/dialup
```

runs the script /home/rich/dialup every 15 minutes of every hour of every day of every month. This is exactly what we need for the pppd program to dial the ISP on a regular basis.

Due to the large command-line entry for the pppd program, it is often beneficial to create a script with the pppd program and its parameters and use the script for the crontab entry.

CAUTION

Be careful with permissions of the script file as well as the pppd program. Remember to set the executable permissions of the script to allow the userid that runs the crontab to execute the script file.

You may have to experiment with the frequency of running the pppd program to balance efficient mail transfer with needless phone calls. Often it is best to have several different crontab entries covering different times of the day and week. While dialing the ISP every 15 minutes is good during business hours, it is wasteful at 1 a.m. in the morning. Here's an example of a multi-entry crontab:

```
0,15,30,45 8-17 * * 1-5 /home/rich/dialup
0,30 0-7,18-23 * * 1-5 /home/rich/dialup
0,30 * * * 6,7 /home/rich/dialup
```

The first entry starts the pppd connection every 15 minutes between 8 a.m. and 5 p.m. every Monday through Friday. The second entry starts pppd every half-hour midnight through 7 a.m. and 6 p.m. through midnight every Monday through Friday. The last entry starts pppd every half-hour on Saturdays and Sundays.

Dial-on-Demand Internet Connection

The third method of connecting the local mail server builds upon the PPP dial-up method. A dial-on-demand server can automatically start the dial-up PPP session when it detects IP traffic destined for a host on the remote network. Figure 12.3 demonstrates how this works.

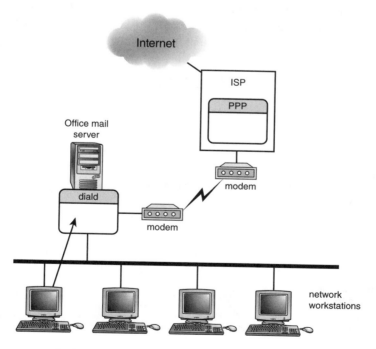

FIGURE 12.3

Dial-on-demand Internet connectivity.

Now that you have your chat script perfected and can dial into the PPP server and establish a connection, you might want to automate things a little more. If you decide to connect your mail server directly to the ISP, you will need to implement a policy on how often your server will connect to the ISP to transfer mail. One method is to use dial-on-demand IP routing. This feature will automatically start the PPP connection whenever it detects data that needs to use the ISP network.

A great program for implementing dial-on-demand routing is the diald program, written by Eric Schenk. FreeBSD and most Linux distributions don't include a binary package for diald. If your UNIX distribution doesn't, you can download a version from the diald Web site at `http://diald.unix.ch`.

The format of the diald program is

`/usr/sbin/diald [device1....] [options...] [-- [pppd options]]`

where *device1* is the TTY line your modem is connected to, *options* is diald options, and *pppd options* is the options that diald will pass to the pppd program when it calls it. It is also possible to set the parameters using a configuration file for diald.

The diald program's configuration file is used to set parameters for it to call the chat and pppd programs as required, as well as list scenarios in which you want diald to start and stop pppd. The configuration file is located at `/etc/diald.conf`. Listing 12.3 shows a sample `diald.conf` file that replaces the options used in the example.

LISTING 12.3 Sample `/etc/diald.conf` Configuration File

```
1  ###
2  # /etc/diald.conf - diald configuration
3  #
4  # see /usr/lib/diald for sample config files
5  #
6  mode ppp
7  connect '/usr/sbin/chat -f /home/rich/isp.chat -t 35000'
8  connect-timeout 180
9  device /dev/ttyS1
10 speed 115200
11 modem
12 lock
13 crtscts
14 local 10.0.0.100
15 remote 10.0.0.2
16 defaultroute
17 include /usr/lib/diald/standard.filter
18 fifo /etc/diald/diald.ctl
```

In Listing 12.3, line 7 shows the diald `connect` parameter that calls the chat program, using the same chat script that was used in the pppd example. Line 8 was added to compensate for the fact that the PPP host modem is set to answer after four rings (so as not to annoy friends and family that call the same line using voice). It allows the chat script up to three minutes to complete. Line 17 includes a `standard.filter` file that diald uses to specify under what conditions it will start the PPP session and when it will stop the session. Line 18 specifies a special file that a companion program dctrl uses to monitor the PPP session. The dctrl program is a graphical program that can be used to monitor the PPP link and report any error conditions, as well as the throughput of the connection.

Once the diald configurations are set, you can test it. Diald runs in background mode, and you must start it as the `root` userid. When diald detects a network condition that warrants a connection to the PPP server, it starts the chat program, which creates the PPP session with the server. Then it starts the pppd program on the local host. When you are satisfied with the performance of diald, you can create a startup script for it and put it in the startup scripts area on your UNIX distribution so that it starts automatically at boot time. Then every time a program needs to access a remote host via IP (such as the ISP mail server), the script will kick in and start the PPP session.

UUCP ISP Connection

Besides PPP sessions, some ISPs support the older UNIX-to-UNIX copy (UUCP) sessions. UUCP was used in the olden days of UNIX to transfer mail and files between UNIX hosts using slow dial-up modems. Its use has been replaced with PPP sessions running FTP and SMTP. However, for security-conscious organizations, there is no better way to get mail to and from the Internet than UUCP.

The nice feature about a UUCP connection is that at no time is the local mail server connected to the Internet. With PPP sessions, the local mail server becomes a node on the ISP'S network and can be reached by remote Internet clients. This creates a risk (although slight) of some adventurous hacker gaining a pathway to your mail server.

The Taylor UUCP package is the most popular UUCP implementation for Linux and FreeBSD. In fact, it is installed by default on FreeBSD systems. The Taylor UUCP package requires several configuration files to define remote UUCP hosts and how to connect to them. The UUCP configuration files are located in the `/etc/uucp` directory and can be edited or created only by `root` permissions.

The first UUCP file to configure is the `config` file, which defines the local UUCP host. No special parameters normally are required in this file. The following is a sample `config` file for the local mail server:

```
1  nodename    shadrach
```

The next file to configure is the sys file, which defines the remote host(s) that will be called. Listing 12.4 shows a sample sys file set to call the ISP UUCP host during normal working hours to check for mail.

LISTING 12.4   Sample Taylor UUCP Master sys File

```
1  system     ispmail
2  time       Wk0800-1730
3  phone      555-1234
4  port       modem
5  speed      38400
6  chat       ogin: shadrach word: guitar
```

The chat script defines what text strings to look for from the remote UUCP host and what text strings to send in response. This allows UUCP to log into the remote server. This sample chat script assumes that the remote UUCP host will automatically run the UUCP program as the default shell for the shadrach userid. If that is not the case, the chat script will need to be extended to look for a user prompt and then send the commands necessary to start UUCP on the remote host.

Next is the port file, which defines the modem used by the mail server to connect with the remote UUCP host. Listing 12.5 shows the sample port file used to define the modem.

LISTING 12.5   Sample Taylor UUCP Master port File

```
1  port       modem
2  type       modem
3  device     /dev/ttyS0
4  speed      38400
5  dialer     normal
```

The last file needed is the dial file, which will tell UUCP how to communicate with the port selected. Listing 12.6 shows the client dial file.

LISTING 12.6   Sample Taylor UUCP Master dial File

```
1  dialer     normal
2  chat       "" ATZ OK ATDT\T CONNECCT
```

Once the configuration files are created, you can test the UUCP configuration. The uucico program can be used to initiate a UUCP call to a remote UUCP host. Once the call is established, any mail or files in the UUCP queue for the remote host will be transferred. Likewise, any mail or files in the remote host's UUCP queue for your host will be transferred back. To test the configuration, enter the following command as the root user:

```
uucico -f -x chat -s ispmail
```

This command tells uucico to dial the `ispmail` UUCP system, ignoring the time restrictions, and to log the chat process. After a few seconds you should hear the modem dialing the remote site. You should be able to look at the UUCP log file (`/var/log/uucp/Log`) to see if the sites connected properly. The debug lines should be in the file `/var/log/uucp/Debug`.

Now that the UUCP connection is working, the next step is to make it run automatically. The best tool for this is the cron program. As the `root` user, enter the following to edit the cron file:

```
crontab -e
```

Add the lines shown in Listing 12.7 to the cron file for the `root` user.

LISTING 12.7   Cron Lines to Execute UUCP Automatically

```
4,9,14,19,24,29,34,39,44,49,54,59 * * * * /usr/sbin/touch
➥ /var/spool/uucp/ispmail/C./C.ispmailA0000
5,10,15,20,25,30,35,40,45,50,55 * * * * /usr/sbin/uucico -s ispmail
```

The first line creates a poll file every five minutes. When uucico notices the file in the spool area, it attempts to contact the remote site. The second line executes the uucico program to process the queued UUCP jobs.

Transferring Messages to the ISP

In the connectivity scenarios mentioned in the previous section, only the UUCP method automatically transfers mail messages when the local mail server connects to the ISP mail server. In all of the PPP-based connection methods, another program must initiate the mail transfer. The qmail program cannot perform this function on its own. Instead, another program is required to accomplish this. The serialmail program was developed by Dan Bernstein to allow the office mail server a method of sending and retrieving mail messages to a remote ISP mail server from a qmail server via a PPP connection. The serialmail program was designed to allow the local mail server to place all outbound mail messages in a single Maildir-formatted mailbox. Also, the ISP must place all inbound Internet messages for the domain in a Maildir mailbox (obviously the ISP must also be running qmail). When the PPP connection to the ISP is established, serialmail performs two operations:

- Any messages in the outbound Maildir mailbox are transferred to the ISP mail server for relaying.

- Any messages in the inbound Maildir mailbox on the ISP mail server are queued for either SMTP or QMTP delivery to the local mail server.

These functions allow the local qmail server to interact with the ISP mail server via the PPP connection to transfer mail messages. Figure 12.4 demonstrates this process.

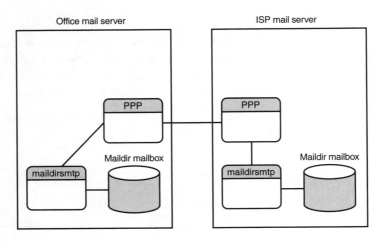

FIGURE 12.4
Using serialmail to transfer messages to and from an ISP mail server.

This section describes how to download, install, and configure serialmail to allow an office mail server running qmail to connect to the remote ISP mail server and transfer mail messages.

Downloading the Serialmail Program

The serialmail program is documented on Dan Bernstein's Web site (http://cr.yp.to/ serialmail.html). At the time of this writing the current version is version 0.75.

FreeBSD includes a port of the serialmail package. It is located in the /usr/ports/mail/ serialmail directory. It can be installed using the normal FreeBSD port method.

If you are not using FreeBSD, you can download the serialmail source code and compile it on your UNIX distribution. Bernstein maintains a location from which the source code can be downloaded at http://cr.yp.to/software/serialmail-0.75.tar.gz.

The serialmail source code comes as a compressed tar file. As with other software distributions, you must unpack it into a working directory. The /usr/local directory is a common place to use as a working directory:

```
tar -zxvf serialmail-0.75.tar.gz -C /usr/local
```

> **CAUTION**
>
> To ensure proper system permissions for the software, remember to be logged in as root when compiling and installing new software distributions.

Compiling and Installing the Serialmail Program

After untarring the serialmail package, the source code should be located in the
`/usr/local/serialmail-0.75` directory. You must change to this directory to compile the
package.

Before compiling and installing serialmail, you must verify that the serialmail configuration
files properly reflect your compiler and qmail environment. There are four configuration files
that are used to compile serialmail:

- `conf-cc`
- `conf-home`
- `conf-ld`
- `conf-qmail`

The `conf-cc` configuration file is used to define the C compiler on your UNIX distribution and
any necessary command-line parameters. By default, serialmail will use the GNU C compiler
with optimizing tuned on. All Linux and FreeBSD distributions include a version of the GNU
C compiler.

The `conf-home` configuration file defines where the serialmail home directory will be located.
Serialmail will place all the executable files in the `$HOME/bin` directory, where `$HOME` is defined
in the `conf-home` file. By default serialmail uses the `/usr/local` directory, thus placing the
serialmail executable programs in the `/usr/local/bin` directory.

The `conf-ld` configuration file is used to define the C linker that will be used to create the executable programs. By default, serialmail uses the GNU C compiler with the `-s` option to link
object files into executable files. This should be fine for Linux and FreeBSD systems using the
GNU C compiler.

Finally, the `conf-qmail` configuration file defines where the qmail home directory is located
on the qmail server. The default points to the default location of the qmail home directory, the
`/var/qmail` directory.

Once the configuration files are modified to reflect the setup of the mail server, the serialmail
program can be compiled and installed.

Compiling and installing serialmail is a two-step process. From the serialmail working directory, enter

```
make
make setup check
```

The first command should compile the source code and man pages for serialmail. The second
command installs and checks the installation of the serialmail program. If both commands are

successfully completed, the serialmail executable programs will be installed in the $HOME/bin directory, where $HOME is defined by the conf-home configuration file. By default this is the /usr/local/bin directory.

The Serialmail Executable Programs

The serialmail package consists of several utilities that allow the local mail server to connect to and retrieve mail messages from a remote ISP mail server running qmail. The two main programs that will be used are the maildirsmtp and maildirqmtp programs. Each allows mail from a Maildir-formatted mailbox to be transferred to a remote mail server, using either the SMTP or QMTP protocol. Figure 12.5 demonstrates how this works.

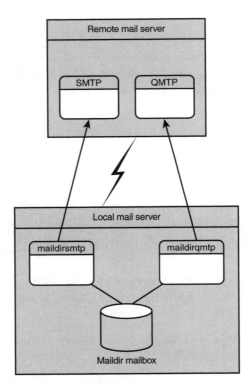

FIGURE 12.5
The maildirsmtp and maildirqmtp programs.

The following sections describe the serialmail utilities.

Transferring Mail via SMTP

The maildirsmtp script is used to read a Maildir-formatted mailbox and send any messages to a remote mail server via the SMTP protocol. The format of the maildirsmtp command is

```
maildirsmtp dir prefix host helohost
```

The maildirsmtp command-line parameters are defined in Table 12.2.

TABLE 12.2   Maildirsmtp Command-Line Parameters

Parameter	Description
dir	A Maildir-formatted mailbox.
prefix	An envelope address prefix.
host	The hostname or IP address of a remote SMTP host.
helohost	The hostname used in the SMTP HELO command when connecting to the remote SMTP host.

The prefix parameter is used to filter messages in the Maildir mail directory. Messages that contain recipient addresses beginning with prefix are forwarded to the remote SMTP host defined in the host parameter. Before they are sent, the prefix is removed from the recipient address. Any messages accepted by host for delivery are removed from the Maildir directory. Any messages rejected by host are bounced back to the original message sender.

Transferring Messages via QMTP

The maildirqmtp script is used to read a Maildir-formatted mailbox and send any messages to a remote ISP mail server using the QMTP mail protocol (see Chapter 5, "SMTP and qmail"). The format of maildirqmtp is

```
maildirqmtp dir prefix host
```

The dir, prefix, and host parameters are used the same as for maildirsmtp. The only difference from maildirsmtp is that maildirqmtp uses Dan Bernstein's QMTP protocol to transfer the messages to the remote ISP. This assumes that the remote ISP is running the qmail-qmtpd program to accept mail messages using the QMTP protocol.

Reading Maildir Mailbox Messages

The maildirserial program is a utility that the maildirsmtp and maildirqmtp programs use to send messages to the remote ISP mail server. The format of the maildirserial command is:

```
maildirserial [ -b ] [ -ttime ] dir prefix client [arg ... ]
```

The maildirserial program reads messages in the Maildir-formatted mailbox *dir*. If a recipient address begins with *prefix*, maildirserial forwards the filename of the message to the program *client*, invoking *client* to use any command-line parameter *args*.

Each filename forwarded by maildirserial to the client program represents a single mail message, as defined in the Maildir format (see Chapter 9, "Using the Maildir Mailbox Format").

A successfully forwarded file is deleted from the Maildir mailbox. There are two parameters that maildirserial uses when processing messages:

- -b bounces rejected messages back to the original message sender.
- -t *time* bounces messages that are more than *time* seconds old back to the original message sender.

The maildirserial utility is used to pass Maildir messages to the serialsmtp and serialqmtp utilities for processing.

Processing Messages for SMTP

The serialsmtp program is used to read a list of filenames from standard input and send their contents via the SMTP protocol to a remote mail server. The format of the serialsmtp program is

```
serialsmtp prefix helohost
```

The prefix and helohost parameters are the same as defined in the maildirsmtp program. In fact, they are usually passed from the maildirsmtp command-line parameters.

The serialsmtp utility accepts a list of filenames from standard input and uses the UCSPI interface via the tcpclient program to contact the remote host via the SMTP protocol to transfer messages. If the remote SMTP server supports ESMTP pipelining, serialsmtp uses it.

Only messages with a recipient address that matches the prefix parameter in the command line are transferred. The maildirsmtp script uses the serialsmtp utility. The maildirsmtp script is written as

```
#!/bin/sh
# WARNING: This file was auto-generated. Do not edit!

exec \
/usr/local/bin/maildirserial -b -t 1209600 -- "$1" "$2" \
tcpclient -RH10 -- "$3" 25 \
/usr/local/bin/serialsmtp "$2" "$4"
```

Notice how messages are detected using the maildirserial utility and transferred using the serialsmtp utility.

Processing Messages for QMTP

The serialqmtp program is used to read a list of filenames from standard input and send their contents via the QMTP protocol to a remote mail server. The format of the serialqmtp program is

```
serialqmtp prefix
```

The `prefix` parameter is the same as defined in the maildirqmtp program. The serialqmtp utility receives filenames via standard input and transfers the contents of the files via the QMTP mail protocol to a remote QMTP mail server. Only messages whose recipient address contains `prefix` are transferred. The maildirqmtp script uses the serialqmtp utility. The maildirqmtp script is written as

```
#!/bin/sh
# WARNING: This file was auto-generated. Do not edit!

exec \
/usr/local/bin/maildirserial -b -t 1209600 -- "$1" "$2" \
tcpclient -RH10 -- "$3" 209 \
/usr/local/bin/serialqmtp "$2"
```

Notice how the maildirqmtp script uses the maildirserial utility to detect messages in the Maildir-formatted mailbox and then transfers the messages via QMTP using the serialqmtp utility.

Checking for a Lock File

The setlock program is used to check for a lock file, open a file for writing, create the lock file, and call another program that uses the file. If the lock file exists when setlock is run, it can either abort the operation or wait until the lock file is removed. The format of the setlock program is

```
setlock [ -nNxX ] file program [ arg ... ]
```

where *file* is the name of the file to open for writing, and *program* is the name of the program that writes to the file. The options for the setlock program are shown in Table 12.3.

TABLE 12.3   Setlock Options

Option	Description
-n	Abort if lock file exists.
-N	If lock file exists, wait until it is removed (default).
-x	If the file cannot be opened, exit with a return code of 0.
-X	If the file cannot be created, opened, or locked, print an error message and exit with a nonzero return code (default).

Using the Serialmail Programs

The serialmail programs are intended to assist the local mail server administrator with functions that are not normally provided by the qmail program. The serialmail package assumes that both the qmail and ucspi-tcp packages are also installed on the mail server. The following sections describe how to use serialmail both from a local mail server and from the ISP mail server.

On a Local Mail Server

The local mail server administrator must ensure that any mail messages from the local domain destined for remote users on the Internet are forwarded to the ISP mail server for remote delivery. Also, the local mail server must be able to retrieve mail messages on the ISP mail server that are destined for users in the local domain.

The serialmail programs can assist the mail administrator in these two functions. The following sections describe the details of implementing these functions using serialmail.

Sending Messages to the ISP

The serialmail programs can be used to transfer messages from a Maildir-formatted mailbox to a remote host, using either the SMTP or QMTP protocol. The trick is to get qmail to place all outbound messages from the mail server in a single mailbox.

The first step is to create a new entry in the `virtualdomains` control file. This entry should define a userid that will receive messages for any host:

```
:ispmail
```

This entry will redirect all messages not destined for the local host to the userid `ispmail`. The next step is to create the userid `ispmail`, complete with a home directory:

```
pw useradd ispmail -d /home/ispmail -c "Mail account for outbound mail"
passwd ispmail
mkdir /home/ispmail
chown ispmail.ispmail /home/ispmail
```

After the userid and home directory are created, you will need to create a Maildir-formatted mailbox. The `maildirmake` command can be used:

```
maildirmake /home/ispmail/Maildir
```

Remember to be logged in as the `ispmail` user when you run this command so that the permissions will be correct.

Once the `Maildir` directory is created, you must let qmail know to deliver mail there. This is accomplished by creating a `.qmail-default` file:

```
echo ./Maildir/ > .qmail-default
```

This should complete creating a `Maildir` directory where all outbound messages are delivered. If `qmail-send` is already running, you can restart it by sending it a `SIGHUP` signal.

Now, if anyone from the local mail server sends a message to a remote user on the Internet, qmail intercepts the message and stores it in the ispmail user account. Listing 12.8 shows a sample message in the mailbox.

LISTING 12.8   Sample Outbound Message in the Mailbox

```
1  $ cat 955047188.98287.meshach.smallorg.org
2  Return-Path: <katie@mail.smallorg.org>
3  Delivered-To: ispmail-postmaster@freebsd.org
4  Received: (qmail 98284 invoked by uid 1004); 6 Apr 2000 18:53:08 -0000
5  Date: 6 Apr 2000 18:53:08 -0000
6  Message-ID: <20000406185308.98283.qmail@meshach.smallorg.org>
7  From: katie@mail.smallorg.org
8  To: postmaster@freebsd.org
9  Subject: Hello
10
11 This message is to tell you that I really like your product!
$
```

In Listing 12.8, line 1 shows how to list a message in the Maildir mailbox. Remember that in Maildir format, each message in contained in a separate file. Line 3 shows that the message was indeed delivered to the ispmail userid. This is the value that the maildirsmtp program will have to search for. After the forwarding information, lines 7–11 show that the rest of the mail message was kept completely intact.

The next step is to run the maildirsmtp program to transfer any messages waiting in the Maildir directory to the ISP mail server. The command for this should be

```
maildirsmtp /home/ispmail/Maildir ispmail- host1.ispnet1.net mail.smallorg.org
```

The maildirsmtp command line tells maildirsmtp to check the /home/ispmail/Maildir mailbox for messages. The prefix that it should look for is ispmail-, which was be added to all messages forwarded to the account. The next two parameters define the ISP mail host address (host1.ispnet1.net) and the local mail server name (mail.smallorg.org). If the PPP connection is up, the maildirsmtp command should automatically start an SMTP session with the remote ISP mail server to transfer any messages in the Maildir directory. Listing 12.9 shows a sample maildirsmtp session with the ISP host.

LISTING 12.9   Sample Maildirsmtp Session

```
$ maildirsmtp /home/ispmail/Maildir ispmail- host1.ispnet1.net smallorg.org
maildirserial: info: new/955047188.98287.mail.smallorg.org succeeded:
➥ host1.ispnet1.net said: 250 ok 955047681 qp 18972
maildirserial: info: new/955047221.98300.mail.smallorg.org succeeded:
```

LISTING 12.9 Continued

```
➥ host1.ispnet1.net said: 250 ok 955047681 qp 18973
maildirserial: info: new/955047204.98294.mail.smallorg.org succeeded:
➥ host1.ispnet1.net said: 250 ok 955047681 qp 18975
$
```

Listing 12.9 shows that three messages were successfully transferred to the ISP mail server. Each message produces a return message from the ISP SMTP server (in this case qmail-smtpd). The ISP mail server should now forward the messages to their intended recipients on the Internet.

Retrieving Messages from the ISP

The serialmail package can also be used to retrieve mail messages being held by the ISP mail server for the local domain. Under this scenario, the ISP has created a virtual domain and is forwarding all messages destined for users in the domain to a single UNIX system account on the mail server. Figure 12.6 demonstrates how this works.

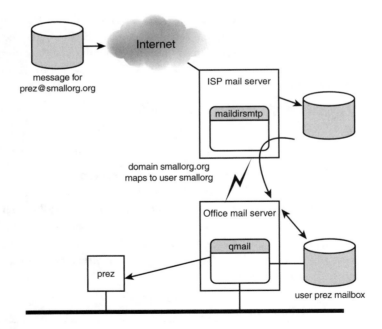

FIGURE 12.6

Retrieving messages for a domain from a single account.

Chapter 11 discussed how the local domain mail server could use the fetchmail program to connect to the UNIX account on the ISP mail server and retrieve messages using the POP3 protocol. If your ISP is running qmail, there is an alternative method that can be used.

The maildirsmtp and maildirqmtp programs can be used on the ISP mail server to trigger messages to be sent back to the local domain mail server. By logging into the ISP mail server and running the maildirsmtp or maildirqmtp command, you can transfer messages in the UNIX account on the ISP mail server to the local domain mail server.

The first step is to make sure that the ISP mail server is using the qmail software package to transfer email. Once this is determined, you can Telnet to the ISP mail server, create a Maildir-formatted mailbox for the user account, and point qmail to deliver messages to the Maildir mailbox:

```
maildirmake /home/smallorg/Maildir
echo ./Maildir/ > /home/smallorg/.qmail-default
```

Now, assuming that the ISP has configured the proper MX record and control files for the virtual domain (see Chapter 11), all mail for the virtual domain should be delivered to the UNIX system account `smallorg` and placed in the Maildir mailbox.

Next, either the maildirsmtp or maildirqmtp program can be run from a Telnet session on the ISP mail server to test transferring messages from the account mailbox back to the domain mail server. The command

```
maildirqmtp /home/smallorg/Maildir smallorg- mail.smallorg.org
host1.ispnet1.net
```

will search the `smallorg` user's Maildir mailbox and transfer any messages via QMTP to the local domain mail server. Once the maildirqmtp command-line syntax has been verified, you can create a crontab entry for the `smallorg` user on the ISP host, calling the `maildirqmtp` command at a regular interval (as described in Chapter 11).

> **CAUTION**
>
> This example assumes two important things: that you have a direct connection to the ISP that is always available, and that your mail server has a static IP address assigned to the `mail.smallorg.org` mail server. If either of these two items is not available, you will have to use an alternative method.

On the ISP Mail Server

The ISP mail server can also benefit from the serialmail program. There are two features that work especially well for ISPs. The maildirqmtp program uses the QMTP protocol to transfer mail messages between qmail servers. If the client mail server is also using qmail, the ISP can take advantage of the quicker message transfer speeds of QMTP to transfer messages with the client mail server. To accomplish this, the ISP mail server also needs to run the `qmail-qmtpd` program to listen for QMTP connection attempts.

Also, many UNIX and non-UNIX mail servers alike use the SMTP ETRN feature to retrieve mail messages. By establishing an ESMTP session with the ISP mail server, a local domain mail server can issue an `ETRN` command to request that the ISP mail server deliver to the domain mail server messages stored in the domain message queue via SMTP (see Chapter 5). The maildirsmtp program can be used to accomplish this function.

Supporting QMTP

With the growing popularity of qmail, many ISPs are finding that transferring mail messages using the quicker QMTP protocol is more efficient. To be able to use the QMTP protocol with the SMTP protocol, both the `qmail-qmtpd` and `qmail-smtpd` programs need to be configured to accept connections.

Using Inetd

If you are using the inetd method of calling `qmail-smtpd`, you can create another entry for the `qmail-qmtpd` program. First, you must ensure that the QMTP protocol port is configured in the `/etc/services` file:

```
qmtp            209/tcp     #The Quick Mail Transfer Protocol
qmtp            209/udp     #The Quick Mail Transfer Protocol
```

Next, an entry must be made in the `/etc/inetd.conf` file to configure the qmtp service:

```
qmtp    stream  tcp     nowait  qmaild  /var/qmail/bin/tcp-env  tcp-env
➥ /var/qmail/bin/qmail-qmtpd
```

As with the `qmail-smtpd` program, `qmail-qmtp` requires certain UNIX environment variables to be present when it starts. Thus, the qmail `tcp-env` program is called from inetd to create those variables. After the `qmail-qmtpd` entry is created in the `/etc/inetd.conf` file, the inetd process can be sent a `SIGHUP` signal to start the `qmail-qmtpd` process. When a QMTP connection request is detected by inetd, the connection will be passed to the `tcp-env` program, which in turn will pass it on to the `qmail-qmtpd` program for processing.

Using Tcpserver

If you are using the tcpserver method of calling `qmail-smtpd`, you can easily create another script file to start the `qmail-qmtpd` program when the mail server starts. A sample script should look like this:

```
tcpserver -v -u 1001 -g 1001 -p -x /etc/tcp.qmtp.cdb 0 qmtp
➥ /var/qmail/bin/qmail-qmtpd
```

This sample assumes that the qmaild uid is 1001 and the nofiles gid is 1001. Again, similar to the qmail-smtpd program, tcpserver allows the mail administrator to create an access control database file to control access to the QMTP server. After the script is created, it should be placed in the same location where the qmail-smtpd boot script is, so that it will be started when the mail server boots.

Supporting ETRN

The ESMTP ETRN function is a popular method of allowing local domain mail servers to retrieve mail messages stored on the ISP mail server. When the ISP mail server receives an ETRN command from the local domain mail server, it must attempt to establish an SMTP connection with the local domain mail server and transfer any messages in the mail queue destined for the local domain mail server.

Unfortunately, the qmail package does not include a program to perform the AUTOTURN function. If a remote ESMTP host sends the ETRN command, an error message is returned:

```
$ telnet localhost 25
Trying 127.0.0.1...
Connected to localhost.
Escape character is '^]'.
220 meshach.ispnet1.net ESMTP
EHLO test.isp
250-meshach.ispnet1.net
250-PIPELINING
250 8BITMIME
ETRN
502 unimplemented (#5.5.1)
QUIT
221 meshach.ispnet1.net
Connection closed by foreign host.
$
```

However, the serialmail package does provide a method to fake out the ETRN functionality to the local domain mail servers. Bernstein describes a technique that uses the maildirsmtp program to initiate an SMTP connection with the local domain mail server and transfer any mail messages waiting in the Maildir mailbox, where the virtual domain mail is stored. By using some sleight of hand, the qmail server can be configured to initiate a maildirsmtp call every time a local domain mail server establishes an SMTP connection to upload messages.

The trick is to replace the qmail-smtpd function call in the tcpserver startup script with a script that calls the maildirsmtp program as well. The sleight of hand comes in ensuring that the correct messages are processed for the correct local domain mail server. This method requires that each local domain mail server be assigned a static IP address by the ISP. For this example, we will use the following configuration:

```
mail server 1:    smallorg.ispnet1.net    10.0.0.30 for domain smallorg.org
mail server 2:    mediumorg.ispnet1.net   10.0.0.31 for domain mediumorg.org
```

First, create a separate directory to hold Maildir mailboxes for all virtual domain hosts that the ISP is servicing. The qmail home directory is a good place to do this:

```
mkdir /var/qmail/autoturn
chgrp qmail /var/qmail/autoturn
chmod 2755 /var/qmail/autoturn
```

Next, a new qmail userid must be created to handle mail for the hosts using the AUTOTURN feature. This is accomplished in the /var/qmail/users/assign database:

```
+autoturn-:qmaild:7770:2108:/var/qmail/autoturn:-::
```

Remember to replace the 7770 and 2108 values with the userid and groupid of your qmaild user. After running the qmail-newu program, the userid should be valid in qmail.

> **NOTE**
>
> If you are already using the qmail-pw2u program, then you must place this entry in the append file to prevent corrupting the generated assign file.

The next step is to create entries in the rcpthosts control file for each AUTOTURN customer and place the virtual domain definition in the virtualdomains control file. The rctphosts file will need the domains to be added for which it is to accept messages:

```
smallorg.org
mediumorg.org
```

The virtualdomains file will need to map a userid to each domain. The trick here is to use the static IP address of each domain mail server to separate where the messages will be stored:

```
smallorg.org:autoturn-10.0.0.30
mediumorg.org:autoturn-10.0.0.31
```

The virtualdomains entries tell qmail to forward any messages received for the domains to the autoturn userid created with the qmail-newu utility, but append the static IP address of each domain server to separate messages for each individual domain.

Now you can create Maildir mailboxes for each domain and create a .qmail file to handle messages for each domain:

```
cd /var/qmail/autoturn
maildirmake 10.0.0.30
maildirmake 10.0.0.31
```

```
chown -R qmaild 10.0.0.30
chown -R qmaild 10.0.0.31
echo ./10.0.0.30/ > .qmail-10:0:0:30-default
echo ./10.0.0.31/ > .qmail-10:0:0:31-default
chmod 644 ,qnail-10:0:0:30-default
chmod 644 .qmail-10:0:0:31-default
```

These commands create individual Maildir-formatted mailboxes for each domain. A `.qmail` file is created in the `autoturn` directory to handle all messages for each domain. Incoming mail for each domain will be placed in the appropriate mailbox according to the IP address of the domain mail server.

Now all the pieces are in place. The final step is to let qmail run the maildirsmtp program to connect to a local domain mail server every time it attempts an SMTP connection. Changing the `qmail-smtpd` script does this.

There should be a script that runs tcpserver with the `qmail-smtpd` program. It should already be in the boot script area of your UNIX server and will look something like this:

```
tcpserver -v -u 1001 -g 1001 -p -x /etc/tcp.qmtp.cdb 0 smtp
➥ /var/qmail/bin/qmail-smtpd
```

This script runs the `qmail-smtpd` program every time an SMTP connection is detected. Instead, you will need to replace `/var/qmail/bin/qmail-smtpd` with the following script:

```
sh -c '/var/qmail/bin/qmail-smtpd
      cd /var/qmail/autoturn
      exec setlock -nx $TCPREMOTEIP/seriallock \
      maildirsmtp $TCPREMOTEIP autoturn-$TCPREMOTEIP- $TCPREMOTEIP AutoTURN'
```

This script runs the maildirsmtp program every time an SMTP connection is established. Notice how the maildirsmtp parameters use the `$TCPREMOTEIP` address to differentiate which `autoturn` mailbox is read and which remote host is called. This should return the proper messages to the proper local domain mail server.

Summary

The qmail program is ideal for use in an office Internet mail environment. It can be used as a central mail hub and on UNIX user workstations to direct all mail to a central point and to collect mail from a central mail hub. Most often the central mail hub is an ISP mail server that implements virtual domains, storing messages for the office domain on a single user account.

The qmail office mail server can connect to the ISP via either PPP or UUCP to retrieve messages. If the office mail server is using PPP, it can use either a regularly scheduled dial method or a dial-on-demand dial method. In either scenario, the office mail server must be able to send and retrieve messages once the PPP connection is established.

The serialmail package is another set of programs to assist the qmail server in transferring messages between an office mail server and an ISP mail hub. The serialmail package includes the maildirsmtp and maildirqmtp programs, which can be used to send mail messages from a Maildir-formatted mailbox to a remote mail server using the SMTP protocol. The ISP mail server can also benefit from the serialmail package. By implementing the qmail-qmtpd program, the ISP can support fast message transfers using the QMTP protocol to remote office mail servers using the maildirqmtp program.

The ISP mail server can also use the maildirsmtp program to implement the ESMTP ETRN command. The ETRN command initiates an AUTOTURN session during which the office mail server can inform the ISP mail server to initiate an SMTP connection to download waiting messages for the domain.

qmail Server Administration

CHAPTER

13

IN THIS CHAPTER

The previous chapters described how to install and configure qmail on a UNIX server. After all the installation and configuration work has been completed, you may think that the mail administrator's job is finished. Unfortunately, it has just begun.

There is always something that must be modified on the mail server. One of the most important tasks is userid maintenance. Users must have valid userids to receive mail on the mail system or log in to retrieve messages from the system. Another task for the mail administrator is to watch the mail server logs to determine if things are going well. Depending on the type of Internet connectivity you choose, you might also have to watch constantly for hackers trying new and improved methods of breaking into your mail server. You always need to be on the lookout for spammers flooding your mailboxes with useless mail or trying to use your mail server as an unknowing relay participant. The job of the mail administrator never ends. This chapter will describe some of the tools and techniques used by UNIX mail server administrators, including a few qmail utilities to help the mail server administrator.

Userid Maintenance

Each user who wants to receive mail via your mail server must have a valid userid and password, either on the system or in the qmail `users` file. An ongoing job of the mail administrator is adding and deleting mail userids. Depending on your organization, this can either be a daily task or a once-in-a-while task. Whichever it is, at some time you will need to add and delete userids. Also, don't forget about the occasional user who forgets his password—at some time you will run across him, too.

For experienced system administrators, this should be old hat. Unfortunately, often in small organizations the new mail administrator might have been recently introduced to UNIX. This section describes the basics of UNIX and qmail userids and passwords and how to manipulate them on Linux and FreeBSD systems.

System User Accounts

All UNIX systems maintain user accounts as flat text files. Some UNIX systems use a complicated system of multiple files to attempt to limit the ability of hackers to obtain usernames and passwords. This section describes the basics of UNIX system userids and how the qmail mail administrator can manipulate system userids using system utilities.

The UserID File

By default, UNIX userids are stored in the `/etc/passwd` file. Listing 13.1 shows an example.

LISTING 13.1 A Sample UNIX /etc/passwd File

```
1  root:unaoBNGut6giH2:0:0:root:/root:/bin/bash
2  bin:*:1:1:bin:/bin:
3  daemon:*:2:2:daemon:/sbin:
4  adm:*:3:4:adm:/var/adm:
5  lp:*:4:7:lp:/var/spool/lpd:
6  sync:*:5:0:sync:/sbin:/bin/sync
7  shutdown:*:6:0:shutdown:/sbin:/sbin/shutdown
8  halt:*:7:0:halt:/sbin:/sbin/halt
9  mail:*:8:12:mail:/var/spool/mail:
10 news:*:9:13:news:/usr/lib/news:
11 uucp:*:10:14:uucp:/var/spool/uucppublic:
12 operator:*:11:0:operator:/root:/bin/bash
13 games:*:12:100:games:/usr/games:
14 man:*:13:15:man:/usr/man:
15 postmaster:*:14:12:postmaster:/var/spool/mail:/bin/bash
16 nobody:*:65535:100:nobody:/dev/null:
17 ftp:*:404:1::/home/ftp:/bin/bash
18 rich:cLafgrY5tfHiw:501:101:Rich B.:/home/rich:/bin/bash
19 usenet:*:502:13:News master:/home/usenet:/bin/bash
20 bbs:*:503:200:BBS User:/home/bbs:/home/bbs:/bin/bash
21 barbara:*:504:100:Barbara B.:/home/barbara:/bin/bash
22 katie:*:505:100:Katie B.:/home/katie:/bin/bash
23 jessica:Ru7vx4rgypupg:506:100:Jessica B.:/home/jessica:/bin/bash
24 haley:WfNervHPbUxUk:507:100:Haley S.:/home/haley:/bin/bash
25 riley:VHA1qqu/pqjMU:508:100:Riley M.:/home/riley:/bin/bash
26 chris:5MLvL/waxN276:509:100:Chris W.:/home/chris:/bin/bash
27 matthew:nZF35ripKCbXQ:510:100:Matthew W.:/home/matthew:/bin/bash
28 alex:9QJ.MQWbSpBG.:511:100:Alex P.:/home/alex:/bin/bash
```

13

QMAIL SERVER
ADMINISTRATION

Listing 13.1 shows the common format of the /etc/passwd file. Each line represents information for one userid. The information is divided into fields separated by colons. The first field is the UNIX username under which the user can log in. The second field is an encrypted version of the user's password. You may notice that for some users the password field is just an asterisk (*). This is equivalent to locking the userid, because no combination of characters can be encrypted to just an asterisk. The third field is the userid number that UNIX uses to track file access for the user. The fourth field is the ID number of the group to which the user is assigned. Users who perform common functions can be assigned to a single group to simplify file access restrictions.

The remaining fields help further identify the user. The fifth field is used as a text identifier of the user. Often, the full name of the user is placed here to help document information for the mail administrator. The sixth field is used to identify the location of the default home directory for the user. If your users are using the Maildir-format mailboxes to store their mail (see Chapter 9, "Using the Maildir Mailbox Format"), it is important that each user have a separate home directory. It is also important that each user have the proper read and write permissions to his home directory.

The last field identifies the default UNIX shell program the user will execute if he logs in interactively. For the purposes of a mail server, it is normally safe to use the default UNIX shell for this field. For Linux systems this is the bash shell (`/bin/bash`), while FreeBSD systems use a shell similar to the Korn shell (`/bin/sh`).

Shadow Passwords

You may have noticed one bad thing about the default UNIX userid file—it is readable by all users. This is necessary because the logon program runs as the user logs in and needs to be able to read the `/etc/passwd` file to compare the attempted password against the real password. The downside to this situation is that creative users can copy the password file and run common cracker programs against it to determine the passwords of other users. This is a potentially bad situation (especially if senior management uses simple passwords that they can remember).

To combat this problem, many UNIX distributions offer the capability to use a shadow password file. The *shadow password file* is a separate file that is used to contain user passwords and other housekeeping information related to passwords. The passwords are not kept in the `/etc/passwd` file. The shadow password file is not readable to normal users, so they won't be able to copy the file and attempt to crack it. Listing 13.2 shows a sample shadow password file.

Listing 13.2   A Sample UNIX Shadow Password File

```
1   root:$1$wkRtbOwr46TSWmezOiXx.ZGAtG/zGKU1:10863:0:99999:7:-1:-1:134537880
2   bin:*:10863:0:99999:7:::
3   daemon:*:10863:0:99999:7:::
4   adm:*:10863:0:99999:7:::
5   lp:*:10863:0:99999:7:::
6   sync:*:10863:0:99999:7:::
7   shutdown:*:10863:0:99999:7:::
8   halt:*:10863:0:99999:7:::
9   mail:*:10863:0:99999:7:::
10  news:*:10863:0:99999:7:::
11  uucp:*:10863:0:99999:7:::
12  operator:*:10863:0:99999:7:::
13  games:*:10863:0:99999:7:::
14  gopher:*:10863:0:99999:7:::
15  ftp:*:10863:0:99999:7:::
16  nobody:*:10863:0:99999:7:::
17  postgres:!!:10863:0:99999:7:::
```

```
18 lists:!!:10863:0:99999:7:::
19 xfs:!!:10863:0:99999:7:::
20 rich:LMQ0vbvbnZpZr1s:10863:0:99999:7:::
21 barbara:$1$OR1Qdo11$GK/H8tjwPGCBUUHMEjXWe1:10863:0:99999:7:::
22 katie:$1$XEd8PKaP$AuwsgfeN3UBcKjB0GeL1d1:10882:0:99999:7:::
23 jessica:$1$ashasfha4hasfhasfhwr$asfgas44rgs:10885:0:99999:7:::
```

Listing 13.2 shows the typical format of the shadow password file. On most Linux distributions it is located at /etc/shadow. On FreeBSD systems it is located at /etc/master.passwd. As in a normal /etc/passwd file, each line represents information for one userid. The information is divided into fields, separated by colons. The first field is the username. This name should match the username field in the /etc/passwd file. The second field is the encrypted password. You may notice a difference between the encrypted passwords in Listing 13.2 and the ones in Listing 13.1. The UNIX system shown in Listing 13.2 was configured to use MD5 encryption of passwords. This produces a stronger encryption than the standard UNIX password encryption technique that is used by default.

The downside to using a shadow password file is that any program that verifies userids needs to be compiled to use the shadow password file. This includes POP3 and IMAP servers, commonly used with mail servers. Fortunately, most common network software packages have this capability already. The qmail-pop3d POP3 server package included with qmail uses the checkpassword program, which can use the shadow password file.

The /etc/group File

The other important file used for user administration is the /etc/group file. This file is used to identify usernames with groups. Assigning users to groups is a common way to allow access to files for a large subset of users. Listing 13.3 shows a sample /etc/group file.

LISTING 13.3   A Sample Linux /etc/group File

```
1   root::0:root
2   bin::1:root,bin,daemon
3   daemon::2:root,bin,daemon
4   sys::3:root,bin,adm
5   adm::4:root,adm,daemon
6   tty::5:
7   disk::6:root
8   lp::7:daemon,lp
9   mem::8:
10  kmem::9:
11  wheel::10:root
12  mail::12:mail
13  news::13:news
```

LISTING 13.3   Continued

```
14 uucp::14:uucp
15 man::15:
16 games::20:
17 gopher::30:
18 dip::40:
19 ftp::50:
20 nobody::99:
21 users::100:
22 postgres:x:101:
23 utmp:x:102:
24 lists:x:500:
25 floppy:x:19:
26 console:x:11:
27 xfs:x:103:
28 pppusers:x:230:
29 popusers:x:231:
30 slipusers:x:232:
31 slocate:x:21:
32 rich::501:
33 dba:x:502:
34 oinstall:x:503:oracle
35 oracle:x:504:
36 pop:x:505:
```

Listing 13.3 shows the common format for the UNIX group file. Each line represents a different group. The group information is divided into fields that are separated by colons. The first field is the group name. The second field is the group password. If this field is blank, no password is required to access group files. As shown in Listing 13.3, this group file uses shadow passwords (identified by the x). The third field is the group ID. The fourth field is the list of userids that have access to the group. An example of this is shown in line 34. The userid `oracle` has access to the group `oinstall`, besides having its own group—`oracle`. This demonstrates how a userid can be a member of multiple groups.

UNIX groups are not commonly used in normal mail server installations. It is often safest to create a new group for each userid that is created, so no accidental sharing of files can occur between users.

> **CAUTION**
>
> Although groups are not important for mail users, don't forget that the qmail mail package itself requires two new mail groups.

UNIX Userid Utilities

There are several different ways to add, delete, and modify userids on UNIX systems. This section describes a few of the more common methods.

> **Caution**
>
> Do not edit the /etc/passwd file directly using a normal text editor such as vi. Corruption can occur in the file and could prevent anyone from logging into the system (including the root user).

Safely Editing the UserID File

Almost all UNIX systems support the vipw program. The vipw program is used to edit the /etc/passwd program directly, using the common UNIX vi editor, but in a safe manner.

The vipw program makes a copy of the passwd file that is edited. When the editor attempts to save the file, the real passwd file is locked, and the new file is copied onto the old file. If the file copy was successful, the file is unlocked. This prevents any other process in the UNIX system from using (or changing) the passwd file during the copy.

Many UNIX system administrators do not like to use the vi editor. You can change the editor that vipw uses by creating an environment variable called EDITOR and giving it the path of the editor of your choice.

Adding User IDs

Most System V systems such as Linux use the useradd program (or its close cousin adduser). The format of the useradd utility is

```
useradd [-c comment] [-d home_dir]
          [-e expire_date] [-f inactive_time]
          [-g initial_group] [-G group[,...]]
          [-m [-k skeleton_dir] | -M] [-s shell]
          [-u uid [ -o]] [-n] [-r] login
```

Table 13.1 explains the command parameters that are available for the useradd utility.

TABLE 13.1   Useradd Parameters

Parameter	Description
-c	Add a comment to the passwd file record.
-d	The home directory.
-e	The expiration date of the password.

continues

TABLE 13.1   Continued

Parameter	Description
-f	The number of days after the password expires that it is disabled.
-g	The default group.
-G	A list of other groups the userid can belong to.
-m	Creates the user's home directory if it does not exist.
-M	Prevents the user's home directory from being created.
-n	In RedHat Linux variants, prevents a group with the same name as the username from being created automatically.
-r	Creates a system account rather than a user account.
-s	Specifies the default logon shell.
-u	Specifies a user ID number.

Listing 13.4 shows an example of creating a new Linux user using the useradd utility.

LISTING 13.4   An Example of Creating a New User

```
1  [root@shadrach /root]# useradd -c "Riley M." riley
2  [root@shadrach /root]# cat /etc/passwd | grep riley
3  riley:x:504:506:Riley M.:/home/riley:/bin/bash
4  [root@shadrach /root]# cat /etc/group | grep riley
5  riley:x:506:
6  [root@shadrach /root]#ls -al /home/riley
7  total 21
8  drwx------   5 riley    riley        1024 Nov  1 16:48 .
9  drwxr-xr-x   7 root     root         1024 Nov  1 16:48 ..
10 -rw-r--r--   1 riley    riley        1899 Nov  1 16:48 .Xdefaults
11 -rw-r--r--   1 riley    riley          24 Nov  1 16:48 .bash_logout
12 -rw-r--r--   1 riley    riley         230 Nov  1 16:48 .bash_profile
13 -rw-r--r--   1 riley    riley         434 Nov  1 16:48 .bashrc
14 -rw-r--r--   1 riley    riley        2626 Nov  1 16:48 .emacs
15 drwxr-xr-x   3 riley    riley        1024 Nov  1 16:48 .kde
16 -rw-r--r--   1 riley    riley        1416 Nov  1 16:48 .kderc
17 -rw-r--r--   1 riley    riley         185 Nov  1 16:48 .mailcap
18 -rw-r--r--   1 riley    riley        3846 Nov  1 16:48 .vimrc
19 -rw-r--r--   1 riley    riley         397 Nov  1 16:48 .zshrc
20 drwxr-xr-x   5 riley    riley        1024 Nov  1 16:48 Desktop
21 drwxr-xr-x   2 riley    riley        1024 Nov  1 16:48 tmp
22 [root@shadrach /root]#
```

Line 1 shows the useradd utility being used to create a new username riley, with a text comment added to the comment field. The default user ID value and login shell will be used for this example. Line 3 shows the result in the /etc/passwd file. A new line is added for the new username with the next available userid (504) and the next available groupid (506). By default, the useradd utility created a default home directory of /home/riley. Also by default, the default logon shell was set to /bin/bash. By listing the newly created home directory in line 6, you can see that there are already several new files that have been created. This is definitely overkill for a simple email userid. Where did all of these defaults come from?

By using the -D option on the useradd utility, you can view the defaults that useradd uses when creating a new user account. Listing 13.5 shows an example of this.

LISTING 13.5   An Example of Useradd -D Output

```
1  [root@shadrach /root]# useradd -D
2  GROUP=100
3  HOME=/home
4  INACTIVE=-1
5  EXPIRE=
6  SHELL=/bin/bash
7  SKEL=/etc/skel
8  [root@shadrach /root]#
```

In Listing 13.5, line 3 shows the default home directory location that useradd appends to the username to create the new directory. You can change this value if you want to create user home directories somewhere other than /home. Line 7 is the line that the mail administrator may be most interested in. This declares a directory that will be copied to the new user home directory when it is created. Listing 13.6 shows the contents of the /etc/skel directory.

LISTING 13.6   A Sample /etc/skel Directory

```
1  [root@shadrach /root]# ls -al /etc/skel
2  total 23
3  drwxr-xr-x   5 root     root      1024 Sep 29 05:18 .
4  drwxr-xr-x  31 root     root      3072 Nov  1 16:48 ..
5  -rw-r--r--   1 root     root      1899 Apr 27  1999 .Xdefaults
6  -rw-r--r--   1 root     root        24 Jul 13  1994 .bash_logout
7  -rw-r--r--   1 root     root       230 Aug 22  1998 .bash_profile
8  -rw-r--r--   1 root     root       434 May 17 21:15 .bashrc
9  -rw-r--r--   1 root     root      2626 Apr 27  1999 .emacs
10 drwxr-xr-x   3 root     root      1024 Sep 29 05:18 .kde
11 -rw-r--r--   1 root     root      1416 May 17 14:44 .kderc
12 -rw-r--r--   1 root     root       185 May 18 10:16 .mailcap
```

13

QMAIL SERVER
ADMINISTRATION

LISTING 13.6   Continued

```
13 -rw-r--r--  1 root    root     3846 May 11 12:49 .vimrc
14 -rw-r--r--  1 root    root      397 Apr 27  1999 .zshrc
15 drwxr-xr-x  5 root    root     1024 Sep 29 05:18 Desktop
16 drwxr-xr-x  2 root    root     1024 May 18 10:12 tmp
17 [root@shadrach /root]#
```

Listing 13.6 looks suspiciously familiar. It is exactly the same as the newly created user home directory shown in Listing 13.4. The useradd utility took the content of the /etc/skel directory and copied it to the user home directory when it was created. As you can see, there are lots of configuration files here that users logging into the system from an X Window session would need, but almost none that an email client would need.

To make user home directories simpler (especially if you are using the IMAP protocol to store mail folders in the users' home directories), you can move the template files from the /etc/skel directory. By leaving the /etc/skel directory empty, nothing will be copied into new users' home directories. If you are using the Maildir mailbox format, you should create a Maildir mailbox in the /etc/skel directory so that it is copied for each new user when his account is created.

FreeBSD UserID Maintenance

FreeBSD systems use the pw program to add, delete, and modify userids. The format of the pw command is:

```
pw command options
```

The function of the pw program depends on the command parameter that is added. Table 13.2 shows the commands that can be used.

TABLE 13.2   The pw Program Commands

Command	Description
useradd	Create a new system user account
userdel	Delete an existing system user account
usermod	Modify an existing system user account
usershow	Display the information for an existing system user account
usernext	Return the next available user and group IDs on the system
groupadd	Create a new system group account
groupdel	Delete an existing system group account
groupmod	Modify an existing system group account

Command	Description
groupshow	Display the information for an existing system group account
groupnext	Return the next available group ID on the system

The command syntax can be used in any order. For example, the commands useradd, adduser, user add, and add user all perform the same function.

The options are used to define additional information when performing operations on the account. Table 13.3 lists the options that are available for the useradd command.

TABLE 13.3 The pw Program Options

Option	Description
-n name	Specifies the username
-u uid	Specifies the system userid
-c comment	Inserts a comment in the text field of the passwd file
-d dir	Specifies the home directory for the user
-e date	Specifies the expiration date for the account
-p date	Specifies the expiration date for the account password
-g group	Specifies a primary group for the account
-G grouplist	Specifies additional group memberships for the account
-L class	Specifies the login class of the account
-m	Instructs pw to attempt to create the home directory for the account
-k dir	Uses the directory dir as the skel directory to copy to all home directories created
-s shell	Specifies a login shell for the account

By default, the useradd command option will create the userid using the next available userid and groupid, not create a home directory, and assign the system default shell (/bin/sh) to the user. An example of the useradd command option would be

```
pw useradd smallorg -c "Mail account for smallorg.org" -m
```

This command creates the username smallorg and assigns it a home directory located at /home/smallorg. Also, the content of the skeleton directory is copied into the user home directory.

The location of the skeleton directory and other default values used for the pw program are defined in the /etc/pw.conf file. Listing 13.7 shows the default pw.conf file.

13

QMAIL SERVER ADMINISTRATION

LISTING 13.7   The Default `/etc/pw.conf` File

```
#
# pw.conf - user/group configuration defaults
#
# Password for new users? no=nologin yes=loginid none=blank random=random
defaultpasswd = "no"

# Reuse gaps in uid sequence? (yes or no)
reuseuids = "no"

# Reuse gaps in gid sequence? (yes or no)
reusegids = "no"

# Path to the NIS passwd file (blank or 'no' for none)
nispasswd =

# Obtain default dotfiles from this directory
skeleton = "/usr/share/skel"

# Mail this file to new user (/etc/newuser.msg or no)
newmail = "no"

# Log add/change/remove information in this file
logfile = "/var/log/userlog"

# Root directory in which $HOME directory is created
home = "/home"

# Colon separated list of directories containing valid shells
shellpath = "/bin"

# Space separated list of available shells (without paths)
shells = "sh","csh"

# Default shell (without path)
defaultshell = "sh"

# Default group (leave blank for new group per user)
defaultgroup = ""

# Extra groups for new users
extragroups =
```

```
# Default login class for new users
defaultclass = ""

# Range of valid default user ids
minuid = 1000
maxuid = 32000

# Range of valid default group ids
mingid = 1000
maxgid = 32000

# Days after which account expires (0=disabled)
expire_days = 0

# Days after which password expires (0=disabled)
password_days = 0
```

After determining the default skeleton directory, you can create a Maildir-formatted mailbox in the skeleton. This ensures that all new system user accounts created automatically have a Maildir mailbox.

qmail User Accounts

As described in Chapter 7, "Changing qmail Operational Parameters," the qmail package has the capability to manipulate its own user accounts. The /var/qmail/users directory contains the assign and cdb database files that qmail can use to determine local users.

The cdb database is a cdb-formatted hashed database that qmail-lspawn uses to determine local mail users. It is created from the assign text file. The format of the assign text file was described in detail in Chapter 7.

The qmail-pw2u program creates qmail accounts for each system userid. The qmail-pw2u command receives the passwd file on standard input and produces the assign text database file on standard output. The command used to create the assign database is

```
cat /etc/passwd | /var/qmail/bin/qmail-pw2u > /var/qmail/users/assign
```

After the assign database file is created, you can use the qmail-newu command to create the cdb database file from the assign text file.

If you use the qmail-pw2u program to create the assign file, only users defined in the /var/qmail/users/cdb database file will be allowed to receive mail messages from qmail. As new system user accounts are added to the /etc/passwd file, the qmail-pw3u and qmail-newu commands need to be run to ensure that the new entries are added to the cdb database.

The UNIX Syslogd Program

The UNIX system has the capability to track events that occur on the system and log messages for each event in system log files. The program that handles this is the syslogd program. As the mail administrator, you should be able to locate the log files and track any problems that may appear in them. You should get in the habit of scanning through the log files at least once a day to watch for possible system or security problems.

This section describes the syslogd program and how to configure it to log events in log files.

Customizing the System Log

The command syntax of syslogd is different on different UNIX systems. For FreeBSD systems, the command syntax is

```
syslogd [-dsuv] [-a allowed_peer] [-f config_file] [-m mark_interval]
➥ [-p log_socket] [-l path]
```

Table 13.4 describes the options available for the FreeBSD version of syslogd.

TABLE 13.4   FreeBSD Syslogd Options

Option	Description
-d	Turns on debugging mode.
-s	Secure mode. Does not log syslog messages from remote hosts.
-u	Unique priority logging. Logs messages only at a specified priority.
-v	Verbose logging. Allows for logging the numeric facility and priority as well as the message.
-a allowed_peer	Logs messages received from the host allowed_peer. Multiple hosts can be defined with additional -a parameters.
-f config_file	Specifies an alternative configuration file to process.
-m mark_interval	Selects the number of minutes between mark messages in the log. Default is 20 minutes.
-p log_socket	Specifies the path of an alternative log socket to use. Default is /var/run/log.
-l path	Specifies location of additional log sockets.

For Linux systems the command syntax for syslogd is

```
syslogd options
```

where *options* is a list of options that are available to modify the behavior of the syslogd program. Table 13.5 shows the options available.

TABLE 13.5 Syslogd Options

Option	Description
-a socket	Specifies additional sockets to listen to for remote connections.
-d	Turns on debugging mode.
-f config	Uses the configuration file specified by config.
-h	Forwards any remote messages to forwarding hosts.
-l hostlist	Specifies a list of hosts that are logged only by hostname.
-m interval	Sets the MARK timestamp interval in the log file. Setting to 0 disables the timestamp.
-n	Avoids auto-backgrounding.
-p socket	Specifies an alternative socket on which to listen for remote syslog connections.
-r	Enables receiving remote syslog connections.
-s domainlist	Specifies a list of domain names that will be stripped out before logging.
-v	Prints syslogd version.

The syslogd program is normally started at boot time by an init script and runs quietly in background mode. Most UNIX distributions start syslogd by default. You can check to see if syslogd is running on your UNIX system by using the command

```
ps ax | more
```

The syslogd program should show up in the list of processes running on your system. When syslogd starts, it reads a configuration file to determine what types of messages to log and how to log them. The next section describes the format of the syslogd configuration file.

Syslogd Configuration File

The syslogd configuration file is located by default at /etc/syslog.conf. It contains directives that instruct the syslogd program what type of events to log and how to log them. There are many types of events that syslogd can log. Table 13.6 shows them.

TABLE 13.6 Syslogd Event Types

Event	Description
auth	Security/authorization events
authpriv	Private security/authorization events
cron	Cron daemon events

13

QMAIL SERVER ADMINISTRATION

TABLE 13.6   Continued

Event	Description
daemon	System daemon events
kern	System kernel events
lpr	Line printer events
mail	Mail program events
mark	Internal check
news	Network News program events
syslog	Internal syslogd events
user	User-level events
uucp	UUCP program events
local*n*	Locally defined events (n = 0–7)

Each event type has a hierarchy of message priorities. Lower priorities mean smaller problems. Higher priorities mean bigger problems. Table 13.7 shows the event priorities that are available.

TABLE 13.7   Syslogd Message Priorities

Priority	Description
debug	Debugging events
info	Informational events
notice	Normal notices
warning	Warning messages
err	Error condition events
crit	Critical system conditions
alert	System alerts
emerg	Fatal system conditions

In Table 13.7, the events are listed by reverse order of priority, with debug having the lowest priority and emerg having the highest priority.

The format of the /etc/syslog.conf file is

```
event.priority    action
```

Each line in the /etc/syslog.conf file represents different actions. There are three actions that can be taken for events:

- Display the event message to the system console.
- Log the event message to a log file.
- Send the event message to a remote log host.

The syslogd configuration file consists of combinations of events and actions that define the characteristics of the syslogd program. This is best explained by an example. Listing 13.8 shows a sample /etc/syslog.conf file.

LISTING 13.8   A Sample /etc/syslog.conf File

```
1  # Log all kernel messages to the console.
2  # Logging much else clutters up the screen.
3  kern.*                     /dev/console
4
5  # Log anything (except mail) of level info or higher.
6  # Don't log private authentication messages!
7  *.info;mail.none;authpriv.none          /var/log/messages
8
9  # The authpriv file has restricted access.
10 authpriv.*                 /var/log/secure
11
12 # Log all the mail messages in one place.
13 mail.*                     /var/log/maillog
14
15 # Everybody gets emergency messages, plus log them on another
16 # machine.
17 *.emerg                         *
18 *.emerg                    @meshach.smallorg.org
19
20 # Save mail and news errors of level err and higher in a
21 # special file.
22 uucp,news.crit                  /var/log/spooler
```

Lines 1 and 2 show how to use comments within the configuration file. These lines are not processed by syslogd. Line 3 is an example of wildcard characters in the file. This indicates that all kernel event messages of any priority will be sent to the system console. Line 7 is a good example of a complex configuration.

Multiple events can be configured for a single action line. A semicolon is used to separate event and priority pairs. The first pair is *.info. This defines all events of priority info and higher. It is important to remember that specifying a particular priority also includes the higher priorities.

The second pair—`mail.none`—may look confusing. You might be wondering that there is no `none` priority. What this event pair is defining is the exclusion of mail events of any priority from the previous definition. The next pair—`authpriv.none`—does the same. This statement in effect is logging all events except `mail` and `authpriv` events and of priority `info` and higher to the log file `/var/log/messages`.

Lines 10 and 13 define what is happening to the `authpriv` and `mail` events. Line 10 defines that all `authpriv` events of any priority get logged to a separate file `/var/log/secure`. Similarly, line 13 defines that all mail events of any priority get logged to a separate file named `/var/log/maillog`. This is an extremely handy way of parsing event messages, by separating them into their own log files. It is a good idea for the mail administrator to define a separate place to put all mail-related event messages. This makes it easier to spot mail problems on the system.

Line 18 shows an example of using a remote syslog server to log messages. Any `emerg` priority messages are sent to the remote host `meshach.smallorg.org`. If there is a serious error on the host, you may not get a chance to see the log file on it, so it is often a good idea to send these messages elsewhere (assuming that the serious error does not prevent the system from sending messages).

The qmail Alternative Logging Program

Much like many of the other UNIX utilities, there has been some debate over the efficiency of the standard syslogd program. Once a message is sent to the syslogd facility, there is no guarantee that it will actually be written to the log file. Also, the syslogd program is not known for its speed in writing log entries.

To compensate for the inadequacies of the syslogd program, Dan Bernstein developed the splogger program and included it with the qmail distribution package. The splogger program is used as a replacement for programs to send messages to the syslog facility running on the UNIX system. The format of the `splogger` command is

```
splogger [tag] [facility]
```

The `tag` parameter is a text tag that will be placed at the front of the message to identify it. The default value for `tag` is splogger. The `facility` parameter defines what facility level messages will be logged as by splogger. The default level is 2.

There are several rules that splogger follows:

- Each message is timestamped, and the timestamp is appended to the message.
- Each message is checked for the keywords `alert:` or `warning:`. If either appears, an appropriate priority level is selected for the message.

- An unprintable character in the message is converted to a question mark (?).
- Blank lines are not logged.
- Messages of more than 800 characters are split into multiple lines of 800 characters per line. Split lines are identified by a plus sign (+) after the timestamp.

By default qmail uses the splogger program to log all of its messages. The `qmail-start` program in the qmail startup script configures this:

```
qmail-start [ defaultdelivery [ logger arg ...  ] ]
```

By using the splogger program as the logger, this command redirects all qmail logs to the splogger program, which then forwards them to the standard UNIX logger. The location of the mail log depends on the values set in the `/etc/syslog.conf` file, described in the previous section. The splogger program logs messages using the `mail` event type. A sample qmail log file is shown in Listing 13.9.

LISTING 13.9   A Sample qmail Mail Log File

```
1  Apr 11 02:02:18 shadrach qmail: 955436538.813320 new msg 18995
2  Apr 11 02:02:18 shadrach qmail: 955436538.815787 info msg 18995:
➥ bytes 603 from <root@shadrach.ispnet1.net> qp 26920 uid 0
3  Apr 11 02:02:18 shadrach qmail: 955436538.892499 starting delivery 103:
➥ msg 18995 to local root@shadrach.ispnet1.net
4  Apr 11 02:02:18 shadrach qmail: 955436538.895936 status: local 1/10
➥ remote 0/20
5  Apr 11 02:02:19 shadrach qmail: 955436539.075785 delivery 103: success:
➥ did_0+1+0/qp_26976/
6 Apr 11 02:02:19 shadrach qmail: 955436539.098222 status: local 0/10
➥ remote 0/20
7 Apr 11 02:02:19 shadrach qmail: 955436539.100838 end msg 18995
```

This log file follows the trail of a new message received by qmail. Line 1 shows the log of qmail accepting the new message. Line 2 identifies the message by the sender, as well as its size. Line 3 indicates that qmail is initiating the delivery. Line 4 indicates the status of qmail. One message is shown waiting for delivery in the local mail queue. Line 5 indicates that qmail was successful in delivering the message to the local user.

13

QMAIL SERVER ADMINISTRATION

NOTE

Bernstein also developed the `daemontools` package, which includes the multilog program, another logger replacement. This is described in detail in Chapter 16, "The Daemontool Utilities."

Reading qmail Logs

Once the qmail log message entries are written to the mail log file, it is the job of the mail administrator to monitor the logs for problems. Often, mail problems appear in the log file but are not noticed by busy mail administrators until it is too late.

> **NOTE**
>
> It is always a good idea to glance at the mail log files at least once a day to watch for any serious problems. Often, mail problems can be detected by warning messages in the log file long before users detect that something is wrong.

As can be seen in Listing 13.9, the qmail entries can seem confusing. There are six types of qmail log messages:

- Status
- Fatal problems
- Serious problems
- Messages
- Deliveries
- Warnings

The following sections describe each of the qmail log types in detail.

Status Messages

Status messages record the operation of qmail on the server. The format of a status message is

```
status: local l/L remote r/R
```

where `l/L` is the number of local messages queued (l) and the size of the local mail queue (L), and `r/R` is the number of remote messages queued (r) and the size of the remote mail queue (R). If you notice the queues filling up with messages frequently, you may need to change the queue sizes.

Fatal Problems

Fatal problems are those that cause qmail to abort and shut down. These problems prevent qmail from running on the mail server and need immediate attention. Table 13.8 shows the fatal problem messages.

TABLE 13.8 qmail Fatal Problem Log Messages

Message	Description
alert: cannot start	qmail-send cannot initialize to start. Often a sign of a configuration file problem.
alert: oh no! lost	A support daemon program such as qmail-lspawn or qmail-rspawn has died, so qmail-send will shutdown.

Serious Problems

Serious problems are situations in which qmail is unable to process a particular event but will try again. Serious problems do not cause qmail to shut down, but if they persist they could cause a fatal problem and a shutdown. Table 13.9 lists the serious problems found in qmail.

TABLE 13.9 qmail Serious Problem Log Messages

Message	Description
alert: unable to append bounce message	qmail-send is unable to process a permanent delivery failure, usually because of no disk space.
alert: out of memory	qmail-send attempted to allocate memory but failed.
alert: unable to opendir	qmail-send is unable to open a file list from disk because of permissions or the descriptor table is full.
alert: unable to switch back	qmail-send received a SIGHUP signal but was unable to read the queue directory.
alert: unable to reread	qmail-send received a SIGHUP signal but was unable to read the controls directory

Messages

qmail creates a log trail for each message that enters and exits the qmail system. These log entries are based on a number assigned to each message. Table 13.10 shows the log entries that may appear for messages.

TABLE 13.10 qmail Message Log Entries

Message	Description
new msg m	qmail-send is processing message number m from the mail queue.
info msg m: bytes b from <s> qp q uid u	Message m contains b bytes, is from sender s, was queued by userid u, and has queue identifier q.

TABLE 13.10 Continued

Message	Description
bounce msg *m* qp *q*	Message *m* had delivery failures. The queue identifier of the bounced message is *q*.
triple bounce: discarding *m*	Message *m* is tagged as an undeliverable double-bounced message and will be deleted.
end msg m	Message *m* is being removed from the queue.

Deliveries

As qmail-send attempts to deliver each message, it logs a status message to the qmail log. Table 13.11 shows the possible delivery log messages.

TABLE 13.11 qmail Delivery Log Entries

Message	Description
starting delivery *d*: msg *m* to	qmail-send is processing message *m* for delivery to one recipient. The delivery ID is *d*.
delivery *d*: success	Delivery *d* was successfully delivered to the recipient.
delivery *d*: deferral	Delivery *d* encountered a temporary delivery failure and will try again.
delivery *d*: failure:	Delivery *d* encountered a permanent delivery failure. The message will be bounced.
delivery *d*: report mangled, will defer	Delivery *d* encountered a problem with either qmail-rspawn or qmail-lspawn and will try again.

Warnings

As errors occur during the processing of mail messages, qmail logs them as warnings to the mail log file. Usually warnings represent temporary problems that qmail can overcome. However, it is possible for a warning to be a sign that something really bad is about to happen. Table 13.12 shows the qmail warning log messages.

TABLE 13.12   qmail Warning Log Entries

Message	Description
internal error: delivery report out of range	qmail-lspawn or qmail-rspawn has returned a delivery report for a non-existent delivery ID.
qmail-clean unable to clean up	qmail-clean was unable to remove a file.
trouble fsyncing	qmail-send was unable to write to the disk.
trouble in select	A possible operating system bug.
trouble injecting bounce message	qmail-send was unable to queue a bounced message.
trouble marking	qmail-send was unable to log the result of an unsuccessful delivery.
trouble opening	qmail-send was unable to open the list of local or remote recipients.
trouble reading	qmail-send was unable to read the recipient list.
trouble writing to	qmail-send was unable to process a queued message.
unable to create	qmail-send was unable to process a queued message.
unable to open	qmail-send was unable to read the envelope of a queued message.
unable to start qmail-queue	qmail-send was unable to queue a bounced message.
unable to stat	qmail-send was unable to obtain information about a file.
unable to unlink	qmail-send was unable to remove a file.
unable to utime	qmail-send was unable to record the next scheduled delivery time.
unknown record type in	A serious bug in qmail-send or qmail-queue.

The qmail log file is a complex set of status messages, delivery messages, and problem messages. Trudging through a log file (especially after a few thousand messages have been processed) is often a difficult and boring task. To help administrators, a separate package to help dissect the log file has been developed.

The Qmailanalog Package

The qmailanalog package is a set of programs developed by Dan Bernstein to help the qmail administrator monitor the operation of the qmail server. The programs contained in the qmailanalog package help parse log messages into more meaningful messages for administrators. The qmailanalog Web site is located at:

```
http://cr.yp.to/qmailanalog.html
```

The qmailanalog package is available as a source code download from the Web site at `http://cr.yp.to/software/qmailanalog-0.70.tar.gz`. The current version at the time of this writing is version 0.70.

After downloading the qmailanalog software, you must untar and uncompress it into a working directory. As usual, you can use the /usr/local directory:

```
tar -zxvf qmailanalog-0.70.tar.gz -c /usr/local
```

This produces the `/usr/local/qmailanalog-0.70` directory, which contains all the source code files. To compile and install the qmailanalog package, use the following commands:

```
make
make setup check
```

The default installation directory for the qmailanalog executable files is /usr/local/ qmailanalog/bin.

If you are using the FreeBSD UNIX distribution, the qmailanalog package is included as a port. It is located in the /usr/ports/mail/qmailanalog directory and can be compiled and installed using these commands:

```
make
make install
```

The default installation directory for the qmailanalog port is also /usr/local/qmailanalog.

The Matchup Program

The most-used qmailanalog utility is the matchup program. The matchup program is used to scan the qmail log and determine the status of delivered mail messages by matching the start and finish delivery log entries for a message. It produces a log that indicates the status of messages and the individual deliveries required for each message.

The matchup program uses the raw splogger information for input. If your qmail server is feeding the splogger messages to the system logger facility (the default), you will need to massage the mail log file a little before feeding it to the matchup program to remove the header produced by the logger utility.

To remove the logger header from the mail log entries, you can use the UNIX awk program. By feeding the mail log to the awk program, you can remove fields that are not needed by matchup. Normally, the first five fields in the log file need to be removed. The command to do this is

```
cat /var/log/maillog | awk '{$1="";$2="";$3="";$4="";$5="";print}' >
➥ maillog.clean
```

This command removes the first five fields from each mail log entry and stores the result in the maillog.clean file. This includes the date, timestamp, hostname, and process name that are placed in the entry by the logger program. All that should be left is the original splogger information. The cleaned-up file can now be sent to the matchup program to produce a status file. Listing 13.10 shows an example of this process.

LISTING 13.10 A Sample Matchup Session

```
1  $ cat maillog.clean | /usr/local/qmailanalog/bin/matchup > maillog.txt
2  $ cat maillog.txt
3  d k 955490845.496211 955490845.578441 955490845.818308 280
➥ <rich@shadrach.ispnet1.net> local.jessica@shadrach.ispnet1.net
➥ 27921 1001 did_0+0+1/
4  m 955490845.496211 955490845.838634 280 1 0 0 <rich@shadrach.ispnet1.net>
➥ 27921 1001
5  d k 955490854.852885 955490854.935059 955490855.133089 290
➥ <rich@shadrach.ispnet1.net> local.katie@shadrach.ispnet1.net
➥ 27930 1001 did_0+0+1/
6  m 955490854.852885 955490855.153612 290 1 0 0 <rich@shadrach.ispnet1.net>
➥ 27930 1001
7  d d 955490866.783966 955490866.866783 955490866.902336 291
➥ <rich@shadrach.ispnet1.net> local.fred@shadrach.ispnet1.net
➥ 27938 1001 Sorry,_no_mailbox_here_by_that_name._(#5.1.1)/
8  ?       955490867.033030 bounce msg 18994 qp 27941
9  m 955490866.783966 955490867.056559 291 0 1 0 <rich@shadrach.ispnet1.net>
➥ 27938 1001
10 d k 955490867.097027 955490867.174458 955490867.364132 861 <>
➥ local.rich@shadrach.ispnet1.net 27941 87 did_0+0+1/
11 m 955490867.097027 955490867.389785 861 1 0 0 <> 27941 87
12 $
```

The file produced by the matchup program details the status of each message and delivery attempt. There are two different types of entries in the matchup file.

The delivery status entries show the status of each delivery attempt that was made by qmail. The format for these entries is

```
d result birth dstart ddone bytes <sender> chan.recip qp uid reason
```

The first field (d in this case) indicates that the entry is for a delivery status. The result field indicates the status of the delivery. Table 13.13 shows the status codes used.

TABLE 13.13   Delivery Status Codes

Code	Description
k	Successful delivery
z	Delivery deferred
d	Delivery failed

The reason field is used to elaborate on the reason for any delivery failures. The birth, <sender>, qp, and uid fields reproduce information from the original message. The dstart and ddone fields are timestamps that indicate the start and finish of the delivery process. The bytes field indicates the size of the message, and the <sender> field indicates the original sender of the message.

The other type of entry is the message status. This entry shows the status of each message that is processed by qmail. The format for this entry is

```
m birth done bytes nk nz nd <sender> qp uid
```

The first field indicates that the entry is for message information. The birth and done fields indicate the creation and deletion timestamps of the message. The bytes field indicates the size of the message. The nk, nz, and nd fields indicate the delivery status of the message:

- nk is the number of successful deliveries.
- nz is the number of deferred deliveries.
- nd is the number of failed deliveries.

Again, the <sender>, qp, and uid fields indicate basic information for the message (the sender, the queue ID identifier, and the uid of the user that queued the message).

By observing both the delivery and message status entries, the qmail administrator can determine if or when problems occur on the qmail system.

The Xrecipient Program

The xrecipient program is another qmailanalog utility that can be used to analyze information in the qmail mail log. It can read the output from the matchup program and display the messages sent to a particular recipient. The format of the xrecipient command is

```
xrecipient chan.recipient
```

where *chan* is the qmail channel and *recipient* is the recipient to check for messages. Listing 13.11 shows an example of using the xrecipient program.

LISTING 13.11   An Example of Xrecipient Session Output

```
$ cat maillog.txt | xrecipient local.katie@shadrach.ispnet1.net
d k 955490854.852885 955490854.935059 955490855.133089 290
➥ <rich@shadrach.ispnet1.net> local.katie@shadrach.ispnet1.net 27930
➥ 1001 did_0+0+1/
$
```

The output shown in Listing 13.11 indicates that there was one message delivered to katie@shadrach.ispnet1.net. Although this is a trivial example, the xrecipient program can be extremely useful when analyzing mail logs with thousands of delivery entries.

The Xsender Program

The xsender program is another qmailanalog utility that helps the qmail administrator manage the mail log file by searching for all messages from a particular sender. The format of the xsender program is

xsender *sender*

where *sender* is the address of the target sender. Listing 13.12 shows an example of using the xsender program.

LISTING 13.12   An Example of Xsender Session Output

```
$ cat maillog.txt | xsender rich@shadrach.ispnet1.net
d k 955490845.496211 955490845.578441 955490845.818308 280
➥ <rich@shadrach.ispnet1.net> local.jessica@shadrach.ispnet1.net
➥ 27921 1001 did_0+0+1/
m 955490845.496211 955490845.838634 280 1 0 0 <rich@shadrach.ispnet1.net>
➥ 27921 1001
d k 955490854.852885 955490854.935059 955490855.133089 290
➥ <rich@shadrach.ispnet1.net> local.katie@shadrach.ispnet1.net
➥ 27930 1001 did_0+0+1/
m 955490854.852885 955490855.153612 290 1 0 0 <rich@shadrach.ispnet1.net>
➥ 27930 1001
d d 955490866.783966 955490866.866783 955490866.902336 291
➥ <rich@shadrach.ispnet1.net> local.fred@shadrach.ispnet1.net
➥ 27938 1001  Sorry,_no_mailbox_here_by_that_name._(#5.1.1)/
m 955490866.783966 955490867.056559 291 0 1 0 <rich@shadrach.ispnet1.net>
➥ 27938 1001
$
```

The output from the xsender program should be all message and delivery entries in the mail log that pertain to the requested sender. Again, this utility is most useful when searching for the status of a particular sender in a 1000-message log.

Summary

The job of a qmail administrator is never finished. There is always something that needs to be attended to on the mail server. New users need to have accounts created so that they can receive mail from qmail. Existing users often forget their passwords or compromise their passwords and need them reset.

There are two methods of handling user accounts with qmail. The normal method is by using the standard UNIX system user account files. The /etc/passwd and /etc/group files are used for the userid database. There are several utilities that can be used to manipulate userids and passwords in these files. The vipw command can be used to create new user accounts manually. Linux users can use the useradd command, and FreeBSD users can use the pw command to create new user accounts.

One nice feature of these two utilities is that they can create user home directories, including the Maildir mailbox, when the account is created. If the mail administrator chooses, he can utilize qmail's user database method. The /var/qmail/users/assign file is a text file that maps qmail usernames to UNIX system usernames. By using the assign database, the qmail administrator can control which system users can receive mail messages.

Another ongoing job of the mail administrator is monitoring the system log files. These files contain important information regarding the operation of the mail server. All UNIX systems run the syslogd program, which writes messages to the log file. The qmail program also uses the splogger program, which has a safer method of writing messages to the appropriate log files.

Once messages are placed in the log file, the qmailanalog package can be used to extract detailed information regarding the operation of the qmail program. Individual messages can be tracked to determine if the delivery process is working properly.

Migrating from Sendmail to qmail

IN THIS CHAPTER

The preceding chapters have described the process of creating a new mail server using the qmail software. Unfortunately, many sites were using other mail server software packages before they decide to migrate to the qmail package. The process of migrating an existing mail server to qmail is slightly different from starting a new mail server. Great care must be taken to ensure that the qmail configuration completely replaces the functionality of the previous mail server. This chapter describes the processes necessary to convert an existing sendmail mail server to a qmail mail server.

What Is Sendmail?

The sendmail software package was designed to be a complete Mail Transfer Agent (MTA) package for UNIX platforms. The sendmail package has been developed under the guidance of the Sendmail Consortium (`http://www.sendmail.org`). Also, Sendmail, Inc., (`http://www.sendmail.com`) provides commercial support as well as a commercial version of the sendmail mail package. A sendmail user's group operates a Web site at `http://www.sendmail.net`.

The sendmail program is one of the most robust and versatile MTA programs available. Because of its versatility, it is also one of the most complicated to configure. Sendmail gets most of its configuration settings from a single configuration file. It is not uncommon for this file to be a few hundred lines in length. Within the configuration file are parameters that control how sendmail handles incoming messages and routes outgoing messages.

Incoming messages are run through a complicated series of rules that can be used to filter messages from the system. The filtering rules are also stored in the configuration file (hence the large file size). Messages can be checked for header content and handled according to either the source or destination information available.

Outgoing messages must be routed to the proper location for delivery. Sendmail must be configured according to the method used to connect the mail server to the Internet. Often a mail server for a small office is configured to pass all outgoing messages to the ISP, which in turn can then relay the messages to the proper destination. This method is called using a *smart host*.

The following sections describe the functionality that sendmail encompasses.

Sendmail Files and Directories

The sendmail program does not work alone. It requires a host of files and directories to do its job properly. This section lists and describes the files and directories needed by a default installation of sendmail.

The Sendmail Mail Engine

There are a few core pieces of the sendmail program that are essential to the operation of the mail system. These pieces are described in the following sections.

The Sendmail Program

Unlike qmail, sendmail uses a single program as the mail engine. The /usr/sbin/sendmail program normally runs as a daemon, waiting for connections for incoming mail, and checks the mail queue at set intervals for outgoing mail. Alternatively, sendmail can be configured to be run by the inetd TCP wrapper program. This saves some server memory by not having the program in the background all the time, but it does decrease performance, because sendmail must read its configuration file every time it starts. The sendmail program is setuid as the root user, so it can access directories owned by root. Non-root users can run sendmail, but they will not have access to many of the default file locations, such as the default mail queue.

The Sendmail Configuration File

For sendmail to operate properly, it must be configured for the specific mail server implementation. The main configuration file for sendmail is /etc/sendmail.cf. All sendmail process definitions are stored in this file. These definitions are called *rule sets*. Sendmail uses rule sets to parse the sender and recipient addresses in messages and determines how to deliver the messages to the intended recipients.

Sendmail reads the configuration file when it starts up. Any changes to the configuration file require the program to be restarted to take effect.

The Sendmail Mail Queue

The mqueue directory is created to contain the queued mail messages waiting to be processed. Unlike qmail, which uses a complicated series of subdirectories to parse messages in the queue, sendmail places all queued messages in the same mqueue directory. The owner of this directory should be the root user. Sendmail ensures that all queue files stored here are set with the proper permissions to prevent users from reading messages in the mail queues. The location of the mail queue directory can be changed. It can be set either by an entry in the sendmail.cf file or by an option on the sendmail command line.

Checking the Mail Queue

The mailq executable file is a symbolic link to the sendmail program. When executed as mailq, sendmail prints a summary of the contents of the mail queue.

User-Controlled Message Forwarding

Each local user on the system can create a .forward file in his $HOME directory. Before sendmail attempts to pass mail for the local user to the local mail processor, it will check for this file. If the file exists and contains valid email addresses, sendmail will instead forward the message to those addresses. The addresses should be in standard format (username@hostname) with one address per line.

The Sendmail Help File

The sendmail.hf file is used to produce a help file for the SMTP HELP command. The help file is in a special format that sendmail can parse as remote SMTP hosts request information using the SMTP HELP command. As shown in Chapter 5, "SMTP and qmail," remote clients can issue either a general SMTP HELP command or specific HELP commands, along with the command they want help on. To parse the information in the help file, sendmail uses tags at the start of each line. Listing 14.1 shows a partial sendmail.hf file.

LISTING 14.1   A Partial /usr/lib/sendmail.hf File

```
1   cpyr
2   cpyr    Copyright (c) 1998 Sendmail, Inc.  All rights reserved.
3   cpyr    Copyright (c) 1983, 1995-1997 Eric P. Allman.  All rights reserved.
4   cpyr    Copyright (c) 1988, 1993
5   cpyr     The Regents of the University of California.  All rights reserved.
6   cpyr
7   cpyr
8   cpyr    By using this file, you agree to the terms and conditions set
9   cpyr    forth in the LICENSE file which can be found at the top level of
10  cpyr    the sendmail distribution.
11  cpyr
12  cpyr    @(#)sendmail.hf 8.18 (Berkeley) 11/19/1998
13  cpyr
14  smtp    Topics:
15  smtp        HELO      EHLO      MAIL      RCPT      DATA
16  smtp        RSET      NOOP      QUIT      HELP      VRFY
17  smtp        EXPN      VERB      ETRN      DSN
18  smtp    For more info use "HELP <topic>".
19  smtp    To report bugs in the implementation send email to
20  smtp        sendmail-bugs@sendmail.org.
21  smtp    For local information send email to Postmaster at your site.
22  help    HELP [ <topic> ]
23  help        The HELP command gives help info.
24  helo    HELO <hostname>
25  helo        Introduce yourself.
26  ehlo    EHLO <hostname>
27  ehlo        Introduce yourself, and request extended SMTP mode.
28  ehlo    Possible replies include:
29  ehlo        SEND        Send as mail              [RFC821]
30  ehlo        SOML        Send as mail or terminal    [RFC821]
31  ehlo        SAML        Send as mail and terminal   [RFC821]
```

```
32 ehlo       EXPN        Expand the mailing list      [RFC821]
33 ehlo       HELP        Supply helpful information   [RFC821]
34 ehlo       TURN        Turn the operation around    [RFC821]
35 ehlo       8BITMIME    Use 8-bit data               [RFC1652]
36 ehlo       SIZE        Message size declaration     [RFC1870]
37 ehlo       VERB        Verbose              [Allman]
38 ehlo       ONEX        One message transaction only     [Allman]
39 ehlo       CHUNKING    Chunking             [RFC1830]
40 ehlo       BINARYMIME  Binary MIME          [RFC1830]
41 ehlo       PIPELINING  Command Pipelining       [RFC1854]
42 ehlo       DSN     Delivery Status Notification     [RFC1891]
43 ehlo       ETRN        Remote Message Queue Starting    [RFC1985]
44 ehlo       XUSR        Initial (user) submission    [Allman]
45 mail   MAIL FROM: <sender> [ <parameters> ]
46 mail       Specifies the sender.  Parameters are ESMTP extensions.
47 mail       See "HELP DSN" for details.
48 rcpt   RCPT TO: <recipient> [ <parameters> ]
49 rcpt       Specifies the recipient.  Can be used any number of times.
50 rcpt       Parameters are ESMTP extensions.  See "HELP DSN" for details.
51 data   DATA
52 data       Following text is collected as the message.
53 data       End with a single dot.
54 rset   RSET
55 rset       Resets the system.
56 quit   QUIT
57 quit       Exit sendmail (SMTP).
```

Lines 14–21 show the standard help message that will be returned in response to an SMTP
HELP command. After that, each individual command is listed with the command on the left
side and the HELP message displayed. For example, the SMTP command HELP MAIL would
result in lines 45, 46, and 47 being sent to the client. To test this, log into the sendmail TCP
port and issue the SMTP command, as demonstrated in Chapter 5 and shown in Listing 14.2.

LISTING 14.2   A Sample SMTP HELP Command

```
1  [kevin@shadrach kevin]$ telnet localhost 25
2  Trying 127.0.0.1...
3  Connected to localhost.
4  Escape character is '^]'.
5  220 shadrach.smallorg.org ESMTP Sendmail 8.9.3/8.9.3; Tue, 5 Oct 1999
➥ 19:19:39 -0500
6  HELP MAIL
7  214-MAIL FROM: <sender> [ <parameters> ]
8  214-    Specifies the sender.  Parameters are ESMTP extensions.
9  214-    See "HELP DSN" for details.
```

14

MIGRATING FROM
SENDMAIL TO
QMAIL

LISTING 14.2   Continued

```
10 214 End of HELP info
11 QUIT
12 221 shadrach.smallorg.org closing connection
13 Connection closed by foreign host.
14 [kevin@shadrach kevin]$
```

The Sendmail Aliases System

The sendmail program contains a method for creating mail aliases on the mail system. Mail aliases can be used to create special-use mail names. When a message is received for the special name, sendmail redirects the message to either a system user mailbox or a program to process the message. This section describes the sendmail alias system.

Creating Sendmail Aliases

The newaliases executable file is also a link to the sendmail program. When sendmail runs as newaliases, it reads the text /etc/aliases file and creates an aliases database using an installed UNIX database package. On Linux and FreeBSD systems, it is common to create a hash database file as the aliases database.

The Sendmail Aliases Table

All sendmail aliases used on the mail server are listed in a common table. The aliases table is normally located at /etc/aliases, but it can be changed in the sendmail configuration file. The aliases file points alias email names to real addresses, programs, or files. One format of the aliases file is

```
name:    name1, name2, name3, ...
```

where *name* is the alias name, and *name1*, *name2*, and so on are the addresses to which the message will be sent instead of the original. There can be one or more different addresses used for the alias. Each address listed receives a copy of the message. Aliases are always considered local to the mail server they are configured on.

Another use of an alias line can be

```
name:    |program
```

where *program* is the full pathname of a program that can process the message. Often this feature is used for mail list programs such as Majordomo.

Still another use of an alias line can be

```
name:    file
```

where `file` is a full pathname pointing to a text file. Any messages sent to the address will be spooled to the text file given. For this feature to work properly, the proper read/write system permissions must be set on both the text file and the directory in which the text file is located.

The last use that the alias line can assume is

```
name:      :include:filelist
```

where `filelist` is the full pathname of a file that can contain a list of email addresses. This has the same effect as listing each of the email addresses on the aliases line separated by commas, as in the first format. This format may be easier to manipulate if you have a large mail list that changes frequently.

Listing 14.3 shows a sample sendmail aliases file.

LISTING 14.3   A Sample `/etc/aliases` File

```
1  #
2  #    @(#)aliases 8.2 (Berkeley) 3/5/94
3  #
4  #  Aliases in this file will NOT be expanded in the header from
5  #  Mail, but WILL be visible over networks or from /bin/mail.
6  #
7  #  >>>>>>>>>>  The program "newaliases" must be run after
8  #  >> NOTE >>  this file is updated for any changes to
9  #  >>>>>>>>>>  show through to sendmail.
10 #
11
12 # Basic system aliases -- these MUST be present.
13 MAILER-DAEMON:  postmaster
14 postmaster: root
15
16 # General redirections for pseudo accounts.
17 bin:        root
18 daemon:     root
19 games:      root
20 ingres:     root
21 nobody:     root
22 system:     root
23 toor:       root
24 uucp:       root
25
26 # Well-known aliases.
27 manager:    root
28 dumper:     root
29 operator:   root
30
```

LISTING 14.3 Continued

```
31 # trap decode to catch security attacks
32 decode:      root
33
34 # Person who should get root's mail
35 root:        rich
36
37 # Program used to auto-reply to messages
38 auto-test:          |/home/rich/auto-test
39
40 # Send all messages to a text file
41 saveme:         /home/rich/test.txt
42
43 # Send all messages to remote site
44 rich:          rich@othercompany.com
45
46 #Create a simple multi-user mail list
47 officenews:          :include:/home/rich/office.txt
```

Lines 13–32 redirect any mail for various standard system usernames to the root user. This is usually a good idea to ensure that no one is trying to hack into the system using one of the default system usernames. If these usernames are not aliased to root, any mail messages generated to them are lost. Line 35 shows another good idea. It redirects any mail for the root user to a common username that should log into the system on a regular basis. Remember, if you are being a good system administrator, you should not be logging in as the root user very often.

Line 38 demonstrates redirecting messages to a program. The program must be shown with its full pathname so that the shell can find it. Line 41 demonstrates using a text file to store any messages sent to an address. Remember to be careful about read/write permissions for the file.

Line 44 demonstrates that, although the alias name must be local to the mail server, the names for which it is an alias do not have to be. You can redirect a mail message for a user to another email account on a completely different system. This is a handy feature when users move to different email machines within the organization or leave the organization.

Line 47 demonstrates the use of a mail list text file in the aliases file. The file /home/rich/office.txt is a plain text file that lists email addresses. When a message is received for the officenews alias, the office.txt file is checked and the message is sent to all addresses in that file. This is sometimes used to create mail lists.

The Sendmail Statistics Programs

Sendmail includes programs to help the mail administrator view mail statistics of the mail server. The following sections describe the sendmail mail statistics files.

Determining Host Mail Statistics

The `hoststat` executable is another link to the sendmail program. When executed as `hoststat`, sendmail will attempt to read a host statistics file and display the status of the last mail transaction to all of the remote hosts where it has sent mail.

Removing Current Host Statistics

The `purgestat` executable is also a link to the sendmail program. When executed as `purgestat`, sendmail will delete all of the information in the host statistics file.

Host Statistics Directory

The directory `/var/spool/mqueue/.hoststat` contains files that contain statistics for each accessed remote host. The hoststat program uses these files to display the status of remote host transactions.

Host Statistics Flag File

The presence of the `sendmail.st` file indicates that the mail administrator wants to collect statistics about the outgoing mail traffic. This is initially created as a null file. Although the `/etc` directory is the default location, many UNIX distributions, including most Linux distributions and FreeBSD, change the default location to `/var/log/sendmail.st`.

Configuring qmail to Use the Standard Sendmail Mailboxes

By default, sendmail uses the local mail delivery program to store local mail messages in the default local mailbox system. The local mail delivery program used on Linux systems is called *binmail*, after its location (`/bin/mail`). For FreeBSD and other BSD-derived systems, the local mail delivery program is called `mail.local`.

The local mail delivery programs deliver mail to a common mailbox directory. Each user's mail is stored in a single file, one file for each user. The common mailbox directory is normally located at `/var/spool/mail`. On FreeBSD systems it has been moved to `/var/mail`.

Each user message is stored at the end of the existing text file containing any previous messages (see Chapter 9, "Using the Maildir Mailbox Format").

On an active sendmail mail server, there could be messages in the standard mailbox locations waiting to be read by users. When changing to the qmail system, it is often easiest to continue using the standard mailbox location to support users with messages there.

To support local mail delivery to the standard mailbox directory, the qmail startup script should point to the appropriate local mail delivery program on your UNIX system (as discussed in Chapter 8, "Using qmail"). For most Linux systems this is

```
exec env - PATH="/var/qmail/bin:$PATH" \
qmail-start \
'|preline -f /bin/mail -f "${SENDER:-MAILER-DAEMON}" -d "$USER"' \
splogger qmail&
```

FreeBSD systems use the following startup script:

```
exec env - PATH="/var/qmail/bin:$PATH" \
qmail-start \
'|preline -f /usr/libexec/mail.local -r "${SENDER:-MAILER-DAEMON}" -d
➥ "$USER"' \
splogger qmail&
```

Both scripts tell qmail-start to use the local mail delivery program on the UNIX system to deliver messages destined to local users to the standard sendmail mailboxes.

By sending messages to the standard mailboxes, you allow users to continue using the same MUA programs to retrieve messages from their mailboxes. After implementing qmail on the mail server, you can slowly migrate users to the qmail Maildir-formatted mailboxes if you want by using individual .qmail files pointing to the Maildir-formatted mailbox (as described in Chapter 9).

CAUTION

Be careful of MUA programs that require /bin/sendmail to forward messages. As mentioned in Chapter 8, you must replace the standard sendmail program with the qmail version for this type of MUA programs.

---

qmail Utilities for Using Sendmail Files

If the UNIX system was running the sendmail mail system previously, many of the sendmail configuration files described in the previous section will be present. To help the qmail administrator migrate the sendmail system to a fully functional qmail system, Dan Bernstein has created two packages. The dot-forward and fastforward packages allow the qmail administrator to migrate existing sendmail configurations into a working qmail configuration. The following sections describe these packages.

Using the Sendmail Alias File

One of the most complicated pieces of the sendmail configuration to duplicate is the use of the sendmail alias file. Sendmail allows the mail administrator to create a text file containing alias names and delivery definitions. By running the sendmail `newaliases` command, the mail administrator converts the text alias file to a binary hash database file called `/etc/aliases.db`. The sendmail program uses the hash database file to determine mail delivery rules for the aliases.

By default, qmail duplicates the sendmail alias function by allowing the mail administrator to create alias files in the `/var/qmail/alias` directory. Each alias name is assigned a separate file containing the delivery instructions. If the existing sendmail configuration contains an aliases file with lots of aliases, creating the individual qmail alias files could become tedious.

The qmail fastforward package contains programs that can be used to read the sendmail `/etc/aliases` file and create a single alias database that qmail can use. This section describes the installation and use of the fastforward package.

Downloading and Installing Fastforward

At the time of this writing, the current version of fastforward is 0.51. The complete source code can be downloaded from Bernstein's Web site at `http://cr.yp.to/software/fastforward-0.51.tar.gz`.

As usual, the software package can be extracted into a working directory using the command

```
tar -zxvf fastforward-0.51.tar.gz -C /usr/local
```

The source code should be in the directory `/usr/local/fastforward-0.51`. To compile the executable programs and install them, use the command

```
make setup check
```

as the `root` user. The fastforward executables will be installed in the `/var/qmail/bin` directory.

If you are using a FreeBSD distribution, the fastforward package is included as a software port. It is bundled with the dot-forward package in a port called `qmail-contrib`. This is located in the `/usr/ports/mail/qmail-contrib` directory. As usual, the port can be installed using these commands:

```
make
make install
```

The fastforward package contains several utilities for migrating a sendmail `/etc/aliases` file to qmail. The following section describes those utilities.

The Fastforward Utilities

Once the fastforward package is installed, you can convert the existing sendmail aliases file to a format that qmail can read and interpret. The fastforward package includes utilities to convert the existing sendmail aliases text file as well as any sendmail mail lists or include files into binary files that fastforward can process. By using binary files instead of the sendmail text files, fastforward can parse the recipient addresses much more quickly and increase response time for the mail server.

Converting the Sendmail Aliases File

The newaliases program is used to convert the text /etc/aliases file into a cdb-formatted database file for qmail. The cdb database file is located at /etc/aliases.cdb.

Unfortunately, the fastforward newaliases command has the same name as the sendmail newaliases command. Be sure to run the qmail version of the program to convert the /etc/aliases database to the proper format. It should be located in the /var/qmail/bin directory.

> **NOTE**
>
> The qmail newaliases program can convert most, but not all, of the standard sendmail aliases file formats. If your /etc/aliases file contains any entries that map an alias name to a text file to archive messages, the qmail newaliases program will not convert those entries and, in fact, will terminate without creating the aliases.cdb database.

Listing 14.4 shows an example of using the newaliases program.

LISTING 14.4   A Sample Newaliases Session

```
shadrach# /var/qmail/bin/newaliases
shadrach# ls -al /etc/alias*
-rw-r--r--  1 root  wheel   1384 Apr 17 15:00 /etc/aliases
-rw-r--r--  1 root  wheel   3226 Apr 17 15:00 /etc/aliases.cdb
-rw-r--r--  1 root  wheel  32768 Apr 17 14:59 /etc/aliases.db
shadrach#
```

A successful newaliases session will not produce a result message. If there are any errors (such as an entry pointing to a text file) newaliases reports the error. As can be seen in Listing 14.4, the database created by the qmail aliases command (/etc/aliases.cdb) is considerably smaller than the database file created by the sendmail newaliases command.

> **NOTE**
>
> If you continue to place new alias names in the /etc/aliases text file, remember to run the fastforward newaliases command to convert them to the /etc/aliases.cdb file.

Processing Sendmail Aliases in qmail

The fastforward utility is used to scan the database file created by the newaliases command and deliver messages appropriately. The format of the fastforward command is

```
|fastforward [-nNpPdD] cdb
```

where cdb is the pathname of the aliases database in cdb format. Table 14.1 shows the command-line options available for the fastforward program.

TABLE 14.1 Fastforward Command-Line Options

Option	Description
-n	No delivery. Fastforward prints a description of what it would do, but no messages are delivered.
-N	Forward messages as defined in the aliases file (default).
-p	Passthrough mode. If the message recipient is not in the aliases file, fastforward exits and allows any other commands in the .qmail-default file to be executed. If found, the message is forwarded and any other commands are skipped.
-P	Do not pass through. If the message recipient is found, the message is forwarded and any other commands in the .qmail-default file are executed. Otherwise, the message is bounced (default).
-d	Use $DEFAULT@$HOST as the recipient address.
-D	Use $RECIPIENT as the recipient address (default).

The section "Using the Fastforward Utilities," later in this chapter, describes how to instruct qmail to use the fastforward command.

Listing the Converted Sendmail Aliases

The printforward utility can be used to list the entries in an existing /etc/aliases.cdb file in an ASCII text format that can be transferred to another mail host. The format of the text file is

```
target: destination, destination
```

target represents the alias name that will be defined in the alias file. *destination* defines actions that will be taken by the mail server for the message. Commands are separated by commas and are terminated with a semicolon.

Destinations can be one of the following:

- Recipient address
- Owner address
- External mailing program
- Program

Listing 14.5 shows a sample printforward file produced from an /etc/aliases.cdb file that was created by the /etc/aliases file defined in Listing 14.1.

LISTING 14.5   A Partial Printforward Output

```
mailer-daemon@:
, &postmaster@shadrach.ispnet1.net
;
postmaster@:
, &root@shadrach.ispnet1.net
;
root@:
, &rich@shadrach.ispnet1.net
;
auto-test@:
, !/home/rich/auto-test
;
rich@:
, &rich@othercompany.com
;
officenews@:
, /home/rich/office.txt.bin
;
```

Listing 14.5 demonstrates the standard output from the printforward command. Each target that was present in the original /etc/aliases file has an at symbol (@) added to enable wild-card matching by qmail. Specific email address recipients have an ampersand (&) appended to the address and the local hostname prepended to specifically identify individual email addresses on the local host.

Notice that the officenews include file that was defined in the original /etc/aliases file has been replaced. The fastforward program uses a binary form of the include file. The original include file must be converted to binary format using the newinclude program, described in the "Converting Sendmail Include Files" section, later in this chapter.

Converting a Sendmail Alias File to a qmail Database

The setforward utility is used to convert the output from the printforward program into a cdb-format database that the fastforward program can process. The format of the setforward command is

```
setforward cdb tmp
```

where cdb is the pathname of the resulting cdb database and tmp is the name of a temporary file that setforward can create while it is converting the data. The printforward file is read from the standard input of setforward. The command to convert the printforward file to a cdb database file is

```
setforward /etc/aliases.cdb /tmp/aliases.tmp < aliases.txt
```

This command assumes that the output from the printforward command has been saved in the aliases.txt file.

Creating a Binary Mail List

The setmaillist utility is used to create a binary mail list for the fastforward program. By using binary mail lists, fastforward can read the mail list and process recipient addresses much more quickly than it can using a text mail list.

The format of the setmaillist command is

```
setmaillist bin tmp
```

where bin is the pathname of the binary mail list produced and tmp is the pathname of a temporary file used by setmaillist. The text mail list is read by setmaillist on standard input.

The setmaillist program can covert a normal ASCII text mail list used by sendmail into a binary mail list used by the fastforward program.

Displaying the Contents of a Binary Mail List

The printmaillist utility is used to print the content of a binary mailing list. The content is parsed onto individual lines, each line representing an entry in the mail list. The lines can be in one of three forms:

- If the line begins with an ampersand (&), the entry is a recipient address.
- If the line begins with a letter or number, the entry is also a recipient address.
- If the line begins with a dot or a slash, the entry is an include file.

The output of printmaillist can be fed into the setmaillist program to produce a binary mail list.

Converting Sendmail Include Files

The newinclude program is used to convert sendmail text include files to a binary format that the fastforward program can interpret and use. The format of the `newinclude` command is

```
newinclude list
```

where `list` is the pathname of the sendmail include file that needs to be converted. The newinclude program will convert the list into a binary file with the name `list.bin`. It will also create a temporary file `list.tmp` while it is processing the mail list.

CAUTION

The fastforward program does not deliver messages to text files or to programs using the newinclude program. Instead, you should create a `.qmail` file to handle those situations.

Using the Fastforward Utilities

Using the utilities in the fastforward package is simple if you follow the right steps. Before you use the fastforward program, you should make sure that all of the appropriate sendmail files have been converted with the appropriate fastforward utilities. The steps necessary for preparing the sendmail files are

1. Convert the `/etc/aliases` file to an `/etc/aliases.cdb` file using the newaliases utility.

2. Convert any sendmail include files using the newinclude utility.

3. Convert any mail lists using the setmaillist utility.

Once the `/etc/aliases` file and any mail lists and include files have been converted using the appropriate utilities, qmail can be configured to use the fastforward program.

The fastforward utility must be placed in an alias file in the `/var/qmail/alias` directory as the default action. This allows qmail to check all recipients against the aliases database. The `.qmail-default` file located in the `/var/qmail/alias` directory is used to define the default action to take on all messages. This is where the fastforward program should be defined. The contents of the `.qmail-default` file should be

```
|fastforward -d /etc/aliases.cdb
```

This command instructs fastforward to check the aliases database for any delivery instructions for the recipient address.

After these steps have been performed, qmail should be able to process the old sendmail aliases file along with any additional mail lists or include files. One remaining item from sendmail's configuration is the user .forward files. Fortunately, Dan Bernstein has developed another utility to handle that.

Using Sendmail .forward Files

The dot-forward package allows qmail to handle any existing sendmail .forward files present in user home directories. The .forward files are used by users to redirect mail messages to an alternate location. The alternate location can be another local user or a remote user.

Downloading and Installing Dot-Forward

The dot-forward package source code is available for downloading from Bernstein's Web site at http://cr.yp.to/software/dot-forward-0.71.tar.gz. At the time of this writing, the current version is 0.71. After downloading, as always, you can unpack the source code into a working directory and run the GNU make utility to create and install the executable code:

```
tar -zxvf dot-forward-0.71.tar.gz -C /usr/local
cd /usr/local/dot-forward-0.71
make setup check
```

The dot-forward package contains one executable file that is placed in the /var/qmail/bin directory (by default).

If you are using the FreeBSD UNIX distribution, you can extract the dot-forward package from the qmail-contrib port file located in the /usr/ports/mail/qmail-contrib directory. To compile and install both the dot-forward and fastforward packages, use the GNU make utility with the install parameter. Just as with the source code installation, the port package places the dot-forward package in the /var/qmail/bin directory on the FreeBSD server.

Using Dot-Forward

The format of the dot-forward command is

```
dot-forward [-nN] file
```

where file is the pathname of the file that dot-forward will read for message forwarding instructions. This file should be in standard sendmail .forward file format—an ASCII text file with each recipient on a separate line.

The dot-forward command uses two command-line options:

- -N to read and forward the message (default).
- -n to parse the file instructions and print them out.

There are two ways to implement the dot-forward command on the qmail system. To enable system-wide processing of .forward commands, you can insert the dot-forward command into the startup script that is used to initialize qmail.

Actually, Bernstein has already provided scripts for this in the /var/qmail/boot directory. All of the standard startup scripts, discussed in Chapter 8, also have a version that includes a +df on the end of the filename. These versions start the qmail processes, but they also add a line for the dot-forward process. Listing 14.6 shows an example of a qmail startup script that also uses the dot-forward command.

LISTING 14.6   A Sample Dot-Forward Startup Script

```
1  #!/bin/sh
2
3  # Using splogger to send the log through syslog.
4  # Using dot-forward to support sendmail-style ~/.forward files.
5  # Using binmail to deliver messages to /var/spool/mail/$USER by default.
6  # Using BSD 4.4 binmail interface: /usr/libexec/mail.local -r
7
8  exec env - PATH="/var/qmail/bin:$PATH" \
9  qmail-start '|dot-forward .forward
10 |preline -f /usr/libexec/mail.local -r "${SENDER:-MAILER-DAEMON}" -d
➥"$USER"' \
11 splogger qmail&
```

Lines 9–11 show the command used to initiate the qmail-start program to start qmail on the mail server. The parameters of the qmail-start command are passed to the qmail-lspawn program to determine how local mail will be delivered. Lines 9 and 10 show that two commands are passed to the qmail-lspawn command.

The first is the dot-forward command. Any message that is for a local user will first be processed by the dot-forward command. The parameter used for the dot-forward command is the file .forward. This allows the program to check if the recipient user has a .forward file in his home directory. If a .forward file exists, dot-forward processes it and forwards the mail message to the listed recipient(s). After the dot-forward command is successfully processed, the script ends. If there is not a .forward file in the user's home directory, the next command in the script is processed, which is a call to the local mail delivery program on the mail server. This should properly deliver the mail message to the appropriate local user.

Other Sendmail Configuration Considerations

By using the fastforward and dot-forward packages, you should be able to process sendmail configurations easily with your new qmail system. Also, by configuring qmail to use the local mail delivery program, your customers should not notice any difference in their email processes (except that they might be processed much faster, with less load on the server).

One final piece of the sendmail puzzle to mention is virtual domains. Sendmail handles virtual domains completely differently than qmail, and to perform the perfect migration you must be prepared to accommodate this. The following sections describe the sendmail `virtusertable` and `sendmail.cw` files and how qmail can duplicate their functionality.

The Sendmail `virtusertable` File

If the previous sendmail server was implementing virtual domains, they should be defined in the `/etc/virtusertable` file.

The `virtusertable` file maps user and domain addresses to local (or even remote) addresses for sendmail to send all messages to. Listing 14.7 shows a sample `/etc/virtusertable` file.

LISTING 14.7   A Sample Sendmail `/etc/virtusertable` File

```
1   prez@smallorg.org      fred
2   @smallorg.org          smallorg
3   @mediumorg.org         mediumorg
4   riley@ispnet1.net      alecia
```

Line 1 shows sendmail mapping an individual email address to a local system username. Lines 2 and 3 show examples of mapping an entire domain name to a local username. Any messages received for the `smallorg.org` domain (except for the `prez` username) are delivered to the local system user name `smallorg`.

The `virtusertable` entries must be replicated in the qmail `virtualdomains` control file. The format of the `virtualdomains` file is similar to the sendmail `virtusertable` file. qmail can define local user addresses to receive messages for an individual user or an entire domain (see Chapter 7, "Changing qmail Operational Parameters"). In the qmail `virtualdomains` file, a colon is used to separate the two values.

The Sendmail `sendmail.cw` File

Besides the `virtusertable`, sendmail also uses the `/etc/sendmail.cw` file to define what domains it should receive mail for. Each domain is listed in a separate line in the `sendmail.cw` file. The mail administrator is responsible for coordinating this file with the DNS MX records for the domains (see Chapter 4, "DNS and qmail").

qmail duplicates this functionality with the `rcpthosts` control file. Any domains that the qmail server will receive messages for must be listed in the `rcpthosts` file. If they are not, qmail will refuse to accept messages for the domain.

Summary

This chapter described the processes required to migrate an existing sendmail mail server to a qmail server. If the sendmail mail server used an alias file, the qmail fastforward package can be installed to allow qmail to process the entries in the alias file with minimum effort. If the sendmail mail users were accustom to using .forward files in their home directories, the qmail dot-forward package can be used to allow qmail to process any mail entries in the existing .forward files.

Finally, the qmail mail administrator should examine the sendmail virtusertable and sendmail.cw files to determine if the sendmail configuration was used to receive messages for any virtual domains. If so, the administrator must transfer any virtusertable entries to the qmail virtualdomains control file and any sendmail.cw entries to the rcpthosts control file. With these few simple steps, a production sendmail mail server can be converted to qmail in no time at all.

Advanced qmail Topics

PART
III

IN THIS PART

Supporting Mail Lists

IN THIS CHAPTER

One of the more common advanced topics for mail servers is the support of mail lists. Customers use mail lists to share information to a widely dispersed group of people. Any person with an email account on the Internet can send and receive messages from a mail list. The mail list automatically replicates all messages received to every address in the mail list.

qmail supports simple mail list functionality by allowing users to create a `.qmail` alias file that can contain multiple email addresses (see Chapter 8, "Using qmail"). The alias filename is appended to the username to create the mail list address. For example, if user `jessica` creates a `.qmail` file called `.qmail-dogs`, then any message sent to the email address `jessica-dogs` would be replicated to every address listed in Jessica's `.qmail-dogs` file.

While this is a great feature of qmail, it by no means takes the place of commercial-quality mail list systems. This chapter describes three mail list systems that can work with qmail to provide full mail list control and functionality.

Types of Mail Lists

You may already be familiar with mail list servers as a subscriber. If you have ever sent a message to a mail list with the word *subscribe* in the body of the message, you probably have interacted with a large mail list system. The capability of remote users to request a subscription is just one feature of real mail list servers. This section describes some of the common ones.

Open and Closed Mail Lists

When you want to become a member of a mail list, you must first send a message asking to subscribe. There are several different options that the mail list server can use to handle new subscription requests.

In an open mail list, anyone is allowed to subscribe. No checks are made to authenticate the email address that is requesting the subscription. This is the simplest type of mail list to administer, because there are almost no functions that need to be administered. There is one drawback to this feature. You assume that the email address requesting the subscription is the actual person who is subscribing. Sometimes this can be dangerous. Just like pranksters who send in magazine subscription cards with other peoples' names on them, pranksters can subscribe someone's email address to the mail list without that person's knowledge.

To combat this, most mail list server programs allow open mail lists but confirm the actual subscription. When a request to subscribe to the mail list is received, the server sends a message back to the email address requesting the subscription, asking for a confirmation reply. Often a special ID code is used so that it is difficult to fake the return confirmation message. When a proper return confirmation message is received, the email address is added to the subscription list.

In a closed mail list, all subscription requests are sent to a special email address called the *list owner*. New email addresses are not added to the mail list unless the mail list owner sends a message okaying the addition. This allows the mail list owner complete control over who is allowed access to the mail list.

Moderated and Unmoderated Mail Lists

Once the mail list is created and email addresses are added to the subscription list, users can send messages to the list to be forwarded to all other members of the list. In an unmoderated mail list, no checking of messages is done. Any member of the list can send a message to the list and it is automatically forwarded to every member of the list.

Some mail list owners are afraid of this feature. You may want or need to control the content that is sent to list members. A moderated mail list allows the list owner to screen all messages sent to the list before they are sent to list members. If the list owner does not want the message forwarded to the list, he can stop the message. If the message is okay, it will be sent to the list as normal. This feature creates a large amount of work for the list owner but, depending on the scope of the mail list, it may be a necessary job.

Remote Administration of Mail Lists

A very nice feature of sophisticated mail list server software packages is the capability to administer the mail list remotely. Most packages allow the list owner to create a special password for access to administration functions on the mail list. When the owner has access, he can then change the configuration of the mail list server via email messages sent to the mail list. Because the configuration is done via email, the list owner can be anywhere in the world, as long as he can send email messages to the server. This is a nice feature to have if the mail list server is located away from the mail list owner.

Each mail list has a separate configuration file that can be maintained by the mail list owner. Features such as whether the list is open or closed and moderated or unmoderated can be configured and changed remotely without any work having to be done on the mail list server.

Digests of Mail Lists

Another feature of full-service mail list servers is the capability to package messages into digests on a daily, weekly, or monthly basis. A user can then receive the digests rather than the individual messages. If the mail list generates lots of messages each day, sometimes it is better to receive just one large message at the end of the day rather than lots of small messages scattered throughout the day. Mail lists that are time sensitive (so that responses are generated frequently) may not be good candidates for digests.

Archives of Mail Lists

Archives are files that contain previous messages sent to the mail list. The list owner can select a daily, weekly, monthly, or yearly archive period. All messages sent to the list in the time period set are also saved to an archive file, and new members of the list can receive archives of past messages. The mail list server can produce lists of available archive files, and members can select which files to receive via email.

The Majordomo Program

One of the most popular mail list programs available for UNIX systems is the Majordomo program. All mail list programs are compared to Majordomo for functionality. The Majordomo program supports all of the mail list functions listed in the previous sections and does them quite well.

The Majordomo package was written to run on a sendmail mail server. It relies on the use of sendmail mail aliases to perform the mail list tasks. The current version of Majordomo at the time of this writing is version 1.94.5. It is rumored that version 2 of Majordomo will have direct support for qmail mail servers. Until then, workarounds are required to allow Majordomo to work with a qmail mail server.

There are several methods that industrious qmail users have used to get Majordomo to work with qmail. This section describes a technique presented by Dan Bernstein, the developer of qmail. It requires that the qmail `fastforward` package (described in Chapter 14, "Migrating from Sendmail to qmail") be installed and configured so that qmail can handle sendmail aliases defined in the `/etc/aliases` file and include files.

Downloading Majordomo

Some Linux distributions include a binary distribution package for Majordomo. The FreeBSD UNIX distribution includes a software port of the Majordomo program. It is located in the `/usr/ports/mail/majordomo` directory and can be installed using the GNU make utility.

If your UNIX distribution does not include a binary distribution of Majordomo or you want to get the latest version, you can download it from the Internet. Many different UNIX and Linux sites have Majordomo distributions available for download. At the time of this writing, Great Circle Associates has offered to host the official Majordomo Web and FTP sites. The Web site is located at `http://www.greatcircle.com/majordomo/`.

The software can be downloaded at the FTP site `ftp.greatcircle.com`, in the `/pub/majordomo` directory. The file `majordomo.tar.gz` is a link that always points to the most current version of Majordomo, which currently is version 1.94.5. Remember to change to the binary FTP mode before downloading the file to your UNIX server.

Installing Majordomo

Once the distribution package has been downloaded, you can begin the installation of Majordomo. The program is distributed as source code, and you will need a C compiler installed on your UNIX system. Both Linux and FreeBSD use the GNU C compiler by default. Several steps are required to install Majordomo. The following sections describe these steps.

Creating a Majordomo User ID

First, Majordomo must be installed from a separate user ID. This is for security purposes, so that Perl programs will not be run under the `root` user ID and create vulnerabilities in the system. For this example, the user ID `majordomo` and group `daemon` were chosen to use as the Majordomo installation account. Use the appropriate user creation program for your UNIX distribution to create the user and group IDs.

The Majordomo distribution file was copied to the Majordomo home directory. To extract the software from the file into a working directory, type

```
tar -zxvf majordomo.tar.gz -C /usr/local/src
```

This creates the directory `/usr/local/src/majordomo-1.94.5` and unpacks the Majordomo source code files. Next, you must modify the Makefile to reflect your particular installation of Majordomo.

Edit the Majordomo Makefile

The Makefile directs what features the Majordomo program will have when it is compiled. Listing 15.1 is a partial listing of the Makefile.

LISTING 15.1   A Partial Listing of the Majordomo Makefile

```
1   #$Modified: Wed Aug 27 17:52:25 1997 by cwilson $
2   #
3   # $Source: /sources/cvsrepos/majordomo/Makefile,v $
4   # $Revision: 1.63 $
5   # $Date: 1997/08/27 15:56:21 $
6   # $Header: /cvsrepos/majordomo/Makefile,v 1.63 1997/08/27 15:56:21 cwils
7   on Exp $
8   #
9
10  #   This is the Makefile for Majordomo.
11  #
12  #------------  Configure these items ---------------#
13  #
14
15  # Put the location of your Perl binary here:
16  PERL = /usr/bin/perl
```

15

LISTING 15.1   Continued

```
17
18 # What do you call your C compiler?
19 CC = gcc
20
21 # Where do you want Majordomo to be installed?  This CANNOT be the
22 # current directory (where you unpacked the distribution)
23 W_HOME = /usr/local/majordomo
24
25 # Where do you want man pages to be installed?
26 MAN = $(W_HOME)/man
27
28 # You need to have or create a user and group which majordomo will run as.
29 # Enter the numeric UID and GID (not their names!) here:
30 W_USER = 507
31 W_GROUP = 2
32
33 # These set the permissions for all installed files and executables (except
34 # the wrapper), respectively.  Some sites may wish to make these more
35 # lenient, or more restrictive.
36 FILE_MODE = 644
37 EXEC_MODE = 755
38 HOME_MODE = 751
39 # If your system is POSIX (e.g. Sun Solaris, SGI Irix 5 and 6,
40 # BSDI or other 4.4-based BSD, Linux) use the following four lines.  Do not
41 # change these values!
42 WRAPPER_OWNER = root
43 WRAPPER_GROUP = $(W_GROUP)
44 WRAPPER_MODE = 4755
45 POSIX = -DPOSIX_UID=$(W_USER) -DPOSIX_GID=$(W_GROUP)
46 # Otherwise, if your system is NOT POSIX (e.g. SunOS 4.x, SGI Irix 4,
47 # HP DomainOS) then comment out the above four lines and uncomment
48 # the following four lines.
49 # WRAPPER_OWNER = $(W_USER)
50 # WRAPPER_GROUP = $(W_GROUP)
51 # WRAPPER_MODE = 6755
52 # POSIX =
53
54 # Define this if the majordomo programs should *also* be run in the same
55 # group as your MTA, usually sendmail.  This is rarely needed, but some
56 # MTAs require certain group memberships before allowing the message sender
57 # to be set arbitrarily.
58 # MAIL_GID =     numeric_gid_of_MTA
```

```
59
60 # This is the env that (along with LOGNAME and USER inherited from the
61 # parent process, and without the leading "W_" in the variable names) gets
62 # passed to processes run by "wrapper"
63 W_SHELL = /bin/sh
64 W_PATH = /bin:/usr/bin:/usr/ucb
65 W_MAJORDOMO_CF = $(W_HOME)/majordomo.cf
66
67 # A directory for temp files..
68 TMPDIR = /usr/tmp
```

Several lines in the Makefile need to be modified to suit your particular UNIX environment. Line 16 defines where Majordomo can find the Perl program. Because the Majordomo scripts are written in Perl, you must have Perl installed on your UNIX system, and Majordomo must know how to find it. Perl is a popular scripting program language developed by Larry Wall and is included with most UNIX distributions. Also, line 19 defines the C compiler used on the UNIX system. For most Linux and FreeBSD distributions, the GNU C compiler gcc is included and should be used.

Besides the compilers, you must specify where Majordomo will be installed. Line 23 defines the home directory for the Majordomo program. Don't get this confused with the home directory for the Majordomo user ID. They can be the same, but it is easier if you select another location that can be used for the scripts and configuration files. I've selected the /usr/local/majordomo location. You will have to create this directory as the root user, and you can change the owner to the majordomo user with the command

```
chown majordomo.daemon /usr/local/majordomo
```

You will have to replace majordomo.daemon with the user ID and group ID with which you installed Majordomo. Speaking of that, the Majordomo user ID and group ID need to be changed in the Makefile. Lines 30 and 31 specify these values to the Majordomo program. You can log in as majordomo and type the command ID to determine the user ID and group ID. On the example system, the majordomo user ID was 507, and the daemon group ID was 2. Remember, the Makefile is looking for the numerical values, not the text names.

Creating and Editing the majordomo.cf File

The majordomo.cf configuration file controls the behavior of the Majordomo installation. To create a new configuration file, you can copy the template file sample.cf, located in the majordomo-1.94.5 directory, to majordomo.cf in the same directory. Listing 15.2 shows a sample majordomo.cf file.

LISTING 15.2   A Sample `majordomo.cf` File

```
1   #
2   # A sample configuration file for majordomo. You must read through this and
3   # edit it accordingly!
4   #
5
6   # $whereami -- What machine am I running on?
7   #
8   $whereami = "smallorg.org";
9
10  # $whoami -- Who do users send requests to me as?
11  #
12  $whoami = "Majordomo\@$whereami";
13
14  # $whoami_owner -- Who is the owner of the above, in case of problems?
15  #
16  $whoami_owner = "Majordomo-Owner\@$whereami";
17
18  # $homedir -- Where can I find my extra .pl files, like majordomo.pl?
19  # the environment variable HOME is set by the wrapper
20  #
21  if ( defined $ENV{"HOME"}) {
22      $homedir = $ENV{"HOME"};
23  } else {
24      $homedir = "/usr/local/majordomo";
25  }
26
27  # $listdir -- Where are the mailing lists?
28  #
29  $listdir = "$homedir/lists";
30
31  # $digest_work_dir -- the parent directory for digest's queue area
32  # Each list must have a subdirectory under this directory in order for
33  # digest to work. E.G. The bblisa list would use:
34  #    /usr/local/mail/digest/bblisa
35  # as its directory.
36  #
37  $digest_work_dir = "/usr/local/mail/digest";
38
39  # $log -- Where do I write my log?
40  #
41  $log = "$homedir/Log";
```

There are several variables that must be set in the `majordomo.cf` file. Line 8 defines the `$whereami` variable, which is the address used for return messages. If qmail is using virtual domains, the return address will be the domain name shown in line 8. If not, the return address will be the fully qualified hostname. Lines 12 and 16 define the `$whoami` and `$whoami_owner` variables based on the `$whereami` variable. You should not need to change these values.

The `$homedir` variable shown on line 24 is important. It must point to the Majordomo program home directory that you configured in the Makefile. This is where Majordomo will look for the Perl scripts as it processes list messages. Line 29 defines the `$listdir` variable. This indicates where Majordomo will store the information for the mail lists. The default location is a subdirectory called `lists` that is located in the Majordomo home directory.

In line 37, `$digest_work_dir` defines where the mail list digest files will be kept. If you plan to use the digest feature, you may need to change this value and create the new subdirectory. Remember that digest files contain the full text of all messages sent during a certain time period. You may need to use a large amount of disk space, depending on the number of mail list messages you will generate.

The last variable described is the `$log` variable in line 41. Majordomo logs all transactions with the mail list server in a log file. You can change the location of this file to match your UNIX distribution's current log file directory, such as `/var/log/majordomo.log`.

Patching Majordomo for qmail

Now is the time to change the Majordomo setup for qmail. Without this patch, Majordomo will not work properly on the qmail system.

Your qmail installation must have the `fastforward` package installed to be able to convert the `/etc/aliases` file to the qmail `/etc/aliases.cdb` file. The `fastforward` package also contains the utility newinclude, which is used to convert include files to binary files for qmail to use. Majordomo must be configured to run the newinclude utility automatically, because it changes include files as new users subscribe and unsubscribe to the mail list.

For Majordomo to run newinclude automatically, newinclude must be added to the Majordomo script file, located in the `/usr/local/majordomo-1.94.5` directory, before the program is compiled. There are two places where it must be inserted: in the `do_subscribe` and `do_unsubscribe` subroutines.

Each subroutine needs the newinclude line added in one place, near the line

```
&lclose(LIST)
```

in the script file. In the `do_subscribe` subroutine, it must be immediately after the `lclose()` line, and in `do_unsubscribe` it must be immediately before the `lclose()` line. Listing 15.3 shows a partial listing of the modified `majordomo` file.

LISTING 15.3   A Partial Listing of the Modified `majordomo` File

```
.
.
.
sub do_subscribe {
.
.
.
        # Send the new subscriber a welcoming message, and
        # a notice of the new subscriber to the list owner
        if ( &cf_ck_bool($clean_list,"strip") ) {
            local($clean_sub) = &valid_addr($subscriber);
            &welcome($clean_list, $clean_sub);
        } else {
            &welcome($clean_list, $subscriber);
        }
    }
    &lclose(LIST) || &abort("Error closing $listdir/$clean_list: $!");
    system("/var/qmail/bin/newinclude", "$listdir/$clean_list");
} else {
.
.
.
sub do_unsubscribe {
.
.
.
    elsif ($match_count == 0) {
        print REPLY "**** No matches found for '$subscriber'\n";
    }
    else {
        print REPLY "**** FAILED.\n";
    }
    unlink("$listdir/$clean_list.new");
    system("/var/qmail/bin/newinclude", "$listdir/$clean_list");
    &lclose(LIST);
} else {
.
.
.
```

In both instances the newinclude command is included in a system call in the script. These system calls enable Majordomo to invoke the newinclude utility when the mail list include file changes. The newinclude utility creates a binary file for the mail list include file, in the same directory as the original Majordomo include file.

Using the GNU Make Utility for Majordomo

After the Makefile and `majordomo.cf` files are configured and the qmail patch completed, you can use the GNU make utility to build the Majordomo executable files. This requires three steps:

1. Run `make wrapper` to verify that the wrapper program will compile cleanly.
2. Run `make install` as the `majordomo` user ID to install the Majordomo scripts and executables in the home directory.
3. Run `make install-wrapper` as the root user ID to install the wrapper program setuid root.

At this point you can run the wrapper program and test the Majordomo installation. Log in as a user without any special rights, and change to the Majordomo program's home directory (`/usr/local/majordomo` for this example). From there, enter

```
./wrapper config-test
```

This runs the wrapper program and tests the configuration. Listing 15.4 shows the final few lines of the long output that the configuration test generates. As you can tell, this configuration passed the test.

LISTING 15.4   Output from a Wrapper Configuration Test

```
.
.
.
-------------------- end of tests ---------------------


Nothing bad found!  Majordomo _should_ work correctly.

If it doesn't, check your configuration file
    (/usr/local/majordomo/majordomo.cf)
closely, and if it still looks okay, consider asking the majordomo-users
mailing list at "majordomo-users@greatcircle.com" for assistance.  Be sure
and fully specify what your problems are, and what type of machine (and
operating system) you are using.

Enjoy!
```

Creating Aliases for Majordomo

After successfully installing the Majordomo software, you must configure qmail to recognize the mail lists. Majordomo processes mail lists using the sendmail aliases file (see Chapter 14).

For the default Majordomo configuration, add the lines shown in Listing 15.5 to the `/etc/aliases` file.

LISTING 15.5   Majordomo Alias Lines

```
1  #  Majordomo aliases
2  majordomo:   "|/usr/local/majordomo/wrapper majordomo"
3  owner-majordomo:    rich
4  majordomo-owner:    rich
```

After new entries are made to the aliases file, you must run the newaliases program for qmail to recognize them. In Listing 15.5, line 2 shows the alias `majordomo` being redirected to the wrapper program with the command-line parameter of `majordomo`. This tells qmail to run the wrapper program when it receives a message.

Lines 3 and 4 are support aliases. If a list member is having difficulties with the mail list, he can send mail to the list owner asking for help or advice. These addresses should point to the real email address of the list owner.

Creating a Majordomo Mail List

With the Majordomo program successfully installed, the next step is to configure an actual mail list. To create a new list, first you must create an empty file that will hold the email addresses in the list. The name of the file must match the name of the mail list. This example will use the mail list name `officenews`. After the file is created, you must ensure that it has the proper access modes set. The commands to create the file and change the permissions are

```
touch /usr/local/majordomo/lists/officenews
chmod 755 /usr/local/majordomo/lists
chmod 644 /usr/local/majordomo/lists/officenews
```

After the file is created, you can create a text information file for the mail list. Majordomo will use the mail list information file when someone requests information on the list and when someone subscribes to the list. The information file should be in this form:

```
list.info
```

where `list` is the mail list name. For this example, the information file will be in the `file/usr/local/majordomo/lists/officenews.info` file and will contain a simple text description of the mail list. Remember not to give out too much information; anyone can request the information file from the mail list server.

Each mail list requires several entries in the sendmail aliases file, depending on what features you want the mail list to support. Table 15.1 shows the aliases that may be used for a mail list named `officenews`.

TABLE 15.1 Sendmail Aliases Used for a Majordomo Mail List

Alias	Description
officenews	The mail list alias
officenews-outgoing	The actual list of subscribers
owner-officenews	The administrator of the mail list
officenews-request	The address for Majordomo requests
officenews-approval	The person who approves postings in moderated lists
officenews-digest	The address for digest lists
officenews-digest-request	The address for digest requests

Listing 15.6 shows a sample entry for the officenews mail list. This will be a simple, no-frills list and will be open to the public, and no digests or archives will be created.

LISTING 15.6 Sample Mail List Alias Entries

```
1  #officenews mail list entries
2  officenews:       "|/usr/local/majordomo/wrapper resend -l officenews
➥ officenews-list"
3  officenews-list:        :include:/usr/local/majordomo/lists/officenews
4  owner-officenews:       rich
5  officenews-owner:       rich
6  officenews-approval:    officenews-owner
7  officenews-request:     "|/usr/local/majordomo/wrapper majordomo -l
➥ officenews"
```

As usual, remember to run the qmail newaliases program as root after adding the mail list aliases to the /etc/aliases file. At this point the mail list should be operational, using the default configurations.

You can create a configuration file by emailing the mail list to the mail list server. The message should be sent to the officenews-request account with the body

```
config officenews officenews.admin
```

Majordomo will automatically create a default configuration file and mail it back to you. One feature of Majordomo is the capability of the administrator to control configuration parameters remotely via email. All you need to do is modify whatever values you need to change in the configuration file and email it back to Majordomo.

Once the mail list is configured to your requirements, users can subscribe to the mail list by sending messages to the officenews-request email account, with the word subscribe

15

SUPPORTING MAIL LISTS

in the body. Once subscribed, users can begin sending messages to the `officenews` email account to be forwarded to all members of the mail list.

A qmail-Specific Mail List Program

Dan Bernstein has developed a mail list program specifically to take advantage of qmail's capabilities. Ezmlm is a mail list package that can compete with Majordomo in functionality and use features of qmail to make it extremely efficient and fast. This section describes how to install and configure the Ezmlm program package.

Downloading Ezmlm

The Ezmlm package can be downloaded from Bernstein's Web site at the URL:

```
http://cr.yp.to/software/ezmlm-0.53.tar.gz
```

At the time of this writing, the current version of Ezmlm is 0.53. Once downloaded, the Ezmlm source code can be extracted into a working directory:

```
tar -zxvf ezmlm-0.53.tar.gz -C /usr/local
```

The FreeBSD UNIX distribution includes a port of the Ezmlm package in the `/usr/ports/mail/ezmlm` directory. The version distributed with FreeBSD 3.4 is the 0.53 distribution. You can use the normal ports installation method to install this software from the FreeBSD port:

```
cd /usr/ports/mail/ezmlm
make
make install
```

In the FreeBSD ports installation, the Ezmlm executable files are installed into the `/usr/local/bin` directory. By installing from the source code download, the executable files are located in the `/usr/local/bin/ezmlm` directory. Table 15.2 shows the executables that are included in the Ezmlm package.

TABLE 15.2   Ezmlm Utilities

Utility	Description
ezmlm-list	Displays mail list addresses.
ezmlm-make	Creates a new mail list.
ezmlm-manage	Handles mail list administration requests.
ezmlm-reject	Rejects incoming messages that don't meet specific criteria.
ezmlm-return	Handles bounced messages.
ezmlm-send	Sends a message to a mail list.

Utility	Description
ezmlm-sub	Manually subscribes a user to a mail list.
ezmlm-unsub	Manually unsubscribes a user from a mail list.
ezmlm-warn	Detects user addresses that bounce mail list messages.
ezmlm-weed	Blocks unwanted messages from the mail list distribution.

Programs in the Ezmlm Package

As can be seen in Table 15.2, the Ezmlm package consists of 10 programs for creating, manip-ulating, and observing mail lists. This section describes these programs and how they interact to produce the Ezmlm system.

Listing Mail List Subscribers

The ezmlm-list program is used to display the addresses contained in a mail list. The format for this command is

```
ezmlm-list dir
```

where dir is the pathname of the mail list directory created.

Creating a New Mail List

The ezmlm-make program is used for creating a new mail list directory structure for a new mail list. Any user on a UNIX system can create a mail list in his home directory. System-wide mail lists can be created by the root user in the qmail aliases directory. The format of the ezmlm-make command is

```
ezmlm-make [ -aApP ] dir dot local host
```

where dir is the pathname of the mail list directory created, dot is the name of the base .qmail file used to control access to the mail list, local is the name of the mail list, and host is the hostname of the local computer hosting the mail list.

Table 15.3 describes the option values possible for the ezmlm-make command.

TABLE 15.3   ezmlm-make Command Option Values

Option	Description
-a	Create a mail list that supports archiving messages (default)
-A	Create a mail list that does not support archiving messages
-p	Create a public mail list (default)
-P	Create a private mail list

By default, `ezmlm-make` will create a mail list with the name specified in the `local` parameter and make it a public mail list (it will respond to remote requests for subscriptions). It will archive all messages posted to the mail list in an archive directory.

User-defined mail lists must include the name of the user so that qmail will know how to handle the mail list. An example of creating a user-defined mail list would be

```
ezmlm-make ~/art ~/.qmail-art katie-art shadrach.ispnet1.net
```

This example creates the mail list `katie-art`, using the `/home/katie/art` directory for the mail list and the `/home/katie/.qmail-art` file as the base `.qmail` file.

> **CAUTION**
>
> Remember that archived mail lists retain copies of all messages posted to the list. This can require lots of disk space, especially if users post binary programs to the list.

Handling Mail List Administration

The `ezmlm-manage` program is used to handle administrative requests made for the mail list. The format of the `ezmlm-manage` command is

```
ezmlm-manage dir
```

where `dir` is the pathname of the mail list directory. Under normal circumstances the `ezmlm-manage` program is invoked from a script file that is in a `.qmail` file.

The program examines an incoming email address and takes a specified action, which is added to the normal mail list address. The format of this is

```
list-action
```

where `list` is the original mail list name, such as `katie-art`. Table 15.4 lists the possible actions that `ezmlm-manage` can handle.

TABLE 15.4   `ezmlm-manage` Mail List Actions

Action	Description
subscribe	Request that a new user be added to the mail list.
sc.cookie	Respond to the subscription request with the required `cookie` value.
unsubscribe	Request that an existing mail list user be removed from the mail list.
uc.cookie	Respond to the `unsubscribe` request with the required `cookie` value.
get.num	Obtain a specific archived message.

The public subscription and unsubscription processes both use a key code method to authenti-cate subscription and unsubscription requests. The process is as follows:

1. The remote user sends the subscription or unsubscription action.

2. `ezmlm-manage` recognizes the request and returns a message to the requesting user with a specific key code.

3. The remote user returns an `sc` or `uc` action including the key code to validate the email address and intention.

4. `ezmlm-manage` adds or removes the email address from the mail list.

Rejecting Mail List Messages

Ezmlm script programs use the `ezmlm-reject` program to reject incoming mail messages according to set options. The format of the `ezmlm-reject` command is

```
ezmlm-reject [-cC-sS]
```

The command-line options used for `ezmlm-reject` are shown in Table 15.5.

TABLE 15.5   `ezmlm-reject` Options

Option	Description
-c	Commands are not permitted in the `Subject:` header field (default).
-C	Commands are permitted in the `Subject:` header field.
-s	A `Subject:` header field is required (default).
-S	A `Subject:` header field is not required.

Messages are read by `ezmlm-reject` on its standard input.

Handling Bounced Messages

Ezmlm script files use the `ezmlm-return` program to handle bounced messages. Ezmlm tracks messages that are bounced from mail list recipients. The format of the `ezmlm-return` command is

```
ezmlm-return dir
```

where `dir` is the mail list directory to check for bounced messages.

Ezmlm takes advantage of a qmail specific feature called Variable Envelope Return Path (VERP). VERP allows for uniquely identifying bounced messages from a mail list.

On a non-VERP mail list, all messages are sent from the same username on the mail list server, often `listname-owner`. If a message bounces back to the mail list server, depending on the remote mail server, it may not be uniquely identifiable.

The VERP system inserts the subscriber's email address into the return address, so bounced messages contain the subscriber's address. This ensures that the mail list administrator can identify what mail list subscriber the bounce came from.

Manually Posting to the Mail List

The `ezmlm-send` program is used to send a mail message to a specific mail list. The format of the `ezmlm-send` command is

```
ezmlm-send dir
```

where `dir` is the pathname of the mail list directory. `ezmlm-send` reads a mail message from its standard input and forwards it to the mail list specified.

This command is used in the `.qmail-list` file for Ezmlm to forward the message received by qmail to the Ezmlm mail list directory.

Manually Subscribing a User to the Mail List

The `ezmlm-sub` program is used to manually subscribe a user to the mail list. The format of this command is

```
ezmlm-sub dir [ user@domain ...  ]
```

where `dir` is the pathname of the mail list directory and `user@domain` is the complete email address of the user to add to the mail list. Multiple users can be added to the mail list with a single `ezmlm-sub` command. Each address should be separated with a space.

Manually Unsubscribing a User from the Mail List

The `ezmlm-unsub` program is used to manually unsubscribe a user from the mail list. The format of the `ezmlm-unsub` command is

```
ezmlm-unsub dir [ user@domain ...  ]
```

where `dir` is the pathname of the mail list directory and `user@domain` is the complete email address of the user that you want to remove from the mail list. Multiple users can be removed in a single `ezmlm-unsub` command. Each address should be separated with a single space.

The `ezmlm-unsub` command can be used by mail list administrators to manually remove users from the mail list without users having to submit an unsubscribe request message.

Detecting Bounced Mail List Messages

The `ezmlm-warn` program is used to detect bounced messages for a mail list recipient and attempt to send him a warning message that he may have missed some messages. As with most of the other Ezmlm commands, the format of the `ezmlm-warn` command is

```
ezmlm-warn dir
```

where `dir` is the pathname of the mail list directory. The mail list directory contains a `bounce` subdirectory that contains messages sent from the mail list server but bounced back. The `ezmlm-warn` command checks these messages and, for any message older than 10 days, sends a warning message to the intended recipient.

The warning message lists the message numbers that bounced. If the intended recipient was experiencing temporary email server problems, he may receive the warning message and use the Ezmlm archive function to retrieve any missed messages.

Filtering Out Unwanted Mail List Messages

Ezmlm scripts use the `ezmlm-weed` program to weed out any warning or success messages returned to the Ezmlm mail list server. The message is read from the standard input. Ezmlm returns a `99` exit code if it receives one of these messages. This causes qmail to drop out of executing the `.qmail` file.

Controlling Ezmlm Features

Once the mail list is created, you can modify its behavior by changing the default files that were created. The files created by the `ezmlm-make` program are used to control the operation of the mail list. Using the command-line options available to the `ezmlm-make` program can give some degree of control over the behavior of the mail list.

The `text` subdirectory in the mail list directory contains text files used for message responses for the mail list. Each response by the mail list server can be customized to the requirements of the mail list administrator. Table 15.6 shows the text files available to modify.

TABLE 15.6 Ezmlm Text Messages

Message File	Description
`bottom`	Generic help text added to responses.
`bounce-bottom`	Tail text message used for bounced messages.
`bounce-num`	Generic text used to inform subscriber how to get an archived message.
`bounce-probe`	Probe message sent to subscriber who bounced a previous message.
`bounce-warn`	Warning message sent to subscriber who bounced a previous message.
`get-bad`	Message in response to an incorrect `get` command.
`help`	Generic message sent in response to an incorrect command.
`sub-bad`	Generic message sent in response to an incorrect subscription confirmation.

TABLE 15.6   Continued

Message File	Description
sub-confirm	Message sent in response to a subscription request.
sub-nop	Message sent in response to subscribing an address already on the mail list
sub-ok	Message sent in response to a valid subscription confirmation.
top	Generic message sent at the top of all correspondence.
unsub-bad	Message sent in response to a bad unsubscribe confirmation.
unsub-confirm	Message sent in response to a valid unsubscribe confirmation.
unsub-nop	Message sent in response to an unsubscribe request of an address not on the mail list.
unsub-ok	Message sent in response to a valid unsubscribe confirmation.

If the mail list administrator wants to change a public mail list to a private mail list, he can remove the ~/list/public file. To change an archived list to an unarchived list, he can remove the ~/list/archive directory.

Creating and Using a Simple Mail List

Creating and maintaining a new mail list using Ezmlm are simple processes. To create a new mail list, use the ezmlm-make program from your $HOME directory:

ezmlm-make ~/art ~/.qmail-art katie-art shadrach.ispnet1.net

This command creates the mail list katie-art, the mail list directory /home/katie/art, and the base .qmail file /home/katie/.qmail-art.

For a new user to subscribe to the mail list, he sends a mail message to the email address katie-art-subscribe@shadrach.ispnet1.net. The message should have an empty Subject: header field and an empty message body. He will receive the response shown in Listing 15.7.

LISTING 15.7   A Partial Sample Mail List Subscription Response

```
From katie-art-return-@shadrach.ispnet1.net Mon Apr 24 15:09:41 2000
Return-Path: <katie-art-return-@shadrach.ispnet1.net>
Delivered-To: jessica@shadrach.ispnet1.net
Received: (qmail 60142 invoked by uid 1002); 24 Apr 2000 20:09:41 -0000
Mailing-List: contact katie-art-help@shadrach.ispnet1.net; run by ezmlm
Date: 24 Apr 2000 20:09:41 -0000
Message-ID: <956606981.60141.ezmlm@shadrach.ispnet1.net>
From: katie-art-help@shadrach.ispnet1.net
To: jessica@shadrach.ispnet1.net
```

```
Reply-To: katie-art-sc.956606981.jbcimndmohbfcfjamkag-jessica=shadrach.isp
net1.net@shadrach.ispnet1.net
Subject: ezmlm response
Delivered-To: responder for katie-art@shadrach.ispnet1.net
Received: (qmail 60137 invoked by uid 1003); 24 Apr 2000 20:09:41 -0000
Status: R

Hi! This is the ezmlm program. I'm managing the
katie-art@shadrach.ispnet1.net mailing list.

To confirm that you would like

   jessica@shadrach.ispnet1.net

added to this mailing list, please send an empty reply to this address:

 katie-art-sc.956606981.jbcimndmohbfcfjamkag-jessica=shadrach.ispnet1.net@shad
rach.ispnet1.net

Your mailer should have a Reply feature that uses this address automatically.

This confirmation serves two purposes. First, it verifies that I am able
to get mail through to you. Second, it protects you in case someone
forges a subscription request in your name.
```

The response to the subscription request is a message requiring the mail list user to resubmit the request using a special cookie number generated by Ezmlm. This helps ensure that the intended recipient really wants to subscribe to the mail list and that the original subscription request was not forged.

Notice in Listing 15.7 that the Return-To: header field contains the proper cookie response. This enables the recipient to simply reply to the generated message to confirm the subscription request.

Once subscribed, the mail list user should receive all messages sent to the katie-art mail list. Each mail list message is sequentially numbered. Any missed messages can be retrieved using the get action. Listing 15.8 demonstrates how a message can be retrieved from the message archive using the get action.

LISTING 15.8   Using the Ezmlm get Command

```
$ mail katie-art-get.2
Subject:
.
EOT
```

LISTING 15.8   Continued

```
No message, no subject; hope that's ok
$ mail
Mail version 8.1 6/6/93.  Type ? for help.
"/var/mail/jessica": 1 message 1 new
>N  1 katie-art-help@shadr  Mon Apr 24 15:19  63/2470  "ezmlm response"
&1
Message 1:
From katie-art-return-@shadrach.ispnet1.net Mon Apr 24 15:19:31 2000
Delivered-To: jessica@shadrach.ispnet1.net
Mailing-List: contact katie-art-help@shadrach.ispnet1.net; run by ezmlm
Date: 24 Apr 2000 20:19:31 -0000
From: katie-art-help@shadrach.ispnet1.net
To: jessica@shadrach.ispnet1.net
Subject: ezmlm response
Delivered-To: responder for katie-art@shadrach.ispnet1.net

Hi! This is the ezmlm program. I'm managing the
katie-art@shadrach.ispnet1.net mailing list.

> Mailing-List: contact katie-art-help@shadrach.ispnet1.net; run by ezmlm
> Delivered-To: mailing list katie-art@shadrach.ispnet1.net
> Received: (qmail 60167 invoked by uid 1001); 24 Apr 2000 20:17:15 -0000
> Date: 24 Apr 2000 20:17:15 -0000
> Message-ID: <20000424201715.60166.qmail@shadrach.ispnet1.net>
> From: rich@shadrach.ispnet1.net
> To: katie-art@shadrach.ispnet1.net
> Subject: New paint brushes
>
> This message is to inform everyone that the new paint brushes have come
> in and are now available for purchase. Please stop by and get your new
> paint brush today.
>
```

The response received from the mail list will include the archived message (indicated by the lines with the > characters).

To unsubscribe from a mail list, send an empty message to the katie-art-unsubscribe address. As with the subscription action, the unsubscribe command returns a message containing a cookie that must be submitted back to the mail list server to confirm the unsubscription request.

Extending the Ezmlm Mail List Package

Although the Ezmlm mail list package performs many of the functions that the Majordomo package does, there are still some functions that have been left out. To remedy this situation, Fred Lindberg developed the Ezmlm-idx package. It extends the functionality of the Ezmlm package by adding the following:

- Moderated mail list support
- Remote mail list administration support
- Remote archive listing support
- WWW access to archived messages
- MySQL and Postgresql database support

The most intriguing feature is the use of an SQL database with Ezmlm-idx. This allows the mail list administrator to tie a mail list into a customer SQL database that contains email addresses.

At the time of this writing, the Ezmlm-idx package is at version 0.40. The Ezmlm-idx package can be downloaded from the following URL:

```
ftp://ftp.ezmlm.org/pub/patches/ezmlm-idx-0.40.tar.gz
```

Once downloaded, the source code can be unpacked into a working directory using the standard method:

```
tar -zxvf ezmlm-idx-0.40.tar.gz -C /usr/local/src
```

The Ezmlm-idx package uses the Ezmlm package to compile, so the contents of the newly created working directory must be copied into the existing Ezmlm-0.53 directory (`/usr/local/ezmlm-0.53`) before the make utilities can be run.

Once the source code files have been copied, you can follow the `INSTALL.idx` instructions included with the Ezmlm-idx package to compile, install, and test the package. For more information on this package, you can consult the Ezmlm-idx Web site at `http://www.ezmlm.org`.

Summary

One of the most-used features of an email server is mail lists. Mail lists enable remote users on a common project to share ideas and comments via their local email system. While qmail supports basic mail list functionality, an add-on software package is needed to support advanced mail list features such as closed mail lists, moderated mail lists, and remotely administered mail lists.

15

SUPPORTING MAIL
LISTS

The Majordomo package is probably the best-known and most frequently used mail list package. It supports all of the advanced mail list features mentioned. It was written to work on a sendmail mail server but can be modified to work on a qmail mail server. The Ezmlm mail list server package was written specifically for the qmail mail server and supports many of the advanced mail list features, including open and closed subscriptions. Another add-on package for Ezmlm is the Ezmlm-idx package, which includes even more advanced mail list functionality for Ezmlm mail lists, including database support.

The Daemontool Utilities

IN THIS CHAPTER

Running a qmail mail server requires lots of administrative tasks. Starting and stopping the qmail service, monitoring the qmail services, and monitoring qmail log files are just a few of them. To help the qmail administrator, Dan Bernstein has developed a set of utilities that simplify some of the administration tasks for qmail. The daemontools package contains several utilities that can be used to make life easier.

The cornerstone of the daemontools package is the *supervise* program, which is used to monitor a running process. If the process should die for any reason, the supervise program will attempt to start another copy. This can be used with the qmail package to ensure that the `qmail-send` and `qmail-smtpd` programs are running at all times.

Another interesting piece of the daemontools package is the *multilog* program, which is intended to be a replacement for the UNIX logger program. It is reported to be safer and more efficient than the logger program. It can be used to separate logs for the `qmail-send` and `qmail-smtpd` programs into separate log files. This makes the job of pouring through log files every day just a little bit easier.

This chapter describes the daemontools package and the utilities that it contains. At the end of this chapter we will discuss how to use the daemontools utilities to help simplify qmail administration.

Downloading and Compiling Daemontools

The daemontools package can be downloaded from Bernstein's Web site at

```
http://cr.yp.to/daemontools/daemontools-0.70.tar.gz
```

At the time of this writing, the current version of daemontools is version 0.70. As always, you can extract the daemontools package into a working directory using the command

```
tar -zxvf daemontools-0.70.tar.gz -C /usr/local
```

This creates the `/usr/local/daemontools-0.70` directory with the source code files.

To compile and install the source code, use the GNU make utility commands:

```
make
make setup check
```

These commands compile the daemontools executable programs and install them in the `/usr/local/bin` directory by default. The FreeBSD UNIX distribution also includes a port of the daemontools package. It is available in the `/usr/ports/sysutils/daemontools` directory. The version included with the most current FreeBSD distribution at the time of this writing is version 0.53. To install software from a FreeBSD port, you can use these commands:

```
make
make install
```

The Daemontool Utilities

CHAPTER 16

393

16

THE
DAEMONTOOL
UTILITIES

These commands will build the daemontools programs and install them in the default `/usr/local/bin` directory. Table 16.1 shows the programs that are included in the daemontools distribution.

TABLE 16.1   Daemontools Programs

Program	Description
envdir	Runs a program with preset environment variables.
envuidgid	Runs a program using preset user and group ID environment variables.
fghack	Prevents a program from running in background mode.
multilog	An alternative log file system.
setlock	Runs a program using a predetermined lock file system.
setuidgid	Runs a program under preset user and group IDs.
softlimit	Runs a program using preset system resource limits.
supervise	Starts a process and monitors it. If the process dies, attempts to restart it.
svc	Controls a process started using the supervise utility. Allows the administrator to start and stop the process.
svok	Checks if a supervise process is running.
svscan	Starts and monitors a group of processes controlled by supervise.
svstat	Returns the status of a process monitored by supervise.
tai64n	Adds a TAI64N formatted timestamp to a log line.
tai64nlocal	Converts a TAI64N timestamp into a local date and time.

Using Daemontools

Once the daemontools utilities are compiled and installed, you can begin using them to assist administrative functions. The following sections describe the daemontools utilities.

Supervising Programs

The supervise program is used to monitor programs that normally run as background processes. If a process dies, supervise attempts to restart it. It accomplishes this by using a script file to start the process and rerunning the script file when it realizes the process has stopped. The format of the supervise command is

```
supervise service
```

where `service` is the pathname of a directory that contains the startup script for the process. The supervise program searches the `service` directory for a file named `run` and executes it. The `run` file should be an executable script file that starts the process that needs to be monitored.

When the supervise program is run, it attempts to create a `supervise` directory below the `service` directory. This directory contains housekeeping files used by supervise. Listing 16.1 shows an example of a `supervise` directory for a service.

LISTING 16.1 A Sample Supervise-Created Directory

```
shadrach# cd supervise
shadrach# ls -al
total 3
drwx------  2 root   qmail  512 Apr 26 14:52 .
drwxr-xr-t  4 root   qmail  512 Apr 25 16:16 ..
prw-------  1 root   qmail    0 Apr 25 16:36 control
-rw-------  1 root   qmail    0 Apr 25 16:15 lock
prw-------  1 root   qmail    0 Apr 25 16:15 ok
-rw-r--r--  1 root   qmail   18 Apr 26 14:52 status
shadrach#
```

The files shown in Listing 16.1 are used by the supervise program to monitor and control the process. Table 16.2 describes these files.

TABLE 16.2 Supervise Directory Files

File	Description
Control	File used by svc to control the status of the supervised process.
Lock	Lock file used to ensure only one supervise program is running on the process.
Ok	Status file used by svstat to determine status of supervised process.
Status	Detailed status information file used by svstat.

The run file created for the supervise program should follow a few important rules:

- Create the file as a shell script:

  ```
  #!/bin/sh
  ```

- Use the UNIX exec command to run scripts and programs:

  ```
  exec /var/qmail/rc
  ```

- Do not run the process as a background process (using the ampersand (&)).
- Do not use shell pipes to transfer data between processes. The data may get lost.

When the supervise program is run, it should appear as a running process, along with the name of the service it is supervising. If the process that supervise is running starts properly, you should also see it as a background process. Listing 16.2 shows an example of a supervise process and a server process that was started by supervise.

LISTING 16.2 A Sample Supervise Process

```
$ supervise /usr/rich/server &
$ ps ax | grep server
32748  p0  S      0:00.09 supervise /usr/rich/server
32749  p0  S      0:00.06 /usr/rich/server/server
32751  p0  S+     0:00.08 grep server
$
```

As shown in Listing 16.2, both the supervise program and the program being supervised are successfully running as background processes. If the program being supervised dies for any reason, the supervise program will restart it, as shown in Listing 16.3.

LISTING 16.3 A Sample of a Restarted Supervised Program

```
$ kill -9 32749
$ ps ax | grep server
32748  p0  S      0:00.12 supervise /usr/rich/server
32754  p0  S      0:00.06 /usr/rich/server/server
32756  p0  S+     0:00.08 grep server
$
```

As can be seen in Listing 16.3, the original server program at PID 32749 was killed, and the supervise program restarted a new server process, now using PID 32754. As long as the supervise program is running, it will attempt to start a new copy of the supervised program when the existing one dies.

To stop the supervised program completely, the supervise process must be stopped as well. Otherwise, it will continue trying to start new copies of the supervised program.

Controlling Supervised Programs

The svc program is used to control programs that are being supervised with the supervise program. The format of the svc command is

```
svc options services
```

where `services` is a list of one or more pathnames of services being supervised. The `options` parameters are used to specify what control should be sent to the service. Table 16.3 lists the options possible for svc.

TABLE 16.3   Svc Options

Option	Description
-a	Alarm—Sends an ALRM signal to the service.
-c	Continue—Sends a CONT signal to the service.
-d	Down—Sends TERM and CONT signals to the service if it is running and does not allow supervise to restart it.
-h	Hangup—Sends a HUP signal to the service.
-i	Interrupt—Sends an INT signal to the service.
-k	Kill—Sends a KILL signal to the service.
-o	Once—If the service is not running, starts it. If it stops, does not allow supervise to restart it.
-p	Pause—Sends a STOP signal to the service.
-t	Terminate—Sends a TERM signal to the service.
-u	Up—If the service is not running, starts it. If it stops, attempts to restart it.
-x	Exit—Removes supervise as soon as the service is down.

The svc command can be used only by the user ID that started the supervise command being controlled or the root user. If the supervise command was started in a boot script, only the root user can send svc commands to the service. Listing 16.4 shows a sample session of controlling a service using the svc command.

LISTING 16.4   A Sample Svc Session

```
1  $ supervise /usr/rich/server &
2  $ ps ax | grep server
3  32854  p0  S      0:00.09 supervise /usr/rich/server
4  32855  p0  S      0:00.06 /usr/rich/server/server
5  $ svc -d /usr/rich/server
6  $ ps ax | grep server
7  32854  p0  S      0:00.11 supervise /usr/rich/server
8  $ svc -u /usr/rich/server
9  $ ps ax | grep server
10 32854  p0  S      0:00.14 supervise /usr/rich/server
11 32862  p0  S      0:00.06 /usr/rich/server/server
```

The Daemontool Utilities

CHAPTER 16

397

16

THE
DAEMONTOOL
UTILITIES

```
12 $ svc -t /usr/rich/server
13 $
14 [1] 32854 Exit 0                supervise /usr/rich/server
15 $ ps ax | grep server
16 32874  p0  S+     0:00.08 grep server
17 $
```

Line 1 shows the `supervise` command being used to start a service. Lines 3 and 4 show the output from the `ps` process listing in line 2. Both the service and supervise programs are shown to be running as normal processes on the UNIX system. In line 5 the `svc` command is used to down the service with the `-d` option. Line 7 shows the output of the process listing. The supervise process for the service is still running, but the actual service process has been stopped, as was expected from the `down` command. Also as expected, the `down` option prevented the supervise program from restarting another copy of the service.

In line 8, the service is restarted using the `-u` option of the `svc` command. The output of the `ps` command in lines 10 and 11 shows that a new copy of the service has been started.

Line 12 shows an example of stopping a running service using the `svc` command and the `-t` option. In this instance, both the running service and the supervise program for the service are stopped. At this point, no more `svc` commands can be issued to the service because the supervise program has been terminated. To restart the service, you must restart another supervise process.

Starting Multiple Supervised Programs

The `svscan` program can be used to start multiple services with a single command instead of having to issue multiple `supervise` commands. The format of the `svscan` command is simple:

```
svscan dir
```

where `dir` is a directory one level higher than the directories of the services that need to be started. Alternatively, you can use the UNIX `cd` command to change to the proper directory and issue the `svscan` command with no parameters. This starts the supervise programs for the subdirectories beneath the current directory.

For example, if you have two processes that need to be supervised, place both their directories under a common directory called `services`. Listing 16.5 shows how this would look.

LISTING 16.5   Sample Supervised Directory Structure

```
1  $ ls -alR /usr/rich/services
2  total 4
3  drwxr-xr-x   4 rich  rich   512 Apr 27 12:06 .
```

LISTING 16.5   Continued

```
4   drwxr-xr-x  10 rich  rich  1024 Apr 27 09:20 ..
5   drwxr-xr-x   2 rich  rich   512 Apr 27 12:10 server1
6   drwxr-xr-x   2 rich  rich   512 Apr 27 12:10 server2
7
8   /usr/rich/services/server1:
9 total 9
10 drwxr-xr-x   2 rich  rich   512 Apr 27 12:10 .
11 drwxr-xr-x   4 rich  rich   512 Apr 27 12:06 ..
12 -rwxr-xr-x   1 rich  rich    49 Apr 27 12:05 run
13 -rwxr-xr-x   1 rich  rich  5527 Apr 27 09:21 server
14
15 /usr/rich/services/server2:
16 total 9
17 drwxr-xr-x   2 rich  rich   512 Apr 27 12:10 .
18 drwxr-xr-x   4 rich  rich   512 Apr 27 12:06 ..
19 -rwxr-xr-x   1 rich  rich    49 Apr 27 09:24 run
20 -rwxr-xr-x   1 rich  rich  5527 Apr 27 09:26 server
21 $
```

Line 1 shows the command to recursively list subdirectories under the /usr/rich/services directory. Lines 2–6 show that there are two subdirectories—server1 and server2. Lines 8–13 show that the server1 directory contains the server program to be supervised and a run script that starts the program. Lines 15–20 show that the server2 directory contains another server program that will be supervised and also contains a run script that is used to start the program.

Notice that in Listing 16.5 no supervise directories are present. The supervise program will create this directory (and the files in it) when it first starts. After the supervise program has been run on a service directory, the normal supervise files as shown in Listing 16.1 will appear. Subsequent supervise processes will write over the existing supervise files to update the control and status information.

To supervise both programs, you could use the following two supervise commands:

```
supervise /usr/rich/services/server1 &
supervise /usr/rich/services/server2 &
```

These two commands would start the supervise program for each of the two programs, running the individual run scripts. Instead, you could use the svscan program to start both programs with one command:

```
svscan /usr/rich/services &
```

The svscan program scans the directory listed and starts an individual supervise program for each separate subdirectory. While this example doesn't save too much effort, imagine if you

The Daemontool Utilities

CHAPTER 16

399

16

THE
DAEMONTOOL
UTILITIES

needed to supervise a dozen or so different programs. By placing them all under a common directory structure, you could use the svscan program to start them all with one command.

> **CAUTION**
>
> Extreme care must be taken when using the svscan program. If it is executed from the wrong location, it will attempt to create supervise directories for all subdirectories beneath where it was executed. More than a few unsuspecting qmail administrators have created lots of supervise directories by accidentally running svscan from the root directory.

Another nice feature of the svscan program is that it supervises the supervise programs! The svscan program remains running as a background process. If a running supervise program stops, svscan will restart it. Listing 16.6 shows the processes that would run, given the example in Listing 16.5.

LISTING 16.6   A Partial Sample Svscan ps Listing

```
$ svscan /usr/rich/services &
$ ps ax
  PID  TT  STAT    TIME COMMAND
33963 p0  S     0:00.08 svscan /usr/rich/services
33964 p0  S     0:00.11 supervise server1
33965 p0  S     0:00.10 supervise server2
33966 p0  S     0:00.06 /usr/rich/services/server2/server
33967 p0  S     0:00.06 /usr/rich/services/server1/server
$
```

Notice in Listing 16.6 that both the server1 and the server2 services are supervised by separate supervise programs. Also, both of the supervised programs are started automatically by the one svscan command.

Still another nice feature of the svscan program is its capability to automatically create a data pipe between a running service and a log service. This allows the mail administrator to use the multilog program (described later in this chapter) to catch any messages that are produced from the running process.

To use the log pipe, you must create another directory beneath the service directory. This directory must be called log, and it must be a run script that starts the multilog program with any parameters that are necessary. But more on this later.

Checking the Status of a Service

The svstat program can be used to check the status of a supervised program. The format of the svstat command is

```
svstat service ...
```

where `service` is a list of one or more services for which you want to get statistics. Wildcards can be used to obtain the status of multiple services under the same directory (as when using the svscan command).

The svstat program uses data stored in the status file in the `supervise` directory created for each service by the supervise program. Listing 16.7 shows a sample output for the `svstat` command.

LISTING 16.7   Sample Output from `svstat`

```
$ svstat /usr/rich/services/*
/usr/rich/services/server1: up (pid 33967) 813 seconds
/usr/rich/services/server2: up (pid 33966) 813 seconds
$
```

Quick Status Check of a Supervised Program

The svok program can be used to do a quick check of a supervised program. The format of the svok command is

```
svok service
```

Unlike the svstat program, the svok program can be used on only one service at a time, and it does not produce a written output. The result of the svok program is an exit code. The svok program produces an exit code of 0 if the service has a supervise process running for it. If there is no supervise process running, the svok program exits with an exit code of 100. It is up to the mail administrator to write a script to handle the exit codes appropriately.

Supervising Programs That Run in Background

You may have noticed that one of the rules for using the supervise program is that the supervised program must not run as a background process. This is to allow the supervise program to properly control the behavior of the program.

If you need to supervise a program that runs as a background process, there is a utility in the daemontools package to help out. The fghack program can be used as a middleman between a background process and the supervise program.

The Daemontool Utilities
CHAPTER 16

401

16

THE
DAEMONTOOL
UTILITIES

The format of the `fghack` command is

```
fghack program
```

where `program` is the pathname of the background process to execute.

When the fghack program is used, supervise can monitor the supervised program, but it cannot control it. This means that if supervise sees that the program has exited, it can start a new copy. However, you will not be able to use the `svc` command to manually stop, pause, or continue the program.

Running a Program with New Resource Limits

The softlimit program can also be used in the run script to modify the system resource limits that are normally placed on a program. When a program is run on the UNIX environment, limits are placed on the program as to how much memory it can use, how large the files it creates can be, and how much CPU time it can consume. These values are set in the system configuration software and apply to all processes running on the system. The softlimit program can be used to modify these values for an individual program without having to modify system-wide values.

The format of the `softlimit` command is

```
softlimit options program
```

The `program` parameter is the pathname of the program to run, including any command-line parameters required to run the program. The `options` are set to specify the resource limits to change that are required for the program to operate properly. Table 16.4 shows the resource limits that can be modified using softlimit.

TABLE 16.4   Softlimit Options

Option	Description
-a n	Limits the total of all memory segments to n bytes.
-c n	Limits the size of core files to n bytes.
-d n	Limits the size of the data segment in memory to n bytes.
-f n	Limits the size of output files to n bytes.
-l n	Limits the size of locked physical memory pages to n bytes.
-m n	Same as using n bytes for the -a, -d, -l, and -s options.
-o n	Limits the number of open file descriptors to n.
-p n	Limits the number of processes per user ID to n.
-r n	Limits the size of the resident set to n bytes.
-s n	Limits the size of the stack segment in memory to n bytes.
-t n	Limits the CPU time for the process to n seconds.

By using the softlimit program, you can manually allocate more system resources to a process than what is defined by the system-wide configuration. This is handy if you have a program that you know may require more resources.

Creating Log Files Without Logger

The logger program has been used for many years as the default message logging program for the UNIX environment (see Chapter 13, "qmail Server Administration"). It is often criticized as being slow and unreliable during system crashes.

Dan Bernstein created the *multilog* program as a replacement to the UNIX logger program. The multilog program is part of the daemontools package and has the capability to read lines from its standard input pipe, pass them through a set of filters, and reliably write them to a specified log file. Multiple multilog programs can be running at the same time, as long as they all write to different log files. The following sections describe the operation of the multilog program.

Multilog Command Format

The format of the multilog program is

```
multilog script
```

where script is a set of patterns and actions that multilog follows to write messages to the log file. The scripts can contain many different elements. The following is a discussion of the different elements that can be incorporated in the multilog script.

Log File Specifications

The log file that is used by multilog can be specified within the script. A string that starts with either a dot or a slash is interpreted to be a log directory. All messages received by multilog (that pass the filters) will be logged in a log file contained in the log directory. Multilog creates several files in the log directory, and Listing 16.8 shows the contents of a typical multilog log directory.

LISTING 16.8   Sample Multilog Log Directory

```
$ ls -al
total 14
drwxr-xr-x  2 qmaill  wheel     512 Apr 26 11:57 .
drwxr-xr-x  3 qmaill  wheel     512 Apr 26 11:57 ..
-rw-r--r--  1 qmaill  wheel   11640 Apr 26 12:05 current
-rw-------  1 qmaill  wheel       0 Apr 26 11:57 lock
-rw-r--r--  1 qmaill  wheel       0 Apr 26 11:57 state
$
```

The Daemontool Utilities

CHAPTER 16

403

16

THE
DAEMONTOOL
UTILITIES

The actual log entries are contained in the file named `current`. The `lock` and `state` files are used to prevent log file corruption.

Log rotation is the capability for the logger to roll a log file into a backup log file due to a pre-determined condition being met. Most often it is due to a time period expiring, such as a requirement to create a new log file every week, or the log file reaching a predetermined size limit.

The multilog program has the capability to perform log rotation. Old logs are identified in the log directory by a leading at sign (@) in the filename. This is followed by a timestamp (see the "Timestamps" section, later in this chapter) that indicates when the log file was written. The reason the log file was written is indicated by a file extension:

- `.u` indicates the log file was created due to a system outage and may not be stable.
- `.s` indicates that the log file was properly written to the disk due to a log rotation condition.

Log rotation conditions are defined by other script parameters. The `s` action can be used to force log rotation when the `current` log file reaches a predetermined size. The format of the `s` action is

```
ssize
```

where `size` is the number of bytes that the log file can reach before a new log file is created. The default value for `s` is `99999`. This means that at 100,000 bytes (100K) a new `current` file will be started and the previous `current` file will be copied as an "old" log file.

The `n` action can be used to control the number of old logs available in the log directory. The format of the `n` action is

```
nnum
```

where `num` is the number of old log files you want to retain. If the act of writing a new "old" log file produces more old log files than defined by the `n` action, the log file with the oldest timestamp is removed.

A final action that can be used to control log files is the `!` action. The `!` action defines a program that the `current` log file can be passed to when it is time for log rotation. This can be a script that compresses the log file before it is saved. The format of the `!` action is

```
!program
```

where `program` is the name of the program to pass the log file to for further processing.

Status Files

The multilog program provides a method to create special status files for a monitored process. A status file will contain the last message sent by a process. The format of the status script element is

`=filename`

where `filename` is the name and path of a file to contain the status. This file contains only one line—the last message sent by multilog. New messages overwrite any existing message. The status action writes only the first 1000 bytes of the message to the status file.

Timestamps

The `t` action provides a timestamp for each entry in the log file. The multilog program uses a different method of timestamping than the standard UNIX logger program does.

The UNIX logger program uses standard UNIX time data elements to represent the time that the message was received from the program. This time value represents the number of seconds since January 1, 1970. It is a well-known bug in UNIX that this value will overflow in the year 2038.

As an alternative to this, an international standard, Temps Atomique International (TAI) was created to represent time using data elements. The TAI64 definition represents time as an 8-byte counter to store a time value equal to the number of seconds since January 1, 1970.

> **NOTE**
>
> The standards committee determined that eight bytes is sufficient to contain the number of seconds left in the scientifically calculated lifespan of the universe, thus avoiding another 2038 problem. I will leave this as an exercise for the reader to determine in what year this value may pose a problem to programmers.

Also defined in the TAI specifications are methods to accurately account for nanoseconds and attoseconds. The TAI64N standard uses 12 bytes to represent nanoseconds, and the TAI64NA standard uses 16 bytes to represent attoseconds.

The multilog timestamp uses the TAI64N standard to represent time to the nanosecond. The format of the multilog timestamp entry is

`@timestamp message`

where `timestamp` is the TAI64N value of the time the message was received by multilog, and `message` is the text of the message received.

If you include the `t` action in your multilog script, it must be the first action listed in the script.

The Daemontool Utilities

CHAPTER 16

405

16

THE
DAEMONTOOL
UTILITIES

Alerts

The e action can be used to quickly print messages to the `stderr` that is defined for the program. This action is usually used with a pattern filter (see the next section, "Message Filtering") to allow only certain important messages to be sent to the `stderr` pipe. Usually the `stderr` device is defined as the system console screen.

Message Filtering

The multilog program uses message filtering to parse incoming messages and decide which messages should be logged. This enables you to create separate multilog processes to look for particular message events and log them to separate log files.

The format of a filter action is

```
codepattern
```

where `pattern` is the pattern to match for the filter and `code` is either a plus (+) or a minus (-), indicating whether the message is passed (+) or dropped (-) if the pattern is matched.

The pattern can be a series of text characters to match the message sent to multilog. Wildcard characters (*) can be used to match multiple unknown characters. The wildcards can also be embedded within known text strings. In this case, multilog will perform exact matches on the text indicated, stopping and starting at the defined text.

For example, the pattern defined as

```
+ftpd[*] *
```

will match any messages from the ftpd server daemon. Normally the PID of the ftpd process would be included in the brackets, and the ftpd text message would follow the brackets. This pattern allows the administrator to log all messages from the ftpd process to a log file.

A Multilog Example

The multilog program is often used with the svscan program. As mentioned in the section "Starting Multiple Supervised Programs," the svscan program can create a pipe to transfer messages from a supervised program to another supervised program in the log directory. This enables the administrator to create a multilog program for each supervised program. The multilog program is usually used for this purpose. An example of this is shown in Listing 16.9.

LISTING 16.9   Supervised Service with a Log Program

```
1  $ ls -alR /usr/rich/services/server1
2  total 11
3  drwxr-xr-t  4 rich   rich    512 Apr 28 14:49 .
4  drwxr-xr-x  4 rich   rich    512 Apr 27 12:06 ..
5  drwxr-xr-x  3 rich   rich    512 Apr 28 14:56 log
```

LISTING 16.9 Continued

```
6  -rwxr-xr-x  1 rich   rich     49 Apr 27 12:05 run
7  -rwxr-xr-x  1 rich   rich   5527 Apr 27 09:21 server
8
9  server1/log:
10 total 4
11 drwxr-xr-x  3 rich   rich    512 Apr 28 14:56 .
12 drwxr-xr-t  4 rich   rich    512 Apr 28 14:49 ..
13 -rwxr--r--  1 rich   rich     69 Apr 28 14:50 run
14 $
```

Line 1 shows a standard UNIX listing of the /usr/rich/services/server1 directory. Lines 3–7 show the content of the directory. Line 5 indicates a log directory. The content of the log directory is shown in lines 11–13 and include a run script. The run script is defined as

```
#!/bin/sh
exec /usr/local/bin/multilog t +incoming* /var/log/server1
```

This script starts the multilog program. The t action defines a timestamp on the output line. The filter is defined as

```
+incoming*
```

which allows any message starting with the text incoming to pass through to the log file. The log directory is defined at /var/log/server1.

For svscan to set up a pipe to the log program, the service directory must be created with the sticky bit set. This can be done with the following command:

```
chmod +t /usr/rich/services/server1
```

When svscan sees the sticky bit set on a directory, it automatically tries to create a pipe to the log directory run program.

> **CAUTION**
>
> Don't forget to create the sticky bit on the service directory. Without it, svscan will not create the pipe to link the log service, and the logs will be empty. This is a problem that is easy to overlook.

The Daemontool Utilities

CHAPTER 16

407

16

THE
DAEMONTOOL
UTILITIES

Adding a Timestamp

The tai64n program can be used to add a TAI64N-formatted timestamp to a message. Entries are received via the standard input (stdin) and written to the standard output (stdout) of the system. The format of the outputted line is

```
@timestamp entry
```

where timestamp is the TAI64N representation of the time the entry was received and entry is the full text of the message received. Listing 16.10 demonstrates the output of the tai64n program.

LISTING 16.10 Sample tai64n Output

```
$ date | tai64n
@40000000390d966d3172591c Mon May  1 09:36:19 EST 2000
$
```

Listing 16.10 shows an example of piping the output of the standard UNIX date command to the tai64n program. The output of the tai64n program is the original message from the date program, plus the TAI64N timestamp in ASCII format.

The tai64n program is used by multilog to accurately timestamp log entries before they are written to the log file.

Converting TAI64N Times to Local Time

The tai64nlocal program can be used to convert a timestamp in the TAI64N format to a time representation using a standard time format. This is most often used for interpreting timestamps in the multilog log files. Listing 16.11 shows an example of this.

LISTING 16.11 Sample tai64nlocal Output

```
1  $ cat /var/log/qmail/current | tai64nlocal
2  2000-04-26 12:05:39.749142500 status: local 0/10 remote 0/20
3  2000-04-26 12:09:56.862247500 new msg 19017
4  2000-04-26 12:09:56.863092500 info msg 19017: bytes 276 from
➡  <rich@shadrach.ispnet1.net> qp 3279 uid 1001
5  2000-04-26 12:09:56.946949500 starting delivery 1: msg 19017 to local
➡  rich@shadrach.ispnet1.net
6  2000-04-26 12:09:56.947816500 status: local 1/10 remote 0/20
7  2000-04-26 12:09:57.203493500 delivery 1: success: did_0+0+2/
8  2000-04-26 12:09:57.221747500 status: local 0/10 remote 0/20
9  2000-04-26 12:09:57.223782500 end msg 19017
```

LISTING 16.11   Continued

```
10 2000-04-27 02:02:17.961389500 new msg 19026
11 2000-04-27 02:02:17.962333500 info msg 19026: bytes 475 from
➥ <root@shadrach.ispnet1.net> qp 4005 uid 0
12 2000-04-27 02:02:18.044884500 starting delivery 2: msg 19026 to local
➥ root@shadrach.ispnet1.net
13 2000-04-27 02:02:18.045772500 status: local 1/10 remote 0/20
14 2000-04-27 02:02:18.219795500 delivery 2: success: did_0+1+0/qp_4063/
15 2000-04-27 02:02:18.238480500 status: local 0/10 remote 0/20
16 2000-04-27 02:02:18.241040500 end msg 19026
$
```

Line 1 shows the command used to list a log file created from the multilog program, piping it to the tai64nlocal program to convert TAI64N timestamps. Lines 2–16 show the log entries as converted by the tai64nlocal program. Each of the timestamps has been converted to a local representation of the timestamp that is much easier for the mail administrator to understand.

Running a Program as Another User ID

Setuidgid, another program in the daemontools utility, is used to allow a mail administrator to run a program in a script file under the user ID and group ID of another user. The format of the setuidgid program is

```
setuidgid user program
```

where `user` is the text username that `program` should be run under. The `program` parameter should include the full command-line syntax of the program to run.

The setuidgid utility is often used with the multilog program to allow the administrator to create a script that can run under the `root` user ID, but also allow him to create a log file under a user ID with fewer privileges, such as one of the standard qmail user IDs. The qmaill or qmaild user ID often is used to create log files for the qmail program.

Running a Program with a User's Environment Variables

The envuidgid program can be used to run a program from a script file using the standard UNIX environment variables set within a specific user's login script. The format of the `envuidgid` command is

```
envuidgid user program
```

where `user` is the username from which the environment variables will be taken, and `program` is the program to execute, complete with the command-line parameters of the program.

Running a Program with Specific Environment Variables

Another daemontools utility is the envdir program, which can be used to run a program from within a script using environment variables defined in a file. The format of the envdir command is

```
envdir dir program
```

where `dir` is the directory from which the environment variables will be read, and `program` is the program to execute, complete with the necessary command-line parameters for the program.

The envdir program reads environment variables from the specified directory using a special format. Each environment variable is created as a separate file within the directory specified. The filename used is the name of the environment variable.

If the file is empty, envdir removes the environment variable if it exists. If the file contains a value, the specified environment variable is set to the value. This feature is helpful for running programs that require preset system environment variables that cannot be set manually before the program is run. Often this is the case with programs run from qmail's `.qmail` files to process incoming messages for a user.

Using a Lock File for a Program

The final utility in the daemontools package is the setlock program, which enables the use of a lock file when running a program. If the lock file is locked, the setlock utility can defer running the indicated program until the lock file is available. The format of the `setlock` command is

```
setlock options file program
```

where `file` is the lock file that setlock will monitor and lock, `program` is the program that setlock will execute if the lock file is open, and `options` is a set of options that defines the behavior of setlock. The options available for use are shown in Table 16.5.

TABLE 16.5   Setlock Options

Option	Description
-n	No delay. If `file` is locked, setlock does not run `program` and exits.
-N	Delay. If `file` is locked, setlock waits until the file is unlocked to run `program` (default).
-x	If `file` is locked, setlock exits with a return code of zero.
-X	If `file` is locked, setlock prints an error message and exits with a nonzero return code (default).

Using Daemontools with qmail

The main purpose of the daemontools package is to create a method that can monitor the qmail background processes and restart them if they should die for any reason. Also, the daemontools multilog utility can be used to create individual log files for the qmail-send and qmail-smtpd processes to help the mail administrator keep log files separate.

To use daemontools for qmail, you must create a common directory to place the supervise scripts for svscan to use. The most common method is to create a supervise directory under the standard /var/qmail directory. Also, the appropriate log directories must be created. Listing 16.12 shows the directory structure that should be used.

LISTING 16.12   A Sample svscan Directory for qmail

```
1  meshach# ls -alR /var/qmail/supervise
2  total 4
3  drw-r-xr-x   4 root  qmail  512 Apr 26 11:46 .
4  drwxr-xr-x  12 root  qmail  512 Apr 26 11:46 ..
5  drwxr-xr-t   4 root  qmail  512 Apr 26 11:57 qmail-send
6  drwxr-xr-t   4 root  qmail  512 Apr 26 11:57 qmail-smtpd
7
8  /var/qmail/supervise/qmail-send:
9  total 5
10 drwxr-xr-t  4 root  qmail  512 Apr 26 11:57 .
11 drw-r-xr-x  4 root  qmail  512 Apr 26 11:46 ..
12 drwxr-xr-x  3 root  qmail  512 Apr 26 11:57 log
13 -rwxr-xr-x  1 root  qmail   29 Apr 26 11:47 run
14
15 /var/qmail/supervise/qmail-send/log:
16 total 4
17 drwxr-xr-x  3 root  qmail  512 Apr 26 11:57 .
18 drwxr-xr-t  4 root  qmail  512 Apr 26 11:57 ..
19 -rwxr-xr-x  1 root  qmail   88 Apr 26 11:48 run
20
21 /var/qmail/supervise/qmail-smtpd:
22 total 5
23 drwxr-xr-t  4 root  qmail  512 Apr 26 11:57 .
24 drw-r-xr-x  4 root  qmail  512 Apr 26 11:46 ..
25 drwxr-xr-x  3 root  qmail  512 Apr 26 11:57 log
26 -rwxr-xr-x  1 root  qmail  228 Apr 26 12:00 run
27
28 /var/qmail/supervise/qmail-smtpd/log:
29 total 4
```

```
30 drwxr-xr-x  3 root   qmail   512 Apr 26 11:57 .
31 drwxr-xr-t  4 root   qmail   512 Apr 26 11:57 ..
32 -rwxr-xr-x  1 root   qmail    94 Apr 26 11:52 run
33
34 meshach#
```

Line 1 shows the command used to list the `/var/qmail/supervise` directory created to contain the svscan scripts. Lines 5 and 6 show the supervise script directories created. Two script directories are created, `qmail-send` and `qmail-smtpd`. Each directory has the sticky bit set to allow log directories.

The `qmail-send` Supervise Scripts

The `qmail-send` directory contains the run script that starts the qmail process (shown in line 13). This run script should be similar to the `/var/qmail/rc` script used previously to start qmail. There are two important differences:

- You must remove the reference to the splogger program.
- The UNIX background process sign (&) must be removed from the script.

A sample startup script using the Dot-Forward program and a local UNIX `mail.local` delivery program would look like this:

```
#!/bin/sh

exec env - PATH="/var/qmail/bin:$PATH" \
qmail-start '|dot-forward .forward
|preline -f /usr/libexec/mail.local -r "${SENDER:-MAILER-DAEMON}" -d "$USER"'
```

This script mimics the standard `/var/qmail/boot/binm1+df` script, except that it has the splogger program removed and is not set to run in background mode.

A log directory is also in the `qmail-send` directory, shown in line 12. The content of the log directory is another run script, configured to run the multilog program that will log any messages produced from the `qmail-send` program. A sample multilog run script would look like this:

```
#!/bin/sh
exec /usr/local/bin/setuidgid qmaill /usr/local/bin/multilog t /var/log/qmail
```

The multilog script uses the setuidgid daemontools utility to ensure that the log files can be created using the standard qmail qmaill username. Each log entry will be timestamped using the TAI64N format and written to the `/var/log/qmail` log directory.

The `qmail-smtpd` Supervise Scripts

Besides the `qmail-send` program, most qmail installations use the `qmail-smtpd` program to accept SMTP connections from remote mail hosts. If you are using the UNIX `inetd` program to run the `qmail-smtpd` program, you do not need to use the supervise program. However, if you are using the tcpserver program to run the `qmail-smtpd` program, you can use the supervise program to monitor and control the tcpserver program running the `qmail-smtpd` program.

Line 6 in Listing 16.12 shows the second supervise service directory created. The `qmail-smtpd` service directory contains a run script used to start the `qmail-smtpd` program. A standard script for this would look like this:

```
#!/bin/sh

QMAILUID=`id -u qmaild`
QMAILGID=`id -g qmaild`

exec /usr/local/bin/tcpserver -v -p -x /etc/tcp.smtp.cdb -u $QMAILUID
➥ -g $QMAILGID 0 smtp  /var/qmail/bin/qmail-smtpd 2>&1
```

This script uses the UNIX `id` program to determine the user ID and group ID of the `qmaild` username. This is used to run the tcpserver program. Also, the tcpserver program is set to point to a filter database stored in the `/etc/tcp.smtp.cdb` file.

As with the `qmail-send` service, the `qmail-smtpd` service directory is created with the sticky bit set, so a log directory can be created to log messages. The format of the run script used for the multilog program should look like this:

```
#!/bin/sh

exec /usr/local/bin/setuidgid qmaill /usr/local/bin/multilog t
➥ /var/log/qmail/smtpd
```

Again, this script uses the daemontools setuidgid utility to allow multilog to log messages as the qmaill user ID. The multilog program itself is configured to timestamp each message and store the `qmail-smtpd` messages in a separate log file in the `/var/log/qmail/smtpd` log directory.

Starting the qmail Svscan Scripts

Once the appropriate supervise run scripts are created, you can create an init script for qmail with the svscan program. The init script should look like this:

```
svscan /var/qmail/supervise &
```

This init script should be located in a place where your particular UNIX distribution will execute it at boot time.

Summary

Dan Bernstein has developed the daemontools package to provide several useful utilities for qmail mail administrators. The supervise program can be used to start, stop, and monitor the `qmail-send` and `qmail-smtpd` programs. While it is monitoring the programs, if either program should die, supervise will restart it.

The svscan utility can be used to simplify the use of the supervise program by running it on multiple services with one command. Each service should be created as a separate subdirectory beneath a common directory.

The multilog utility can also be used to log messages from supervised programs to separate log files. Each multilog entry can be configured to log a particular process and to log only particular types of messages from the process. The use of the svscan and multilog utilities from the daemontools package can greatly simplify the work of the qmail mail administrator.

Installing and Configuring POP3 and IMAP Servers

IN THIS CHAPTER

After you have successfully installed the qmail software, your mail server should be receiving email messages from both local users and remote users on other mail hosts. However, this only gets the messages to the user mailboxes on the mail server. It is still up to the individual email clients on the mail server to retrieve their own mail.

Users who have physical access to the mail host can log into an interactive session such as a console screen or an X Window session. Once he is logged into the mail server, a user can use a Mail User Agent (MUA) program such as pine, elm, or kmail to access the local mailbox and manage his messages. These types of programs allow users to view and delete mail messages from an interactive session on the local mail server.

Unfortunately, many users do not have physical access to the mail server host. In fact, in most cases it is impossible for all users on the network to have physical access to read email messages on the same mail server. The next possible solution for remote email clients is to use the Telnet or X terminal programs to establish a connection with the remote mail server. Although this works, it is extremely inefficient for reading mail messages. Both Telnet and X terminal sessions create a large network overhead for just reading a few lines of text messages.

The best solution mail administrators have available is Mail Delivery Agents (MDAs). MDAs offer a method for remote users to access their mailboxes on the local mail server without a lot of network overhead. The MDA can access the remote mailbox and download just the information necessary for the client computer to present the message to the user. Figure 17.1 shows remote clients accessing mail messages residing on the mail server using an MDA.

Two protocols that allow remote access of mailboxes are the Post Office Protocol (POP3) and the Interactive Mail Access Protocol (IMAP). The POP3 and IMAP protocols allow remote users to view and delete mail messages on the local mail server from a remote workstation using an email client program. The UNIX mail server must run server software that supports either the POP3 or IMAP protocol to allow remote users access to their mailboxes.

This chapter describes three server software packages that allow the UNIX mail server to support the POP3 and IMAP retrieval of email messages. qmail includes a POP3 server software package—qmail-pop3d, which can be used to retrieve messages from Maildir-formatted mailboxes. Qualcomm's qpopper program can also be used to support POP3 access of normal UNIX mailboxes from remote email clients. The University of Washington IMAP program supports both the POP3 and IMAP protocols to access local mailboxes.

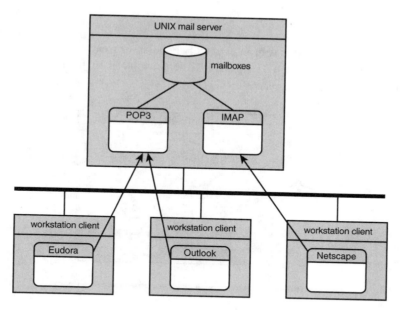

FIGURE 17.1

Remote network clients retrieving mail messages from the server.

Email MDA Protocols

Although POP3 and IMAP programs perform similar functions, the methods they use to access mailboxes are totally different. This section compares and contrasts the two most common email client MDA protocols to help the mail administrator decide which protocol(s) to implement and for what reasons.

The main difference between the IMAP and POP3 protocols is where mail is located. For POP3, the mail messages are spooled on the mail server and downloaded to the client for further manipulation. Often the messages on the server are deleted as soon as the client downloads them.

In contrast, the IMAP protocol maintains all of the messages in folders on the server. Each user has a default folder named the Inbox. New messages are placed in the Inbox to be read. Each time the client connects to the IMAP server, a listing of the Inbox messages can be obtained, and any of the messages can be retrieved—even from different client computers.

POP3

The Post Office Protocol (POP) has been extremely popular. Currently, it is on its third official release version (thus the name POP3). Figure 17.2 demonstrates how the POP3 protocol can be used to retrieve mail from a mail server.

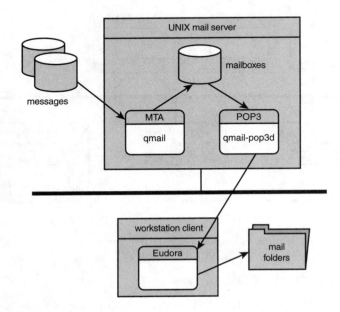

FIGURE 17.2
An overview of the POP3 protocol.

The user's client computer can use the POP3 protocol to download messages from the user's mailbox on the mail server. After it is downloaded, the message can be deleted form the mail server, or the user can elect to keep the mail message on the mail server. In either situation, the message is downloaded in its entirety for the user to view on the remote client computer using email client software.

The POP3 protocol is popular with Internet service providers (ISPs) that must maintain hundreds of email mailboxes on servers. POP3 allows the ISP to force the messages to be deleted from the server as they are downloaded, thus saving on server disk space. One unfortunate consequence of this scenario is that the user's mail is kept on the computer that he checks the mail from. If this is always the same computer, there is not a problem. However, in today's world many people must have the capability to check email messages from home as well as from the office. This is where POP3 becomes a problem. If the user checks for email at home and downloads 20 new messages, those messages will remain on the home computer. When the user gets to work, the messages will not be on the email server and will thus be unobtainable. This is where IMAP comes in.

POP3 is a text-based protocol that relies on the client sending a text command to the server. The server responds to the command with either the result of the command or an error message. Table 17.1 shows the POP3 commands that can be sent by the client.

TABLE 17.1   POP3 Commands

Command	*Description*
user *name*	Sends a username to the POP3 server.
pass *password*	Sends a user password to the POP3 server.
apop *name digest*	Sends a username and an encrypted value to authenticate the user.
auth *method*	Negotiates the authentication method used with the POP3 server.
stat	Retrieves a short summary of the user's mailbox.
list *num*	Retrieves a short listing of the messages (or message number *num*) for the mailbox.
retr *num*	Retrieves the entire text of message number *num*.
dele *num*	Removes message number *num* from the mailbox.
noop	Solicits a response from the server.
rset	Resets the POP3 connection state.
quit	Terminates the POP3 session with the server.
top *msg num*	Retrieves the first *num* lines from message number msg.
uidl	Displays the unique message identification number for each message.

> **NOTE**
>
> In RFC 1939, the Post Office Protocol defines commands in uppercase. It has been common practice though that all implementations of POP3 servers accept commands in either uppercase or lowercase. The examples used in this chapter use all lowercase commands.

The POP3 protocol is very simple in the way the client interacts with the remote mail server. The POP3 server listens for TCP connections on port 110. You can test your POP3 server software by Telneting to port 110 on the local mail server. Listing 17.1 demonstrates a sample POP3 session with the local mail server.

LISTING 17.1   A Sample POP3 Session

```
1  $ telnet localhost 110
2  Trying 127.0.0.1...
3  Connected to localhost.ispnet1.net.
4  Escape character is '^]'.
5  +OK QPOP (version 3.0) at shadrach.ispnet1.net starting.
6  user rich
7  +OK Password required for rich.
8  pass guitar
9  +OK rich has 4 visible messages (0 hidden) in 1637 octets.
10 stat
11 +OK 4 1637
12 list
13 +OK 4 visible messages (1637 octets)
14 1 408
15 2 409
16 3 410
17 4 410
18 .
19 retr 1
20 +OK 408 octets
21 Return-Path: <rich@shadrach.ispnet1.net>
22 Delivered-To: rich@shadrach.ispnet1.net
23 Received: (qmail 25364 invoked by uid 1001); 3 May 2000 14:39:52 -0000
24 Date: 3 May 2000 14:39:52 -0000
25 Message-ID: <20000503143952.25363.qmail@shadrach.ispnet1.net>
26 From: rich@shadrach.ispnet1.net
27 To: rich@shadrach.ispnet1.net
28 Subject: Test message one
29 X-UIDL: J0J"!@KQ!!XNN!!M*]!!
30
31 This is the first test message
32
33 .
34 dele 1
35 +OK Message 1 has been deleted.
36 list
37 +OK 3 visible messages (1229 octets)
38 2 409
39 3 410
40 4 410
41 .
42 uidl
43 +OK uidl command accepted.
44 2 -mI!!M1Z!!S]<!!fd4"!
```

```
45 3 c~T!!;+*#!8Fa!!mPL!!
46 4 b6g"!WbE"!f6a!!%Z~"!
47 .
48 top 3 5
49 +OK Message follows
50 Return-Path: <rich@shadrach.ispnet1.net>
51 Delivered-To: rich@shadrach.ispnet1.net
52 Received: (qmail 25388 invoked by uid 1001); 3 May 2000 14:40:14 -0000
53 Date: 3 May 2000 14:40:14 -0000
54 Message-ID: <20000503144014.25387.qmail@shadrach.ispnet1.net>
55 From: rich@shadrach.ispnet1.net
56 To: rich@shadrach.ispnet1.net
57 Subject: Test message three
58 X-UIDL: c~T!!;+*#!8Fa!!mPL!!
59
60 This is the third test message
61
62 .
63 quit
64 +OK Pop server at shadrach.ispnet1.net signing off.
65 Connection closed by foreign host.
66 you have mail
67 $
```

In Listing 17.1, line 1 shows the command to Telnet to the POP3 port on the local mail server. After receiving the welcome banner from the POP3 software, you can user the user and pass commands to log into the POP3 server as a local user (shown in lines 6–9). Line 9 shows a banner provided by the POP3 server, giving a synopsis of the user's mailbox. In line 10 the user sends the stat command, which provides the same synopsis of the mailbox.

Line 12 shows the POP3 list command being sent to the mail server to obtain an individual account of each mail message. Lines 13–18 show the results returned by the list command. Each message is listed with a message number and the number of bytes required to store the message. In line 19 the user sends the retr command, requesting to download the first mail message. The complete mail message including the RFC822 headers is downloaded, as shown in lines 20–33.

Line 34 shows the user sending the dele command to remove the first mail message from the mailbox. In line 36 a list command is sent to verify that the message has been removed.

Each message is numbered sequentially for the POP3 session. As shown in lines 37–41, when message 1 was removed, messages 2, 3, and 4 keep the same message numbers. However, if this POP3 session was terminated and a new one started, the messages would be renumbered for the new session, starting with message number 1.

This could be disastrous if you do not pay attention to which message has which number. To solve this problem, POP3 provides a system for identifying each message uniquely. The uidl command can be used to display the unique message number for each message. Line 42 shows an example of using the uidl command to display the unique message numbers for each message. These numbers do not change between POP3 sessions.

Finally, line 48 shows the use of the POP3 top command. This allows clients to request a subset of the message text instead of having to download the entire message. This comes in handy for client MUA programs that want to display the message subject headers without having to download the entire message.

IMAP

The Interactive Mail Access Protocol (IMAP) has been a lesser-known protocol in the email world, but it is quickly gaining popularity. Currently it is at release version 4, revision 1 (commonly called IMAP4rev1). Figure 17.3 demonstrates how the IMAP protocol works.

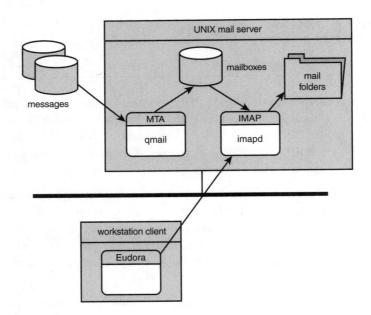

FIGURE 17.3
An overview of the IMAP protocol.

The IMAP protocol also uses a series of text commands that can be sent from the network client to the mail server. Each command instructs the mail server to perform a particular function. Table 17.2 shows the IMAP commands that can be used by the network client.

TABLE 17.2   IMAP Commands

Command	Description
login	Uses a plain text user ID and password to log into the IMAP server.
authenticate	Negotiates an alternative login authentication method with the server.
select	Opens a specific mailbox folder on the server.
examine	Opens a specific mailbox folder for read-only.
create	Creates a new mailbox folder.
delete	Deletes an existing mailbox folder.
rename	Renames an existing mailbox folder to a new name.
subscribe	Adds a specific mailbox folder to a subscription list.
unsubscribe	Removes a specific mailbox folder from a subscription list.
list	Lists all mailbox folders available for the user on the server.
lsub	Lists all mailbox folders that the user has subscribed to.
status	Displays the current status of a mailbox.
append	Places a message at the end of a specific mailbox file.
check	Marks a checkpoint for mailbox operations. Forces the IMAP server to delete any messages marked for deletion.
close	Closes an open mailbox folder.
expunge	Removes all messages marked for deletion from a folder without closing the folder.
search	Searches for a message in a mailbox folder based on specified criteria.
fetch	Displays the message header, body, or both for a specific mailbox message.
store	Alters flag information for a mailbox message.
copy	Copies messages from one mailbox folder to another.
uid	Displays the internal unique identification number for the mailbox messages.
capability	Displays a list of IMAP capabilities that the IMAP server supports.
noop	Tests the connectivity of the IMAP server.
logout	Terminates the current session from the IMAP server.

17

INSTALLING AND
CONFIGURING
POP3 AND IMAP

> **NOTE**
>
> As with the POP3 protocol, RFC 2060 defines the IMAP protocol commands as upper-case, but all of the implementations of IMAP servers accept either uppercase or low-ercase commands.

Most of the IMAP commands use parameters indicating the mailbox folder or message that needs to be processed. Also, the IMAP protocol requires that each command line sent to the server be identified with a unique tag. This enables the client to send multiple commands to the server and identify which responses are associated with which commands. The format of an IMAP command is

```
tag command parameters
```

where tag is the unique identifier for the command line.

To test the IMAP server, you can Telnet to the IMAP TCP port (143) on the local mail server and issue IMAP commands. Listing 17.2 shows a sample IMAP session with the local mail server.

LISTING 17.2   A Sample IMAP Session

```
1   $ telnet localhost 143
2   Trying 127.0.0.1...
3   Connected to localhost.ispnet1.net.
4   Escape character is '^]'.
5   * OK localhost.ispnet1.net IMAP4rev1 v12.250 server ready
6   a1 login rich guitar
7   a1 OK LOGIN completed
8   a3 lsub "" *
9   a3 OK LSUB completed
10  a4 create newbox
11  a4 OK CREATE completed
12  a5 subscribe newbox
13  a5 OK SUBSCRIBE completed
14  a6 create stuff/junk
15  a6 OK CREATE completed
16  a7 subscribe stuff/junk
17  a7 OK SUBSCRIBE completed
18  a8 lsub "" *
19  * LSUB () "/" newbox
20  * LSUB () "/" stuff/junk
```

```
21 a8 OK LSUB completed
22 a9 select inbox
23 * 4 EXISTS
24 * 0 RECENT
25 * OK [UIDVALIDITY 957373049] UID validity status
26 * OK [UIDNEXT 5] Predicted next UID
27 * FLAGS (\Answered \Flagged \Deleted \Draft \Seen)
28 * OK [PERMANENTFLAGS (\* \Answered \Flagged \Deleted \Draft \Seen)]
➡ Permanent flags
29 a9 OK [READ-WRITE] SELECT completed
30 a11 fetch 2:3 body[header.fields (date from subject)]
31 * 2 FETCH (BODY[HEADER.FIELDS ("DATE" "FROM" "SUBJECT")] {98}
32 Date: 3 May 2000 16:56:42 -0000
33 From: rich@shadrach.ispnet1.net
34 Subject: Second test message
35
36 )
37 * 3 FETCH (BODY[HEADER.FIELDS ("DATE" "FROM" "SUBJECT")] {97}
38 Date: 3 May 2000 16:56:56 -0000
39 From: rich@shadrach.ispnet1.net
40 Subject: Third test message
41
42 )
43 a11 OK FETCH completed
44 a12 copy 2:3 stuff/junk
45 a12 OK COPY completed
46 a13 select stuff/junk
47 * 2 EXISTS
48 * 0 RECENT
49 * OK [UIDVALIDITY 957373506] UID validity status
50 * OK [UIDNEXT 3] Predicted next UID
51 * FLAGS (\Answered \Flagged \Deleted \Draft \Seen)
52 * OK [PERMANENTFLAGS (\* \Answered \Flagged \Deleted \Draft \Seen)]
➡ Permanent flags
53 a13 OK [READ-WRITE] SELECT completed
54 a14 fetch 1:2 body[header.fields (date from subject)]
55 * 1 FETCH (BODY[HEADER.FIELDS ("DATE" "FROM" "SUBJECT")] {98}
56 Date: 3 May 2000 16:56:42 -0000
57 From: rich@shadrach.ispnet1.net
58 Subject: Second test message
59
60 )
61 * 2 FETCH (BODY[HEADER.FIELDS ("DATE" "FROM" "SUBJECT")] {97}
62 Date: 3 May 2000 16:56:56 -0000
63 From: rich@shadrach.ispnet1.net
```

LISTING 17.2   Continued

```
64 Subject: Third test message
65
66 )
67 a14 OK FETCH completed
68 a15 capability
69 * CAPABILITY IMAP4 IMAP4REV1 NAMESPACE IDLE SCAN SORT MAILBOX-REFERRALS
➥ LOGIN-REFERRALS AUTH=LOGIN THREAD=ORDEREDSUBJECT
70 a15 OK CAPABILITY completed
71 a16 logout
72 * BYE shadrach.ispnet1.net IMAP4rev1 server terminating connection
73 a16 OK LOGOUT completed
74 Connection closed by foreign host.
75 $
```

In Listing 17.2, line 1 demonstrates the command used to initiate an IMAP session with the local mail server. If the IMAP server software is running, you should get a welcome banner, as shown in line 5. Line 6 shows a sample login command sent to the IMAP server. Line 7 indicates that the login attempt was successful. Line 8 shows an example of using the lsub command to check for subscribed mailbox folders. Line 9 indicates that none exist. In lines 10 and 14, two new mailbox folders are created on the IMAP server, and in lines 12 and 16 they are subscribed to. The next lsub command, issued in line 18, indicates that now both of the new mailboxes are subscribed (as shown in lines 19–21).

Line 22 shows the client selecting the standard Inbox mailbox, where all new messages are stored. The response from the IMAP server, shown in lines 23–29, indicates that there are four messages in the Inbox.

Line 30 shows an example of using the fetch command to retrieve the header information from a subset of messages in the Inbox. The IMAP server responds by sending the requested information from the messages in lines 31–43. In line 44 the client requests that the second and third messages in the Inbox be copied to the stuff/junk mailbox folder on the server. To verify this operation, the client selects the new mailbox (in line 46) and fetches the header information (in line 54). Notice that now both messages have been relocated to the stuff/junk folder.

Line 68 shows an example of using the capability command. The IMAP server responds with the current capabilities of the server.

The use of folders on the IMAP server is a great advantage to users who must check mail from multiple workstations throughout the day. No matter what workstation is used, the mail messages and folders always remain constant.

The `qmail-pop3d` Program

The qmail package includes a POP3 server package. The `qmail-pop3d` program can accept POP3 sessions from remote clients and connect them to their mailboxes. The main benefit from using the `qmail-pop3d` program is that it can work with qmail Maildir-formatted mailboxes. Of course, the main disadvantage with the `qmail-pop3d` program is that it works only with Maildir-formatted mailboxes. If you need to also run an IMAP server that cannot read Maildir-formatted mailboxes, you will not be able to use `qmail-pop3d` at the same time. The `qmail-pop3d` program was introduced and discussed in Chapter 9, "Using the Maildir Mailbox Format."

The `qmail-pop3d` program must run in Background mode to monitor the network for POP3 connection requests. This can be accomplished using either the UNIX inetd or the ucspi-tcp tcpserver programs. Chapter 9 describes using the inetd program to run `qmail-pop3d`. This section describes how to use the tcpserver program.

There are actually three pieces of software required for the `qmail-pop3d` program to operate properly:

- The `qmail-popup` program, used to obtain the user ID and password
- The checkpassword program, used to verify the user ID and password
- The `qmail-pop3d` program, used to establish the POP3 session to read the user's mailbox

Each program is called in sequence during the POP3 connection. This means that the program called by the tcpserver program needs to be the `qmail-popup` program. The command used to run the `qmail-pop3d` program using the tcpserver program would look like this:

```
tcpserver -v -R 0 pop3 /var/qmail/bin/qmail-popup host  /bin/checkpassword
➥ /var/qmail/bin/qmail-pop3d Maildir 2>&1 |  /var/qmail/bin/splogger
➥ pop3d &
```

The `host` parameter should define the full hostname of the local mail server. Also, ensure that the `pop3` tag is defined in your `/etc/services` file.

> **NOTE**
>
> Alternatively, instead of using the `pop3` service tag, you can use the port number (110). For some administrators this method is easier to remember.

Listing 17.3 shows a sample POP3 session with the `qmail-pop3d` server.

LISTING 17.3   A Sample POP3 Session Using `qmail-pop3d`

```
1  $ telnet localhost 110
2  Trying 127.0.0.1...
3  Connected to localhost.
4  Escape character is '^]'.
5  +OK <44208.957474028@meshach.ispnet1.net>
6  user frank
7  +OK
8  pass soccer
9  +OK
10 stat
11 +OK 3 1049
12 list
13 +OK
14 1 349
15 2 351
16 3 349
17 .
18 retr 1
19 +OK
20 Return-Path: <rich@meshach.ispnet1.net>
21 Delivered-To: frank@meshach.ispnet1.net
22 Received: (qmail 44191 invoked by uid 1001); 4 May 2000 21:00:01 -0000
23 Date: 4 May 2000 21:00:01 -0000
24 Message-ID: <20000504210001.44190.qmail@meshach.ispnet1.net>
25 From: rich@meshach.ispnet1.net
26 To: frank@meshach.ispnet1.net
27 Subject: First test message
28
29 This is the first test message.
30
31 .
32 quit
33 +OK
34 Connection closed by foreign host.
35 $
```

In Listing 17.3, line 1 shows the command used to create a POP3 session with the local mail server. The `qmail-pop3d` program produces the welcome banner shown in line 5.

The username and password are entered in lines 6 and 8. The checkpassword program can be used to validate usernames and passwords entered in using the standard user and pass commands. If you want to use a different type of authentication method, you must download and install a different authentication program other than checkpassword.

After the user is validated, he can interact with the POP3 server using any of the standard POP3 commands shown in Table 17.1.

The Qpopper Program

The qpopper program is freeware originally released by the University of California at Berkeley but now maintained by the Qualcomm corporation. It also supports the Eudora email client software. Qpopper was written to provide POP3 server software for most types of UNIX servers. It works just great on Linux and FreeBSD servers.

Qpopper supports both the normal user and password POP3 logins and a special APOP POP3-encrypted authentication. By default, the user/password login method sends user IDs and passwords across the network in clear text format. The APOP authentication method allows the client to send a user ID in clear text and then submit a password that is an encryption of the password and a known secret value.

The user/password login feature supports using the standard Linux and FreeBSD password files, as well as a special feature for Linux shadow password files. The APOP feature supports encrypted passwords using a separate password database file that must be maintained separately by the mail administrator.

Information about qpopper can be found on its Web site at `http://www.eudora.com/qpopper/index.html`. The current release version of qpopper at the time of this writing is version 3.0. There is also a beta version that is available for use—version 3.0.1b2.

CAUTION

If you happen to come across a version of qpopper earlier than version 2.41, don't use it. There were some serious buffer overflow problems with the earlier versions that could allow a hacker to gain root access to your mail server.

Downloading Qpopper

The Qualcomm FTP site hosts the most current version of qpopper. The FTP server is located at `ftp.qualcomm.com`. The directory where qpopper is located is `/eudora/servers/unix/popper`.

> **NOTE**
>
> Don't get confused by the qpopper package name. Although the package name is qpopper, the executable program name is popper. Often you will see these names interchanged in documentation and Web sites. I try to maintain the proper consistency in this chapter.

At the time of this writing, there are four qpopper distributions in this directory: versions 2.53, 3.0, 3.0.1b1, and 3.0.1b2. All four use the UNIX tar and compress utilities to compact the distribution files. Make sure you are using the FTP binary mode and download the version that you want to use. For this example, the file qpopper3.0.tar.Z will be used:

```
ftp://ftp.qualcomm.com/eudora/servers/unix/popper/qpopper3.0.tar.Z
```

Once the file is downloaded (the 3.0 version is a little over 2.4MB), you can extract the source code files into a working directory:

```
tar -zxvf qpopper3.0.tar.Z -C /usr/local
```

The UNIX tar utility creates a subdirectory /usr/local/qpopper3.0 and places the source code files in subdirectories beneath it.

Configuring Qpopper

The qpopper program uses the configure program to examine the operating environment and create a Makefile that references the specific locations of the C compiler, libraries, and include files. The configure program also uses command-line parameters to change specific features that you may want to include in your implementation of the qpopper server. These will be described later.

The default qpopper configuration environment uses no extra command-line parameters and can be built using the following commands:

```
./configure
make
```

This creates a default POP3 server that does not recognize the APOP authentication method or the shadow password database on Linux systems. This configuration will work on FreeBSD systems, though.

The qpopper executable program is called popper and is located in the popper subdirectory beneath the qpopper3.0 directory. You will need to copy this program to a common location as the root user. The qpopper documentation recommends using the /usr/local/lib directory.

The popper program can use command-line parameters to modify the behavior of the POP3 server. Table 17.3 shows the available command-line parameters.

TABLE 17.3 Popper Command-Line Parameters

Parameter	Description
-b	Changes the default directory for bulletins
-c	Changes all usernames to lowercase
-d	Enables debugging
-e	Sets POP3 extensions
-k	Enables Kerberos support
-s	Enables statistics logging
-t	Defines an alternate debug and log file
-T	Changes the default timeout waiting for reads
-R	Disables reverse client address lookups

The qpopper program uses the inetd program to execute. Alternatively, you can use the tcpserver program from the ucspi-tcp package, as discussed in Chapter 10, "The ucspi-tcp Program." Both the inetd and tcpserver programs listen for network connections and pass those connections to the appropriate program according to the TCP or UDP port number on which the connection is established.

If you are using the inetd program, the first part of the inetd configuration is to make sure that it recognizes the POP3 TCP port (number 110). This information is in the /etc/services file. The pertinent line should look like the following:

```
pop-3       110/tcp             # POP version 3
```

After ensuring that the /etc/services file supports POP3, the next step is to configure the inetd configuration file to support POP3. The inetd configuration file is /etc/inetd.conf. A line should be added to the configuration file that corresponds to the tag in the /etc/services line (pop-3) and identifies the program to start when a connection is established. The new line should look like the following:

```
pop-3  stream  tcp nowait  root    /usr/local/lib/popper   popper -s
```

This inetd.conf entry assumes that the popper program is located in the /usr/local/lib directory and that statistics logging is enabled (the -s option). By default, statistics will be logged in the UNIX default syslog file (usually /var/log for Linux and FreeBSD).

To activate the new inetd.conf settings, the currently running inetd daemon must be restarted. This can be accomplished by sending a SIGHUP signal to it. The following commands can be used to accomplish this:

```
[root@shadrach rich]# ps ax | grep inetd
  327 ?        S       0:00 inetd
12600 pts/2    S       0:00 grep inetd
[root@shadrach rich]# kill -HUP 327
[root@shadrach rich]#
```

You can test the qpopper installation by using the Telnet program and connecting to port 110 on the mail server, as shown in Listing 17.4.

LISTING 17.4 A Sample POP3 Session

```
1  [erin@shadrach erin]$ telnet localhost 110
2  Trying 127.0.0.1...
3  Connected to localhost.
4  Escape character is '^]'.
5  +OK QPOP (version 3.0b18) at shadrach.smallorg.org starting.
6  QUIT
7  +OK Pop server at shadrach.smallorg.org signing off.
8  Connection closed by foreign host.
9  [erin@shadrach erin]$
```

In Listing 17.4, line 1 shows the user Telneting to port 110 of the localhost. Line 5 shows the greeting banner produced by the qpopper program.

The default qpopper configuration will work in some simple POP3 implementations running on basic UNIX mail servers. However, there are other features that can be implemented to make qpopper more versatile.

Supporting Shadow Passwords

A common UNIX feature is to make use of shadow passwords. This helps prevent unauthorized users from accessing the encrypted password file to try a brute force attack. FreeBSD supports shadow passwords using the /etc/master.passwd file. By default, qpopper recognizes the FreeBSD shadow password file without any modifications.

However, many Linux distributions have incorporated the use of a different shadow password file system. The normal /etc/passwd file still contains user IDs, but the encrypted passwords are stored in a separate file that can be made inaccessible to other users. When a shadow password file is used, programs that verify user IDs must be aware of its existence. For qpopper to work with Linux shadow password files, additional parameters must be included in the configure command line.

If you have previously compiled a version of qpopper, you must clean the object and executable files from the `build` directory. You can accomplish this by using the following command from the `qpopper3.0` directory:

```
make clean
```

This command removes files that have been added or modified by the install script. The next
step is to run the configure script with the parameter that includes shadow password support.
The format of this command is

```
./configure --enable-specialauth
```

This re-creates the Makefile using parameters necessary for the GNU gcc compiler to add support for shadow password files. After the configure program finishes building the Makefile,
you can then run the GNU `make` against it to create a new popper executable program in the
popper subdirectory. Again, you must copy this file to the location specified in the `inetd.conf`
file as the `root` user. There is no need to restart the inetd daemon, because the configuration
file `/etc/inetd.conf` was not modified.

After copying the new executable popper program to the appropriate directory, you can test the
configuration by Telneting to port 110 and attempting to log in as a user. An example of this is
demonstrated in Listing 17.5.

LISTING 17.5 A Sample POP3 Login Session

```
1  [riley@shadrach riley]$ telnet localhost 110
2  Trying 127.0.0.1...
3  Connected to localhost.
4  Escape character is '^]'.
5  +OK QPOP (version 3.0b18) at shadrach.smallorg.org starting.
6  USER riley
7  +OK Password required for riley.
8  PASS firetruck
9  +OK riley has 3 messages (1162 octets).
10 QUIT
11 +OK Pop server at shadrach.smallorg.org signing off.
12 Connection closed by foreign host.
13 [riley@shadrach riley]$
```

In Listing 17.5, line 1 shows a Telnet session to port 110 (the POP3 port) of the local mail
server. Line 5 shows the greeting banner produced by Qpopper, indicating that it is indeed up
and running. In lines 6 and 8 the user enters his user ID and password, and in line 9 qpopper
accepts the login attempt and informs the user that he has 3 messages waiting to be downloaded.

17

INSTALLING AND
CONFIGURING
POP3 AND IMAP

Supporting Encrypted Logons

As shown in Listing 17.5, our poor email client had to send his user ID and password in clear text to the qpopper server. Had Riley been checking his mail from across the Internet, it is possible that this information could have been captured by a hacker and used for illegal purposes. However, the POP3 protocol provides a solution to this problem.

The POP3 protocol can use alternative methods to authenticate a user. The qpopper program supports the APOP method of authenticating a user. This method uses encrypted passwords, which greatly reduces the risk of being compromised. To accommodate the different passwords, the APOP method requires that the mail administrator create a separate user password database.

It is often best to create a new system user (often called pop) to control the qpopper access database. This reduces the risk of logging in as root to add new users.

To add this capability to the popper executable program, you must recompile the program. First you must use the following command to remove the object and executable files that were created from any previous builds:

```
make clean
```

Next, you must run the configure script again, including parameters to define the location of the APOP password database and the user ID of the APOP administrator:

```
./configure --enable--apop=/etc/pop.auth --with-popuid=pop
```

This creates a new Makefile, using the values /etc/pop.auth for the authentication database location and the user pop as the database administrator. You can then create the new executables by using the GNU make command as before. With the APOP option, two executable files are created: popper and popauth.

As before, copy the popper executable file to the location specified in the inetd.conf file (such as /usr/local/lib). The popauth file allows the APOP administrator to add users to the APOP authentication database specified in the configure command line.

To test the new qpopper configuration, you can Telnet to port 110 and observe the new greeting banner. Listing 17.6 shows an example of a qpopper server using APOP authentication.

LISTING 17.6 A Sample Qpopper Greeting Banner Using APOP

```
1  [carol@shadrach carol]$ telnet localhost 110
2  Trying 127.0.0.1...
3  Connected to localhost.
4  Escape character is '^]'.
```

```
5   +OK QPOP (version 3.0b18) at shadrach.smallorg.org starting.
➥<17166.940368317@shadrach.
6   smallorg.org>
7   QUIT
8   +OK Pop server at shadrach.smallorg.org signing off.
9   Connection closed by foreign host.
10  [carol@shadrach carol]$
```

In Listing 12.6 line 1 shows the telnet command to connect to the POP3 service port. Line 5 shows the new greeting banner that is generated by qpopper. It differs from the greeting banner shown in Listing 17.5 in that it includes the APOP seed information. The POP3 server supplies this seed value on the greeting banner for the client to use in the encryption of the password. Both sides of the POP3 connection must know the secret word so the hashed value can be matched. The qpopper server stores the secret words in the authentication database.

To create the APOP authentication database, as the root user enter this command:

```
./popauth –init
```

This creates a new authentication database in the location specified (/etc/pop.auth in the example). The user ID specified in the -with-popuid parameter is now the APOP administrator and can add users to the authentication database. One strange characteristic about qpopper is that when a user ID is added to the authentication database, that user *must* use APOP authentication to connect to the POP3 server.

To add a new user to the authentication database, the APOP administrator can type this command:

```
popauth –user user1
```

where user1 is the UNIX system username of the user. popauth will query the administrator for a password for the user to be used for APOP authentication. This password can be different from the normal UNIX system login password. To remove a user from the authentication database, the administrator can enter

```
popauth –delete user
```

where user is the UNIX system username of the user to be removed. An individual user can change his APOP passwords by using the popauth command without any parameters.

Using Bulletins

Another feature that can be added to qpopper is the use of bulletins. Bulletins allow users to send messages to all POP3 users. When a user connects via POP3 to the mail server, qpopper checks the bulletins directory and determines which bulletins have not been read by that user. Any unread bulletins are added to the normal mail messages for that user. The mail administrator can restrict who can send bulletins by controlling the access of the `bulletins` directory.

As before, if you have already compiled a version of qpopper, you must delete any existing object and executable files:

```
make clean
```

Next, the configure program must be run with the `bulletins` parameter added. You can run the configure program with multiple parameters if you also need shadow password or APOP support as well as bulletins. The format for using bulletins with shadow password support is this:

```
./configure --enable-bulletins=/var/spool/bulls --enable-specialauth
```

where the `--enable-bulletins` parameter points to the directory where you want the bulletins to reside. After the configure script finishes, you must run the GNU make utility to create the popper executable. When this finishes, you must again copy the `popper` executable to the directory pointed to by the `inetd.conf` configuration file.

To use the bulletins feature, you must create a separate file for each bulletin and place them in the `bulletins` directory. The filenames should be in this format:

```
nnnnn.string
```

where nnnnn is a five-digit number to identify the bulletin number and `string` is text used to identify the bulletin. An example would be `00001.Test_Bulletin`. Bulletins must be numbered sequentially for qpopper to be able to keep track of which bulletins each user has seen. Once a POP3 client has downloaded the bulletin, it will not appear in the user's mailbox again. The text of the bulletin file must follow strict RFC822 message formats. Listing 17.7 shows a sample bulletin.

LISTING 17.7 Sample Qpopper Bulletin Text

```
1   From pop Wed Oct 20 18:25:00 1999
2   Date: Wed, 20 Oct 1999 18:25:00 (EST)
3   From: "Mail Administrator" <postmaster@shadrach.smallorg.org>
4   Subject: Test bulletin
5
6   This is a test of the Qpopper mail bulletin system.  This is only a test
7   Had this been a real bulletin you would have been instructed to do
8   something important, like log off of the system.
9   This is the end of the bulletin test.
```

The bulletin will be checked for download as long as it is in the `bulletins` directory. If you remove the bulletin file, new POP3 clients will not see the bulletin in their mail.

University of Washington IMAP

The most common POP3 and IMAP package used on the UNIX platform was developed by the University of Washington. It includes both a POP3 server and an IMAP4rev1 server. This section describes how to install and configure the UW IMAP software to support remote POP3 and IMAP clients from your UNIX mail server.

Downloading and Installing UW IMAP

Many Linux distributions already come with a UW IMAP binary package. The FreeBSD UNIX distribution includes the IMAP portion of the UW package, but it replaces the POP3 server part with its own POP3 server implementation—popper. You can install UW IMAP from the distribution that came with your UNIX system, or you can download the current source code file and build it yourself.

The University of Washington currently supports a Web site for the IMAP software project. The URL of this site is `http://www.washington.edu/imap/`.

The site contains information about the UW IMAP project at the university, as well as links to the current release of UW IMAP. The current release at the time of this writing is version 4.7c2.

You can download the source code distribution of this version by the link provided at the Web site. Alternatively, you can connect directly to the FTP site at `ftp.cac.washington.edu` and check the `/imap` directory for the current release version. A link named `imap.tar.Z` is always set to the current release version. The source code distribution comes as a compressed tarred file—`imap-4.7c2.tar.Z`. Remember to use binary mode when retrieving the file.

Once the source code distribution file is downloaded, it can be untarred into a working directory using this command:

```
tar –zxvf imap-4.7c2.tar.Z -C /usr/local
```

This produces a subdirectory named `imap-4.7.BETA` and places the source code in subdirectories beneath it.

The UW IMAP program does not have any feature options that are necessary to add at compile time like qpopper does. The main requirement for building the IMAP distribution executables is to know what type of system you are compiling the source code on and use the appropriate Makefile section. Table 17.4 shows common IMAP make options for UNIX systems.

TABLE 17.4   UW IMAP Make Options

Option	Description
bsf	FreeBSD systems
lnx	Traditional Linux systems
lnp	Linux with Pluggable Authentication Modules (PAM)
sl4	Linux using -lshadow for passwords
sl5	Linux using shadow passwords
slx	Linux using -lcrypt for passwords

Note that there are different Makefile sections for Linux, depending on the type of user authentication method your system uses. For a FreeBSD system, you can use the bsf option:

```
make bsf
```

This compiles the source code and produces the IMAP executables located in the subdirectories in the distribution. The next step is to install and configure the individual pieces of IMAP.

Configuring UW POP3

For the UW POP3 server software to work properly, it must be set up and configured after it is compiled. The first step is to copy the executables into a common directory. The ipop3d and imapd programs were written to be used by the tcpd wrapper program, and it is best to locate them in the same directory—/usr/local/libexec on a FreeBSD system. The ipop3d program is located in the ipopd subdirectory under the imap-4.7c directory. Also included in this directory is a POP2 server—ipop2d. This is mainly for compatibility with older mail clients that do not support the POP3 protocol. If you are establishing a new email system, you should stick with the POP3 implementation. There are plenty of new clients available that use the POP3 protocol.

> **CAUTION**
>
> Make sure you are the root user when copying the ipop3d program to the /usr/local/libexec directory or the copy will fail.

Once the executable is placed in the proper directory, the inetd configuration files must be modified. The first file to modify is /etc/services. You must make sure that the POP3 TCP port is configured. The POP3 line should look like this:

```
pop-3        110/tcp          # POP version 3
```

This indicates that the inetd program will monitor TCP port 110 and pass off any connection attempts to the program defined by the pop-3 tag in the /etc/inetd.conf file, which should indicate where the executables are located when a connection is passed off to it. The necessary POP3 line in the /etc/inetd.conf file is

```
pop-3    stream  tcp       nowait  root      /usr/local/libexec/ipop3d  ipop3d
```

The pop-3 tag in the inetd.conf file relates the ipop3d program to the pop-3 TCP port tag in the /etc/services file.

To activate the new inetd.conf settings, the currently running inetd daemon must be restarted. This can be done by sending a SIGHUP signal to it. The following commands can be used for this:

```
[root@shadrach barbara]# ps ax | grep inetd
  327 ?         S       0:00 inetd
12600 pts/2     S       0:00 grep inetd
[root@shadrach barbara]# kill -HUP 327
[root@shadrach barbara]#
```

With the inetd daemon restarted, you can test the UW IMAP installation. Listing 17.8 shows an example of testing the POP3 server.

LISTING 17.8   A Sample POP3 Session

```
1  [lizzy@shadrach lizzy]$ telnet localhost 110
2  Trying 127.0.0.1...
3  Connected to localhost.
4  Escape character is '^]'.
5  +OK POP3 localhost v7.63 server ready
6  USER lizzy
7  +OK User name accepted, password please
8  PASS SINGING
9  +OK Mailbox open, 5 messages
10 QUIT
11 +OK Sayonara
12 Connection closed by foreign host.
13 [lizzy@shadrach lizzy]$
```

In Listing 17.8, line 1 shows a Telnet session to the POP3 port—110. Line 5 shows the greeting banner generated by the UW POP3 server, indicating that it is indeed running.

An optional feature that is available for the UW POP3 server is the capability to use APOP user authentication. The method of implementing APOP that UW POP3 uses is not as sophisticated as that of the qpopper POP3 server, but it serves its purpose.

If the UW POP3 server detects that the file /etc/cram-md5.pwd exists, it will support the APOP and CRAM-MD5 authentication protocols. Both methods use the same technique of hashing a seed value with a secret word to create the encrypted password used for authentication. The APOP seed value is displayed on the POP3 greeting banner. Both the server and the client must already know the secret word that will be hashed with the seed value.

In the case of UW POP3, the secret words are stored in the /etc/cram-md5.pwd file. Each line of the file contains the username and the secret word that the user will use. Listing 17.9 shows a sample /etc/cram-md5.pwd file.

LISTING 17.9   A Sample /etc/cram-md5.pwd File

```
1  rich       guitar
2  barbara    reading
3  riley      firetruck
4  haley      starwars
5  katie      boxcar
6  jessica    sharks
```

As seen in Listing 17.9, the cram-md5.pwd database is a plain text database. To protect the passwords, you should ensure that the file is set to mode 600 so that normal users cannot view it. This means that the mail administrator must have root access to modify passwords. Also, this means that users cannot modify their own passwords.

To check if the APOP feature is available, Telnet to the POP3 port. The new greeting banner should show the seed value. Listing 17.10 shows an example of an APOP-enabled POP3 server.

LISTING 17.10   A Sample APOP-Enabled POP3 Server Greeting Banner

```
1  [kevin@shadrach kevin]$ telnet localhost 110
2  Trying 127.0.0.1...
3  Connected to localhost.
4  Escape character is '^]'.
5  +OK POP3 v7.63 server ready <4d61.380e35cc@localhost>
6  USER kevin
7  +OK User name accepted, password please
8  PASS dinosaur
9  +OK Mailbox open, 0 messages
10 QUIT
11 +OK Sayonara
12 Connection closed by foreign host.
13 [kevin@shadrach kevin]$
```

In Listing 17.10, line 1 again shows a sample Telnet session to the POP3 server port. This time, line 5 shows a different greeting banner than the example in Listing 17.8. Included in the greeting banner is the APOP seed value. Line 6 demonstrates a nice feature of the UW POP3 server implementation of APOP. Unlike qpopper, in which a user defined as using APOP cannot connect in any other way, UW POP3 will allow a user to connect using either the APOP method or the user/password method. This is especially good for users who connect to the mail server using different computers and different email client software packages.

Configuring UW IMAP

Much like the POP3 server software, the UW IMAP software uses the inetd program. This requires new lines in the inetd configuration files to specify the actions for the IMAP server. The first line required is in the /etc/services file:

```
imap            143/tcp       imap2 imap4        # Interim Mail Access Proto v2
```

Although the comment indicates that the service is for IMAP version 2, both IMAP version 2 and IMAP version 4 will be recognized. The UW IMAP program uses the IMAP version 4, revision 1 protocol.

The /etc/inetd.conf file should also be modified to contain the information necessary for the IMAP server. This is an example of what the configuration line should look like:

```
imap    stream  tcp    nowait  root    /usr/local/libexec/imapd  imapd
```

This example assumes that the imapd program is located in the /usr/local/libexec subdirectory. You must change this to the proper location on your UNIX system.

To activate the new inetd.conf settings, the currently running inetd daemon must be restarted. This can be accomplished by sending a SIGHUP signal to it. The following commands can be used to accomplish this:

```
[katie@shadrach katie]# ps ax | grep inetd
  327 ?        S      0:00 inetd
12600 pts/2    S      0:00 grep inetd
[katie@shadrach katie]# kill -HUP 327
[katie@shadrach katie]#
```

Once the inetd daemon is restarted, you can test the installation of the IMAP server by Telneting to the IMAP port—number 143. Listing 17.11 shows an example of this.

17

INSTALLING AND
CONFIGURING
POP3 AND IMAP

LISTING 17.11   A Sample IMAP Session

```
 1  [jessica@shadrach jessica]$ telnet localhost 143
 2  Trying 127.0.0.1...
 3  Connected to localhost.
 4  Escape character is '^]'.
 5  * OK localhost IMAP4rev1 v12.261 server ready
 6  a1 LOGIN jessica sharks
 7  a1 OK LOGIN completed
 8  a2 SELECT INBOX
 9  * 0 EXISTS
10  * 0 RECENT
11  * OK [UIDVALIDITY 940284862] UID validity status
12  * OK [UIDNEXT 2] Predicted next UID
13  * FLAGS (\Answered \Flagged \Deleted \Draft \Seen)
14  * OK [PERMANENTFLAGS (\* \Answered \Flagged \Deleted \Draft \Seen)]
➥Permanent flags
15  a2 OK [READ-WRITE] SELECT completed
16  a3 LOGOUT
17  * BYE shadrach.smallorg.org IMAP4rev1 server terminating connection
18  a3 OK LOGOUT completed
19  Connection closed by foreign host.
20  [jessica@shadrach jessica]$
```

Summary

As the mail server receives mail, the mail is placed in user mailboxes. It is up to the user to connect to the mail server using an MDA protocol to retrieve the mail messages. The two most popular MDA protocols in use are the Post Office Protocol (POP3) and the Interactive Mail Access Protocol (IMAP4rev1). There are several software packages that can be used in the UNIX environment that support either the POP3 or IMAP protocols. qmail includes the qmail-pop3d software package, which can be used as a POP3 server. Also, the Qualcomm corporation supports the qpopper program, which can use the POP3 protocol to connect remote mail users. The University of Washington developed the UW IMAP software package, which can support both IMAP and POP3 clients. All three software packages can be installed to work with a qmail mail server.

Configuring a PPP Server

IN THIS CHAPTER

After the qmail, POP3, and IMAP software packages are installed and configured, you will need some method to establish a TCP/IP connection with your customers. Whether you are an ISP needing a method to connect remote office mail servers to your qmail server or an office administrator needing to connect dial-in customers to your POP3 or IMAP server, somehow you must support dial-in TCP/IP access.

This is where the Point-to-Point Protocol (PPP) comes in. PPP allows a remote customer to establish a TCP/IP connection with the mail server through a modem. Once the PPP session is established, any type of TCP/IP packet can be transferred, whether it is an SMTP packet, a POP3 packet, or an IMAP packet. In this day of widespread ISP connectivity, PPP is an important piece of any mail server.

This chapter describes PPP and the software that can be used on a UNIX server to connect to a remote site using PPP.

The Point-to-Point Protocol

Many small organizations cannot afford direct connections to the Internet. Instead, they use a cheaper method. Most ISPs allow customers to connect via a modem. A dedicated modem can use an ISDN or DSL line to establish a full-time connection with the remote host. A dial-up modem can use a common analog telephone line as well as an ISDN line to transfer data between hosts by establishing a connection when necessary. Both techniques require a method to pass TCP/IP packets between the ISP host and the office host.

Also, most offices that support remote users must support a method for users to connect to the mail server to read mail messages. Most often the remote users are at home or in a hotel room miles away. If the office mail server is not on a dedicated Internet connection, a remote user cannot just dial into a local ISP and connect to his mailbox. He must have some method to dial into the mail server to read his mail messages efficiently.

In both scenarios, PPP can be used across a standard dial-up connection to establish a TCP/IP connection with the mail server. PPP allows a common network protocol such as IP or IPX to be transferred across a modem connection using a serial communication protocol, such as HDLC. Figure 18.1 demonstrates this principle.

What Is PPP?

A normal PPP session consists of four phases:

- Link establishment
- Authentication (optional)
- Protocol negotiation
- Link termination

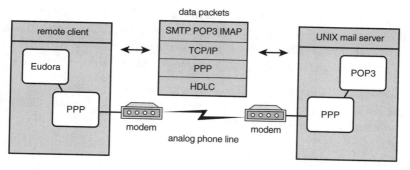

FIGURE 18.1
How PPP is used to transfer TCP/IP packets across a modem link.

PPP uses several different protocols during each of the four phases. At the core of PPP is a framing protocol that encapsulates the PPP frames for transmission across a serial modem link—the High-Level Data Link Control (HDLC) protocol.

Before any data can be sent across the line, the link between the two peer devices must be established. PPP employs a special protocol for negotiating the link—the Link Control Protocol (LCP). LCP's main purpose is to negotiate options that the two devices must use to successfully transfer packets between themselves. Items such as packet size must be determined before the two devices can transfer data successfully. Once the link is in established, the next phase can begin.

The authentication phase is officially listed in the RFC as optional, but in these days of network security it is often required to establish a PPP connection. PPP currently supports two different types of user ID authentication—the Challenge Handshake Authentication Protocol (CHAP) and the Password Authentication Protocol (PAP). CHAP is the more secure of the two protocols, but PAP is easier to implement and thus the more popular of the two. Once the remote host has successfully authenticated the connection, the next phase of the PPP cycle can begin.

The protocol negotiation phase of the PPP connection is what makes PPP unique among other serial network connections. Its predecessor, the Serial Line Internet Protocol (SLIP) supported only one protocol type (IP) to transmit across the serial line. PPP allows for virtually any network protocol to be transmitted across the modem connection, as long as both peer devices support the protocol.

After the connection is authenticated, the client PPP device must establish which protocols it wants to use over the connection. It is the PPP server's responsibility to refuse requests for protocols that it does not support. The Network Control Protocol (NCP) is used to allow the two devices to negotiate which protocols will be supported on the connection. During the

18

CONFIGURING A
PPP SERVER

protocol negotiation, the host and client can determine options for each individual protocol. For example, during an IP protocol negotiation, the host can supply the client's IP address and DNS server required for the client to properly talk on the host's network. After a protocol has been successfully negotiated, data packets can be transferred between the host and the client.

When the client wants to disconnect the PPP session, another LCP session is started to properly terminate the session. The host PPP server must recognize this request and drop the modem connection with the client.

PPP Protocol Frames

PPP can use modem connections to transfer network packets to another host that is connected to the Internet. A specific protocol is used to establish the connection between the modem on the office UNIX server and the modem on the ISP's host computer. A standard method of transferring frames across a serial connection is the High-Level Data Link Control (HDLC) protocol. This protocol can be used in several different modem environments using several different types of modems. PPP also has a specific frame format for transferring packet information to the host computer. This section discusses the HDLC and PPP frame specifications and how they are used to transfer the information between the client and host computer systems.

HDLC Frame

HDLC has been in use for many years in the mainframe computer environment. It has proven to be a stable method of transferring data between two devices connected with modems. RFC 1662 defines the method used to encapsulate PPP in an HLDC frame. Figure 18.2 shows the basic frame format for an HDLC frame.

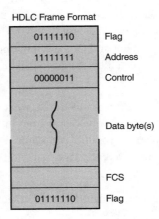

FIGURE 18.2
The HDLC frame format.

The HDLC frame format consists of five separate fields that encapsulate the PPP data sent on the modem line.

The Flag field is used to identify the start of an HDLC frame. It is defined as the binary value 01111110, or 0x7e in hex. The HDLC software should be able to detect this field and recognize it as the start of a new frame.

The Address field is always set to binary 11111111, or 0xff in hex. This is the broadcast address. Each station should recognize data sent to this address. Because there are only two devices in an HDLC "network," it is obvious that any data received with the broadcast address is intended for the device.

The HDLC Control field for PPP packets is always set to binary 00000011, or 0x03 in hex. The receiving device should discard frames with any other Control field values.

Because the Address and Control fields are always the same value, they are often omitted from the frame to conserve bandwidth. Thus, the first value after the Flag field could be the start of the PPP packet, or the Protocol field (see the following section, "PPP Frames"). Because of this situation, the PPP Protocol field does not use the values 0xff and 0x03, because the receiver could confuse the PPP Protocol field with the HDLC Address and Control fields. This method of omitting HDLC fields is called *frame compression*.

The Frame Check Sequence (FCS) field is used for error detection during the transmission. The FCS is calculated using the Address, Control, and Data fields of the HDLC packet. The Flag field and any start and stop bits or transparency bits inserted for various modem configurations are not included in this calculation.

The last Flag field identifies the end of the transmitted frame. If another frame follows, then the closing Flag field must be omitted. The single Flag field identifies both the end of one frame and the start of a new frame until it is the last Flag field received, indicating the end of the transmission.

It is possible that PPP data might have the same value as the HDLC Flag field and confuse the receiving device into thinking the frame has ended. To avoid this, a method called *frame transparency* is used. After the FCS computation, the sending device examines the fields between the two proper Flag fields and inserts a Ctrl+Escape octet (binary 01111101 or hex 0x7d) in front of any data value that matches the Flag value. It then performs an exclusive OR of the data value with the value 0x20 to make it not equal to the Flag value. Of course, if a data value is equal to the Ctrl+Escape data value, it also must be replaced by putting a Ctrl+Escape value inserted before it, and exclusive ORing the value with 0x20. When the receiving device sees the Ctrl+Escape octet, it should know that the next data value should be converted back to its original value.

It is possible for a PPP host to autodetect a PPP connection request from a remote modem by examining the first group of octets transmitted from the client. A PPP connection can be identified by one of these three octet groups:

```
7e ff 03 c0 21
7e ff 7d 23 c0 21
7e 7d df 7d 23 c0 21
```

The first example shows a standard HDLC frame (7e ff 03) with a standard PPP LCP protocol field (c0 21). The second and third examples show methods of frame transparency that create the same frames. When any one of these three frame sequences is received on the modem line, the PPP server can assume that the client is attempting to initiate a PPP connection and can act accordingly. mgetty+sendfax is a popular UNIX program that uses this technique to autodetect a PPP session on a standard dial-in modem line. If one of the three frame sequences is not received, it can assume that the data is not a PPP session. It then could be a user typing in his user ID for a normal terminal session across the modem connection or a fax connection being attempted on the modem. This allows the same modem line for terminal, fax, and PPP sessions to be shared without forcing an individual user to select a special phone number that supports his type of connection.

PPP Frames

The PPP frames are placed within the data fields of the HDLC frame. The basic PPP frame is shown in Figure 18.3.

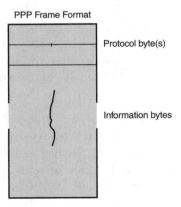

PPP Frame Format

Protocol byte(s)

Information bytes

FIGURE 18.3

The PPP protocol frame format.

The Protocol field identifies the protocol used in the Information fields and may be either one or two octets in length. Table 18.1 shows some of the currently supported Protocol field types in PPP.

TABLE 18.1   PPP Protocol Field Values

Value	Description
0001	Padding Protocol
0021	Internet Protocol
002b	Novell IPX
002d	Van Jacobson Compressed TCP/IP
x002f	Uncompressed TCP
8021	IP Control Protocol
802b	Novell IPX Control Protocol
c021	Link Control Protocol (LCP)
c023	Password Authentication Protocol (PAP)
c223	Challenge Handshake Authentication Protocol (CHAP)

The Information field is used to hold the data packets for the next layer protocol. Notice that there are no fields indicating the length of the PPP packet. It is the responsibility of the next layer protocol to provide this information to the remote device.

PPP Negotiation Phases

There are several protocols that must be established for the PPP connection to pass data across the serial line. Each of these protocols is identified as a different phase of the complete PPP protocol. The link establishment phase negotiates values for the low-level protocol used for PPP. Once the link has been established, the client can authenticate itself to the server using the PPP authentication phase. After authentication, each of the higher-level protocols that will be used on the link must be established in the network protocol establishment phase. The following sections describe these phases in more detail.

Link Establishment Phase

After an HDLC modem connection is made between the two peer devices, the initiating device must attempt to negotiate the parameters necessary for the link to transfer data between the devices. Much like a TCP connection, several connection states are used to identify the connectivity status of the devices. The Link Control Protocol (LCP) is used to accomplish this task. These connection states are shown in Figure 18.4 and described in the following sections.

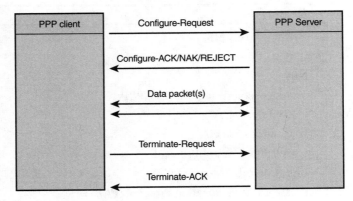

FIGURE 18.4

The LCP connection states.

LCP Protocol

The LCP protocol consists of formatted packets that transfer information between two peer devices to negotiate connection parameters. Figure 18.5 shows the basic format of an LCP packet.

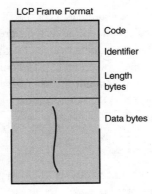

FIGURE 18.5

The Link Control Protocol packet format.

The Code LCP field is one byte in length and is used to identify the LCP packet type. LCP packets are mainly used for negotiating parameters of the link but can also change the current state of the link (such as link termination, described later). Eleven different LCP packet types are defined in RFC 1661 and shown in Table 8.2.

TABLE 8.2   Link Control Protocol Code Field Values

Code	Description
1	Configure-Request
2	Configure-Ack
3	Configure-Nak
4	Configure-Reject
5	Terminate-Request
6	Terminate-Ack
7	Code-Reject
8	Protocol-Reject
9	Echo-Request
10	Echo-Reply
11	Discard-Request

The Identifier field is used to uniquely identify the LCP packet so that the sending and receiving devices can match the proper reply to the proper request. It is one octet in length.

The Length field is two octets in length and is used to indicate the entire length of the LCP packet (including the Code, Identifier, Length, and Data fields). The total length of the LCP packet must not exceed the maximum receive unit (MRU) of the link.

The Data fields are multiple octets in length, as specified in the Length field, and contain data as specified by the Code field.

The Code field controls the purpose of the LCP packet. As shown in Table 8.2, there are many different types of LCP packets.

LCP Negotiated Options

During the Configure-Request phase of the link negotiation, the client PPP device can request parameter changes for the link. If an option is not included in the Configure-Request packet, the default value for it is assumed. Figure 18.6 shows the format of the LCP Option portion of the Configure-Request packet.

The Type field is used to identify the option being negotiated. Table 18.3 shows the available options.

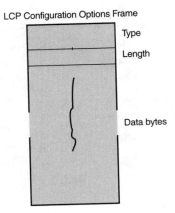

LCP Configuration Options Frame

Type

Length

Data bytes

FIGURE 18.6
The LCP Configure-Request Option fields.

TABLE 18.3   LCP Configure-Request Options

Type	Description
0	Reserved
1	Maximum Receive Unit
3	Authentication Protocol
4	Quality-Control
5	Magic-Number
7	Protocol Field Compression
8	Address and Control Field Compression

The Length field is one octet in length and indicates the length of the Option fields. This value includes the Type, Length, and Data fields.

PPP Authentication Phase

In an attempt to improve on a plain text user ID/password authentication system, two different authentication methods have been devised. PAP has been more popular in PPP implementations, but the CHAP method is more secure and is gaining in popularity. The PPP implementation for Linux supports both authentication methods.

The Challenge Handshake Authentication Protocol (CHAP)

The Challenge Handshake Authentication Protocol (CHAP) is used to implement a level of security in PPP authentication. CHAP uses a three-way handshake method to authenticate the client to the host. RFC 1994 describes the method used to implement the CHAP protocol. The basic CHAP packet format is shown in Figure 18.7.

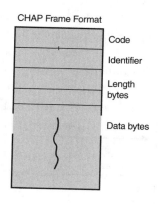

CHAP Frame Format

Code

Identifier

Length
bytes

Data bytes

FIGURE 18.7

The CHAP packet format.

18

The Code field is one octet in length and identifies the type of CHAP packet. Table 18.4 shows the possible values for this field.

TABLE 18.4   CHAP Code Field Values

Code	Description
1	Challenge
2	Response
3	Success
4	Failure

The Identifier field is one octet in length and identifies the CHAP packet to help the client and host match the reply and requests together.

The Length field is two octets in length and indicates the length of the CHAP packet. The Length value should include the octet count from the Code, Identifier, Length, and Data fields.

The Data fields can be zero or more octets in length and are used to support the functions identified by the Code value of the CHAP packet.

Figure 18.8 demonstrates the handshake protocol that CHAP uses to authenticate a client. The CHAP three-way handshake uses the following system:

- The host sends a Challenge CHAP packet based on a random value to the client.
- The client responds with a Response CHAP packet indicating a value calculated using the Challenge value and a secret word that are combined using a one-way hash function.
- The host checks the client's Response value with the value that it calculates itself for the Challenge value and secret word. If they match, the host sends a Success CHAP packet and the PPP session is continued. If not, the host sends a Failure CHAP packet and the PPP session is terminated with a Terminate-Request LCP packet.

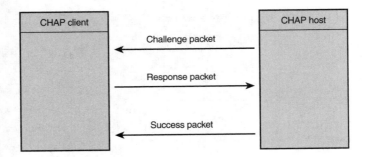

FIGURE 18.8
CHAP handshake phases.

Another feature of the CHAP protocol is that the PPP host can reissue a request for the client to authenticate at any time during the PPP session. This feature can be used to prevent session hijacking by another device.

Password Authentication Protocol (PAP)

The Password Authentication Protocol (PAP) is not as sophisticated as the CHAP protocol. It authenticates the user through a simple user ID/password mechanism. The user ID is sent as plain ASCII text. The password may be encrypted or not, depending on the capability of the client. After the client is authenticated, the PPP session is continued and is not reauthenticated for the duration of the session. If the client does not authenticate properly, the PPP session may be terminated by the PPP host or not.

The PAP authentication method is the easier of the two methods to implement, but it is the least secure. One reason why it has become so popular with ISPs is that, even though it does not have the highest level of security, security on a dial-up connection is not often a determining factor. Tapping a phone connection to intercept a PPP session is much more difficult than observing a password sent in text mode across an ethernet network. Thus, ease of configuration and use overrule level of security.

Network Protocol Establishment Phase

After the link layer has been established through the LCP negotiation phase, individual network layer sessions can be initiated. PPP allows for multiple network protocols to be transported across the connection simultaneously. To negotiate the network layer parameters, PPP uses the Network Connection Protocol (NCP) for each individual protocol that can be transmitted during the PPP session. For the UNIX mail server, only one protocol is necessary: IP. The NCP used to negotiate an IP connection in a PPP session is IP Control Protocol, or IPCP.

IP Control Protocol (IPCP)

To support an IP network across a PPP session, both PPP devices must support IP Control Protocol (IPCP), which is used to negotiate the IP connection parameters for both sides of the connection. The PPP Protocol field will have a value of 8021 when it contains an IPCP packet (as shown previously, in Table 18.1).

IPCP uses the same frame format as LCP (refer to Figure 18.4). The IPCP Code field also uses the same codes as the LCP packet, but it recognizes only codes 1 through 7 (refer to Table 18.2). The negotiation method is just like LCP negotiation. A Configure-Request packet is sent with any options that the client wants to negotiate with the host. The host can respond with a Configure-Ack if it agrees with the options or a Configure-Nak if it does not agree with any of the options.

IPCP Options

IPCP allows the two PPP devices to negotiate IP parameters before the IP connection is established. IPCP options are sent in the Configure-Request packet, similar to LCP. Table 18.5 shows the IPCP options listed in the RFC.

TABLE 18.5   IP Control Protocol Options

Option	Description
1	IP Addresses
2	IP Compression Protocol
3	Remote IP Address

Option 1 has been deprecated from the RFC and is no longer in use. Its purpose was to allow the PPP devices to negotiate the IP addresses used on the link. It was found through experimentation that it was often difficult for the devices to converge on a mutually agreeable set of IP addresses. Option 3 has been added to replace the functionality of this option.

Option 2 is used to negotiate a method of IP packet compression to conserve bandwidth on the PPP session. Currently, the Van Jacobson method of TCP/IP header compression is supported by PPP. This method allows the device to reduce the TCP/IP header to as few as three octets. The Configure-Request value for requesting IP compression is 002d.

Option 3 is used to negotiate an IP address for the client device. The option allows the client to specify a desired IP address. If the PPP host is unable to support that address for some reason, it can return an alternative address for the client to use in the Configure-Nak packet. The client and host can negotiate a proper IP address for the client to use. The default is no address.

After a successful IPCP negotiation, IP packets can be passed in the PPP session using one of three PPP Protocol field values: 0021 for normal uncompressed IP, 002b for compressed TCP/IP using Van Jacobson compression, or 002f for uncompressed TCP with compressed IP headers (also called *Van Jacobson uncompressed*).

Link Termination Phase

When the client wants to drop the PPP session, it can issue the Terminate-Request LCP packet (refer to the earlier discussion). When the PPP server sees a Terminate-Request LCP packet, it must reply with a Terminate-Ack LCP packet and drop the connection. This is not dependent on the current state of any IP connections active at the time the Terminate-Request command is issued. A client can terminate a PPP session with IP sessions still active. The PPP server cannot keep the PPP session active until the IP sessions are closed. After the PPP session is closed, the client must reissue the proper LCP connection request packets to restart a new session, even if the physical layer did not disconnect.

UNIX PPP Server Configuration

There are two software elements that are required for UNIX servers to support PPP connections. Figure 18.9 demonstrates them.

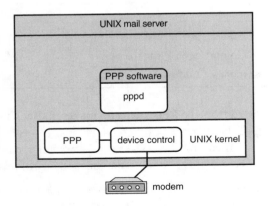

FIGURE 18.9
PPP support on UNIX systems.

The first element is in the UNIX kernel software. Because the PPP software uses modem connections, the kernel software is configured to support many of the low-level device control protocols to increase PPP performance.

The second element is an application program. The pppd program, developed by Al Longyear, Paul Mackerras, and Michael Callahan, provides this piece for most UNIX systems. The pppd program can establish a PPP session with a remote client using a modem device and transfer IP packets between the remote client and the UNIX host.

This section describes the pppd program, how to install it, and how to configure it on a UNIX server.

Installing the pppd Program

Most UNIX distributions include a binary distribution of the pppd program. Both Linux and FreeBSD include binary packages that install the pppd program and its configuration files. On FreeBSD systems, pppd is installed as a default application. On most Linux systems, it must be installed as a separate package.

If you want the latest version of the pppd program, you can download it from the pppd FTP site at `ftp://cs.anu.edu.au/pub/software/ppp`. At the time of this writing, the latest version of pppd software available is version 2.3.11. The source code download file is called `pppd-2.3.11.tar.gz`.

> **CAUTION**
>
> If your UNIX distribution includes a binary distribution of the pppd program, I strongly recommend you use it. The pppd software is very tightly coupled with the PPP software in the UNIX kernel. If your UNIX distribution already has PPP support compiled into the kernel, use it. If it doesn't, then you have no choice but to bite the bullet and install it manually.

If you downloaded the source code from the pppd FTP site, you must untar the distribution package to a working directory:

```
tar -zxvf pppd-2.3.11.tar.gz -C /usr/local/src
```

After it is untarred, install it with the following steps:

1. Run the `./configure` program from the `ppp-2.3.11` directory. This configures the Makefile to your specific UNIX distribution.

2. Run the GNU make program with the `kernel` option (`make kernel`). This creates the `include` files for your version of UNIX with the new kernel pieces for `pppd`.

3. Recompile and install your new kernel with the new pppd support (refer to your UNIX distribution documentation for specific details on how to do this).

4. Run the GNU make program to compile the pppd program.

5. As the root user, run the GNU make program with the install option (make install) to place the new executables in their proper places.

After you have installed pppd, either by your UNIX distribution's binary distribution file or by compiling the source code, you can configure pppd to work as a PPP server.

> **CAUTION**
>
> Recompiling and installing a new UNIX kernel is not for the beginner. If you have any doubts, refer to your UNIX distribution's documentation on recompiling the kernel, or obtain a precompiled kernel with PPP support. A miscompiled kernel can render your UNIX server unbootable.

Configuring the pppd Program

Once a modem connection has been established and the remote user has logged into the UNIX system, he can use the pppd program to start the PPP session. To use pppd in server mode, you must supply some options that help it connect to the PPP client and establish the PPP session properly. The basic format for the pppd command is

```
pppd tty line speed [options]
```

where *tty line* is the serial port device to which your modem is connected and *speed* is the speed at which you want to connect to the modem. The art of using the pppd program comes in choosing the proper options for the server commands.

The passive and silent options are used to allow the pppd program to wait for an LCP Configure-Request packet to initiate the PPP session. The proxyarp option is used to allow the PPP host computer to respond to ARP requests on the local network on behalf of the PPP client. This allows other computers on the network to connect to the remote PPP client.

> **CAUTION**
>
> The proxyarp option allows other computers to connect to the PPP client. When you establish a PPP connection to the ISP, your UNIX server becomes a network device on your ISP's network and is susceptible to the same network hacks as any other device directly connected to the network. It is strongly recommended to use firewall

software to control access to the UNIX server by external clients. Extreme care should be taken if no firewall software is being used on the PPP connection. Please watch the system logs for invalid access attempts.

The `lock` option creates a UUCP lock file for the modem used in the PPP session. This prevents other communications programs from attempting to use the modem while pppd is running.

The `auth` option can be used to require the client to authenticate itself within the PPP session. If the client runs the pppd program from an interactive session, it probably does not need internal PPP authentication.

The `login` option is used to allow pppd to verify the requested authentication username from the system `/etc/passwd` table.

The `chap` and `pap` options are used to configure pppd to use either CHAP or PAP authentication for the username.

The `Local_IP:Remote_IP` option allows pppd to assign IP addresses to remote devices. The `Local_IP` address is that of the PPP host, and the `Remote_IP` address is the address that will be assigned to the remote PPP client.

A sample pppd command line run by a remote client would look like this:

```
pppd ttyS1 38800 lock proxyarp silent 192.168.1.1:192.168.1.100
```

If this line looks like a lot of keyboard entry from remote users, it is. To make life easier for remote clients, instead of using command-line options for pppd, you can place options in configuration files. By default, pppd will check the `/etc/ppp/options` file for a list of options to use. All of the options used in the example pppd script could be placed in the `/etc/ppp/options` file, one per line. Then, when the remote user connects, he can just enter the `pppd` command.

Another handy feature is that the pppd program also checks another options file, depending on the tty line that it is initialized from. This enables you to specify specific options for each tty line, such as the remote IP address. If you have three modems on tty lines `ttyS0`, `ttyS1`, and `ttyS2`, you can have three separate pppd options files: `/etc/ppp/options.ttyS0`, `/etc/ppp/options.ttyS1`, and `/etc/ppp/options.ttyS2`. Each option file will have a different `Local_IP:Remote_IP` pair specified. That way, multiple PPP clients will not accidentally have duplicate IP addresses assigned to them.

Using the pppd Program

For a client to establish a PPP session with the server requires five steps:

1. The client connects to the server using the modem.
2. The server issues a standard login prompt.
3. The client logs into the server using a standard system username and password.
4. The client starts the pppd program on the server from the command prompt.
5. The client initiates the PPP software on the client host.

After the client initiates the PPP software on the client host, both the client and server should be able to communicate using PPP.

If this seems to be a complicated process, it is. The remote client must manually log into the PPP server and issue the pppd command. Even with pppd option files, this is a hassle. Alternatively, the mail administrator can create a profile script that starts the pppd program automatically when the client logs in. Some administrators create separate user IDs for PPP accounts. This is better, but it still requires that the client manually log into the system.

Many PPP client software packages such as Windows 98 Dial-Up Networking (described in Chapter 19, "Supporting Dial-In Clients") support automatic CHAP or PAP authentication on the PPP connection. For the UNIX PPP server to support these client features, it must be able to detect the PPP connection attempt and authenticate the CHAP or PAP session. The next section describes an easy way that this can be done.

The mgetty+sendfax Program

The mgetty+sendfax program was developed by Gert Doering to be a multifunctional device control program. It is multifunctional in that it can detect different types of connections on a terminal line and automatically start the appropriate software. The types of connections that it can detect are

- Fax connections
- PPP connections
- UUCP connections
- Text connections

By setting parameters in the mgetty+sendfax configuration file or on the command line, you can control the type of connections that the mail server will accept and what software the connection is passed to for handling. This allows the administrator to configure dial-in lines to automatically detect incoming PPP connections and pass them directly to the pppd program for authentication. The following sections describe how to install and use the mgetty+sendfax software.

Installing the mgetty+sendfax Program

Many UNIX distributions include a binary distribution of the mgetty+sendfax program. The FreeBSD distribution version 3.4 includes mgetty+sendfax version 1.1.21 as a port that can be compiled and installed using the normal FreeBSD port method.

If you do not have a copy of mgetty+sendfax, you can connect to the mgetty+sendfax Web site at `http://alpha.greenie.net/mgetty/` and download the source code distribution. At the time of this writing, the current release version is 1.0.0 (version 1.1.21, distributed with FreeBSD, is a beta version). You can download the source code from `ftp://alpha.greenie.net/pub/mgetty/source/1.0/mgetty+sendfax-1.0.0.tar.gz`.

After the source code is downloaded, you can extract it to a working directory with the normal method:

```
tar -zxvf mgetty+sendfax-1.0.0.tar.gz -C /usr/local/src
```

After the source code is extracted, you can compile and install the executables with the following steps:

1. Change directory to the newly created `mgetty-1.0.0` directory.
2. Edit the `policy.h-dist` file to match your desired environment, and copy it to `policy.h`.
3. Run the GNU make utility.
4. Run the GNU make utility with the parameter `testdisk`.
5. Run `make install` to place the binary executables in their proper locations.

After compiling and installing mgetty+sendfax, you can use it in the `/etc/inittab` file as a controlling process for the modem line. The mgetty program is used to control the modem connection. The format of the `mgetty` command is

```
mgetty [options] ttydevice
```

where `options` are mgetty options that control the behavior of the modem line and `ttydevice` is the Linux tty line that mgetty will monitor. Table 18.6 shows the options available for mgetty.

18

CONFIGURING A
PPP SERVER

TABLE 18.6   mgetty Command-Line Options

Option	Description
-x *level*	Sets debugging level to *level*
-s *speed*	Sets line speed to *speed*
-a	Tries to autodetect the modem connection speed
-k *space*	Sets number of kilobytes required in the incoming fax spool directory to *space*
-m 'EXPECT SEND'	Sets a modem initialization chat script
-r	Indicates a direct line
-p LOGIN_PROMPT	Sets the login prompt for the modem line
-n RINGS	Sets the number of rings before mgetty will answer the modem
-D	Locks modem to data mode
-F	Locks modem to fax mode
-R SEC	Enables ring-back mode—callers must call twice
-i 'issue'	Specifies an issue file to display on a connection
-S 'FAX DOC'	Specifies a default fax document to send to polling fax machines

A sample /etc/inittab line using mgetty will look like this:

```
s1:12345:respawn:/sbin/mgetty -D -s 38400 -n 4 ttyS0
```

The sample line shows the mgetty program being used for a data connection on line /dev/ttyS0. It is set to a constant baud rate of 38400, and it is set to answer after the fourth ring.

One word of caution: mgetty listens for the RINGS value when the phone rings and then picks up the line. Whereas with uugetty the modem might still answer the line even if the process hangs, if mgetty hangs, it will not answer the phone. Oddly, if your modem has an autoanswer LED on it, it won't be lit, but that is a feature of mgetty, not a problem.

To configure mgetty to autodetect a PPP connection requires settings in the mgetty configuration file as well as a new file to control PPP access. The following section describes the steps necessary to configure mgetty to autodetect PPP connections.

Configuring mgetty for PPP Support

Enabling automatic PPP connections from Windows clients starts with the mgetty configuration file. The default location for the configuration file is /etc/mgetty+sendfax/ login.config. For FreeBSD systems it is located in the /usr/local/etc/mgetty+sendfax directory. If you build the mgetty executable yourself from the source code, you can change this location.

The login.config file tells mgetty how to handle the different types of connection attempts that it detects. Listing 18.1 shows a sample login.config file.

LISTING 18.1   A Sample login.config File

```
1   # login.config
2   #
3   # This is a sample "login dispatcher" configuration file for mgetty
4   #
5   # Format:
6   #       username userid utmp_entry login_program [arguments]
7   #
8   # Meaning:
9   #       for a "username" entered at mgettys login: prompt, call
10  #       "login_program" with [arguments], with the uid set to "userid",
11  #       and a USER_PROCESS utmp entry with ut_user = "utmp_entry"
12  #
13  # username may be prefixed / suffixed by "*" (wildcard)
14  #
15  # userid is a valid username from /etc/passwd, or "-" to not set
16  #  a login user id and keep the uid/euid root (needed for /bin/login)
17  #
18  # utmp_entry is what will appear in the "who" listing. Use "-" to not
19  #  set an utmp entry (a must for /bin/login), use "@" to set it to the
20  #  username entered. Maximum length is 8 characters.
21  #
22  # login_program is the program that will be exec()ed, with the arguments
23  #  passed in [arguments]. A "@" in the arguments will be replaced with the
24  #  username entered. Warning: if no "@" is given, the login_program has
25  #  no way to know what username the user entered.
26  #
27  #
28  # SAMPLES:
29  # Use this one with my Taylor-UUCP and Taylor-UUCP passwd files.
30  #  (Big advantage: tuucp can use the same passwd file for serial dial-in
31  #   and tcp dial-in [uucico running as in.uucpd]). Works from 1.05 up.
32  #
33  #U*    uucp    @       /usr/lib/uucp/uucico -l -u @
34
35  #
36  # Use this one for fido calls (login name /FIDO/ is handled specially)
37  #
38  # You need Eugene Crosser's "ifmail" package for this to work.
39  #  mgetty has to be compiled with "-DFIDO", otherwise a fido call won't
40  #  be detected.
41  #
```

LISTING **18.1**   Continued

```
42 /FIDO/   uucp     fido    /usr/local/lib/fnet/ifcico @
43
44 #
45 # Automatic PPP startup on receipt of LCP configure request (AutoPPP).
46 #  mgetty has to be compiled with "-DAUTO_PPP" for this to work.
47 #  Warning: Case is significant, AUTOPPP or autoppp won't work!
48 #  Consult the "pppd" man page to find pppd options that work for you.
49 #
50 #  NOTE: for *some* users, the "-detach" option has been necessary, for
51 #        others, not at all. If your pppd doesn't die after hangup, try it.
52 #
53 #  NOTE2: "kdebug 7 debug" creates lots of debugging info. If all works,
54 #         remove those!
55 #
56 /AutoPPP/  -   ppp   /usr/sbin/pppd auth -chap +pap login modem crtscts lock
➥ proxyarp
57
58 #
59 #
60 # An example where no login name in the argument list is desired:
61 #  automatically telnetting to machine "smarty" for a given login name
62 #
63 #telnet-smarty  gast    telnet  /usr/bin/telnet -8 smarty
64 #
65 # This is the "standard" behavior - *dont* set a userid or utmp
66 #  entry here, otherwise /bin/login will fail!
67 #  This entry isn't really necessary: if it's missing, the built-in
68 #  default will do exactly this.
69 #
70 *          -          -           /bin/login @
```

Line 56 shows the entry that is required for mgetty to autodetect a PPP connection. The configuration file is case sensitive, so make sure that the /AutoPPP/ header is entered exactly as shown or mgetty will not recognize it. The line also includes the pppd command exactly as it would be entered if using pppd from the command prompt. If you already have entered pppd command-line parameters in a pppd configuration file, you do not need to enter them here.

Line 70 is important. It instructs mgetty on what to do if it does not autodetect a special signal such as a fax or PPP connection. In this case it assumes that it must be a normal terminal connection and passes it to the login program to produce the standard login prompt.

The next step needed to enable automatic PPP connections is a method to authenticate user IDs and passwords automatically. You might notice that one of the parameters used in the pppd command line in line 56 is +pap. This instructs mgetty to use pppd's PAP authentication method when initializing the PPP connection.

For pppd to use PAP authentication, there needs to be a password file that contains user IDs and passwords of users who will dial into the Linux mailserver. The default location of the file is /etc/ppp/pap-secrets. Listing 18.2 shows a sample pap-secrets file.

LISTING 18.2 A Sample /etc/ppp/pap-secrets File

```
1  # Secrets for authentication using PAP
2  # client        server   secret      IP addresses
3  rich            *        guitar      192.168.1.100
4  barbara         *        aslsign     192.168.1.100
5  katie           *        boxcar      192.168.1.100
6  jessica         *        clifford    192.168.1.100
```

Each line in the pap-secrets file represents information for a separate user. The format of the pap-secrets file is

```
client    server    secret    address
```

where client is the username that the user is assigned, server is the server that this entry applies to, secret is the password entered into the Microsoft dial-in software, and address is the local IP address that the user can use. In Listing 18.2, an asterisk (*) is used to enable the client username to be used on any server the user connects to. This feature is generally used if the client dials out to several different servers and needs a different secret word for each server. The IP address field can also be left blank if you do not know what IP address will be assigned to the user, such as if there are multiple dial-in lines.

The mgetty Log Files

After configuring the mgetty and pppd software, you can test it out by connecting with a Microsoft Windows 95, 98, or NT 4.0 workstation (see Chapter 19). When a client connects or attempts to connect, mgetty produces an entry in a log file. On most UNIX distributions, the log file is located in /var/log/mgetty.log.ttyxx, where xx is the tty line that the mgetty process is monitoring. FreeBSD uses the mgetty.log.cuaax file, where x is the cuaa line number. Listing 18.3 shows a sample mgetty log file.

LISTING 18.3 A Sample /var/log/mgetty.log.ttyS0 File

```
1  11/07 07:16:13 yS0   mgetty: experimental test release 1.1.14-Apr02
2  11/07 07:16:13 yS0   check for lockfiles
3  11/07 07:16:13 yS0   locking the line
4  11/07 07:16:14 yS0   lowering DTR to reset Modem
```

LISTING 18.3   A Sample /var/log/mgetty.log.ttyS0 File

```
5  11/07 07:16:14 yS0   send: \dATQ0V1H0[0d]
6  11/07 07:16:15 yS0   waiting for ``OK'' ** found **
7  11/07 07:16:15 yS0   send: ATS0=0Q0&D3&C1[0d]
8  11/07 07:16:15 yS0   waiting for ``OK'' ** found **
9  11/07 07:16:16 yS0   waiting...
10 11/07 07:16:16 yS0   checking if modem is still alive
11 11/07 07:16:16 yS0   mdm_send: 'AT' -> OK
12 11/07 07:16:16 yS0   waiting...
13 11/08 07:16:27 yS0   checking if modem is still alive
14 11/08 07:16:27 yS0   mdm_send: 'AT' -> OK
15 11/08 07:16:28 yS0   waiting...
16
17 11/08 07:44:10 yS0   waiting for ``RING'' ** found **
18 11/08 07:44:10 yS0   waiting for ``RING'' ** found **
19 11/08 07:44:16 yS0   waiting for ``RING'' ** found **
20 11/08 07:44:22 yS0   waiting for ``RING'' ** found **
21 11/08 07:44:46 yS0   send: ATA[0d]
22 11/08 07:44:46 yS0   waiting for ``CONNECT'' ** found **
23 11/08 07:44:59 yS0   send:
24 11/08 07:44:59 yS0   waiting for ``_'' ** found **
25 11/08 07:45:02 ##### data dev=ttyS0, pid=10089, caller='none',
➥ conn='38400/ARQ/26400 LAP-M', name='', cmd='/usr/sbin/pppd',
➥ user='/AutoPPP/'
```

Lines 1–12 show the log entries generated by starting mgetty. The date, time, and device name are all logged on the lines. Lines 13–15 show the periodic checks that mgetty makes to ensure that the modem is still operating properly. Mgetty continues checking the line until a connection is made. In line 17, the first sign of activity appears. Mgetty detects the first RING string from the phone line. This particular mgetty is set in the command-line parameters to answer after the fourth ring (one method used to fool hackers looking for a modem to answer on the first ring). As shown in line 21, after mgetty receives the fourth ring, it issues the ATA command to instruct the modem to pick up the line and then waits for a CONNECT string from the modem. Lines 25 and 26 show the result of the connection: Mgetty detected a PPP signal and started the pppd program.

After viewing the mgetty log and determining that a PPP connection was detected, you can then look at the pppd program log to determine if pppd was able to establish a connection. In both the Linux and FreeBSD distributions, the pppd program sends its event logs to the /var/log/messages file. Listing 18.4 shows sample entries from the pppd program after mgetty has established the modem connection.

LISTING 18.4 Sample pppd Log Entries in /var/log/messages

```
1  Nov  8 07:45:02 shadrach mgetty[10089]: data dev=ttyS0, pid=10089,
➥ caller='none'
2  , conn='38400/ARQ/26400 LAP-M', name='', cmd='/usr/sbin/pppd',
➥ user='/AutoPPP/'
3  Nov  8 07:45:04 shadrach kernel: CSLIP: code copyright 1989 Regents
➥ of the University of California
4  Nov  8 07:45:04 shadrach kernel: PPP: version 2.2.0 (dynamic channel
➥ allocation)
5  Nov  8 07:45:04 shadrach kernel: PPP Dynamic channel allocation code
➥ copyright 1995 Caldera, Inc.
6  Nov  8 07:45:04 shadrach kernel: PPP line discipline registered.
7  Nov  8 07:45:04 shadrach kernel: registered device ppp0
8  Nov  8 07:45:04 shadrach pppd[10089]: pppd 2.3.5 started by ppp, uid 0
9  Nov  8 07:45:04 shadrach pppd[10089]: Using interface ppp0
10 Nov  8 07:45:04 shadrach pppd[10089]: Connect: ppp0 <--> /dev/ttyS0
11 Nov  8 07:45:06 shadrach PAM_pwdb[10089]: (ppp) session opened for
➥ user rich by (uid=0)
12 Nov  8 07:45:06 shadrach pppd[10089]: user rich logged in
13 Nov  8 07:45:07 shadrach pppd[10089]: found interface eth0 for proxy arp
14 Nov  8 07:45:07 shadrach pppd[10089]: local  IP address 192.168.1.1
15 Nov  8 07:45:07 shadrach pppd[10089]: remote IP address 192.168.1.100
16 Nov  8 07:45:10 shadrach pppd[10089]: CCP terminated by peer
17 Nov  8 07:45:10 shadrach pppd[10089]: Compression disabled by peer.
18 Nov  8 07:51:19 shadrach pppd[10089]: LCP terminated by peer
19 Nov  8 07:51:22 shadrach pppd[10089]: Hangup (SIGHUP)
20 Nov  8 07:51:22 shadrach pppd[10089]: Modem hangup
21 Nov  8 07:51:22 shadrach PAM_pwdb[10089]: (ppp) session closed for
➥ user shadrach.smallorg.org
22 Nov  8 07:51:22 shadrach pppd[10089]: Connection terminated.
23 Nov  8 07:51:23 shadrach pppd[10089]: Exit.
24 Nov  8 07:53:03 shadrach kernel: PPP: ppp line discipline successfully
➥ unregistered
```

Line 1 shows the mgetty log entry indicating that a PPP session was detected. Lines 3–7 indicate that the UNIX kernel loaded the PPP kernel support software dynamically when the PPP connection was detected. Lines 8–17 show the pppd program starting and attempting to run through the configured command-line parameters. Line 12 shows that the remote user ID was detected and that the authentication method was successful. Line 13 indicates that the prox-yarp command-line parameter was used and that now the remote client has access to the local network via the eth0 network device on the UNIX mail server. In lines 14 and 15, the pppd program assigns an IP address of 192.168.1.100 to the remote client. After the PPP session has ended, line 18 indicates that the remote client has initiated a disconnect signal on the PPP Link Control Protocol, and lines 19–23 show the pppd program terminating the PPP session. In line 24, the UNIX kernel unregisters the PPP kernel support.

Summary

The Point-to-Point Protocol (PPP) plays an important role for mail servers. It allows remote mail servers to connect via modems to transfer mail and allows remote clients to connect via modems to read mail messages in their inboxes. PPP is used to encapsulate TCP/IP packets in the modem connection. Once the TCP/IP packet is transferred between systems, any third-layer protocol, such as SMTP, POP3, and IMAP, can be used across the connection.

Most UNIX servers use the pppd program to support PPP connections. The pppd program has several command-line parameters that can be used to customize the PPP connection, such as automatic authentication support, assigning an IP address to the remote client, and locking the modem so no other application attempts to use it. The pppd command-line parameters can also be placed in either a common configuration file or one that is specific to the different modem lines on the UNIX system. This allows the mail administrator to preconfigure pppd so that remote clients do not have to worry about running the proper command-line parameters when they use the program.

Most UNIX systems also support the mgetty+sendfax program, which has the capability of autodetecting an incoming PPP session without the remote client having to log in on a terminal session. This allows remote Microsoft Windows clients to establish PPP connections automatically without any manual intervention.

Both the pppd and mgetty programs can produce detailed log files to enable the mail administrator to monitor the dial-in activity on the UNIX server.

Supporting Dial-In Clients

IN THIS CHAPTER

Unless you are extremely fortunate, most likely at some point you will have to support dial-in clients. Many organizations allow employees to connect to the email system from a location outside the office, such as a remote office, home, or a hotel room. Once connected, the remote user can use standard POP3 or IMAP client software to read messages in his mailbox just as if he were on the LAN in the office.

Supporting dial-in clients requires that the UNIX server be configured to handle modems. This chapter first describes how modems are used on a UNIX system and how to configure the UNIX system to communicate with a remote client using modems. Next, several different dial-in clients are discussed. Finally, an example of a client MUA program is discussed that can allow a remote client to read his mailbox on the qmail server.

Configuring Dial-In Modems

Before the UNIX server can receive dial-in connections, it must recognize and communicate with any modem connected to it. UNIX deals with modems differently than Microsoft Windows operating systems do. This section describes how UNIX systems communicate with modems.

Using Modems in UNIX

Most network administrators are familiar with the way Microsoft MS-DOS and Windows operating systems interact with serial ports on IBM-compatible computers. The IBM-compatible architecture supports serial devices as COM ports. The ports are numbered 1 through 4, each port having a separate IRQ and I/O address pair.

UNIX systems running on an IBM-compatible computer recognize the same COM ports but do not use the same naming convention. In Linux they are called tty devices. Specifically, they are located at /dev/ttySx, where x is the number of the communication port. FreeBSD systems call them cuaa devices, which are also located in the /dev directory. As with the tty devices, cuaa devices are numbered sequentially.

Unfortunately, UNIX uses a different numbering scheme than Microsoft. UNIX starts numbering serial ports at port 0, not port 1. Table 19.1 shows how the Linux and FreeBSD serial ports match MS-DOS serial ports.

TABLE 19.1   Linux Serial Ports

MS-DOS	Linux	FreeBSD	IRQ	I/O Address
COM1	ttyS0	cuaa0	4	0x3f8
COM2	ttyS1	cuaa1	3	0x2f8

MS-DOS	Linux	FreeBSD	IRQ	I/O Address
COM3	ttyS2	cuaa2	4	0x3e8
COM4	ttyS3	cuaa3	3	0x2e8

NOTE

UNIX systems can also support multiport serial devices. These devices contain multiple serial ports that may share a single IRQ. They use special software drivers to differentiate between ports. In this situation, UNIX continues the naming convention sequentially, using the same device names (either ttyS or cuaa) and continues for however many ports are available. Often these devices require special drivers installed in the UNIX kernel.

While FreeBSD automatically assigns existing COM ports to cuaa devices when it is installed, Linux does things a little bit differently. Listing 19.1 shows the ttySx devices for a standard Mandrake Linux system on an IBM-compatible PC with two COM ports and an internal modem using COM4.

LISTING 19.1   /dev/ttySx Device Listing

```
1  [alex@shadrach /dev]$ ls -al ttyS*
2  crw-------  1 root     tty        4,  64 Nov 29 16:09 ttyS0
3  crw-------  1 root     tty        4,  65 May  5  1998 ttyS1
4  crw-------  1 root     tty        4,  66 May  5  1998 ttyS2
5  crw-------  1 root     tty        4,  67 May  5  1998 ttyS3
6  [alex@shadrach /dev]$
```

In Listing 19.1, it can be seen that, although there are only three COM ports used in the PC, by default the Linux system creates entries for all of the four basic COM ports. Attempting to use the non-existent device ttyS2 would produce an error.

Linux also supports a mirror set of devices named /dev/cuax for each /dev/ttySx device. The purpose of the cua devices is to simplify the programming that is required to control the devices. The cua devices allow programs to connect to the device without a DCD signal being present. The DCD signal is provided by the modem to indicate that a connection is present. This feature is used mainly for dial-out software, because no connection will be present when dialing out. Thus, the Linux convention was started to use cua for dial-out programs and ttyS for dial-in programs.

19

SUPPORTING
DIAL-IN CLIENTS

> **NOTE**
>
> When using both dial-in and dial-out programs, modem locking becomes a problem. It is easier to write the controlling software for the ttyS type of devices rather than try to maintain code for two different types of device names for the same device. Although the cua devices are present, many software programs now produce a warning message when cua device names are used, indicating that the cua devices may not be used in future releases of Linux.

Another special device that may be present is the /dev/modem device. This is a symbolic link to the cua device that the modem is connected to. It was intended to simplify programs that needed to communicate with the modem by creating a standard device to communicate with. Many UNIX distributions create this link when the operating system is first installed as part of the setup program. In some Linux distributions, if you install a modem later, you can use the modemtool X Windows program to create the /dev/modem link. Figure 19.1 shows the modemtool program window.

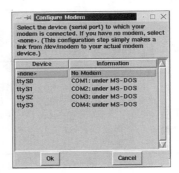

FIGURE 19.1
The modemtool utility.

Controlling FreeBSD Serial Ports

FreeBSD serial port configurations are stored in the system kernel. To change a configuration for a serial port, the system administrator must add the new configuration values directly to the kernel. These values must be added every time the system is rebooted. This can be accomplished using the comcontrol program. The following sections describe the FreeBSD serial port configuration and how to add, delete, and change serial port information.

Setting Modem Port Parameters in FreeBSD

The `sio` device driver controls modem ports on a FreeBSD system. Each modem port is configured in the kernel using the `device` command:

```
device sio0 at isa? port "IO_COM1" tty irq 4
device sio1 at isa? port "IO_COM2" tty irq 3
device sio2 at isa? port "IO_COM3" tty irq 5
device sio3 at isa? port "IO_COM4" tty irq 9
```

Once the serial port devices have been configured in the kernel you can change serial port parameters using the comcontrol program. The format of the `comcontrol` command is

```
comcontrol sio_device [options]
```

where `sio_device` is the device name of the modem port. There are two options that can be controlled by the comcontrol program:

- `dtrwait` *number*, which sets the time to wait after dropping DTR to *number* in hundredths of a second. The default value is 300.
- `drainwait` *number*, which sets the time to wait for output drain to *number* in seconds. The default value is 0, which means to wait forever.

The FreeBSD `ttys` File

On FreeBSD systems, the `/etc/ttys` file controls which devices allow logins. For the modem port to accept login requests, it must be configured in the `/etc/ttys` file. A sample `ttys` file is shown in Listing 19.2.

LISTING 19.2 Partial `/etc/ttys` File

```
console none                                unknown off secure
#
ttyv0   "/usr/libexec/getty Pc"             cons25  on   secure
# Virtual terminals
ttyv1   "/usr/libexec/getty Pc"             cons25  on   secure
ttyv2   "/usr/libexec/getty Pc"             cons25  on   secure
ttyv3   "/usr/libexec/getty Pc"             cons25  on   secure
ttyv4   "/usr/libexec/getty Pc"             cons25  on   secure
ttyv5   "/usr/libexec/getty Pc"             cons25  on   secure
ttyv6   "/usr/libexec/getty Pc"             cons25  on   secure
ttyv7   "/usr/libexec/getty Pc"             cons25  on   secure
ttyv8   "/usr/X11R6/bin/xdm -nodaemon"      xterm   off  secure
# Serial terminals
# The 'dialup' keyword identifies dialin lines to login, fingerd etc.
ttyd0   "/usr/libexec/getty std.9600"       dialup  off  secure
ttyd1   "/usr/libexec/getty std.9600"       dialup  off  secure
```

LISTING 19.2   Continued

```
ttyd2    "/usr/libexec/getty std.9600"    dialup   off secure
ttyd3    "/usr/libexec/getty std.9600"    dialup   off secure
cuaa1    "/usr/local/sbin/mgetty -D -n 7"          unknown on insecure
# Pseudo terminals
ttyp0    none                    network
ttyp1    none                    network
ttyp2    none                    network
```

The format of an entry in the `ttys` table is

```
trminal program type status allow
```

The `terminal` field identifies the device name that is associated with the terminal in `/dev` directory. The `program` field indicates the program that the connection will be passed to. The `type` field defines the type of terminal that is defined in the `/etc/termcap` file. This is used to control screen-painting functions on the terminal.

The `status` field is used to control whether the terminal is active (`on`) or inactive (`off`). This allows the system administrator to inactivate a terminal without having to delete its entry in the `ttys` file. The `allow` field can be set to either allow (`secure`) the root user to login or not allow (`insecure`) the root user to login.

Once the `ttys` file is configured you can use the UNIX `init` command with the q option.

```
init q
```

This instructs the init program to re-read the `ttys` file and reinitialize the terminal ports.

The sample `ttys` file shown in Listing 19.2 allows logins to the `cuaa1` serial port (COM2). The program that any connection will be passed to is the mgetty program. This program was discussed in Chapter 18, "Configuring a PPP Server." It is often used to autodetect an incoming PPP connection and start the pppd program.

The FreeBSD `rc.serial` Script

Once the `ttys` file has been configured, you must ensure that the modem ports are initialized every time the FreeBSD system boots. To do this, you must have a startup script.

The default location of the master startup script on a FreeBSD system is the `/etc/rc` file. This file is run every time the server is booted. The serial port configurations are kept in the `rc.serial` file, also in the `/etc` directory. The `rc` script file calls the `rc.serial` script to initialize serial ports. Listing 19.3 shows a partial `rc.serial` script file.

LISTING 19.3 Partial /etc/rc.serial File

```sh
#!/bin/sh
# $FreeBSD: src/etc/rc.serial,v 1.11.2.1 1999/08/29 14:18:58 peter Exp $

# Change some defaults for serial devices.
# Standard defaults are:
#       dtrwait 300 drainwait 0
#       initial cflag from <sys/ttydefaults.h> = cread cs8 hupcl
#       initial iflag, lflag and oflag all 0
#       speed 9600
#       special chars from <sys/ttydefaults.h>
#       nothing locked
# except for serial consoles the initial iflag, lflag and oflag are from
# <sys/ttydefaults.h> and clocal is locked on.

default() {
        # Reset everything changed by the other functions to initial defaults.

        ci=$1; shift    # call in device identifier
        co=$1; shift    # call out device identifier

        for i in $*
        do
                comcontrol /dev/tty$ci$i dtrwait 300 drainwait 0
                stty </dev/ttyi$ci$i -clocal  crtscts  hupcl 9600 reprint ^R
                stty </dev/ttyi$ci$i -clocal -crtscts -hupcl 0
                stty </dev/cuai$co$i -clocal  crtscts  hupcl 9600 reprint ^R
                stty </dev/cual$co$i -clocal -crtscts -hupcl 0
        done
}

maybe() {
        # Special settings.

        ci=$1; shift
        co=$1; shift

        for i in $*
        do
                # Don't use ^R; it breaks bash's ^R when typed ahead.
                stty </dev/ttyi$ci$i reprint undef
                stty </dev/cuai$co$i reprint undef
                # Lock clocal off on dialin device for security.
                stty </dev/ttyl$ci$i clocal
                # Lock the speeds to use old binaries that don't support them.
```

19

SUPPORTING DIAL-IN CLIENTS

LISTING 19.3   Continued

```
                        # Any legal speed works to lock the initial speed.
                        stty </dev/ttyl$ci$i 300
                        stty </dev/cual$co$i 300
                done
        }

        modem() {
                # Modem that supports CTS and perhaps RTS handshaking.

                ci=$1; shift
                co=$1; shift

                for i in $*
                do
                        # may depend on modem
                        comcontrol /dev/tty$ci$i dtrwait 100 drainwait 180
                        # Lock crtscts on.
                        # Speed reasonable for V42bis.
                        stty </dev/ttyi$ci$i crtscts 57600
                        stty </dev/ttyl$ci$i crtscts
                        stty </dev/cuai$co$i crtscts 57600
                        stty </dev/cual$co$i crtscts
                done
        }
```

The rc.serial script uses the comcontrol utility to set the serial ports. Also, the FreeBSD stty utility is used to set device-specific parameters for the serial port.

Controlling Linux Serial Ports

Much like FreeBSD, Linux serial port configurations are stored in the Linux kernel. Changing kernel values requires precise programming to add parameters to the kernel. Fortunately, there is also a utility program for Linux that can change the serial port values in the kernel. The setserial program can be used to configure new serial ports in the kernel. This section describes how to add, delete, and change serial port information on a Linux system.

Setting Modem Port Parameters in Linux

Serial port settings must be set in the Linux kernel by an external program. The setserial command is used to set and modify the configuration information for the individual serial ports on the Linux system.

Each serial port that Linux uses must be configured with the setserial command. As shown in Listing 19.1, the four standard COM ports are configured by default. If you are using a modem that does not use standard IRQ or I/O port settings or are using multiport serial devices, you will need to use the setserial program to properly configure the serial ports for Linux.

There are two formats of the setserial command. They are

```
setserial [-abqvVW] device [parameter 1 [arg] ] ...
setserial -g [-abv] device1 ...
```

The -g option is used to retrieve information regarding the devices listed. Listing 19.4 shows the output from the setserial command on the sample Linux system.

LISTING 19.4   Sample Output from setserial

```
1  [root@shadrach rich]$ /sbin/setserial -g /dev/ttyS0 /dev/ttyS1 /dev/ttyS2
➥ /dev/ttyS3
2  /dev/ttyS0, UART: 16550A, Port: 0x03f8, IRQ: 4
3  /dev/ttyS1, UART: 16550A, Port: 0x02f8, IRQ: 3
4  /dev/ttyS2, UART: unknown, Port: 0x03e8, IRQ: 4
5  /dev/ttyS3, UART: 16550A, Port: 0x02e8, IRQ: 3
6  [root@shadrach rich]$
```

In Listing 19.4, line 1 shows the setserial command entered using the -g option to display the serial port information. You must be the root user to be able to run the setserial command. Lines 2–5 show the output of the command for the Linux system. Each line shows the information for a single serial port. Notice in Line 4 that the ttyS2 port, which is unused, produces an unknown UART type. This may be misleading, because in reality it does not exist.

NOTE

There appears to be no standard for where the setserial command is located in Linux. Many distributions place it in the /sbin directory, while others place it in the /bin directory. You may have to use the Linux find or whereis command to locate the setserial command on your Linux distribution.

You can modify the output from the setserial program by using one of the three available command-line options. The default output is the -v option, which produces the output shown in Listing 19.4. The -b option produces a more summarized version of the output. An example of this output would be

```
/dev/ttyS0 at 0x03f8 (irq = 4) is a 16550A
```

This produces the same information but in a more compact method. The -a option can be used to produce more verbose output. An example of this output would be

```
/dev/ttyS0, Line 0, UART: 16550A, Port: 0x03f8, IRQ: 4
Baud_base: 115200, close_delay: 50, divisor: 0
closing_wait: 3000, closing_wait2: infinite
Flags: spd_normal skip_test auto_irq session_lockout
```

The -a option displays values for the internal parameters used by Linux to control the device. These parameters can be set and modified by using the first format of the setserial command that was shown. Table 19.2 shows the parameters that are available to use with the setserial command.

TABLE 19.2 setserial Command-Line Parameters

Parameter	Description
port N	Sets the I/O port number of the device to N.
irq N	Sets the hardware IRQ of the device to N.
uart type	Sets the UART type of the device to type.
autoconfigure	Attempts to autodetect the serial device information.
auto_irq	Attempts to determine the IRQ of the serial device.
^auto_irq	Does not attempt to determine the IRQ of the serial device during autoconfigure.
skip_test	Skips the UART test during autoconfigure.
^skip_test	Does not skip the UART test during autoconfigure.
baud_base	Sets the base baud rate of the serial device, normally the clock rate divided by 16.
spd_hi	Uses 57.6kb when the application requests 38.4kb.
spd_vhi	Uses 115kb when the application requests 38.4kb.
spd_cust	Uses a custom divisor to set the speed when the application requests 38.4kb, set to the baud_base divided by the divisor.
spd_normal	Uses 38.4kb when the application requests 38.4kb.
divisor	Is used to set the spd_cust value.
sak	Sets the Break key as the Secure Attention key.
^sak	Disables the Secure Attention key.
fourport	Sets the device as an AST Fourport card.
^fourport	Disables AST Fourport configuration.
close_delay D	Sets the amount of time that DTR should remain low on a line after the device is closed, in hundredths of a second. Default is 50.

Parameter	Description
closing_wait D	Sets the amount of time that the kernel should wait for data to be transmitted from the serial port while closing the port, before the receiver has been disabled, in hundredths of a second. Default is none to cause the kernel to wait indefinitely.
closing_wait2 D	Sets the amount of time the kernel should wait for data to be transmitted from the serial port while closing the port, after the receiver has been disabled, in hundredths of a second. Default is 30.
session_lockout	Locks out the dial-out port (cua) access by other sessions when in use.
^session_lockout	Does not lock out the dial-out port access by sessions when in use.
pgrp_lockout	Locks out the dial-out port (cua) access by other processes when in use.
^pgrp_lockout	Does not lock out the dial-out port access by other processes when in use.
hup_notify	Notifies a process waiting on the dial-out line when it is available.
^hup_notify	Does not notify a process waiting on the dial-out line when it is available.
split_termios	Treats the termios settings used by the dial-out and dial-in devices as separate.
^split_termios	Does not treat the termios settings used by the dial-out and dial-in devices as separate.
callout_nohup	If the serial port is opened as a dial-out device, does not hang up the tty when carrier detect is dropped.
^callout_nohup	If the serial port is opened as a dial-out device, hangs up the tty when the carrier detect signal is dropped.

19

SUPPORTING
DIAL-IN CLIENTS

The setserial command must always identify the device that it is operating on. If the default IRQ and I/O address for the port are being used, they can be omitted from the command line. After that, parameters can be entered on the command line in any order. A sample setserial command would look like this:

```
setserial /dev/ttyS3 autoconfigure auto_irq skip_test
```

This command will attempt to autodetect the serial device in COM4. Entries made by the setserial program in the kernel table will disappear when the Linux server is rebooted. Thus, the setserial command should be executed for each COM port present in the server at each boot time. As this is a common function, most Linux distributions include init scripts to run the setserial commands.

The Linux `inittab` File

The Linux system determines what terminal ports to activate by reading the `inittab` file. The `/etc/inittab` file is used by Linux to execute specific processes at specific init run levels. In this situation, it is being used to define the Linux devices to which users can log in and know how to handle each individual device.

The init program reads the `/etc/inittab` file and spawns the required programs to listen to the indicated devices for login attempts. Listing 19.5 shows an example of an `/etc/inittab` file.

LISTING 19.5   Sample `/etc/inittab` File

```
1  # inittab       This file describes how the INIT process should set up
2  #               the system in a certain run-level.
3  #
4  # Author:       Miquel van Smoorenburg, <miquels@drinkel.nl.mugnet.org>
5  #               Modified for RHS Linux by Marc Ewing and Donnie Barnes
6  #
7  # Default runlevel. The runlevels used by RHS are:
8  #    0 - halt (Do NOT set initdefault to this)
9  #    1 - Single user mode
10 #    2 - Multiuser, without NFS (The same as 3, if you do not have
➥ networking)
11 #    3 - Full multiuser mode
12 #    4 - unused
13 #    5 - X11
14 #    6 - reboot (Do NOT set initdefault to this)
15 #
16 id:3:initdefault:
17 # System initialization.
18 si::sysinit:/etc/rc.d/rc.sysinit
19 l0:0:wait:/etc/rc.d/rc 0
20 l1:1:wait:/etc/rc.d/rc 1
21 l2:2:wait:/etc/rc.d/rc 2
22 l3:3:wait:/etc/rc.d/rc 3
23 l4:4:wait:/etc/rc.d/rc 4
24 l5:5:wait:/etc/rc.d/rc 5
25 l6:6:wait:/etc/rc.d/rc 6
26
27 # Things to run in every runlevel.
28 ud::once:/sbin/update
29
30 # Trap CTRL-ALT-DELETE
31 ca::ctrlaltdel:/sbin/shutdown -t3 -r now
32
33 # When our UPS tells us power has failed, assume we have a few minutes
```

```
34 # of power left.   Schedule a shutdown for 2 minutes from now.
35 # This does, of course, assume you have powerd installed and your
36 # UPS connected and working correctly.
37 pf::powerfail:/sbin/shutdown -f -h +2 "Power Failure; System Shutting Down"
38
39 # If power was restored before the shutdown kicked in, cancel it.
40 pr:12345:powerokwait:/sbin/shutdown -c "Power Restored; Shutdown Cancelled"
41
42# Run gettys in standard runlevels
43 1:12345:respawn:/sbin/mingetty tty1
44 2:2345:respawn:/sbin/mingetty tty2
45 3:2345:respawn:/sbin/mingetty tty3
46 4:2345:respawn:/sbin/mingetty tty4
47 5:2345:respawn:/sbin/mingetty tty5
48 6:2345:respawn:/sbin/mingetty tty6
49
50 # Set serial line for modem
51 s1:2345:respawn:/sbin/uugetty ttyS0 38400 vt100
52
53 # Run xdm in runlevel 5
54 x:5:respawn:/usr/bin/X11/xdm -nodaemon
```

The format of each record in the `inittab` file is

`id:runlevels:action:process`

where `id` is a unique ID within the `inittab` file used to identify the action, `runlevels` is a list of `init` run levels when the action will be taken, `action` is the `init` action that will be performed on the process, and `process` is the specific program that will be run. In Listing 19.5, lines 43–48 demonstrate this format. These lines define the virtual terminals present in most Linux distributions. They use the standard mingetty program to monitor the appropriate `tty` line. Each record represents one `tty` line, which is set to the `respawn` action, which "respawns" a new terminal session when you log off. You may also notice that `tty1`, the main console screen, is started at all run levels, but `ttys2`–`ttys6` start at run level 2. In Linux, init run level 1 is considered the single user mode, thus, only one terminal session is required.

Line 51 defines the dial-in modem on the Linux mailserver. It specifies the `inittab` ID `s1`, which is activated on init run levels 2, 3, 4, and 5. The `respawn` action indicates that the process defined will be restarted by init whenever the process terminates. This allows the program to be restarted automatically after a user terminates the dial-in session. The program that will be run is the uugetty program. It also contains a few command-line parameters to define its behavior. The uugetty program handles any login attempts coming in on the modem connected to device `/dev/ttyS0` (due to the command-line parameter `ttyS0`).

Linux Serial Port init Scripts

The default location for the setserial scripts is the /etc/rc.d/rc.serial file. Some Linux distributions include a generic version of this script that can be edited for the particular server configuration. The script contains many lines for special situations, such as multiport serial boards and specially configured modem cards. Listing 19.6 shows an excerpt from a sample rc.serial script.

LISTING 19.6   Excerpt from an /etc/rc.d/rc.serial Script

```
1   STD_FLAGS="session_lockout"
2   SETSERIAL=/sbin/setserial
3   WILD=false
4   SUMMARY=true
5
6   echo -n "Configuring serial ports...."
7
8   ############################################################
9   #
10  # AUTOMATIC CONFIGURATION
11  #
12  # Uncomment the appropriate lines below to enable auto-configuration
13  # of a particular board.  Or comment them out to disable them....
14  #
15  ############################################################
16
17  # Do AUTOMATIC_IRQ probing
18  #
19  AUTO_IRQ=auto_irq
20
21  # These are the standard COM1 through COM4 devices
22  #
23  SetSerial /dev/ttyS0 ${AUTO_IRQ} skip_test autoconfig ${STD_FLAGS}
24  SetSerial /dev/ttyS1 ${AUTO_IRQ} skip_test autoconfig ${STD_FLAGS}
25  SetSerial /dev/ttyS2 ${AUTO_IRQ} skip_test autoconfig ${STD_FLAGS}
26  SetSerial /dev/ttyS3 ${AUTO_IRQ} autoconfig ${STD_FLAGS}
27
28  ############################################################
29  #
30  # MANUAL CONFIGURATION
31  #
32  # If you want to do manual configuration of one or more of your
33  # serial ports, uncomment and modify the relevant lines.
34  #
35  ############################################################
36
```

```
37 # These are the standard COM1 through COM4 devices
38 #
39 #SetSerial /dev/ttyS0 uart 16450 port 0x3F8 irq 4 ${STD_FLAGS}
40 #SetSerial /dev/ttyS1 uart 16450 port 0x2F8 irq 3 ${STD_FLAGS}
41 #SetSerial /dev/ttyS2 uart 16450 port 0x3E8 irq 4 ${STD_FLAGS}
42 #SetSerial /dev/ttyS3 uart 16450 port 0x2E8 irq 3 ${STD_FLAGS}
43
44 echo "done."
45
46 ##############################################################
47 #
48 # Print the results of the serial configuration process
49 #
50 ##############################################################
51
52 if [ -n "$SUMMARY" ]; then
53   SetSerial -bg /dev/ttyS?
54
55   if [ '/dev/ttyS??' != /dev/ttyS?? ]; then
56     SetSerial -bg /dev/ttyS??
57   fi
58 fi
```

In Listing 19.6, lines 23–26 use setserial commands that attempt to autodetect the first four serial ports in the server. If you prefer that the server not attempt to autodetect the serial ports, you can comment these lines out and uncomment lines 39–42. These lines use the specific IRQ and I/O port addresses for each serial port in the setserial command. If you are using a modem that is configured with a non-standard IRQ and I/O port setting, you can customize the appropriate setserial command to the proper values.

> **NOTE**
>
> If your Linux distribution does not include an rc.serial script, you can still create one in the /etc/rc.d directory. Just make sure that it is called from one of the boot scripts such as /etc/rc.d/rc.sysinit.

19

SUPPORTING
DIAL-IN CLIENTS

Configuring UNIX Dial-In Clients

Almost all UNIX clients use the pppd program to establish a PPP session with the remote host (see Chapter 18). The pppd program can be configured as a PPP client, allowing your UNIX server to connect to an ISP PPP host and establish an IP network connection to pass mail and other IP traffic. There are other programs available to assist the PPP client process. This section describes some of them.

Using the pppd Program

To use pppd in client mode, you must supply some options that help it connect to the PPP server and establish the PPP session properly. The basic format for the pppd command is

```
pppd tty line speed [options]
```

where tty line is the Linux COM port to which your modem is connected and speed is the speed at which you want to connect to the modem. The art of using the pppd program comes in choosing the proper options for the client and server commands. Here are some of the options available to use pppd as a client.

- The connect option allows the pppd program to use an executable or shell script to set up the serial link before the pppd program will attempt to connect.
- The crtscts option uses RTS/CTS hardware flow control on the serial line.
- The defaultroute option adds a default route to the kernel routing table, pointing to the remote IP address of the PPP server. The route table entry is deleted when the PPP session is terminated. This allows your Linux server to know to send IP traffic destined for other network devices out of the PPP connection.
- The lock option is used to create a UUCP-style lock file to indicate that the modem is in use.
- The mru and mtu options allow the client to attempt to set the Maximum Receive Unit (MRU) and Maximum Transmit Unit (MTU) sizes during the LCP negotiation phase. It is up to the PPP server to agree to the new sizes. Often this is used on slower modem connections to reduce the PPP packet size.
- The modem option allows the UNIX system to use the modem control lines. With this option, the pppd program will wait for the CD (carrier detect) modem signal when opening the modem line and will drop DTR (data terminal ready) briefly when the PPP connection is terminated.

Using the Chat Program

The chat program is a part of the pppd distribution and is used to simplify the connect string for pppd. The chat program can use a simple script file and communicate with the modem to initiate the connection with the PPP server. The chat script uses text strings that it can send to the remote server in response to text strings received. It tries to match the text strings in a chat session—one response for each string received. Listing 19.7 shows an example of a sample chat script used for pppd.

LISTING 19.7   Sample Chat Script `isp.chat`

```
 1  " "
 2  ATDT5551234
 3  CONNECT
 4  " "
 5  "ogin:"
 6  rich
 7  "word:"
 8  guitar
 9  "rich]$"
10  "exec /usr/sbin/pppd silent modem crtscts proxyarp 10.0.0.100:10.0.0.2"
```

In Listing 19.7, line 2 shows the command that pppd will send to the modem to dial the ISP phone number. Line 3 shows what text string pppd should wait for to establish that a connection has been made to the PPP server. Line 4 indicates that, when the chat program receives a connection notice from the modem, it should send a single carriage return. Line 5 shows what text string to wait for from the server. If the server is allowing terminal logins from this modem line, it should issue a welcome banner with a login prompt. In line 6, pppd sends the user ID to the PPP server, and in line 8 it sends the password. When pppd gets a command prompt from the PPP server (as shown in line 9), it then issues the host pppd command on the PPP server.

Once a successful chat script has been created, it can be used in the client's pppd configuration to dial the PPP server when the pppd program is executed. The connect pppd option calls the chat script using the following format:

```
pppd ttyS1 38400 connect '/usr/sbin/chat -v -f /home/rich/isp.chat' modem
➥ crtscts defaultroute
```

The connect option uses the chat program in its script to connect to the PPP server. The preceding command line will automatically call the PPP server, and start the pppd program on the server. The -v option, used in the chat program, allows for extremely verbose output to the /var/log/messages file. Use this for testing purposes, and then remove it when you have all the bugs worked out. Listing 19.8 shows the lines that the pppd and chat programs place in the message log during a client PPP session.

LISTING 19.8   Lines from `/var/log/messages` for pppd and Chat

```
1  Sep 22 06:56:56 shadrach pppd[663]: pppd 2.3.5 started by root, uid 0
2  Sep 22 06:56:56 shadrach kernel: registered device ppp0
3  Sep 22 06:56:57 shadrach chat[664]: send (ATZS7=100^M)
4  Sep 22 06:56:57 shadrach chat[664]: expect (OK)
5  Sep 22 06:56:57 shadrach chat[664]: ATZS7=100^M^M
```

LISTING 19.8 Continued

```
 6  Sep 22 06:56:57 shadrach chat[664]: OK
 7  Sep 22 06:56:57 shadrach chat[664]:  -- got it
 8  Sep 22 06:56:57 shadrach chat[664]: send (ATDT5551234^M)
 9  Sep 22 06:56:58 shadrach chat[664]: expect (CONNECT)
10  Sep 22 06:56:58 shadrach chat[664]: ^M
11  Sep 22 06:57:18 shadrach chat[664]: ATDT5551234^M^M
12  Sep 22 06:57:18 shadrach chat[664]: CONNECT
13  Sep 22 06:57:18 shadrach chat[664]:  -- got it
14  Sep 22 06:57:18 shadrach chat[664]: send (^M)
15  Sep 22 06:57:18 shadrach chat[664]: expect (ogin:)
16  Sep 22 06:57:18 shadrach chat[664]:  28800/V42BIS^M
17  Sep 22 06:57:19 shadrach chat[664]: ^M
18  Sep 22 06:57:19 shadrach chat[664]: ^MRed Hat Linux release 5.2 (Apollo)
19  Sep 22 06:57:19 shadrach chat[664]: ^MKernel 2.0.36 on an i486
20  Sep 22 06:57:19 shadrach chat[664]: ^M
21  Sep 22 06:57:19 shadrach chat[664]: ^M^M
22  Sep 22 06:57:19 shadrach chat[664]: mail1.isp.net login:
23  Sep 22 06:57:19 shadrach chat[664]:  -- got it
24  Sep 22 06:57:19 shadrach chat[664]: send (rich^M)
25  Sep 22 06:57:19 shadrach chat[664]: expect (word:)
26  Sep 22 06:57:19 shadrach chat[664]:  rich^M
27  Sep 22 06:57:19 shadrach chat[664]: Password:
28  Sep 22 06:57:19 shadrach chat[664]:  -- got it
29  Sep 22 06:57:19 shadrach chat[664]: send (guitar^M)
30  Sep 22 06:57:20 shadrach chat[664]: expect (rich]$)
31  Sep 22 06:57:20 shadrach chat[664]:  ^M
32  Sep 22 06:57:20 shadrach chat[664]: Last login: Tue Sep 21 20:45:47^M
33  Sep 22 06:57:21 shadrach chat[664]: [rich@mail1 rich]$
34  Sep 22 06:57:21 shadrach chat[664]:  -- got it
35  Sep 22 06:57:21 shadrach chat[664]: send (exec /usr/sbin/pppd passive
➥ silent modem crtscts^M)
36  Sep 22 06:57:22 shadrach pppd[663]: Serial connection established.
37  Sep 22 06:57:23 shadrach pppd[663]: Using interface ppp0
38  Sep 22 06:57:23 shadrach pppd[663]: Connect: ppp0 <--> /dev/ttyS1
39  Sep 22 06:57:27 shadrach pppd[663]: local  IP address 10.0.0.100
40  Sep 22 06:57:27 shadrach pppd[663]: remote IP address 10.0.0.2
```

Using the chat script and the pppd client commands establishes a PPP session with the PPP
server. This can be placed in a script file to create a method to start the PPP session when
needed. However, this method still needs some external event to trigger it to startup, such as
the cron process running the PPP script whenever mail needs to be checked. The next program
allows the PPP client to be started automatically when it is needed.

The Diald Program

Now that you have your chat script perfected and can dial into the PPP server and establish a connection, you might want to automate things a little more. If you decide to connect your UNIX mail server directly to the ISP, you will need to implement a policy on how often your server will connect to the ISP to transfer mail. One method is to use dial-on-demand IP routing. This feature will automatically start the PPP connection whenever it detects data that needs to use the ISP network.

A great program for implementing dial-on-demand routing is the *diald* program, written by Eric Schenk. Some UNIX distributions include a binary package for diald. If yours doesn't, you can download a version from the new diald Web site at `http://diald.unix.ch`.

The format of the diald program is

```
/usr/sbin/diald [device1....] [options...] [-- [pppd options]]
```

where `device1` is the Linux `tty` line your modem is connected to, `options` are diald options, and `pppd options` are the options that diald will pass to the pppd program when it calls it. It is also possible to set the parameters using a configuration file for diald.

The diald program's configuration file is used to set parameters for it to call the chat and pppd programs as required and list scenarios in which you want diald to start and stop pppd. The configuration file is located at `/etc/diald.conf`. Listing 19.9 is a sample `diald.conf` file that replaces the pppd options used in the pppd example above.

LISTING 19.9 A Sample `/etc/diald.conf` Configuration File

```
1   ###
2   # /etc/diald.conf - diald configuration
3   #
4   # see /usr/lib/diald for sample config files
5   #
6   mode ppp
7   connect '/usr/sbin/chat -f /home/rich/isp.chat -t 35000'
8   connect-timeout 180
9   device /dev/ttyS1
10  speed 115200
11  modem
12  lock
13  crtscts
14  local 10.0.0.100
15  remote 10.0.0.2
16  defaultroute
17  include /usr/lib/diald/standard.filter
18  fifo /etc/diald/diald.ctl
```

In Listing 19.9, line 7 shows the diald `connect` parameter, which calls the chat program using the same chat script that was used in the pppd example. Line 8 was added to compensate for the fact that the PPP host modem is set to answer after four rings (so as not to annoy friends and family who would call the same line). It allows the chat script up to 3 minutes to finish. Line 17 includes a file `standard.filter` that diald uses to specify under what conditions it will start the PPP session, and when it will stop the session.

Line 18 is used to specify a special file that a companion program dctrl uses to monitor the PPP session. The dctrl program is a graphical program that can be used to monitor the PPP link and report any error conditions as well as the throughput of the connection.

Once the configurations are set, you can test diald, which runs in background mode. You must start it as the `root` user ID. After diald detects a network condition that warrants a connection to the PPP server, it starts the chat program, which creates the PPP session with the server and then starts the pppd program on the local host. Once you are satisfied with the performance of diald, you can create a startup script for it and put it in the boot script area on your UNIX server so that it starts automatically at boot time. Then, every time a program needs to access a remote host via IP (such as fetchmail), it will kick in and start the PPP session.

The Kppp Program

If you are using a UNIX distribution that has the K Desktop Environment (KDE) window manager, you can use another option to simplify your PPP connection. The kppp program is a graphical interface that helps you configure and start the pppd program. Figure 19.2 shows the main screen that appears when you start the program.

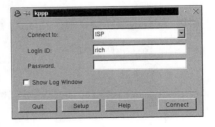

FIGURE 19.2

The kppp program main screen.

From the main screen, you can select a configured PPP host and start the pppd connection simply by entering your password and clicking on the Connect button. Clicking on the Setup button on the main screen starts the kppp Configuration screen. Multiple accounts can be preconfigured using the Accounts tab on the Configuration screen. Figure 19.3 shows the Accounts tab.

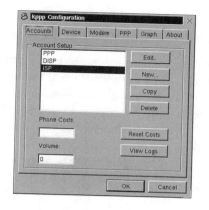

FIGURE 19.3

The kppp account configuration tab.

By clicking the New button, individual accounts can be configured. The account configuration screen is shown in Figure 19.4.

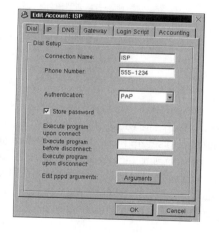

FIGURE 19.4

The kppp account setup screen.

Each property for the new account can be configured on the Edit Accounts screen. You can input the phone number and authentication method required to initiate the PPP session. Authentication methods available include PAP, CHAP, a chat script, and a pop-up terminal session that allows you to manually log in and issue the pppd command on the remote PPP server. The IP tab allows you to determine how your local IP address will be configured—either dynamically by the PPP host or statically by you. You can also use the DNS and Gateway tabs to select how the PPP client will obtain the DNS server and IP router addresses—either dynamically from the PPP host or statically by you.

Figure 19.5 shows the kppp Configuration window Device tab settings. This allows you to configure the modem that will be used for dialing the ISP and various settings that will affect the modem, such as the flow control method and the line termination method. The Use Lock File check box allows you to utilize the pppd lock option to create UUCP style modem lock files so that another process won't try to use the modem at the same time.

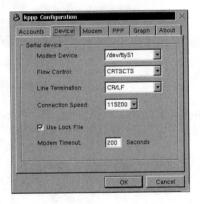

FIGURE 19.5

The kppp device configuration tab.

Figure 19.6 shows the kppp Configuration window Modem tab settings. These settings allow you to set parameters for the modem. The Modem Commands button allows you to add initialization parameters to your modem to set up the modem for the connection. The Query Modem button allows you to send query strings to the modem to check current configuration settings. Up to eight settings can be shown with this option. The Terminal button is handy when trying to create dial-up scripts for the first time. It brings up a mini-terminal that allows you to talk with the modem and dial into the PPP server. This feature is great for dialing into the server to observe return strings required to set the dial-up script settings properly.

Once all of the account parameters are configured, it is just a matter of selecting the account you want to dial into, supplying the proper user ID and password, and clicking the Connect button. The kppp program will automatically start pppd, using the parameters that you configured for the account. Speaking of accounts, there is also a handy feature that will log your total session times and produce a nicely formatted report showing all of your connections.

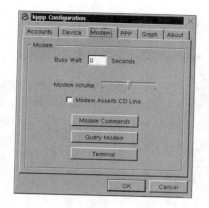

FIGURE 19.6

The kppp modem configuration tab.

Configuring Windows 95/98 Clients

The first step to using PPP dial-up support on a Windows 95 or 98 workstation is to ensure that you have a modem installed. You can select Start, Settings, Control Panel, Modems to view the installed modems or to add a new modem. Figure 19.7 shows this window.

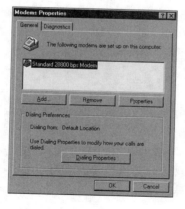

FIGURE 19.7

The Windows 95 and 98 Modems Properties window.

After selecting the modem type that is installed and loading the drivers, the next step is to use the Windows Wizard to configure a new Dial-Up Networking (DUN) session. Running the

Windows Explorer program and selecting the Dial-Up Networking icon starts the wizard.
Follow the instructions in the wizard to create a new connection using a configured modem.
Figure 19.8 shows a sample wizard window.

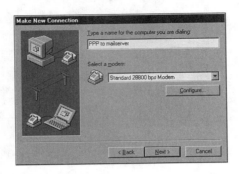

FIGURE 19.8
The Windows 95 and 98 Make New Connection Wizard window.

After creating the new DUN session, you must enter the phone number required to connect to
the remote server. When the wizard is done, the new DUN session should appear as an icon in
Windows Explorer under the Dial-Up Networking section. The Entry name should match the
name you gave it in the wizard configuration. Figure 19.9 shows the connection window when
you double-click the DUN session icon.

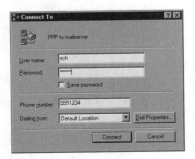

FIGURE 19.9
The Windows 95 and 98 Dial-Up Networking Connection window.

After typing in your assigned username and password, click the Connect button to start the
connection. If all goes well, the Windows workstation should dial the UNIX mail server and
establish a PPP session. If the Windows workstation dials the mail server but fails to establish
a PPP session, you can check the UNIX system log files (as described in Chapter 13, "qmail
Server Administration") to determine where the problem might be. Most often it is a problem
with the /etc/ppp/pap-secrets file.

Once the PPP session is established, an icon of two terminals appears in the Windows system tray. Each terminal will flash when data is transmitted in that particular direction. The email client software package can then be started to connect to the UNIX mail server.

To stop the PPP session, you must right-click on the DUN icon in the system tray and select the Disconnect menu item. The workstation modem should hang up the phone connection. The UNIX mail server should also reset the modem and respawn the mgetty process to wait for another incoming call.

Configuring Windows NT and 2000 Clients

Configuring Windows NT and 2000 Remote Access Software (RAS) is similar to but different than Windows 95 and 98 DUN software. Again, the first step is to ensure that you have a modem installed on the workstation. By selecting the Modem icon in the Control Panel area, you will see the Modems Properties window, shown in Figure 19.10.

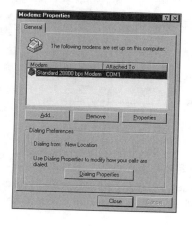

FIGURE 19.10

The Windows NT 4.0 Modems Properties window.

As with the Windows 95 and 98 software, you can view the current modem configuration or add a new modem using the Add button. After the modem is configured, you can begin to configure the RAS information. To select the Dial-Up Networking feature, you can double-click on the Dial-Up Networking icon in Windows Explorer. If Dial-Up Networking has not been installed, the main installation window, shown in Figure 19.11, is displayed.

To start the installation wizard, click the Install button. To properly communicate with the remote PPP server, the RAS software must recognize the modem. The first dialog box is Add RAS Device, which allows you to select the modem that will be used to dial in to the remote server. Figure 19.12 shows the Remote Access Setup window, which allows you to select the modem to connect to the remote PPP server.

FIGURE 19.11
Windows NT 4.0 Dial-Up Networking installation.

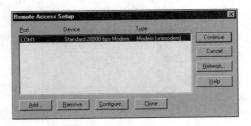

FIGURE 19.12
The Windows NT 4.0 Remote Access Setup window.

After the modem is selected, the RAS software is installed on the workstation. You will need to use the media with the Windows NT or 2000 software to install the necessary files to support Dial-Up Networking services. When the installation is complete, the wizard will reboot your workstation.

After the workstation is rebooted, you can select the Dial-Up Networking icon from Windows Explorer. Unlike Windows 95 and 98, which have a separate icon for each DUN session, a Windows NT or 2000 workstation has just one icon to access the RAS software. The first time you select the RAS software, it starts a wizard to help you add a new session to the phonebook. The New Phonebook Entry Wizard main window is shown in Figure 19.13.

After following the wizard and entering the phone number information for the new PPP session, the main Dial-Up Networking window shown in Figure 19.14 is displayed.

The main window shows the drop-down box that allows you to select configured sessions in the phonebook. Select the Edit Entry and Modem Properties menu item to configure the new phonebook entry. The Edit Phonebook Entry window appears, as seen in Figure 19.15. Select the Server tab to modify the connection entries.

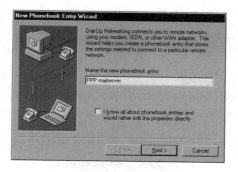

FIGURE 19.13

The Windows NT 4.0 New Phonebook Entry Wizard.

FIGURE 19.14

The Windows NT 4.0 Dial-Up Networking main window.

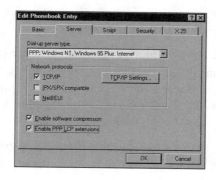

FIGURE 19.15

The Windows NT 4.0 Edit Phonebook Entry window.

The last entry that needs to be modified in this section is under the Security tab. For PPP authentication to work correctly, you must select the Accept Any Authentication Including Clear Text method of authentication.

For the Dial-Up Networking software to connect to the UNIX mail server, you must select the PPP Dial-Up server type and ensure that the TCP/IP protocol check box is checked. You can also enable compression and the PPP LCP extensions. The UNIX pppd program supports both of these functions. Figure 19.16 shows the PPP TCP/IP Settings window.

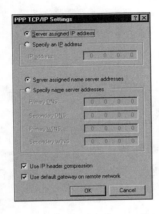

FIGURE 19.16
The Windows NT 4.0 PPP TCP/IP Settings window.

Depending on the configuration of the UNIX mail server pppd program, you will have to either assign static IP and DNS server addresses to the Windows NT workstation or allow the pppd program to assign them. Also, you can check the check boxes to enable IP compression and to use the default gateway on the UNIX mail server.

After the configuration parameters are finished, you can go back to the Dial-Up Networking main window shown in Figure 19.14, select the phonebook entry for the UNIX mail server, and click the Dial button. This produces the window shown in Figure 19.17. After entering the appropriate username and password, click the OK button to allow RAS to attempt to connect to the UNIX mail server.

Similar to the Windows 95 and 98 DUN, when the connection is established, an icon appears in the system tray, indicating that the connection has been made. The two bars indicate sending and receiving packets across the PPP link.

After the PPP connection has been established, you can start the email client software package and connect to the mail server and use the POP3 or IMAP protocol to retrieve your mail messages. When you are finished, you can right-click on the DUN icon in the system tray and select Close from the menu. This stops the PPP session and disconnects the modem connection.

FIGURE 19.17
The Windows NT 4.0 Connect window.

One feature on the Windows NT and 2000 workstation is the addition of the Dial-Up Networking Monitor. By right-clicking on the RAS icon in the system tray, you can select the Open System Monitor menu item. This produces the Dial-Up Networking Monitor window, shown in Figure 19.18.

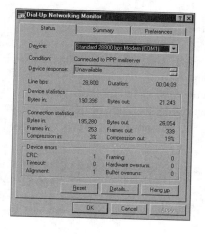

FIGURE 19.18
The Windows NT 4.0 Dial-Up Networking Monitor.

The Dial-Up Networking Monitor does a nice job of showing you how your PPP client is behaving by showing you statistics on the amount of traffic that has gone across the PPP connection and the number of errors it has encountered. You can also keep tabs on the compression rates that are being used on the PPP session if you enabled compression on both the Windows NT/2000 workstation and the UNIX mail server pppd program.

The Eudora POP3 Client Software

After the remote client has established a PPP session, it requires software to connect to the qmail server to read messages stored in the user's mailbox. There are lots of commercial and free software mail packages available that allow a workstation to establish either a POP3 or IMAP connection with the remote server across the PPP link. One of the most popular free packages is Qualcomm Eudora.

The Qualcomm Corporation was already mentioned once before in this book. Chapter 17, "Installing and Configuring POP3 and IMAP Servers," discussed using the qpopper POP3 server program for the UNIX mail server. Qualcomm also maintains the Eudora email client package as well. The Eudora package has three levels of support:

- Light mode—A free version with fewer features.
- Paid mode—You pay for all of the features.
- Sponsored mode—You get all of the features, but the package contains ads that are displayed.

Customers can download the Eudora package for free and decide which version is best for them from the configuration menu. This section describes how to download, install, and use the Eudora Sponsored mode email client package.

Downloading Eudora

The Eudora software package can be downloaded from the Eudora Web site at `http://www.eudora.com/`. The current version at the time of this writing is version 4.3.1. You must fill in a short questionnaire before it allows you to download the software. If you are not into doing questionnaires, you can FTP a copy of the beta version of version 4.3.2 from the Eudora FTP server at `ftp://ftp.eudora.com/eudora/eudorapro/windows/english/beta432/e432b6.exe`.

The file is about 6MB in size. As before, remember to use the binary FTP mode when downloading. The `e432b6.exe` file contains the complete Eudora installation program, so it can be copied and used on any workstation that needs to have email client software installed.

Installing Eudora

Eudora uses InstallShield to install the software, so installation is easy. There are a few questions that you will have to answer first regarding where you want the software installed.

After the InstallShield program is finished, there should be a new program group in the Programs listing named Eudora, which will contain the Eudora 4.3.2 executable program icon.

Configuring Eudora

After Eudora is installed, it must be configured. Start Eudora by clicking on the Eudora program icon from the Eudora program group in the Programs listings. The main client window appears, as shown in Figure 19.19.

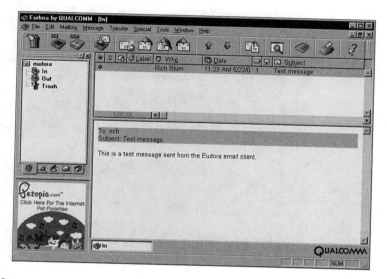

FIGURE 19.19

The Eudora main client window.

The first time you use Eudora, a Connection Wizard assists you in configuring Eudora to connect to your qmail server. To manually get to the configuration window from the main client window, select the Tools, Options menu items. The Options window shown in Figure 19.20 appears.

There are several options that need to be configured for Eudora to work properly with the UNIX mail server. First, you must select the Getting Started icon to configure basic information on where your mailbox is located. As shown in Figure 19.20, you must enter your username and the IP address of the mail server in the Return Address field. One nice feature of Eudora is that it supports encrypted POP authentication methods. The Incoming Mail icon allows you to select an authentication method. Remember that the POP3 server must also be configured to support the APOP authentication or the client will not be able to log into the POP3 server.

After the Getting Started fields have been completed, you must select the Sending Mail icon to configure how Eudora will send messages. As in the other software packages, use the IP address of the mail server as the SMTP server. Also, as before, ensure that the qmail program on the mail server is configured to relay SMTP messages from clients on your local network. The `qmail-smtpd` program supports SMTP authentication, so you can check the Allow Authentication check box on Eudora for added security.

FIGURE 19.20
The Eudora Options window.

Using Eudora

When you start Eudora, it will ask you for your password to your account on the UNIX mail server. Then it attempts to connect to the mail server and download any new messages. To check for new messages after you have logged into the mail server, click the Check Mail icon at the top of the main window.

The main window (previously shown in Figure 19.19) shows the message headers in the right window and the mailbox folders on the left side. To view a message, double-click on the message header. The message header list will be replaced with the message body. To return to the Inbox listing, double-click on the In icon on the left side.

To compose a new message, click on the New Message icon at the top of the main window (the fifth icon from the left). This produces the new message window shown in Figure 19.21.

In the new message window you can insert recipient addresses on the To: and Cc: lines. You can configure commonly used email addresses in the Address Book to simplify adding them to email messages. After composing the new message, click on the Send button to forward the message via SMTP to the mail server.

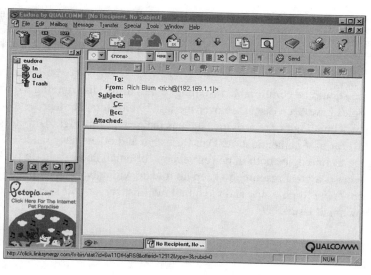

FIGURE 19.21

The Eudora new message window.

Eudora supports reading mail in HTML format by spawning an external Web browser. It also supports binary file attachments directly within the client package.

Eudora is a nice lightweight email client package that can meet the basic email needs of any office. It works great for offices that have some older, underpowered workstations still in use.

Summary

This chapter discusses the requirements for supporting dial-in mail clients. For the UNIX mail server to support dial-in clients, the system must first recognize serial ports. Both FreeBSD and Linux have utility programs that enable the system administrator to configure the kernel to communicate with serial ports on the system. The FreeBSD comcontrol and Linux setserial programs allow the system administrator to enable serial ports to communicate with both internal and external modems. Once the system recognizes the serial port, it must use software to handle any incoming connection attempts. The mgetty program can automatically detect incoming PPP connection requests.

The second part of the chapter describes how to configure various types of remote clients to establish a PPP session with the mail server. Linux clients can use the pppd program to initiate a PPP session with the server. Microsoft Windows 95 and 98 clients can use the Dial-Up Networking (DUN) feature built into the operating system to establish a PPP session. Microsoft Windows NT 4.0 and 2000 can use the Remote Access Server (RAS) feature to establish the PPP session. Once the PPP session is established with the remote client, the user can read messages stored in his mailbox using standard MUA software. The Qualcomm Eudora MUA package is a freely available package that provides POP3 access to the mail server from a remote client.

At this point you should be comfortable installing, configuring, and running a qmail mail server. Many topics have been discussed over the last 19 chapters, but there is always more to know. Many new technologies are arriving, such as the new Lightweight Directory Access Protocol (LDAP) for user authentication. Dan Bernstein and others have made efforts to include emerging technologies both in newer versions of qmail and in add-on packages to qmail. The Internet is a great resource to keep up to date with advances in qmail. The qmail Web site at `http://www.qmail.org` and the qmail mail list server will keep you informed and educated on new qmail issues.

INDEX

Symbols

A

creating aliases, 350
listing converted aliases,
357-359
processing aliases, 357
include files, 360
mail engine, 347-350
mailboxes, 353-354
Majordomo mail list aliases,
378
qmail, compared, 44
sendmail.cw file, 363
statistics program, 353
virusertable file, 363
Web site, 346
**Sendmail Consortium Web
site, 12**
**sendmail wrapper program,
204-205**
sendmail.cw file, 363
**sendmail.hf help file (send-
mail), 348-350**
**Serial Line Internet Protocol
(SLIP), 445**
serial ports
FreeBSD, 472
options, 473
rc.serial script, 474-476
ttys file, 473-474
Linux, 470, 476
init scripts, 482-483
inittab file, 480-481
options, 476-479
multiport devices, 471
serialmail program, 301-302
compiling, 303-304
configuration files, 303
downloading, 302
installing, 303-304
ISP mail server, 311-312
ETRN support, 313-315
QMTP support, 312-313
local mail server, 308-311
source code, 302
utilities, 304-307
serialqmtp program, 306-307
serialsmtp program, 306
**serious problem log
messages, 337**

**server (qmail), configuring,
188**
aliases, 189
control files, 188-189
*existing local mail deliv-
ery method, 191-193*
*local mail delivery
method, 190-191*
*Mailbox local mail deliv-
ery method, 193-195*
*Maildir local mail deliv-
ery method, 195-196*
servers
client identification, 108
DNS. *See* DNS servers
external DNS, 102-103
ISP mail
features, 268
*hosting virtual domains,
268*
mail relaying, 268
*selective relaying, 268-
272*
*serialmail program,
311-315*
*virtual domains. See vir-
tual domains*
local caching DNS, 101-102
local mail
*hostname specifications,
172*
*serialmail program,
308-311*
office mail
*dial-on-demand Internet
connection, 297-299*
*dial-up Internet connec-
tion, 292-297*
*full-time Internet connec-
tion, 291*
requirements, 290
*UUCP connection,
299-301*
qmail, configuring, 188
aliases, 189
control files, 188-189
*existing local mail deliv-
ery method, 191-193*

*local mail delivery
method, 190-191*
*Mailbox local mail deliv-
ery method, 193-195*
*Maildir local mail delivery
method, 195-196*
sendmail, 346
aliases system, 350-352
mail engine, 347-350
sendmail.cw file, 363
statistics program, 353
virusertable file, 363
Web site, 346
SMTP, 259
UCSPI tools, 246
workstation cache DNS, 96-99
zone DNS, 99-100
**service response codes
(SMTP), 117-118**
services directory, 397
services file, 242
**session lockout option (set-
serail command), 479**
sessions (POP3), 235
setforward utility, 359
**setlock program, 307, 393,
409**
setmaillist utility, 359
setserial command, 476-479
setuidgid program, 393, 408
sh shell, 65
**shadow passwords, 320-321,
432-433**
shared memory areas, 50
shells, 65-67
**silent option (pppd com-
mand), 458**
**Simple Mail Transfer
Protocol.** *See* SMTP
single user accounts
creating, 275
mail retrieval, 280-283
message delivery configuration, 277
qmail configuration, 275-276
virtual domain configuration,
274-277

The IT site
you asked for...

InformIT is a complete online library delivering
information, technology, reference, training, news,
and opinion to IT professionals, students,
and corporate users.

Find IT Solutions Here!

www.informit.com

InformIT is a trademark of Macmillan USA, Inc.
Copyright © 2000 Macmillan USA, Inc.

Read This Before Opening

By opening this package, you are agreeing to be bound by the following agreement:

What's on the CD-ROM?

The companion CD-ROM contains FreeBSD 4.0 with the source code for qmail, dot-forward, fast-forward, and qmailanalog.

Accessing the Source Code for qmail and Its Utilities

The source code for qmail, dot-forward, fast-forward, and qmailanalog is located on the companion CD-ROM. Once you have mounted the CD-ROM, you can find the source code in the xtras directory.

Installing FreeBSD from a Bootable CD-ROM

Before you begin an installation, you should make backups of your valuable data.

1. Place the CD-ROM in the CD-ROM drive.
2. Restart your computer. The FreeBSD installation program will start if you have a CD-ROM drive that can autoboot. If FreeBSD does not start up, you may have to change your BIOS boot-order or boot from floppies. See below for instructions on how to install FreeBSD from a floppy.
3. Follow the onscreen prompts to finish the installation of FreeBSD 4.0.

Installing FreeBSD from Boot Floppies

You will need two blank, DOS formatted 1.44MB floppy to set up boot floppies; label one as mfsroot and the other one as kernel. These instructions assume that your system's CD-ROM drive is D:. If your CD-ROM drive is not D:, substitute your system's drive letter for the one in the examples.

1. Open a Command Prompt or DOS Prompt.
2. Insert the CD-ROM into your CD-ROM drive.
3. Type `d:` and press the ENTER key.
4. Make sure you are at the root of the CD-ROM by typing `cd \` and press the ENTER key.
5. Type `makeflp` and press the ENTER key. Follow the onscreen prompts to finish creating the disks.
6. When you are finished creating the boot disks, insert the floppy labeled kernel into your floppy drive and restart your computer. If the FreeBSD install process does not start, check your BIOS settings to make sure you have booting from floppies enabled, or to make sure that your floppy drive is selected to boot before your hard drive.
7. Follow the onscreen prompts to finish the installation.